RENAISSANCE DRAMA

New Series I ❧ *1968*

Renaissance Drama

New Series I

Essays Principally on Masques and Entertainments

Edited by S. Schoenbaum

Northwestern University Press

EVANSTON 1968

Copyright © 1968 by Northwestern University Press
Library of Congress Catalog Card Number: 67–29872
Manufactured in the United States of America

THE ILLUSTRATION on the front cover is from *C'est la Deduction* . . . (Rouen, 1551). The illustration on the back cover is "Truth," from Henry Peacham, *Minerva Brittanna* (London, 1612), and is reproduced by courtesy of the Folger Shakespeare Library, Washington, D. C.

Editorial Note

RENAISSANCE DRAMA, an annual publication, provides a forum for scholars in various parts of the globe: wherever the drama of the Renaissance is studied. Coverage, so far as subject matter is concerned, is not restricted to any single national theater. The chronological limits of the Renaissance are interpreted liberally, and space is available for essays on precursors, as well as on the utilization of Renaissance themes by later writers. Investigations shedding light on theatrical history and actual stage production are especially welcome, as are comparative studies. Editorial policy favors articles of some scope. Essays that are exploratory in nature, that are concerned with critical or scholarly methodology, that raise new questions or embody fresh approaches to perennial problems are particularly appropriate for a publication which originated from the proceedings of the Modern Language Association Conference on Research Opportunities in Renaissance Drama.

This volume initiates a new series of RENAISSANCE DRAMA. Past numbers have been collections of miscellaneous essays; the new policy is to build the volume around a specified subject, but also to allow for a few papers on unrelated topics. Most of the articles this year are concerned with masques and entertainments.

The 1969 volume will be devoted mainly to studies in dramatic theory and form. Contributions offered for publication should be addressed to the Editor, Renaissance Drama, Northwestern University, 619 Emerson Street, Evanston, Illinois 60201. Prospective contributors are requested to follow the recommendations of the *MLA Style Sheet* (revised edition) in preparing manuscripts.

Contents

RENAISSANCE DRAMA

New Series I ~ *1968*

The Evolution of the Early Tudor Disguising, Pageant, and Mask

SYDNEY ANGLO

E NTERTAINMENTS AT THE EARLY TUDOR COURT are scarcely an unworked field. Most writers who deal with the evolution of drama, and especially of court festivals, include a cursory statement on these shows, for it has long been recognized that they contained, in embryonic form, the elements of the full-fledged Stuart masque. But, in general, the literary historians' approach has been both too selective and too static. Anxious to proceed to more congenial material, critics have seized upon what seem to them the most striking features of these entertainments— those most relevant to later developments—without any regard for chronology. A few contemporary narratives, recording fairly unusual entertainments, have been employed as though they were typical of the period, so that the general impression given has been of a homogeneous Tudor court culture.[1] But the truth of the matter is that there was only one

1. By far the fullest account of Early Tudor festivals is included in Paul Reyher, *Les Masques anglais* (Paris, 1909), though Reyher's thematic treatment precludes any sense of chronological development in these embryonic masks. C. W. Wallace, *The Evolution of the English Drama up to Shakespeare* (Berlin, 1912), gives a fairly full chronological account, but it is marred by inaccuracy and a truly wondrous tendency to attribute virtually all pre-Shakespearian drama to William Cornish. Enid Welsford, *The Court Masque* (Cambridge, Eng., 1927), is very useful for background and comparative material, but the treatment of Early Tudor antecedents to

3

significant period in the history of Early Tudor court festivals, when
England, having long lagged behind the Continent in semi-dramatic
spectacle, made up for some—though by no means all—of the time lost
in the mid-fifteenth century. Innovation and experimentation, based
principally upon a limited number of Continental models, were confined
within the first three decades of the sixteenth century. In this article I
attempt nothing more ambitious than a straightforward chronological
account of these entertainments, preceded by a note on the knotty problem
of the mask "after the maner of Italie" and interrupted by an examination
of some parallel Continental festivals which seem to me especially relevant
to the matter in hand.

I   *The Mask* "after the maner of Italie": *Epiphany 1512*

Twelfth-night 1512 was not an especially splendid occasion in the annals
of Henry VIII's court festivals; but it was celebrated with an entertainment in which the King, with eleven companions, went "disguised, after
the maner of Italie, called a maske, a thyng not seen afore in Englande."
The banquet had just concluded when

these Maskers came in, with six gentlemen disguised in silke bearyng staffe
torches, and desired the ladies to daunce, some were content, and some that
knewe the fashion of it refused, because it was not a thyng commonly seen.
And after thei daunced and commoned together, as the fashion of the Maske
is, thei tooke their leaue and departed, and so did the Quene, and all the ladies.

This passage is one of the most discussed sections in Edward Hall's
Chronicle, having been the source of much fruitless controversy amongst
historians.[2] The controversy is of small moment; but the entertainment,

the Stuart masque is disorganized and far too selective to give any impression of a
changing court culture. E. K. Chambers' volumes on the medieval and Elizabethan
stage are, as ever, full of all kinds of valuable information but are very thin and
highly selective on the Early Tudors. More recent scholarship has tended to concentrate upon the Jonsonian masque.

2. Edward Hall, *The Vnion of the Two Noble and Illustre Famelies of Lancastre
& Yorke,* ed. Henry Ellis (London, 1809), p. 526; hereafter cited as "Hall." Welsford, *The Court Masque,* pp. 130–142, discusses the arguments advanced by earlier
authorities and decides in favor of Reyher's opinion. The novelty is held to subsist
principally in the dancing together of maskers and ladies in the audience; and it is

described by Hall, though of slight importance in the development of the structure of English court festivals, did help introduce a new word into the language of literary form. This was the "maske," indicating "a thyng" eventually apotheosized in the much grander "masque" of the late sixteenth and early seventeenth century.

There is no doubt that Hall considered this Twelfth-night entertainment to have included a twofold innovation. In the first place it witnessed dancing of the disguised persons in the company of undisguised ladies from the audience; secondly, this dancing was accompanied by informal talk, or *communing,* between the two parties. It is, however, by no means apparent that these innovations were of any importance to the development of dramatic entertainments at court. Prunières long ago pointed out that this adaptation of the Italian *maschera* was essentially undramatic and could not have led to the organized court mask: and arguments to the contrary have tended to depend upon an altogether too rigid attitude toward the terminology of sixteenth-century authorities.[3] The disguising and mask have been sharply differentiated in a way which would have surprised Hall who, though fairly consistent, sometimes interchanges the terms or uses them inexactly—especially noteworthy since the chronicler was writing some twenty or more years after the majority of the entertainments he describes.

As a matter of fact, the contemporary authority for the 1512 festivity, Richard Gibson, Serjeant of the Tents, refers merely to "long govns and hodes and hats after the maner of messkelyng in etaly," as though all the novelty subsisted in the costumes.[4] Thereafter Gibson, in his *Revels*

---

suggested that some of the ladies refused to join in because they recognized that the King was introducing the notorious Italian *maschera*—a risqué social pastime. But instead of all the lengthy argument and hypothesis one may merely examine the significance of the word "commoned" for Hall. That this did not merely indicate mixed dancing is apparent from Hall's description of the disguising at Newhall in September 1519. See below, p. 30.

3. Henri Prunières, *Le Ballet de cour en France avant Benserade et Lully* (Paris, 1914), p. 27, writes that Reyher's work does not explain how "un genre dramatique aussi déterminé que le Mask anglais a pu sortir d'un usage aussi peu dramatique que celui de se masquer et de se déguiser pour danser. Le *disguishing* [sic] du Moyen âge (équivalent de l'*entremets*) contient un germe dramatique autrement intéressant."

4. Public Record Office, E.36/229, fol. 175; S.P.2/Fol. A, No. 4.

Accounts, uses the word-root in every conceivable variety both of form and meaning. An entertainment at Greenwich in March 1519, which Hall calls a "disguysing," is referred to by Gibson as a "maskalyne after the maner of etaly," though it was, apparently, lacking in the two necessary ingredients later diagnosed by Hall as essential to the mask.[5] Sometimes, as in September 1519, Gibson would write that he had to prepare coats "for a meskeler," or, as in Christmas 1524/5, that "yt was the kynges plesyer that meskelers and other plesyers schoulld be had"—as though the word indicated a type of entertainment.[6] But for that same Christmas 1524/5 he also records payment for silver of damask used by "vj maskelers that had heedes and berds," as though the word meant either a visor or the person who wore it.[7] In January 1526 Gibson wrote of a "meskeler of vj gentylmen in govnes of cloothe of syllver and cloothe of golld," and of "viij maskelers, viij long govnes of taffata and viij hoodes," implying both a type of revel and a type of garment.[8] On the other hand, sometimes it is clear that "meskeller" indicates the person engaged in the revelry.[9] Most revealing of all, perhaps, is the reference in the accounts for 31 December 1519 where Gibson records his disbursements for a "meskeller or mvmry," thus conflating two forms of entertainment customarily regarded as quite separate.[10] Gibson, of course, was not alone in his confusion and variant spellings; and it is not till June 1527 that the form "maske" is encountered, when Viscount Lisle, English ambassador at the French court, reporting the entertainments he had witnessed, described how the French

5. S.P.1/18, fol. 53.

6. E.36/217, fol. 89; S.P.1/32, fol. 275. This is the most common usage, and there are dozens of examples throughout Gibson's accounts.

7. S.P.1/32, fol. 274.

8. S.P.1/37, fol. 14[v].

9. For example, Gibson's account for revels at a banquet at Tournai in 1513 refers to material for hose for the "iiij meskellers" (S.P.1/7, fol. 75), whereas in another draft of the same account the reference is to the "iiij mynstrelles" (E.36/217, fol. 73). Quite unambiguous is Gibson's reference in his account for 5 January 1520 to silk points spent "vn the maskellyers apparell" (E.36/217, fol. 104).

10. E.36/217, fol. 100. Cf. College of Arms MS. 1st M.6, fols. 10[v], 12, where, in the course of a narrative of the Field of Cloth of Gold, the entertainments of 17 and 24 June, described by Hall and Gibson as "maskers" or "meskelers," are each designated "momery."

king and some of the young lords "whent in maskyr" and "daunsyd." He wrote that there were several sorts of "maskes," two being "after the turkys facion"; a play followed, after which the "maskers daunsyd agen." A few months later Gibson himself employs "maske" for the first time, which suggests that the word was already beginning to gain currency.[11] By the early 1540's it was well-established; and in Cawarden's *Revels Accounts* for Edward VI's reign "maske" is always the form used.[12]

The historian looking back on this period is, naturally, in a position to distinguish between various elements which made up a court entertainment, and he can discern that the disguising, the pageant, and the mummery, as well as the mask, were separate forms, each having its own peculiar characteristics. But he must also recognize that, to contemporaries, the names of these revels were not so clearly differentiated and that—much more important—the festivals, like their names, could be interchanged or combined. The fluidity of all forms of entertainment in the period under discussion, the way in which combats, dances, and disguisings could appear upon almost any social occasion, and the fact that these spectacles were all developing concurrently throughout Europe render suspect any attempt at a unilinear approach singling out a particular entertainment as the key influence. More especially suspect must be the choice of the vague *maschera* at the expense of court disguisings, interludes, pageants, and even tournaments, as the foundation of dramatic court revels. That Henry VIII took the trouble to introduce an ostensibly novel revel from Italy is more important as an illustration of the King's desire to be fashionable and to create a dazzling impression upon the European stage than for its influence upon English court festivities. There is no reason why the entry of gentlemen in disguise who dance with women from the audience should have had any more epoch-shattering effect than the entry of disguised gentlemen who dance with dis-

---

11. Lisle's letter is at the P.R.O., S.P.1/42, fol. 74. Gibson, in his account for the entertainments of 10 November 1527, mentions black sarsenet "spente for iij meskelyng hodes for the gret maske"; and under expenses of yellow sarsenet he mentions "vj gyrdylls for the blacke maskelers," "vj gyrdylls for the gret maske," and "vj gyrdylls for the friste maske" (S.P.1/45, fol. 34).

12. See Albert Feuillerat, *Documents Relating to the Revels at Court in the Time of King Edward VI and Queen Mary* (Louvain, 1914).

guised ladies, or than undisguised men who dance with undisguised women. This general dance was scarcely ever part of the dramatic proceedings.

The problem is largely one of nomenclature and false emphasis. The evolution of the *mask* into the *masque* and the extinction of the *disguising* and *mummery* have tended to suggest that the mask was in some way responsible for that extinction and took to itself certain elements of the old entertainments. But what could the mask add to the disguising? What have informal chatter, possibly flirtation, and dancing with members of the audience to do with the dramatic court masque? The truth of the matter is that the spectacular disguising merely took over the name *mask;* while the form introduced in 1512—which should be seen as merely one experiment among several—became popular either as a simple masquerade or as a useful bridge between the more specialized dancing of the maskers and the general ball with which court festivals customarily ended. The future (and the future was a very long way off) lay, in fact, with the traditional English forms such as the *débat* and disguising, enriched not by the *maschera* but by other Continental forms, some of which made a belated but spectacular appearance at the Tudor court on 19 November 1501.

II *The Festivals of 1501 and Their European Context*

In November 1501 Catharine of Aragon was married to Henry VII's elder son, Prince Arthur. This dynastic triumph was celebrated in London by civic pageantry of unprecedented complexity, at court by tilts, tourneys, and barriers within the lists, and by disguisings with pageant cars within the banquet hall. Especially noteworthy among this remarkable series of magnificences was an entertainment devised by an up-and-coming Gentleman of the Chapel Royal, William Cornish, to mark the very first banquet on the evening of Friday, 19 November.[13] This was a "moost goodly and pleasaunt disguysing, conveyed and shewed in pagents proper and subtil." The first pageant was a castle:

13. On Cornish's authorship see my article, "William Cornish in a Play, Pageants, Prison, and Politics," *R.E.S.,* N.S., X (1959), 350–353. For the narrative of this disguising see F. Grose and T. Astle, *The Antiquarian Repertory* (London, 1807–1809), II, 300–302.

right cunyngly devysed, sett uppon certain whelys, and drawen into the seid hall of IIII°ᵗ great bestis, with cheynys of gold; two of the first bestis were lyons, oon of them of gold, and the other sylver; oon of the other was an harte, with gilt hernys, and the secunde of the same was a ibex; with in evrych of the which IIII bests were II men, oon in the fore parte, and another in the hynde parte, secretly hide and apparellid, no thing seene but their leggs, and yet thoes were disguysid aftr the proporcion and kynde of the bests that they were in.

Within this castle, looking out of the windows, were eight disguised ladies; and at the top of each of its four towers was a young girl—all four children "syngyng full swettly and ermenuously in all the commyng of the lengeth of the hall." When the castle had taken its station before the King, the second pageant entered. This was

a shippe in like wise sett uppon whelys, without any leders in sight, in right goodly apparell, havyng her mastis, toppis, saylys, her taclyng, and all other appertenauns necessary unto a semely vessell, as though it hade been saylyng in the see; and so passid thorugh the halle, by his hool lengeth till they cam byfore the Kynge, sumwhat beside the castell (at the which tyme the masters of the shippe, and their company, in their countenauns, spechis, and demeanour, usid and behavyd them self after the maner and guyse of marynours) and there cast their ankkers sumwhat beside the seid castell.

Now the action really began. Down a ladder let over the side of the ship there descended two "weelbeseen" persons calling themselves Hope and Desire, whose banners proclaimed them to be ambassadors from certain Knights of the Mount of Love. They immediately attempted to win over the ladies of the castle, entreating them, "as wowers and brokers of the mattr of love," on behalf of the knights. The ladies, however, refused all their blandishments and denied that they were ever "myndid to th'accomplisshement of any such requests." Whereupon the ambassadors waxed wrath and warned the ladies that the knights would make battle and so assault the castle that it "shuld be grevous to abyde there power and malesse." Now the third pageant made its appearance in the form of a great hill or mountain in which were enclosed the eight goodly knights, with their banner "spred and displaied, namyng themself the Knights of the Mounte of Love." This pageant took its place beside the ship whence the two ambassadors again issued forth, this time to report to their masters concerning the ladies' total lack of response. The knights were in no wise content at this snub, and "with moch malés and curvagyous myend,"

marched across to the castle and began siege operations. Ere long the
ladies yielded, descended from their stronghold, and joined their conquerors in "many goodly daunces" in the course of which the pageants
were removed. Finally, the disguisers "avoyded and evanyshed ought of
the sight and presens," and the ball was opened first by Prince Arthur and
then by Catharine of Aragon, his bride.

At first sight none of this seems remarkable. It is what we have grown
accustomed to regard as a typical late-medieval English court festival—
principally because it is always cited as such. Certainly song and dance
had been the normal mode of *divertissement,* both popular and courtly,
at all times and everywhere. They still are. Mimesis, too, is ubiquitous and
sempiternal, while the courtly form of an entry of disguised lords and
ladies may be traced back in English festivals to the fourteenth century
and the *débat* had been popularized at court by Lydgate more than sixty
years previously. Furthermore, the assault on the castle of love was a
literary and artistic commonplace, and there is scarcely a romance manuscript which does not include illustrations of such a scene.[14] Yet Cornish's
show—with its spectacular combination of music, scenic display on mobile
stages, speeches in the form of a dramatic argument, mock combat or
siege, and final resolution in a well-regulated dance—appears, from all
available evidence, to have been an innovation at the English court. It is
true that Lydgate's disguisings may have included pageants of some kind,
though the evidence for this is scant and ambiguous.[15] There seems to be
as wide a gulf between Lydgate's static speechifyings and the action-filled
disguising of 1501 as there is between the latter entertainment and the
poetically polished, and mechanically elaborate, Stuart masque. Moreover,
there is no other indication in the fifteenth century that the pageant car
had ever been translated from the city street into the banquet hall. This
was, of course, a common practice elsewhere in Europe: but not in England. And certainly, though disguisings are frequently come upon in the

14. For a few convenient examples see R. S. Loomis, "The Allegorical Siege in the
Art of the Middle Ages," *American Journal of Archaeology,* 2d ser., XXIII (1919),
255–269; G. R. Kernodle, *From Art to Theatre* (Chicago and London, 1944),
pp. 76–84.

15. I think it by no means safe to assume, as does Glynne Wickham, *Early English Stages 1300–1600* (London, 1959), I, 216, that such scenic devices were certainly
used in Lydgate's entertainments.

accounts of the Treasurer of the Chamber for Henry VII's reign, the word *pageant* does not occur prior to 1501.[16] When it is recalled that these same Anglo-Spanish marriage festivals were also the very first occasion when an English tournament was enhanced by a complete series of pageant-car entries into the lists, of the kind favored in the greatest Burgundian and Italian magnificences, then it becomes clear that a deliberate attempt was being made, indoors and out, to vie with the Continental courts and to bring England up-to-date.[17]

I have already suggested that Tudor Englishmen were not too fussy about the terms they used to describe their entertainments. One can go much further than this, however, for flexibility extended far beyond England, far beyond the sixteenth century (in both directions), and far beyond mere matters of nomenclature. Plays, pageants, tournaments, disguisings, dances, interludes, and mummeries all developed together, and with much mutual interchange both of theme and form.

Undoubtedly the most important spectacle and pastime, up to the sixteenth century, was the tournament. This was the normal chivalric exercise; it was the show usually organized to entertain one's friends or visiting dignitaries; it was the customary mode of signalizing diplomatic coups, military triumphs, noble marriages, and joyful, noteworthy events of every kind; and the tournament remained the focal point of any great series of courtly magnificences even into the seventeenth century. Combats on horseback, modified by the introduction of the tilt, and combats on foot, modified by the introduction of the barriers, were everyday affairs. The tournament, moreover, had always given opportunity for semidramatic spectacle and the demonstration of artistic ingenuity, though—since such shows, as well as real battles, skirmishes, and sieges, were all an integral part of medieval life—it is impossible to draw clear distinctions between the influence of romance literature on mock combats and the in-

16. See my article, "The Court Festivals of Henry VII: a Study Based upon the Account Books of John Heron, Treasurer of the Chamber," *BJRL,* XLIII (1960), 12–45. The account of the festival for Epiphany 1494 in Brit. Mus. Additional MS. 6113, fol. 169, mentions a "pageant of St. George with a castle"; but this is a much later MS which is not corroborated by the contemporary descriptions in London chronicles. See also my article, "William Cornish in a Play," pp. 348–350.

17. On this tournament and its place within the European tradition see my forthcoming book, *The Great Tournament Roll of Westminster* (Oxford at the Clarendon Press), pp. 19–40.

fluence of such combats on romance literature. There is evidence that the mock siege, as a kind of social custom as well as entertainment, had been organized as early as 1214 when there was the oft-cited *Castello d'amore* at Treviso. On this occasion the besieged maidens defended themselves against an assault waged with a hail of fruit, dates, raisins, quinces, roses, lilies, violets, balsam, rose water, and many other spices and flowers which "redolent vel splendescunt." They withstood the fruit and flowers but succumbed to gold—thereby causing a riot, and ultimately war.[18] Thus was the mock assault brought back to its brutal origins.

England had played a part in the early development of the artistic potentialities of the tournament by the introduction of allegorical challenges and disguisings and by the elaboration of ritual. In the fifteenth century, however, England did not keep pace with the employment of the romantic allegory, fantastic costuming, pageant spectacle, and semidramatic speech-making which were increasingly favored on the Continent both within the lists and within the banquet hall. The great festivities at Westminster in 1501 seem to have been a deliberate attempt to catch up. Especially interesting is the fact that Cornish's disguising with three pageants was to usher in a long series of banquet battles and castle-stormings. These, ultimately, took their origin in the tournament and in the mock combats long since introduced into all forms of European public and courtly spectacle, such as civic pageantry, entremets or intermezzi, and as part of the dance.

I have discussed elsewhere the way in which the tournament itself became increasingly allegorical, and there is no point in going over this material again. But clearly, not only was there a relationship between the Continental pageant tournaments and the Westminster tournament of 1501, there was also little distance between an allegorical pageant tournament such as the *Pas de l'Arbre d'Or* in 1468, or the *Castello d'amore* tournament at Ferrara in 1464, and Cornish's indoor pageants with disguising.[19] The assault on a stronghold as part of a tournament, with or without allegorical adornment, already had a long history by the begin-

---

18. *Rolandini Patavini cronica in factis et circa facta Marchie Trivixane,* ed. A. Bonardi (Città di Castello, 1903–1905), p. 25. See also W. A. Neilson, *The Origins and Sources of the Court of Love* (Boston, 1899), pp. 255–256.

19. Olivier de la Marche, *Mémoires,* ed. Henry Beaune and J. d'Arbaumont (Paris, 1883–1888), III, 101–201; *Diario Ferrarese dall'anno 1409 sino al 1502 di autori incerti,* ed. G. Pardi (Bologna, 1928–1933), p. 45.

ning of the sixteenth century, and its kinship both with real warfare on the one hand, and with indoor simulations on the other, is manifest.[20] Nevertheless, the extent to which mock sieges and mock combats were incorporated into spectacle and entertainments other than the straight tournament has not been generally appreciated—though the material is not especially unfamiliar.

Even in civic pageantry, conceived principally for royal entries as spectacle mounted at fixed stations, this combative element is frequently encountered. The entry of Queen Isabelle of Bavaria into Paris in 1389 was enlivened by a castle defended by Saladin and his Saracens against Richard Coeur de Lion and his Christian knights.[21] In 1431 one of the pageants for Henry VI's entry into Paris consisted of a running fight between three wild men and a wild woman; and in 1443 Alphonso's entry into Naples included a battle between Saracens and Spaniards.[22] Milan, in 1453, prepared, as part of the annual festivities in the piazza before the cathedral, a representation of Coriolanus, showing an attack on Rome—signified by a fierce assault on a castle.[23] Louis XI, during his

20. For examples see the following: in 1458 at Venice, *Armilustre e Torneo con Armi di Battaglia Tenuti a Venezia Addi XXVIII e XXX Maggio MCCCCLVIII* (Turin, 1866); in 1464 at Ferrara, see preceding note; in 1481 at Forli, Andrea Bernardi, *Cronache forlivesi .... dal 1476 al 1517,* ed. G. Mazzatinti (Bologna, 1895–1897), I, 58–60. The sport grew in popularity in the first half of the sixteenth century. For examples see the following: in France as a military training, Maréchal de Fleuranges, *Mémoires,* ed. Michaud and Poujoulat (Paris, 1838), p. 7; in 1501 at Rome, F. Clementi, *Il Carnevale romano* (Rome, 1899), p. 108; in 1507 at Milan, Jean d'Auton, *Chroniques de Louis XII,* ed. R. de Maulde La Clavière (Paris, 1889–1895), IV, 313–319; in 1519 at Nozeroy, B. Prost, *Traicté de la forme et devis comme on faict les tournois* (Paris, 1878), pp. 236–237, 254–259; Christmas 1524/5 at Greenwich, Hall, pp. 688–691; in 1543 at Fontainebleau, D. Godefroy, *Le Cérémonial françois* (Paris, 1649), II, 144–146; in 1549 at Bologna, Lodovico Frati, *La Vita privata di Bologna* (Bologna, 1900), p. 179; in 1549 at Rome, Clementi, *Il Carnevale romano,* pp. 203–204; in 1549 at Binche, *Le Siège et les fêtes de Binche,* ed. Charles Ruelens (Mons, 1878), pp. 93–103.

21. Jean Froissart, *Chroniques,* ed. J. A. C. Buchon (Paris, 1824–1826), XII, 11–12.

22. Monstrelet, *Chroniques,* ed. J. A. C. Buchon (Paris, 1836), p. 652; *Alphonsi Regis Triumphus* in *Antonii Panormitae de Dictis et Factis Alphonsi Regis Aragonum* (Basle, 1538), pp. 234–235.

23. Pietro Ghinzoni, "Trionfi e Rappresentazioni in Milano (Secolo XIV e XV)," *Archivio Storico Lombardo,* XIV (Milano, 1887), 826–827.

Paris entry of 1461, was greeted by a pageant of wild men and women who "combatoient et faisoient plusieurs contenances"; and subsequently there was a scene showing the capture of the castle of Dieppe (a feat actually performed by Louis when Dauphin), and, after a marvelous assault, the English were captured and all their throats were cut.[24] The year 1473 witnessed the triumphal return of Cardinal Caraffa to Rome, where he was entertained at a carnival including two pageant cars, "uno per il Turcho, l'altro per il Re di Mazedonia; e ciascheduno haveva circha venti homeni armati e molti fanti." The two parties quickly began "una scaramuccia," first with batons and then with lances, till eventually the King defeated the Turk and led him captive through the streets.[25] A rather different military sport greeted Charles VIII during his coronation procession at Rheims in 1484 when, on the river, three boats filled with young men tilted at a quintain with such energy that two or three of the warriors tumbled into the water.[26] Finally, another mock siege took place in 1492 at Rome where, to celebrate the Christian victory at Granada, Spanish troops successfully assaulted a great wooden castle defended by Moors.[27]

Perhaps the earliest recorded occasion when mock combat enlivened a banquet was at Avignon in 1308, when Cardinal Pelagru entertained Pope Clement V at a feast during which ten mounted knights in armor began a "torniamento" one against one—their blows resounding marvelously for about an hour. The horses were fashioned of cloth mounted upon a frame and were carried by six men who could not be seen. But the knights were real enough, and the spectacle was deemed very fine and recognized as a "nuova giuoco." Later, in the same banquet, six "ischermidori" appeared, shouting and brandishing swords, till they came before the Pope's table, when they began a combat, very fierce and bitter while it lasted. This skirmish, like the mounted combat, was thought to be a new kind of show—"una schermagla disusata"—but it is not till seventy years

24. Godefroy, Le Cérémonial françois, I, 180, 183.
25. Clementi, Il Carnevale romano, p. 75, quoting a letter written by Ludovico Genovesi, physician of the court of Mantua.
26. Godefroy, Le Cérémonial françois, I, 187.
27. Clementi, Il Carnevale romano, pp. 91–92.

later that there is record of a similar *divertissement*.[28] At a banquet, celebrating Epiphany 1378, given in Paris by Charles V of France for the
Emperor Charles IV, there was brought into the hall a representation of
Jerusalem, "faicte en bois et d'un beau travail," occupied by Saracens.
This was followed by a ship carrying Godfrey of Bouillon who led an
assault upon the city and effected its capture.[29] Then, a few years later,
the marriage celebrations for Isabelle of Bavaria in 1389 included several
dramatic representations of battle, first during the royal entry, and subsequently during the banquets. One of the latter concluded with the appearance of two mounted knights who jousted against each other before
being joined by other warriors who continued the sport for a further two
hours. At another banquet, the city of Troy (made of wood in the form
of a castle and mounted on wheels for easy transportation) was attacked
by Grecian troops who entered the hall within a mobile pavilion and a
huge ship. However, within the auditorium, even more stirring events
were afoot; for several ladies were overcome by the excessive heat, and a
scaffold collapsed, precipitating the onlookers to the floor, so that the
mock siege had to be abandoned.[30]

Evidence for the early history of this type of entertainment is rather
scattered, but the form may be more readily traced in the latter half of the
fifteenth century, when it became increasingly allegorical and romantic.
Burgundian festivals afford several examples, as at the Feast of the Pheas-
ant celebrated at Lille in 1454 to initiate a grand crusade. The entremets
at this banquet consisted of short dramatic scenes representing various
exploits of Jason, which gave obvious scope for fighting in the scenes with
the brazen bulls, the serpent, and especially the warriors who sprang from
the dragon's teeth—these bellicose men scarcely regarded each other before joining a violent battle which ended with the curtain falling on a
stage littered with dead bodies.[31] Again, at the marriage festivities for

28. *I due sontuosissimi conviti fatti a papa Clemente V nel MCCCVIII ec.* cited
in D'Ancona and Bacci, *Manuale della Letteratura Italiana* (Florence, 1906), I,
232–233.

29. Christine de Pisan, *Le Livre des fais et bonnes meurs du sage roy Charles,*
ed. Michaud and Poujoulat (Paris, 1836), p. 110.

30. Froissart, *Chroniques,* XII, 20–22, 30.

31. Olivier de la Marche, *Mémoires,* II, 357–361.

Margaret of England and Charles of Burgundy in 1468, there was a similar series of Hercules entremets including several fights: against a giant, a sea monster, lions, Cerberus, a monster with seven heads, Caucus, a wild boar, two archers, and two Amazons. Another entremets, presented on the last day of these magnificences, was a pageant like a vast whale which entered the hall emitting songs sung by sirens concealed within. These sirens emerged, still singing, followed by two knights of the sea—"ayans en l'une des mains talloches et en l'autre battons deffensables"—who danced "en maniere de morisque," till a drum was heard from inside the whale. The singing thereupon ceased, and the sirens danced with the knights who, becoming jealous of each other, engaged in a "debat et tournay" until parted.[32]

It can be seen how these combats readily became associated with music; and it was in Rome, especially, that this tendency was first fully developed to the stage when the combats themselves were fought to music and took the form of a well-ordered dance. In 1473, at a banquet given in Rome by Cardinal Riario, honoring the return of Cardinal Caraffa from the war in the Levant, moriscoes were danced, and a representation of a battle "con bastoni e lance" was fought between the Turk and the King of Macedon—thus repeating the theme of Caraffa's triumphal entry into the city.[33] In the following year Rome witnessed the complete identification of combat with dance at a banquet held in honor of Leonora, daughter of Ferdinand of Naples, when she passed through the city on her way to marry Ercole d'Este. The show was presented in the Piazza de' Santi Apostoli which had been temporarily roofed with curtains. In the course of the banquet there entered eight disguised couples, including Hercules with Deianira, Jason with Medea, and Theseus with Phaedra. Musical instruments began to play, and the lovers and nymphs began a dance only to be interrupted by centaurs, armed with shields and maces, who tried to abduct the ladies. This led to "una bella scaramuzza," resulting in the defeat of the centaurs who were driven from the stage by Hercules.[34] In 1475, this time at Turin, a *Castello d'amore* supplied the setting

32. *Ibid.*, III, 197–198.

33. Clementi, *Il Carnevale romano*, pp. 75–78.

34. Bernardino Corio, *L'Historia di Milano* (Venice, 1554), p. 419ᵛ. Cf. Clementi, *Il Carnevale romano*, p. 83 (p. 79, n. 2) who cites a contemporary MS: "Levata la tavola lu ballo de Hercules con cinque mascoli et nove donne. Fra lu ballo ven-

for "un gran ballo fantastico" which included a combat between a dragon, wild men, and an assortment of other characters, waged with "materie infiammabili."[35] Then, in the following year, again in Rome, at a banquet given by Cardinal Gonzaga, there was a choreographic dispute between the Virtues and the Vices. The Vices, swords in hand, danced to the attack, but were beaten off by the Virtues whose victory brought the show to a close.[36]

Probably the high point in the history of this form of spectacle was reached in the festivals connected with the marriage of Lucrezia Borgia, early in 1502, which were the occasion for several indoor battles arranged as dances. The entertainments began at Rome in January with a comedy in the Vatican, preceded by "uno spettacolo allegorico coreografico." This opened with a controversy between Virtù and Fortuna, during which Cesare Borgia's deeds were cited in connection with a demonstration that Caesar and Hercules had overcome Fortuna by their Virtù. The figure of Hercules himself then engaged in a fight with Fortuna whom he overcame and held prisoner till Juno pleaded for her release. At last Fortuna was set free, on condition that she did not harm the house of Borgia.[37] The whole conception gains special interest from the fact that it was not long before the house of Borgia crumbled, and Machiavelli, trying to demonstrate how Fortuna may be overcome by Virtù, cites Cesare Borgia as his prime exemplar—though Cesare was ultimately overthrown through the malignity of Fortuna and an error of judgment.

It was in Ferrara that the Borgia entertainments reached their climax.[38] Throughout a week of rejoicing banquets were given, each followed by performances of a series of five Plautine comedies. On 3 February the *Epidicus* was played in five parts between which were inserted various "moresche." The first consisted of ten warriors armed in antique fashion,

---

nero li centauri et fecese una bella bactaglia. Li centauri vinti da Hercule retornaro et formose lu ballo."

35. Text cited in Leone Luzzato, "Una rappresentazione allegorica in Urbino nel 1474," *Atti e Memorie della R. Accademia Petrarca di Scienze, Lettere ed Arti in Arezzo*, N.S., I (1920), 192–193.

36. Alessandro D'Ancona, *Origini del teatro italiano* (Turin, 1891), II, 69.

37. Clementi, *Il Carnevale romano*, p. 111.

38. Bernardino Zambotti, *Diario Ferrarese*, ed. G. Pardi (Bologna, 1934–1937), pp. 325–331. Cf. *I Diarii di Marino Sanuto*, ed. F. Stefani (Venice, 1879–1902), IV, cols. 225–230.

some with knives, others with maces or two-handed swords, and each with a dagger at his side. Their movements were carried out to a strict tempo, "con movimenti tuti acomodati a uno tempo," dancing on the stage "a la morescha" to the sound of drums. Suddenly they raised their hands against each other with rapid movements, as if they wished to kill each other, and aimed blows both with their hands and feet, yet all without breaking the rhythm—"senza alchuna differentia conformi al sono." They next seized their swords and continued the combat with great dexterity and agility; then they dropped their swords, at exactly the same moment, and fought with daggers until half dropped simultaneously to the floor as though dead. The others then raised them, and all made their exit together. The second interlude began with the entry of twelve armed men who paraded before the audience and then, dancing a *morescha* to the sound of drums, rained blows upon each other "con grande arte e destreza," before leaving the stage still smiting vigorously to the time of the music. On the 6th, the *Miles gloriosus* was presented with various intermezzi, one of which consisted of twelve youths dancing a *morescha* which ended with a dagger combat fought "con destreza grandissima." On the 7th, during the *Asinaria,* there was an intermezzo consisting of an elaborate hunting scene danced to music. And finally, on 8 February, the *Casina* was acted with intermezzi, the last of which showed twelve men, dressed in the Swiss fashion and armed with halberds, who danced a *morescha* and fought with great skill, "tuti a tempo senza alchuna discrepantia."

III *Early Tudor Court Festivals: 1501–1522*

It is within this context that festivals at the Early Tudor court must be considered, for the mock combat—though by no means providing the only theme and form for these entertainments—was one of the most popular and certainly gave the greatest opportunity for developing the old disguising into a semidramatic spectacle.

In the week following Cornish's three-pageant disguising of 19 November 1501, the court witnessed three other disguisings with pageants, though these were all nondramatic and served merely as allegorical introduction to the dancing, first of the disguisers alone and then of the spectators—but the arbor, the lantern, the vegetable and mineral mountains, and the mobile tabernacle drawn by sea horses and mermaids were all prophetic of things to come. As a matter of fact these things did not come very rapidly, and for the rest of Henry VII's reign, apart from a few scattered references to disguisings and interludes, I have only found two further documented pageant entertainments—another lantern during the festivals for the Scottish ambassadors in January 1503, and a castle, a tree, and a mountain for the Flemish ambassadors in December 1508.[39]

However, the atmosphere at court was soon to undergo a remarkable transformation, for "King Henrie the Eight, after the death of his re-nowned father, coming at once to a flourishing kingdome and a plenti-full fortune, spent most part of the two first yeares of his reigne in masques and revells, and those other oblectations which usually attend youthfull and galliard spiritts." [40] Certainly the vain, vigorous, and ambitious young monarch's accession provided a perfect outlet for the long-repressed en-ergies of painters, decorators, tailors, embroiderers, carpenters, minstrels, musicians, actors, singers, and everyone about the court who could con-tribute to pleasures and pastimes. Indeed, the reign opened with the first English tournament for which there is evidence not only of the pageantry and disguising elements already employed in 1501, but also of allegorical speechmaking.[41] And this neo-Burgundian feat of arms set the tone for much that was to take place in the revels department, within both the banquet hall and the lists, not merely for the "two first yeares" but for the two first decades of Henry's reign.

From the very outset there are references to disguisings and revels at court. Sometimes these were of considerable unorthodoxy, as on one morn-ing in January 1510 when the King surprised the Queen in her chamber by appearing with ten companions disguised as Robin Hood's men and a woman dressed as Maid Marian: "whereof the Quene, the Ladies, and

39. John Leland, *De Rebus Britannicis Collectanea,* ed. Thomas Hearne (London, 1770), IV, 263; P.R.O., L.C.9/50, fols. 143–147ᵛ.

40. This succinct character sketch introduces the last chapter of an early seven-teenth-century biography, *A short view of the long life of that ever wise, valiaunt, and fortunat commander, Rice ab Thomas etc.,* published in *The Cambrian Register for the Year 1795* (London, 1796), p. 134. I must thank my friend Rhys Robinson for drawing my attention to this very circumstantial and amusing text.

41. Hall, pp. 510–512; *The Great Chronicle of London,* ed. A. H. Thomas and I. D. Thornley (London, 1938), pp. 341–343; Anglo, *Great Tournament Roll of Westminster,* pp. 46–49.

al other there, were abashed, aswell for the straunge sight, as also for their sodain commyng, and after certain daunces, and pastime made, thei departed." [42] On the last day of February the foreign ambassadors at court were entertained at a more elaborate festivity which established a form subsequently in great favor. It began with a banquet from which Henry, who had been chatting amiably with the Queen and the visitors, suddenly absented himself. He returned in a disguising made "by the advyse of the erll of essex," in which the King and Earl appeared as Turks, with companions attired after the fashion of Russia and Prussia and twelve torch-bearers "lyke Moreskoes, their faces blacke." A mummery ensued, when members of the court were invited to play, presumably at "mumchance," before all the disguisers withdrew to change their apparel for the ball. Then, when the dancing was in full swing, "and euery man toke muche hede to them that daunsed," Henry and his chosen companions again withdrew, returning shortly in a second sumptuously-costumed disguising. They were followed by a disguising of ladies in which Henry's sister Mary and a companion were dressed in a fine black material called "lumbardyn," giving them the appearance of being "nygrost or blacke Mores." [43] This mixture of disguisings, mummery, and ball, together with the constant comings and goings and surprise appearances and disappearances, was to remain a feature of Henry VIII's early festivals, for the King seems to have derived considerable, and undiminishing, glee from "abashing" the ladies.

May Day 1510 was celebrated with archery contests, and the summer season passed in a lively progress during which Henry tried his hand at almost every courtly diversion:

exercisyng hym self daily in shotyng, singing daunsyng, wrastelyng, casting of the barre, plaiyng at the recorders, flute, virginals, and in setting of songes, makyng of balettes, & dyd set. ii. goodly masses, euery of them fyue partes, whiche were songe oftentimes in hys chapel, and afterwardes in diuerse other

42. Hall, p. 513. Cf. E.36/217, fol. 14, "the xj yn grene cottes and grene hosyn of kentyshe kendall the facyon lyke Robyn hodes men the woman lyke meyd maryan." The earliest reference to an indoor festival is a payment to Sir Andrew Wyndesor, for disguisings before the ambassadors of Flanders in September 1509 (*Letters and Papers, Foreign and Domestic, of the Reign of Henry VIII*, II.ii, 1443; hereafter cited as "*L.P.*").

43. Hall, pp. 513–514; E.36/217, fols. 14–24.

places. And whan he came to Okyng, there were kept both Iustes and Turneys: the rest of thys progresse was spent in huntyng, hawkyng and shotyng.[44]

The court returned to Greenwich in the autumn and enjoyed a succession of foot combats, while in November Henry entertained the Imperial ambassadors with another of his disguising-mummery-ball pastimes, complete with sudden materializations.[45]

It was for Epiphany 1511 that the first indoor pageant spectacle of the reign was arranged to take place in the banquet hall at Richmond. This pageant was a great mountain, "glisteringe by night, as though it had bene all of golde and set with stones." The scene was surmounted by a golden tree and other artificial flowers and fruits, the whole structure being "with vices brought vp towardes the kyng." There issued forth a "morryke dancyd by the kynges yong gentyllmen as hynsmen and ther to a lady," after which the revelers re-entered the pageant which was drawn back to make room for the "wassaill or banket."[46] Apparently this pageant was a great success, for preparations were immediately set afoot to celebrate the birth of a prince (the Queen had been delivered on New Year's Day) with even more splendid shows. These took place on 12 and 13 February and consisted of a two-day tournament with pageant entries and disguising and, on the second evening, concluded with a banquet and entertainment in the White Hall. Here, after an interlude with songs, performed by the Gentlemen of the Chapel Royal, a grand ball commenced during which the King, as was his wont, crept away unnoticed. Soon the trumpets flourished, and four torchbearers entered the hall preceding a huge pageant car, *The golldyn arber in the arche yerd of plesyer,* which was garnished with a vast array of trees, flowers, and a "vyen of syllver beryng grapes of goold." Grouped within and about this arbor were six ladies, six lords (including the King), eight minstrels, Kyte, Crane, Cornish of the Chapel Royal, and six children who participated in the singing. It is no wonder that Gibson, in his *Revels Account,* commented that the structure was "mervelvs wyghtty to remevf and karry as yt dyd bothe vp and down the hall and turnyd rovnd." At first the pageant came only part of the way into the hall, where it remained concealed behind a "great cloth of Arras,"

---

44. Hall, p. 515.
45. *Ibid.,* p. 516; E.36/217, fols. 27–33; E.36/229, fols. 1–9.
46. Hall, pp. 516–517; E.36/217, fols. 33–40; E.36/229, fols. 9–23.

while a gentleman, possibly Cornish, came forward to outline the allegory of the scene and ask permission of the Queen to demonstrate the pastime. The Queen assented, and the cloth "that did hang before thesame pageaunt was taken awaye, & the pageaunt brought more nere"—a process of unveiling employed, as will be seen, in subsequent entertainments. The disguisers now descended from the pageant and danced to the music of the minstrels who themselves joined in the dancing so "that it was a pleasure to beholde." Unfortunately the revelry degenerated into a wild scramble by the "rude people" for souvenirs—first they attacked the pageant and then the King and his companions, trying to pluck off the golden letters adorning the costumes. Order was at last restored, and the rest of the evening passed merrily, though it was not long before "sorrowful chaunce" ensued. The prince died within a fortnight, and Henry paused in his revelries for two whole months before returning to the lists in a May Day tournament.[47]

Continental politics, as well as infant mortality, now interrupted the calm succession of court entertainments, though the English court was still able to celebrate New Year's Day 1512 in the banquet hall at Greenwich with a pageant entitled *Le Fortresse Dangerus*. This was built like a castle, with towers and bulwarks fortified by ordnance, "as govns hagbochys kanvns kortawes chynes of iern werke and seche lyke." The dungeon of this grim stronghold was lit by two cressets and displayed a banner with a sheaf of arrows beaten thereon; and its walls were adorned with a "rosyer reed and whyght of sarsenet, well and kunnyngly kut and wrowght, kround with a kroun of golld." Within this castle were six ladies clad in the Milanese fashion. After the pageant had been carried about the hall, the King and five other lords began an assault upon the fortress until the ladies, "seyng them so lustie and coragious," were content to "solace with them" and, "vpon farther communicacion," to yield the castle. The ladies then descended and danced with the lords for a time, after which they led the knights back into the castle which "sodainly vanished"—a feat of scenography inexplicable unless the curtain of 1511 was repeated in reverse.[48]

Twelfth-night 1512 was the occasion for the entertainment in which

47. Hall, pp. 517–519; E.36/217, fols. 41–71; E.36/229, fols. 23–87. See also Anglo, *Great Tournament Roll of Westminster*, pp. 55–58.

48. Hall, p. 526; S.P.2/Fol. A, No. 4; E.36/229, fols. 175–205.

Henry and his eleven companions were "disguised, after the maner of Italie, called a maske." Thereafter the times—being occupied with war preparations or active campaigning—were not propitious for revelry, though the court managed to stage a sumptuous pageant with disguisings, *The ryche movnt,* for Epiphany 1513. This was a rock or mountain of gold and precious stones, set with a profusion of artificial flora. On the summit, clustered around a blazing beacon, were the King and five companions:

and foure wood houses drewe the Mount till it came before the quene, and then the king and his compaignie discended and daunced: then sodainly the Mount opened, and out came sixe ladies all in Crimosin satin and plunket, enbroudered with Golde and perle, with French hoddes on their heddes, and thei daunced alone. Then the lordes of the Mount tooke the ladies and daunced together: and the ladies reentred and the Mount closed, and so was conueighed out of the hall.[49]

The following year Epiphany was celebrated with an "interlevt in the weche contaynet a morreske." This moresque included the lady "kalld bewte" and the lady "kalld venvs"—a circumstance which led that ingenious and imaginative scholar, John Payne Collier, to stumble across a "singular paper folded up in a roll, and in a different handwriting, giving an account of the exhibitions before the King on this occasion. Two interludes were performed, one by Cornyshe and the Children of the Chapel and the other by English and the rest of the King's players." Collier continues by citing the document itself:

Venus dyd synge a songe with Beawte, which was lykyd of al that harde yt, every staffe endyng after thys sortte:
> Bowe you downe, and doo your dutye
> To Venus and the goddes Bewty:
> We tryumphe hye over all,
> Kyngs attend when we doo call.

The whole story is delightful but, sadly, is amongst the numerous flights of fancy which led to Collier's being castigated by Chambers as "this slovenly and dishonest antiquary."[50]

49. Hall, p. 535; E.36/217, fols. 170–185.
50. E.36/217, fols. 74–76; S.P.1/7, fols. 74–76; John Payne Collier, *History of English Dramatic Poetry to the Time of Shakespeare* (London, 1831), I, 64–65; E. K. Chambers, *The Mediaeval Stage* (Oxford, 1903), I, v.

It was not until the end of 1514 that festive activity was seriously renewed by a mummery and dance on New Year's Day and by a mock
assault upon a castle to mark Twelfth-night 1515. The court on this occasion was filled with ambassadors and visitors from France, Spain, and
Germany, and they were treated to an elaborate pageant entitled *The
pavyllyon vn the plas parlos*. This name was written over the portals of the
pavilion which was made of crimson and blue damask surmounted by a
golden crown and rosebush. At the four corners of the structure were
brickwork towers, each containing a lord dressed in purple satin embroidered with the gold letters *H* and *K;* on the main stage of the pageant were six minstrels playing sackbuts, shawms, and viols; and at the
foot of the pavilion were two armed knights "maintaining the place."
Three Gentlemen of the Chapel Royal, led by Cornish, entered with the
pageant and declared what it was all about—an analysis to which Gibson
might have listened with profit, for his *Revels Account* is confused and is
only loosely followed by Hall. The discrepancies between the two authorities are difficult to reconcile; but the main action appears to have
been first an assault by a second group of armed knights upon the pavilion
accompanied by the "noyse of drombyllslades." This was possibly a danced
combat to rhythmic accompaniment similar to those at the Italian courts—
although this is merely a hypothesis. Then came an interruption by wild
men, "all apparayled in grene mosse, made with slyued sylke, with Vggly
weapons and terrible visages," who emerged from a place like a wood and
fought a desperate, though losing, battle with the knights. Eventually,
when the wild men had been driven off, the tent opened, and six ladies
descended to dance with the knights. Finally they all re-entered the pavilion, which was conveyed out of the hall—though not before it had been
spoiled by the press of the spectators.[51]

The year 1515 passed pleasantly with numerous jousts and other shows,
including a striking May festival which greatly impressed the Venetian
ambassadors. This was based upon a Robin Hood theme and began with
the outlaws' invitation to the King, Queen, and nobles to attend a banquet
in the woods outside Greenwich where bowers had been prepared filled
with singing birds which "carolled most sweetly." There was a special
arbor made of boughs—with a hall, great chamber, and inner chamber,

51. Hall, p. 580; E.36/217, fols. 195–204; S.P.2/Fol. A, No. 6.

"couered with floures & swete herbes"—where the revelers dined off venison to the music of organ, lute, and flute. Such open air revels were not unprecedented: Edward IV had entertained the Mayor of London at a similar banquet in 1483, when "the said mayer by the conveyaunce of certayn knygthys was browgth unto a lusty and plesaunt lodge made of Grene bowhhys and othyr thyngys of pleasure." [52] But the Henrician version was enhanced, on the return journey, when the company encountered

ii. ladyes in a ryche chariot drawen with. v. horses and euery horse had hys name on his head, and on euery horse sate a ladye with her name writen. On the first courser called Cawde, sate *humidite,* or *humide.* On the. ii. courser called *Memeon,* roade lady vert. On the iii. called *pheton* sate lady vegetaue. On the. iiii. called *Rimphon* sate lady pleasaunce. On the. v. called *lampace,* sate swete odour, and in the Chayre sate the lady May, accompanyed with lady *Flora,* rychely appareled, and they saluted the kinge with diuerse goodly songes, & so brought hym to Grenewyche.

The entire revel seems to have been a curious hybrid of May game, pageant triumph, and allegorical music-making. The ladies mentioned by Hall are all obviously relevant to the seasonal festivity; but the horses—apart from Hall's tortured version of Phaeton and Lampos, the two steeds of Aurora—are obscure. The Venetian, Sagudino, adds to the confusion by mentioning the presence of tall pasteboard giants in the pageant car; but he confirms the musical nature of the show by describing how the musicians sang the whole way home, sounding trumpets and other instruments. It was, he wrote, a very fine triumph and very pompous and was watched by a crowd of more than 25,000 persons. [53]

Henry hunted throughout the summer on his progress westward but returned late in the year to London where preparations were set afoot for the Christmas revels. Epiphany 1516 was the occasion for an interesting show devised by Cornish and staged, as always, by Richard Gibson. The festival began with a play—performed by Cornish and the Children of the Chapel Royal—about "troylous and panrdor," in which the dramatis

52. Thomas and Thornley, *Great Chronicle,* pp. 228–229.

53. Hall, p. 582; Rawdon Brown, *Four Years at the Court of Henry VIII* (London, 1854), I, 79–81; E.36/229, fols. 125–137. The Venetian Pietro Pasqualigo further complicates the issue by mentioning an encounter, on the outward journey, with a triumphal car, "full of singers and musicians, drawn by griffins with human faces" (Rawdon Brown, *Four Years at the Court of Henry VIII,* I, 90–91).

personae included "allso kallkas and kryssyd inparylled lyke a wedow of
onovr in blake sarsenet and other abelements for seche mater, dyomed
and the greks inparylld lyke men of warre," and a "eulyxes" played by
one of the children. After this drama there ensued a vigorous disguising
with pageant to fulfill the King's pleasure to "hauf reuelles for yoyvs
pastym . . . as well by the avyes of wyllyam kornyche as by the avyes of
the master of the revelles." Gibson had taken pains to provide a "castel
of tymbyr fyne and fast in the kyngys hall garnechyd after seche devyces
[as the sayd master kornyche cummandyd]": but it is not apparent
whether this pageant was used as the setting for the play or whether it
entered the hall after the performance. The disguising began with the
appearance of a herald—played by Cornish who had already acted the
part of "kallkas"—proclaiming that three strange knights had come to do
battle with the knights of the castle. Thereupon three men at arms sallied
forth from the fortress, bearing "punchyng speres, redy to do feets at the
barryers," and when the strange knights entered with similar weapons
they all "with speers mad sartayn strooks." After this the two groups
fought with naked swords "a fayer batayll of twelve strooks," and so
ended the contest. From the pageant there next descended a queen with
six ladies in attendance who delivered "spechys after the devyse of master
kornyche." Minstrels now appeared on the walls and towers of the castle
and played a melodious song, accompanying the dancing of six new lords
and six ladies who had emerged from the capacious castle.[54]

The summer of 1516 was occupied with the reception of Henry's sister
Margaret and the preparation of a tournament in her honor; and there is
scant record of court festivals till Epiphany 1517, when another pageant
entertainment graced Henry's court. This time it was the *Gardyn de
esperans,* "Rayllyd with bankys all sett with goodly flowers arttyfycyall."
Six knights and six ladies walked about in this garden, the center of which
contained a pillar supporting six "partyd antyks" set with stones and
pearls and a rose tree bearing red roses and pomegranates, richly "Inornyd
and korwnyd with golld of gret bygnes." No dramatic action has been
recorded for this occasion, and one may assume, since Cornish rode in on
a horse and "shewyd by speche the effectte and Intent," that the interest
was largely allegorical. The pageant was brought through the hall "with

54. Hall, p. 583; E.36/229, fols. 139–157; *L.P.,* II.ii, 1470.

noyse of mynstrells and melody," the disguisers descended and danced before the court, and finally—having remounted the pageant—they were conveyed out of the hall. The existing narratives of this show cannot be complete, for the *Revels Accounts* reveal that Cornish was provided with three garments, so that there must have been some sort of interlude or play presented; but it is impossible to determine whether or not this was connected with the pageant.[55]

Later in 1517 the revels department at court was occupied with the reception of the Flemish ambassadors and preparations for the tournament at which they were entertained, and there is no further reference to significant indoor festivities until October 1518, during the celebrations for the Treaty of Universal Peace in London.[56] On Thursday, 5 October, after a banquet at Greenwich, the King, his court, and the visiting dignitaries were all entertained by a large-scale political disguising and pageant. The action began with the entry of sundry Turks playing on drums. These were followed by the principal characters, a winged horse, and his rider "called Reaport." The horse introduced himself as Pegasus, who had been flying about the world spreading news of the peace and the impending Anglo-French marriage, and he called upon two children to sing an excellent composition on these topics. When they had finished Pegasus said, "You will now see a fine castle. We shall see who will be able to explain it." Immediately a curtain was lowered to reveal a triumphal car with a castle and a rock, all green and gilded. Inside the rock was a gilded cave, the entrance to which was furnished with wooden gates hung with silk curtains. In this recess were nine beautiful damsels holding wax candles—their appearance through the veil being that of radiant goddesses, so handsome were they. Cunningly hidden within the rock were musicians, and outside the cave, seated about the pageant, were nine youths all dressed in identical livery. Planted about the rock were five

55. Hall, pp. 585–586; E.36/217, fols. 252–262.

56. Hall, p. 595; *Calendar of State Papers, Venetian,* II, No. 1088; hereafter cited as "*CSP, Ven.*" A curious *divertissement* enlivened the banquet given for the Flemish ambassadors in July 1517, when the viands were carried to the King's table by an elephant, lions, panthers, and other animals, marvelously designed, to the sounds of constant music (Rawdon Brown, *Four Years at the Court of Henry VIII,* II, 102). Two pageants for July 1517 are mentioned in the King's Book of Payments (*L.P.,* II.ii, 1479), but no details survive.

trees: an olive tree bearing the Pope's arms; a fir tree with those of the Emperor; a lily, with the arms of the King of France; a rose tree, with the English King's; and finally a pomegranate, with the arms of the King of Spain. Between the olive tree and the rose tree was a girl, dressed as a queen, lying prostrate—one hand touching the base of the olive and her feet at the base of the rose. In her lap was a dolphin. Reaport now took the stage and explained the allegorical significance of the scene, commenting that the whole world rejoiced at the Universal Peace. One of the Turks, who had all been waiting while the speeches and songs were performed, hereupon stepped forward to dispute this rash claim: "Thou speakest not the truth: I, who am of this world, rejoice not at it." Reaport, naturally, reiterated his boast, and the ensuing argument resulted in a challenge to battle.

Immediately fifteen armed men appeared on either side and fought a tourney, the result of which is not recorded. Then the triumphal car was drawn up in front of the King, and the music of lutes and other instruments played beautifully. After this musical interlude the car was returned to its place, and the youths, each holding a damsel by the hand, descended from the pageant and performed a goodly dance. There followed fresh viands and wines, and the King made a gift of fifty-two large silver drinking vessels to the French visitors. Finally, removing his royal robe of gold brocade and ermine, he presented it to the Admiral of France. The entertainment lasted until two o'clock in the morning before the party retired to their beds.

The authorship of this political disguising is not known with certainty. The *Revels Accounts* for this occasion do not survive, although there is a record, in the King's Book of Payments, of money allowed to Richard Gibson for both a mummery, which took place at Wolsey's palace on 3 October, and for the disguising at Greenwich.[57] But, despite the lack of positive evidence, I think it safe to assume that William Cornish was responsible for the show. Cornish dominated the revels at this period and had figured, as deviser and actor, in most of the pageant entertainments given at court. During the pageant for Epiphany 1517 he had made his entry riding upon a horse and had explained the symbolism of the scene

57. *L.P.,* II.ii, 1479.

to the audience—a form so closely followed in 1518 that it justifies the supposition that Cornish acted the role of Reaport. He was, moreover, the author of a later political play, performed at Windsor in 1522 before the Emperor Charles V, so that the political allegory of 1518 could well have been an early essay in this genre.

The staging of the performance seems to have been fairly straightforward. The allegorical scene was set on a pageant car which also contained the disguisers and musicians. The car was mounted on wheels, for it had to be moved about the hall at various phases of the action: in its original place during the explanatory speeches and combat; drawn before the King's seat for the performance of the musical interlude which was, apparently, entirely instrumental; then taken back to its first position prior to the dancing. The only unusual feature was the lowering of a curtain to reveal the pageant car in the first instance—"et subito abassato un panno se uide un bello carro Triumphale." This suggests that the car was hidden from sight until the curtain was drawn. A similar device had been used in February 1511 and was later employed in the great Greenwich spectacle of May 1527, though on the latter occasion the pageant was not moved about the hall.

Records for the entertainments over Christmas 1518/9 are lacking, but later in the year there were two important experimental revels without pageantry, both staged to entertain the French hostages held by Henry VIII against the delivery of Tournai to Francis I. The first of these shows took place on 7 March when Henry

> prepared a disguysyng, and caused his greate chambre at Grenewiche to be staged, and great lightes to be set on pillers that wer gilt, with basons gilt, and the rofe was couered with blewe sattin full of presses of fine gold and flowers: and vnder was written, *iammes,* the meanyng wherof was, that the flower of youth could not be oppressed.

Within this chamber there was "a goodly commedy of Plautus plaied." This was, perhaps, the first such classical performance at court, though it is impossible to discover whether or not the work was given in translation and whether, as seems likely, it was performed on a fixed stage. The play was followed by the entry of eight ladies, "tired like to the Egipcians very richely," and eight lords, who danced together "all beyng viserd." There was, on this occasion, no dancing of the disguisers with members of the audience, though Gibson still refers to it as a "maskalyne after the maner of etaly." [58]

The second of these entertainments was presented at Newhall in Essex on 3 September 1519:

And after the banket ended, with noise of minstrelles entered into the chamber eight Maskers with white berdes, and long and large garmentes of Blewe satten pauned with Sipres, poudered with spangles of Bullion Golde, and they daunsed with Ladies sadly, and communed not with the ladies after the fassion of Maskers, but behaued theimselfes sadly. Wherefore the quene plucked of their visours, and then appered the duke of Suffolk, the erle of Essex, the Marques Dorset, the lorde Burgainy, sir Richard Wyngfeld, sir Robert Wyngfelde, sir Richard Weston, sir Willyam Kyngston: all these wer somwhat aged, the youngest man was fiftie at the least. The Ladies had good sporte to se these auncient persones Maskers. When they wer departed, the kyng and the foure hostages of Fraunce, and the erle of Deuonshire with. vi. other young gentlemen entered the chamber, of the whiche sixe wer al in yelowe sattin, hosen, shoen, and cappes, and sixe other wer in like maner in Grene: the yelowe sattin was freted with siluer of Damaske, and so was the grene very richely to behold: and then euery Masker toke a ladie and daunsed: and when they had daunsed & communed a great while their visers were taken of, and then the ladies knewe them, & there the king gaue many brooches & proper giftes to the ladies. And after this done, the quene made a banket to the kyng & his lordes and thother strangers.

Hall's description is of particular interest, for it clarifies his account of the 1512 mask: "thei daunced and commoned together, as the fashion of the Maske is." This "commoning" was nothing more than lively conversation—in contrast to dancing silently or "sadly." Furthermore, what we have in this double entry of maskers, with the first acting as a foil to the second, is clearly an antimask, nearly a century before Jonson's supposed innovation.[59] This festival also included an interlude performed

58. Hall, p. 597; S.P.1/18, fols. 53–58. Apparently Cornish and the Children of the Chapel played an interlude on this occasion (L.P., III.ii, 1536), and Wallace, *Evolution of the English Drama,* identifies this with the Plautine comedy. Such a conclusion is just possible, but it is based on the assumption that Hall mentioned everything which occurred during the festival, a dangerous assumption in view of other omissions by the chronicler, as, for example, his scanty account of the entertainments for Epiphany 1516, which are so fully detailed in Gibson's *Revels Accounts.*

59. Hall, p. 599.

by the Children of the Chapel Royal. Gibson refers to it as the "pastym that master kornyche maad," and it was probably acted prior to the double mask. William Cornish had coached the cast of seven children who appeared as Summer, Lust, the Moon, the Sun, Winter, Wind, and Rain. John Browne, the King's Painter, one of the regular team engaged in the production of court spectacle, was entrusted with the task of decorating the costumes for the minstrels and the children, whose garb reflected the seasonal nature of the interlude, being powdered with golden suns and clouds, moons, silver drops, silver honeysuckles, golden stars, and silver snowflakes.[60]

Revels, "kalld a meskeller or mvmry," held on New Year's Eve 1519/20, welcomed in one of the most festival-filled years of Henry VIII's spectacular reign. On 5 January the King went "in meskellyng apperell," with nineteen gentlemen, by river to visit Cardinal Wolsey. Then on Twelfth-night Henry commanded Gibson to prepare and "make Redy yn all hast . . . a dysgysyng with a pagent convenyent for the same." [61] This is the first reference to a pageant entertainment since that of October 1518, and, in view of the extremely short notice and the meager cost of 22 s. Gibson must merely have refurbished an existing pageant car. The poor Serjeant of the Tents was really under pressure, for on the following day, 7 January, he was ordered by the King "to purvay a new and an other meskeller"—an easier task, however, merely requiring the alteration of masking costumes from the King's store. Masks were, in any case, far simpler and far cheaper to organize, and the popularity of the pageant with disguising seems to have been waning: though on 1 February some gentlemen of the court, "clothyd yn blew saten with meskelyn," used a "tryke wagyn or spell wagvn" to present a challenge before the King and Queen for a tilting match to be fulfilled on 19 February.[62] But, just as the pageant entry for tournaments—in such high favor at the beginning of Henry VIII's reign—had quickly been super-

60. E.36/217, fols. 89–97.
61. E.36/217, fols. 100–105.
62. E.36/217, fol. 108: "entred iiij gentyllmen clothyd yn blew saten with meskelyn and with them browght a tryke wagyn or spell wagvn and ther yn a lady. vn the pyllers of the sayde spell wagvn beyng iiij hed peces of armytes with sartayn devyces." Cf. Hall, pp. 600–601: "before the quenes chamber there blewe a trompet sodainly,

seded by sumptuously-costumed processions in which all the ingenuity
of artists and embroiderers was concentrated in chivalric devices and im-
prese, so the pageant entry into the banquet hall more slowly gave way
to the simpler forms of disguising and mask. It was in many ways a
regression. Both these changes are strikingly evidenced at the entertainments given at the Field of Cloth of Gold in June 1520 when, though both
English and French were vying with each other in displays of artistic
virtuosity, there were no pageant cars either in the tournament or in the
indoor entertainments which were entirely devoted to "meskellers." And,
though Cornish was appointed to devise "pageants" for a banquet at Calais
for the subsequent Anglo-Imperial interview, there is no record of anything other than masks being performed on that occasion.[63] Thereafter
it was one "meskeller" after the other in rapid succession at the end of
1520 and early 1521.[64]

It was not till 4 March 1522, at an entertainment given by Wolsey, with
the aid of the royal revels department, for the Imperial ambassadors, that
another pageant show was devised—and this, entitled the *schatew vert,*
stood firmly within the romantic tradition of castles, imprisoned lovers,
and mock assaults.[65] At the far end of a special chamber, decorated with
arras and brilliantly illuminated with candelabra, stood the castle, its three
towers painted green and its battlements covered with green tin foil. A
great deal of timber had been "spent and inployd vn the boos of the pagent
wher vn hyng all the edyfyes the bord spent vn the stayers in to the havt
plaas set vn the wyndow and spred from the jams of the saam and all so
bord and tymbyr for plaas and stonddyng of the mynstrells with vyalls
and other instrements." Each tower was surmounted with a banner: three

---

and then entred into the Quenes Chamber foure gentlemen appareled in long and
large garmentes of blewe damaske bordred with gold, and brought with them a
tricke waggon, in the which sat a ladie richely appareled with a canapy ouer her hed,
& on the. iiii. corners of the waggon, wer. iiii. hed peces called Armites, euery pece
beyng of a sundery deuice."

63. See my article, "Le Camp du drap d'or et les entrevues d'Henri VIII et de
Charles Quint," *Fêtes et cérémonies au temps de Charles Quint,* ed. Jean Jacquot
(Paris, 1960), pp. 112–134. Cornish's responsibility for "pageants" is referred to in
the *Rutland Papers,* ed. W. Jerdan (Camden Society; London, 1842), p. 56.

64. S.P.1/29, fols. 208^v–215^v.

65. Hall, p. 631; S.P.1/29, fols. 224^v–233.

rent hearts, a lady's hand gripping a man's heart, and a lady's hand turning a man's heart. Within this lovelorn fortress eight ladies of "straunge names" were imprisoned: Beautie, Honor, Perseueraunce, Kyndnes, Constance, Bountie, Mercie, and Pitie. The *Revels Accounts* name, as retaining their garments from the pageant, eight ladies of the court (including Mary, the Dowager Queen of France, and one Mistress Anne Boleyn) who presumably acted the nonspeaking parts of the eight prisoners whose romantic names were embroidered on their headgear. Guarding the battlements were "other eight ladies, whose names were, *Dangier, Disdain, Gelousie, Vnkyndenes, Scorne, Malebouche, Straungenes,* these ladies were tired like to women of Inde." This unpleasant group, who had more violent parts to play than the passive beauties whom they held prisoner, were played by Children of the Chapel Royal, as appears from a payment for "reparacyvn doon for vn garmentes for ladyes the chylldern of the chappell" and another referring to eight cauls, of which three were lost "by the chyldern of my lordes chappell by kasttyng down ovt of the kastell." [66] The scene having been set, nine lords entered to begin the action. Their leader, Ardent Desire, played by the King, appropriately clad in crimson satin decorated with "burnyng flames of gold," asked the evil defenders to surrender the castle. Scorne and Disdain refused, and the lords, encouraged by their leader, ran to assault the battlements, "at whiche tyme without was shot a great peale of gunnes." The attack was waged with dates, oranges, and other "fruites made for pleasure"; while the defenders responded with a desperate hail of rose water, "Comfittes," and "boows and balles," and, of course, the three hats hurled down by the enthusiastic Children of the Chapel when, one imagines, the rest of their ammunition had given out. But the heroic stand was in vain. The sinister ladies were forced to take flight, abandoning the eight beauties to the lords who led them onto the floor where they "daunced their fill" before removing the visors which had hitherto concealed their identity. A costly banquet, as ever, completed the entertainment.

There is no direct evidence in the *Revels Accounts* concerning the authorship of the *schatew vert;* but, since the Children of the Chapel were involved, and since, stylistically, the entertainment is in the tradition established at the Tudor court in 1501, it seems most likely that Cornish

66. S.P.1/29, fols. 232–233.

was responsible. Corroborative, though somewhat enigmatic, evidence for this attribution may be deduced from one of Cornish's surviving songs, *Yow and I and Amyas,* which has several similarities to the *schatew vert* both in characters and setting. It concerns a knight called Desyre who knocks at a castle gate and is answered by a lady, Strangenes. He says that he has been asked to present a petition:

> Kyndnes said she wold yt bere,
> And Pyte said she wold be ther.
> Thus how thay dyd we cannot say—
> We left them ther and went ower way.[67]

Perhaps Cornish wrote the *schatew vert* as a sequel at the request of some of those who, having heard the song, wished to discover "how thay dyd."

Three months later the Emperor Charles V himself visited the English court where he was entertained with tilting and, on two evenings, with masks. The latter *divertissements* were characterized, as usual, by a double entry with the second group arriving "sodainly" to displace the first.[68] The Emperor's visit was also the occasion for Cornish's last major production at court. This was a political play, performed at Windsor on 15 June, showing the French king as a wild horse eventually tamed by Friendship, Prudence, and Might—all representing the Anglo-Imperial alliance which was formally agreed on the following day.[69] England was now on the verge of a disastrous war. Court festivals were again to pass through a lean period, and, when the time next came for major festivities, the faithful William Cornish was no longer available to devise, produce, and perform them. He died late in 1523, and his demise marks the end of a distinct period in the history of English court festivals—though not yet the end of all experimentation in Henrician revelry nor the end of his influence.

---

67. B.M. Additional MS. 31,922, fols. 45ᵛ-46, printed in John Stevens, *Music and Poetry in the Early Tudor Court* (London, 1961), pp. 402–403. Stevens acutely notes (p. 402): "the verses read like the 'story' of a disguising."

68. Hall, pp. 635–637; S.P.1/24, fols. 225ᵛ–233.

69. *El Emperador Carlos V y su Corte según las Cartas de Don Martín de Salinas Embajador del Infante Don Fernando (1522-1539),* ed. Antonio Rodriguez Villa (Madrid, 1903), pp. 40–41. This letter is calendared in *Calendar of State Papers, Spanish,* II, No. 437; hereafter cited as *"CSP, Span."* See also, Hall, p. 641; S.P.1/24, fols. 233ᵛ–235ᵛ.

IV Classics and Politics: The Last Phase of Henrician Experiment

After the Anglo-Imperial entertainments of 1522 the record of court festivals dwindles dramatically, with regard to both tournaments and indoor spectacle. Indeed, I have so far located only four references relating to banquet hall *divertissements* prior to Christmas 1526/7: a "maske" on 29 December 1524; "disguisynges" on 18 June 1525; an unspecific and scathing allusion by Hall to Wolsey's Christmas celebrations 1525/6, when the Cardinal treated himself to "plaies and disguisyng in most royall maner"; and a brief *Revels Account* relating to a "meskeller" for 14 January 1526.[70]

Admittedly, this paucity of material may be partly accidental. But, on the whole, it seems to reflect a waning interest in lavish spectacle for its own sake. Whatever the cause, it is not until January 1527 that we again encounter large-scale revelry within doors. This was an entertainment, presented at Wolsey's palace at Hampton Court, which, while including many of the old favorite forms of display, also introduced a new note into English court life—a note far more Italianate than the minor innovation of Epiphany 1512.[71] The day of 3 January had been spent in jousting; then, in the evening, Henry and a group of companions dressed themselves in masking apparel like shepherds, donned their beards of gold and silver wire, and took barge to Wolsey's abode, where an extravagant sup-

---

70. Hall, pp. 689, 703, 707; S.P.1/37, fols. 8–16.

71. This entertainment is described in a letter from Gasparo Spinelli, secretary to the Venetian ambassador in London, to his brother Lodovico. It is printed in Stefani, *I Diarii di Marino Sanuto,* XLIII, cols. 703–704, and calendared in *CSP, Ven.* Hall, p. 719, briefly mentions the entertainment without describing the dramatic performances. J. S. Brewer, *The Reign of Henry VIII from His Accession to the Death of Wolsey* (London, 1884), II, 107, n. 2, points out that this festival was a classic event in Wolsey's career and suggests that Cavendish's well-known long general account of Wolsey's entertaining of Henry VIII is based largely upon this occasion. Certainly—though the King had previously visited Wolsey by river, with a company of maskers (see above p. 31)—the similarity between Cavendish and Spinelli is such that I have accepted Brewer's suggestion and have filled out the Venetian's description with a few details from Cavendish. For the best-edited text, see *The Life and Death of Cardinal Wolsey by George Cavendish,* ed. Richard Sylvester (EETS, 1959), pp. 25–28. Sylvester, in his notes, misses the connection with the festival of January 1527.

per was being given to various important guests, including the Papal, French, and Venetian ambassadors, and the leading English nobles. The arrival of the maskers, by river, at the palace was signalized by the firing of cannon, and the revelers entered the banquet hall "with such a number of drums and fifes," writes Cavendish, "as I have seldom seen together at one time in any maske." These visitors played dice, or "mumchance," with the Cardinal and his lady guests before unmasking to join in the banquet.[72] When replete the entire company repaired to another chamber to witness the dramatic performances which were the crowning point of the evening's entertainment. Spinelli, the Venetian Secretary, who has left an account of the show, writes that "una molto ben intesa scena" had been prepared, on which the Cardinal's gentlemen recited Plautus' Latin comedy, the *Menaechmi*. As we have seen, this was not the first time that a Plautine comedy had been staged in England as part of a courtly revel. In March 1519 the French hostages had been similarly entertained at a festival for which a fixed stage had probably been provided. In 1527 the fixed stage seems a certainty, and Spinelli's unfortunately ambiguous "scena" must indicate something architecturally more ambitious than a plain wooden platform.

After the play the actors, one after the other, presented themselves to the King, reciting Latin verses in his honor. An interval followed in which the guests returned to the banquet hall for choice confections before another diversion. Again Spinelli suggests the provision of some sort of stage set, and, though his account is vague, he seems to indicate a setting different from that provided for the comedy: "apresso così meravigliosa colatione, fu scoperto uno solaro sopra el qual eravi Venere con 6 damisele." This suggests a process of unveiling similar to that already encountered in 1511 and 1518; but it is impossible, without further evidence, to say more. Whilst everybody was intent upon the agreeable sight of Venus and her nymphs, the trumpets flourished and a car appeared, drawn by

---

72. Spinelli (col. 703) describes this part of the entertainment thus: "Et cenando, sopragionse il Re con molta bella compagnia de maschare, qual presentatosi al reverendissimo Cardinal gioco alli dati al mumo el fato questo si levo la maschera; il che da tutti li altri parimente fu osservato." Hall, p. 719, calls the revelers "Maskers"; but when he says that they danced before unmasking he is clearly relying on his imagination. The brevity and inaccuracy of Hall's description suggest that he had neither original documents nor eyewitness accounts for Wolsey's show.

three stark-naked boys, "nudi come naquero." On the car was Cupid dragging after him, by a silver rope, six old men clad in pastoral fashion. Cupid presented them to his mother explaining, in an elegant Latin oration, how they had been cruelly wounded, whereupon Venus compassionately replied in equally choice language and caused the nymphs, described by Spinelli as the sweethearts of the old men, to descend. Venus commanded the beauties to afford their lovers all solace and to requite them for their past pangs of love. Each lover then took his nymph and, to the sound of trumpets, performed "una molto bella danza." The evening's revelry later ended with a ball led by the King.

The show is not structurally, or even thematically, all that different from Cornish's tripartite revels, with their play, pageant of unrequited lovers, and dance. But it is, undeniably, reminiscent of Italian court entertainments—with their classical plays (Plautus was a great favorite) and their intermezzi of classical characters, brief dialogue, and final well-designed dance or "spettacolo allegorico coreografico." There is no precise indication that the dance of nymphs and old men, which terminated Wolsey's show, had a planned choreography, but for Early Tudor revels, this is one of the features most difficult to elucidate. In English court festivals for this period only one of the numerous dance entertainments is described in such a way as to suggest the degree to which it had been planned and rehearsed. Nevertheless, the fact that there is this one account of a complex dance routine at the English court as early as 1494 suggests that other dances were similarly the result of careful design and may have approximated an incipient ballet.[73] By 1527, when an Italian as distinguished as Spinelli writes of "una molto bella danza," it is reasonable to conclude that the choreography was of some intricacy—a view which may be corroborated by the even more elaborate entertainments presented at court in May 1527.

Late in February 1527, a great French embassy arrived in England to negotiate an alliance against the Emperor Charles V. Already, at the beginning of the month, work had started on the construction of a banquet hall and separate theater for the treaty celebrations at Greenwich. This was the second temporary theater for masks and disguisings built for

73. Thomas and Thornley, *Great Chronicle*, pp. 251–252. See also my "William Cornish in a Play," pp. 349–350.

Henry VIII. The first had been constructed from timber and canvas at Calais for the Anglo-Imperial interview in July 1520, after the Field of Cloth of Gold. Circular in conception, it was, in fact, like the later London theaters, polygonal with sixteen sides; the three levels of spectators' galleries were set one above the other—each fronted by a low parapet—and, though no seats were provided, the floors sloped so that "they that stode behynd myght see over the hedes that stode before." A vast circular *mappa mundi* adorned the roof, and its culmination in a representation of the heavens and the celestial sphere completed this remarkable anticipation of the English public theater as it was to develop later in the century. Unfortunately the Calais theater—intended for "pageants" to be devised by Cornish and for "mummeries" which were "referred to the Kinges pleasure"—succumbed to the wind and was destroyed before the festivities could begin. The 1527 theater, complete with an astronomical ceiling by Holbein, was more fortunate with the weather. Unlike its predecessor, it followed a traditional form for court entertainments, being rectangular in shape with three sloping tiers of seats, one behind the other, rather than galleries, one above the other, for standing spectators.[74]

The festival of 5 May 1527 began with a colossal feast in the banquet hall, after which the company made their way to the adjoining disguising house. When all had settled in their seats, eight choristers appeared, in

74. On these theaters see my forthcoming book, *Spectacle, Pageantry, and Early Tudor Policy,* chaps. IV, VI. More especially on the 1527 theater see my article, "La Salle de banquet et le théâtre construits à Greenwich pour les fêtes franco-anglaises de 1527," *Le Lieu théâtral à la Renaissance,* ed. Jean Jacquot (Paris, 1964), pp. 273–288. Cavendish, *The Life and Death of Cardinal Wolsey by George Cavendish,* ed. Sylvester, pp. 72–73, describes this festival very inaccurately, confessing that "I do bothe lake wytt in my grosse old hed & Cunnyng in my bowelles to declare the wonderfull and Curious Imagynacions in the same Inventyd & devysed." He maintains that the foot combat was followed by a tourney on horseback—in the midst of the banquet—and that both preceded the "disguysyng or enterlude made in latten & frenche." Sylvester, *ibid.,* pp. 222–223 (notes to p. 72/11-12, and p. 73/7-8), confuses this entertainment with the November festival at Greenwich. As a matter of fact Cavendish himself confuses the whole series of entertainments for the French embassy for November with that for May (*ibid.,* pp. 65 ff.). For May 1527, Hall, pp. 723–724, records three companies of maskers—as does Cavendish, though Cavendish has two companies of ladies and one of gentlemen, whereas it was the other way round. Sylvester says that Hall records four companies—he does, but for November, not May, 1527.

the midst of whom was a youth clad in a blue silk gown scattered with golden eyes and a golden cap garlanded with laurel and berries of fine gold. After the choristers had performed certain English songs they withdrew, leaving the elaborately-clad youth, in the guise of Mercury, to deliver a Latin oration in praise of the Anglo-French alliance, Henry VIII, Francis I, and Cardinal Wolsey. He then announced that Jupiter, having listened frequently to disputes between Love and Riches concerning their relative authority and being unable to decide the question, had appointed Henry as judge and had asked him to pass his sentence. Mercury then departed and was immediately succeeded by eight choristers—four led by Cupid ("Amore") and four led by Plutus ("Richeza"). Between these groups walked the figure of Justice who came before the King and, in English, outlined the controversy between the two parties. Cupid then stated his case, to which Plutus replied—support being given by their choristers who each recited verses. The altercation being at an end, neither side could agree, and it was decided to have recourse to battle. Three knights thereupon appeared for each party and fought, one against one, over a barrier across the triumphal archway of the hall. After the combat, an old, silver-bearded gentleman entered and tritely pronounced that both love and riches were necessary for princes: "by loue to be obeied and serued, and with riches to rewarde his louers and frendes."

The next part of the entertainment followed immediately after this dialogue, combat, and verdict. At the nether end of the disguising house, writes Hall,

> by lettyng doune of a courtaine, apered a goodly mount, walled with towers and vamures al gilt, with all thinges necessarie for a fortresse, & all the mount was set ful of Christal coralles, & rich rockes of rubie cureously counterfaited & full of roses & pomgranates as though they grewe.

Spinelli reports that, at the end of the hall, there fell to the ground a painted canvas "che si trovava all'ingresso del luoco" and revealed a verdant cave to which entrance was gained by four steps ("et si scoperse un viridissimo antro al qual si saliva per 4 gradi"). Both these accounts are vague and suggest that the curtain was in the nature of a painted scene which might, therefore, have served as a back cloth to the preceding dialogue. Gibson's *Revels Accounts* refer to this curtain: first under a general entry for linen, as "the travas for the pagent," and again in a payment to tailors for sewing the new "cloothe for the pagent and the ij ends." It is impossible to determine the way in which the curtain was drawn, or dropped, but the "lettyng doune" recalls the usage in 1511 and 1518; and the scene thus revealed, though stationary, is exactly like the pageants favored earlier in the reign. Apart from the verdant cave, the removal of the curtain also revealed a fortress and mountain on which were grouped eight damsels, including the Princess Mary; and on either side of the pageant stood a group of four youths bearing torches. Spinelli's account of the ensuing dances differs from Hall, for, whereas the English chronicler merely talks of "diuers daunces," the Italian observer is much more specific. His account implies, as well as the dances by men accompanied by women, two groups of elaborate figure dances performed first by women and then by the men without intermingling of the sexes—a procedure long customary at the Tudor court. The ladies first of all descended from their seats to the sound of trumpets and then, presenting themselves before the King, they performed a dance which was delightful for its variety and for the groups and figures executed—"La danza loro fu molto diletevole per la varietà, imperò che vi intervenivano certi nodi insieme et svilupi poi, grati al veder." This certainly suggests that the dance had been carefully designed and rehearsed and that it was of some considerable complexity. When the ladies had finished, the youths relinquished their torches, came down from the pageant, and performed their own dance. It was only after this that they took their ladies by the hand and led them in the coranto. Six maskers then entered to dance with ladies of the audience, interrupting (as was the tradition) the original entertainment. After these maskers had "daunced lustely about the place," a second group, including the King, made their entry. All members of this second mask wore black velvet slippers so that Henry, who wore such a slipper owing to a foot injury sustained at tennis, might not be distinguished. The usual dancing and unmasking followed, and the evening ended with another repast in the great banquet hall amidst "ioy, myrth and melody."

The very day after this celebration, the Imperialist troops broke into the city of Rome and gave it to the sack. This act of sacrilege was to provide a major theme of political propaganda throughout the year, both on the Continent and in England where it was exploited in two dramatic entertainments. The first of these took place within the new Greenwich theater—carefully refurbished by laborers, craftsmen, and artists—where, on 10 November, a Latin play united all the major contemporary political themes.[75] Virtually nothing survives concerning the staging of this play, but the main course of action seems straightforward. The Church was falling and the Pope was captive; succor was provided by Henry VIII and Wolsey in their writings and actions against Luther; St. Peter gave the Cardinal authority to free the Pope and resuscitate the Church; and Wolsey interceded between the kings of France and England who, by united action, were able to liberate the Pope. After all this, Francis I's two children, who were being held hostage by the Emperor, begged Henry and Wolsey to help them since their custodian would not come to a reasonable agreement with their father. King and Cardinal agreed that, if the Emperor would not release the hostages, they themselves would challenge him—a threat which induced the Emperor's Chancellor to come forward and conclude a peace, whereupon the two young princes were released. The show concluded with the entry of maskers, including a group led by the King, who danced with the ladies grouped about a fountain at the end of the hall, "and so with disport al this night passed."

In December Charles V allowed Pope Clement to escape to Orvieto. It was difficult, after this, for the Emperor's enemies to continue their diatribes against him, but Wolsey was able to employ the Pope's escape for one more political drama. The news of the liberation was celebrated on 5 January 1528 at St. Paul's, and two days later the Cardinal invited all the ambassadors to a banquet followed by a double dramatic performance—Terence's *Phormio* and a political dialogue.[76] This program arrangement, with a classical comedy followed by a new work, had already been used in Wolsey's entertainment of the preceding January, though on that occasion there had been no political symbolism. The hall in which the guests had dined, and where the play was given, was decorated at its head with a large garland of boxwood, inscribed with gilt letters, *Terentii Phormio*. Then on one side, inscribed upon paper in Gothic letters, was *Cedant arma togae* (a favorite Ciceronian tag), and on the other, *Foedera*

75. Hall, pp. 734–735; *CSP, Span.,* III.ii, No. 240. See also Anglo, "La Salle de banquet," pp. 285–287.

76. Stefani, *I Diarii di Marino Sanuto,* XLVI, col. 595, calendared in *CSP, Ven.* IV, No. 225.

pacis non movebitur. Beneath the garland was written *Honori et laudi Pacifici,* with reference to Cardinal Wolsey, who was styled in his favorite role, *Cardinalis Pacificus.* Other mottoes relating to peace, such as *Pax cum homine et bellum cum vitiis,* were scattered over the sides of the hall. The entire decoration was thus an affirmation of Wolsey's assumed position as the pacifier of Europe. *Phormio* was delivered by the Children of St. Paul's, and their performance had such good spirit and their acting was so accomplished that Spinelli was obliged to confess astonishment. After the classical comedy, three richly-clad girls appeared, representing Religion, Peace, and Justice. They complained that they had been expelled from well-nigh all Europe by heresy, war, and ambition; and they detailed the iniquities perpetrated by the enemy, saying that they had no other refuge than in their most generous Father whom they besought to defend and protect them. Each of these characters concluded her speech with the lines: "Ast tibi pro meritis meritos tribuemus honores / Et laudes cecinit nostra Thalia tuos." When the girls had said their piece, a little boy, who had already recited the prologue of the comedy, delivered a Latin oration celebrating the day as one of great thanksgiving owing to the release of the Pope, who had escaped from the hands of the "most iniquitous men in the world—worse than the Turks." He attacked the cruelty of these people and also of the Emperor, *omisso nomine,* and showed that all these calamities proceeded "ab unius libidine, qui cuncta sibi subjicere cupide admodum conabantur." Spinelli ends with a word of praise for the manner in which the little fellow delivered his lines but gives no further information relating to the performance.

Considered as a series, the entertainments between January 1527 and January 1528 evince striking common characteristics, though no two shows are exactly similar. All the dialogues were primarily in Latin; the two January shows began with a Latin classical comedy; the performances of January and May 1527 included classical deities; and the performances of November 1527 and January 1528 were both political, having the characters Religion and Peace in common, together with praise of Henry VIII and Cardinal Wolsey and an attack on heresy. The Plautine play of 1527 was, according to Spinelli, performed by the Cardinal's gentlemen, though the actors and dancers in the ensuing triumphal-car scene are not specified. The performers in May 1527 are similarly not identified, but the dialogue of Love and Riches, in Latin and English, with its Cornish-like resolution at the barriers, seems to have been devised by John Rastell, painter, printer, playwright, pageanteer, and a noted stalwart on the production side of the Henrician revels.[77] The last two performances appear to have had a common authorship. In Gibson's accounts for the November revels, there are two payments relating to John Rightwise, Master of St. Paul's School. The first is for "dobelletes hossis and showise for the chyldryn that wer powir menys sonys and for fyar in tyme of Lernynge of the play"; the second is for the hiring of boats to carry the Master and his children to and from Greenwich.[78] This establishes that the actors, in November, were the Children of St. Paul's and that they were coached in their parts by Rightwise; this, in turn, strongly suggests that the Master was author of the play. The January entertainment, on Spinelli's testimony, was again given by the Children of St. Paul's and was very similar in theme to the earlier play. Both plays were in Latin—and Rightwise was a noted Latinist. It is virtually certain, therefore, that the Master of St. Paul's was the author and producer on both occasions. Interesting corroboration for this view is obtained from a fragmentary petition addressed by Rightwise to Henry VIII about the year 1530. The old pedagogue was by that time disabled by sickness and was hoping for some aid, especially as he had in times past, by the command of King and Council, written and played comedies for the entertainment of ambassadors and other strangers visiting the realm.[79] In so short a time had the playwright fallen from favor into hardship, along with the Cardinal whose greatness he had recently lauded.

Elaborate court festivals, too, seem to have suffered an eclipse. The entertainments from January 1527 to January 1528 are, astonishingly, the last in Henry VIII's reign for which we have any detailed record. The major sources for our knowledge of Henrician entertainments—Hall's *Chronicle,* Gibson's *Revels Accounts,* and the Venetian ambassadors' reports—become suddenly meager. There is evidence for later masks and entertainments, but no worthwhile narratives survive, while the *Revels Accounts* indicate both that the money expended on these shows was minimal and that the easily-organized nondramatic form of the mask—designated by Chambers as the "mask simple," that is, a mere entry of

77. Anglo, "La Salle de banquet," pp. 282–283; Anglo, "Le Camp du drap d'or," pp. 130–131.

78. S.P.1/45, fol. 39.

79. S.P.1/236, fol. 380 (*L.P. Addenda,* I.i, No. 717).

disguised persons to begin the dancing—became the normal mode of revelry. The "mask spectacular," having reached its peak, was suddenly abandoned.

V

The basic form of dramatic court entertainment—with pageant entries, disguising, *débat*, combat, music, and incipient ballet—introduced into England in 1501, had been enhanced and complicated, though only intermittently, by various innovations: the increased emphasis on rehearsed combat; the addition of the "mask simple"; the performance of a play of some kind on a fixed stage, prior to the entry of disguisers; the double-mask and the rudimentary antimask; and the appearance of classical deities, faintly foreshadowing the divine epiphanies so much in vogue nearly a century later. All these elements were combined only once, in May 1527, but then the period of innovation and experimentation was virtually at an end. The kind of display favored by Henry VIII, when he was trying to establish himself as a dazzling European potentate, and later employed to publicize the ambitious foreign policy pursued by the King and Cardinal Wolsey, became an expensive and unnecessary adornment for a policy of religious reformation. The whole evolution of the court mask form, wrote Chambers, "as we find it in the seventeenth century was already complete under Henry VIII." [80] This is largely true. But it is important to remember that this evolution was the result of self-conscious innovation, that it was a fairly rapid and circumscribed process, and that later, and strikingly similar, developments should not be seen as entirely contiguous to it.

80. Chambers, *The Elizabethan Stage* (Oxford, 1923), I, 155.

The First Progress of Henry VII

JOHN C. MEAGHER

WHEN HENRY TUDOR came to London from Bosworth Field, "with great pompe & triumphe he roade through the cytie to the cathedral churche of S. Paule wher he offred his iii. Standardes." London responded in kind, with a formal welcome, a substantial gift of money, and public acclamation, followed by "playes pastimes & pleasures" and by religious processions which displayed "their hartye and humble thankes" to God "whiche had deliuered them." Shortly after his solemn coronation, Henry appeared before his first Parliament to emphasize that the crown had come to him both by hereditary succession and by the true judgment of God given in battle; the Parliament acknowledged his title unqualifiedly, dutifully voted the expected attainders and subsidies, and then secured a few concessions before dissolving. These were important achievements for the stabilizing of Henry's throne, but they were also restatements, in a legal key, of themes already richly embodied in the grand gesture of Henry's triumphant visit to St. Paul's and in the celebrations and solemnities with which London had answered him then. The first Tudor Parliament affirmed and continued the work of the earliest Tudor pageantry. After Parliament dissolved, Henry's marriage effected another decisive step in the securing of his throne by uniting it with the heiress of the rival house. London responded with general rejoicing and magnificent festivities, Bernardus Andreas reports. Looking over the achievements of his first five months, Henry VII might well feel that "al things . . . were appeased at London & that he had set & appoynted all his affaires in good ordre and sure state." [1]

But London was not England, and although the enthusiasm that had been manifested there was not peculiar to London alone, Henry nevertheless had reason to suspect that the feeling elsewhere might be more reserved. In York, for instance: for Richard III had been kind to York, and Henry VII knew that the city's old loyalties had not died with his own accession. When his first emissary to York, Sir Roger Cotam, had arrived to proclaim the new King, the city officials had visited him at his inn to receive the proclamation, because "the forsaid Sir Roger Cotam durst not for fere of deth come thrugh the Citie to speake with the Maire and his Brethre"—and indeed, the mayor and aldermen had only the day before registered their sorrow for the late and lawful King Richard, "pitiously slane and murderd, to the grete hevyness of this Citie." Nor had the difficulties ceased with the proclamation. During the following months Henry had had repeated diplomatic problems with York over its recorder, Miles Metcalfe, one of the eight men specifically excepted from the general pardon offered by the new King to those in the northern counties who had supported Richard. Despite a letter received from the King in early October, reminding the York council that the "seditious" Metcalfe was unfit for office and preferring Richard Greene as his successor, the council a few days later not only continued to list Metcalfe as recorder but included in the day's business a reference to "the moost famous prince of blessed memory, King Richard, late decesid." Until Metcalfe's death at the end of the following February eased an awkward situation, York had continued to stall the election of a new recorder and to protect Metcalfe's interests against the pressure of intermittent letters from the King. Henry might well have a few misgivings about the fervor of York's loyalty.[2]

1. Edward Hall, *The Vnion of the Two Noble and Illustre Famelies of Lancastre & Yorke,* ed. Henry Ellis (London, 1809), pp. 423, 426; hereafter cited as "Hall." See also Sydney Anglo, "The Foundation of the Tudor Dynasty: The Coronation and Marriage of Henry VII," *The Guildhall Miscellany,* II (1960), 3–11.

2. *York Civic Records,* Vol. I, ed. Angelo Raine (The Yorkshire Archaeological

York was not the only problem. There had been strong loyalty to Richard III elsewhere in England, and some of the supporters of the late and vanquished King were still at liberty and disposed to further rebellion. Henry VII therefore, in the words of Hall's *Chronicle,* "thought it best to make a peregrinacion & take his progresse into the other quarters of his realme, that he might wede, extirpate and purdge the myndes of men spotted & contaminate with the contagious smoke of dissencion, & prevy faccions, & especially the countie of Yorke . . ." [3] Thus it was that at about the time of year when other folk once longed to go on pilgrimages, King Henry VII set out on progress to secure the civil reverence of the doubtful parts of his new kingdom.

An account of Henry's first progress is preserved in Cottonian MS. Julius B. xii, in the form of a tract entitled "A shorte and a brief memory by licence and corveccon of the first progresse of our souueraigne lorde King Henry the vij^th." [4] To judge from the mood of triumph in which this *Memory* recalls the tour, Henry's doubts about the loyalty of the provinces had been unwarranted: his affairs appear consistently to be in good order and sure state in all quarters of the realm. Needless to say, the happy recollections of the *Memory* do not tell the whole story of those three months. The editorial policy which shaped its account—probably determined in part by the terms of its license and correction—resulted in the tactful omission of a few events which would have qualified its optimistic view. It resulted also in an unusually detailed concentration on the incidents of the progress most redolent of harmony and solidarity— the ceremonies and shows with which the King was received all along his route. That is how the *Memory* happens to preserve, in its descriptions

---

Society, Record Series), XCVIII, 119–120, 125–126. Subsequent quotations from this volume will be designated by *YCR.*

3. Hall, p. 426.

4. The *Memory,* which begins on fol. 8ᵛ of the MS, was reprinted in John Leland's *Collectanea,* ed. Hearne (London, 1774), IV, pp. 185–203. Although marred by inaccuracies and eighteenth-century typographical mannerisms, this is the best, because it is the only, edition yet available, and subsequent references to the MS will include cross-references to the Hearne version, designated by "(1774)." In quoting from the MS, I have silently expanded the abbreviations, supplied sparingly the almost total lack of punctuation, and ignored the random and whimsical capitalizations of the original.

and extensive quotations, the earliest detailed examples of the striking variety of techniques in Tudor pageantry.

Yet despite its peculiar specialization, and despite its omissions, the *Memory* is not an unreal account of the progress. The shows themselves protect it from falsifying. The language of pageantic display was a remarkably versatile instrument in the service of royal propaganda and of civic diplomacy; in a pageantic show, a city could create a privileged meeting place between itself and its king and define the real relationship between them in ways that transcended both the neutrality of convention and the tact of silence. The *Memory,* especially when illuminated by other documents, discloses the various and occasionally brilliant uses made of this privilege during the first progress of Henry VII, and reveals that the story of the civic receptions is in many ways the real story of the progress after all. In even more ways, it is the story of Tudor pageantry in general.

I

Not that the progress or the pageantry belonged to the cities alone, of course. A royal progress was necessarily a reciprocal display. While the main burden fell naturally to the hosts, the royal guest with equal propriety seized the occasion to manifest his noble qualities. After passing through Cambridge, Huntingdon, and Stamford (the nature of whose receptions is not recorded in the *Memory*), Henry paused at Lincoln to observe the feast of Easter in a manner that would reveal his regal piety: he who had characterized his role at Milford Haven, Bosworth Field, and London by the offering of prayers, now "full like a cristene prince hard his dyuyne seruice in the cathedrall chirche and in no priue chapell," being present daily for both the morning's High Mass and for Evensong. On Holy Thursday he carefully observed the ancient custom of washing the feet of poor men, one for each of his twenty-nine years, "hum[b]ly and cristenly for Christez loue," afterwards distributing alms to them and to other of the poor "besides great almes to poore freres, prisoners, and lazares howsez of that countrey." [5]

5. *Memory,* fol. 8ᵛ, (1774), p. 185; see also the transcription in A. H. Smith, "A York Pageant, 1486," *London Mediaeval Studies,* ed. R. W. Chambers *et al.* (London, 1948 [for 1939]), p. 384. Smith's article is a parallel text edition of the account

After Easter, Henry made a brief stop at Nottingham, where he was formally received by the civic officials and the religious houses, and then turned northwards toward Yorkshire. The city of York had been warned some two weeks before that he might visit after Easter and had promptly sought the good advice of the Archbishop of York as to "how we shuld demeane us ayenst this supposid commyng of the King." Their burden was lightened in one respect; for although York had managed to present Richard III with a gift of over £300 on the occasion of his visit less than three years before, both their parliamentary representatives and the Archbishop of York had successfully pleaded the present poverty of the city and Henry had agreed not to expect a cash gift. But, on the other hand, this made it all the more important

that some conuenyent Shew be had ayenst the Kings said commyng by the counsell of some which can devise the same, wherby his highnesse may the rather be movid to think that the said Maior, Aldremen, Sheriffs and other inhabitaunts heyr be gladded and joifull of the same his commyng, as thei have be in tymes past of seing commyng of other Kings ther soverain lords.[6]

The council remembered Henry Hudson, a priest at Spofford who had been one of the devisers of the shows for the visit of King Richard in 1483, and entrusted him with "the making and directing of the Shew to be maide ayenst the Kings next commyng heder," promising him a stipend of five marks. The time was short, and Hudson set to work—possibly with the aid of hints from those near to the King and almost certainly with direction from the collective diplomatic wisdom of York.[7]

of the York shows from the MS. *Memory* and from the York *House Book*. Smith's transcriptions from these MSS are generally superior to those of both Hearne in (1774) and Raine in *YCR*, and will be used hereafter to correct the latter. The Smith texts will be designated in the notes by the symbol *LMS*.

6. *YCR*, pp. 80, 150, 152. It is ironic that this latter quotation appears in the York *House Book* just after an entry noting the King's nomination of Thomas Middleton for the now vacated post of recorder and just before an entry stating that the council filled the position by the unanimous election of John Vavasour.

7. *Ibid.*, pp. 77, 153. There is no mention of advice from the court, but it is not an improbable hypothesis. When Richard III had come on progress three years before, he had been preceded by a letter to York from his secretary, John Kendal, who asked that York provide pageants for the occasion and added that "Maister Lancastre, of the Kings counsell, this brynger, shall sumwhat advertise you of my mynd in that behalve" (*YCR*, p. 78). It appears that London had the guidance of the court

As King Henry moved toward Yorkshire, his role was appropriately adjusted: for there he was concerned to display not his piety but his strength and magnificence. He had set out from London "wele and nobley accompanyed," but it was only as he drew near to York that his train gathered the full strength of attendance noted by the *Memory*—not only a considerable group of bishops, earls, lords, and knights, but a "merveolous great nombre of so short a warnyng of esquiers, gentilmen, and yomen in defencible array."[8] A commentator was later to observe, anent the processions of the last Tudor monarch, that "in pompous ceremonies a secret of government doth much consist, for that the people are naturally both taken and held with exteriour shewes,"[9] and this kind of thinking surely motivated in part the grand display of Henry's train. For at least the last stage of his journey to York, he himself was dressed in ermine and cloth of gold, and his retinue, "also in golde smythez werk were richely besene."[10] But Tudor pomp was a two-edged sword—it was a way of winning the hearts and minds of true subjects, but also a way of striking the false with awe and terror. Henry was keenly aware of the importance of such tactics at that critical moment, for he had learned during his stay at Lincoln that Francis Lord Lovell and Humphrey Stafford, attainted in Parliament, had both left sanctuary, and he was now informed that they were attempting to raise insurrections.[11] These were serious threats, to judge from other records; but the author of the *Memory,* quite in harmony with the view of the royal power and presence which the King himself wished to promote, says of armed opposition merely that "in that tyme ther were certeyne rebelles aboute Rypon and Midlem whiche, vndrestanding the kinges myght and nere approching,

---

for the preparation of shows for the reception of Catherine of Aragon in 1501: a booklet published shortly thereafter, entitled *The traduction & mariage of the princesse,* reproduces a directive that suggests as much: "Item the forth attendaunce shalbe made by the Maire of London & by the citezeins of the same lyke as it is agreed bitwene the saide maire & dyuers of the kinges counsell to deuyse the maner therof with all other solempnytes / & ceremonyes necessary for the honour of the cyte and of the feste."

8. *Memory,* fol. 10; (1774), p. 187; *LMS,* p. 386.
9. *Haward's Annals* (Camden Society, Vol. VII; London, 1840), p. 15.
10. *Memory,* fol. 10; (1774), p. 187; *LMS,* p. 386.
11. Hall, p. 427.

within ij dayes disperclede." [12] With that he turns to Henry's triumphant entry into York.

Tadcaster Bridge, at the extremity of the York franchises, was the traditional point at which the process of a York reception began. On this occasion, the city had decided to outdo its usual welcome, noting in the council meeting that while the ordinary practice had been for the two sheriffs to wait at Tadcaster Bridge with twenty horsemen, this time they would add two of the aldermen and raise the number of horsemen to forty. Like that of the King himself, this was a calculated and rhetorical pomp. One may presume that it was tactfully communicated to the King that York had outdone itself at Tadcaster Bridge and likewise that the mayor and the rest of the aldermen were meeting him farther from York than was customary. The compiler of the *Memory* does not seem aware that there was anything extraordinary about these arrangements, but then, neither does he seem to appreciate the irony that "Vavasoure recordre of the same citie had the speche in bidding the king welcome and also recommaundede the citie and theinhabitauntes of the same to his good grace." [13] The presence of Vavasour, elected against Henry's preferment of Greene and Middleton, would be no great pleasure to the King, and York probably softened the blow by making their extraordinary arrangements known to the King himself. However, when Henry came within a half mile of York and encountered not only the processions of friars and parish churches but a "merveolous great nombre of men, women, and childern on foote whiche in rejoysing of his commyng criden King Henry, King Henry," it is probable that York's ambassadors tactfully concealed the fact that the common council had also ordained "a certaine nowmbre of childrine as shal be gaddard togiddre aboute sanct Iames Chappell, calling ioyfully 'king Henrie' after the maner of children." [14] King Henry and his advisers may well have suspected that this spontaneity was contrived and would probably have approved; but the fictions of diplomacy are privileged pretenses.

Apart from the places of encounter outside the city itself, the first tradi-

12. *Memory,* fol. 10; (1774), p. 187; *LMS,* p. 386.

13. This and the following quotation are from *Memory,* fol. 10; (1774), p. 187; *LMS,* p. 387.

14. *YCR,* p. 156; corrected according to *LMS,* p. 387. Subsequent *YCR* citations will be similarly corrected.

tional station for a formal welcome to York was Micklegate Bar, the
main gate to the city—corresponding to the use of London Bridge for the
initial pageantic display in early receptions by the city of London. Here
the King and his train found the first of the shows which the council had
ordained, and the *Memory* describes it as "a paiaunt with dyuers personages and mynstrelsyez and therby stode a king coronede whiche had
his speche that folowith whos name was Ebraucus." [15]

The "dyuers personages and mynstrelsyez" mentioned in the *Memory*
were of course a standard feature of civic pageantry: it was normal to
adorn a city show with singers or instrumentalists who could provide
interim celebration or entertainment while the distinguished visitor was
approaching or studying the visual display before the speeches began.
Had we only the *Memory* account, we could properly assume that the
music at Micklegate Bar came from a group of nondescript musicians
stationed unobtrusively on the pageant. Fortunately, however, we can
supplement the *Memory*. The scenario and speeches prepared under
Hudson's direction were copied into the York *House Book* after the
council had approved them and the text in the *House Book* details a
more elegant show at Micklegate Bar: "at the entre of the citie and first
bar of the same shal be craftely conceyvid a place in maner of a heven of
grete ioy and anglicall armony . . ." [16] The depiction of a heaven full of
angelic musicians is such a common motif in fifteenth-century art that
one hardly needs to look for specific sources; but in this case it is probable
that the idea and the costumes—perhaps the scaffold as well—had merely
been taken over wholesale from one of the musical heavens of the York
cycle. The next part of the show likewise borrows from local tradition.
According to the plans approved by the York common council, the area
under the heaven was to be decorated to represent an uninhabited world
"full of treys and floures"—a simplified version of the Eden in which two
of the cycle plays are set. Within this area was ordained an ingenious
vegetable dumb show, made possible by the traditions of York stage mechanics. After the King had arrived in place (presumably to the accompaniment of angelic harmony from the top of the pageant), within this
quasi-Eden "shall spryng vp a rioall rich rede rose convaide by viace,

15. *Memory*, fol. 10ᵛ; (1774), p. 187; *LMS*, pp. 387–388.
16. *YCR*, p. 156; *LMS*, pp. 387–388.

vnto the which rose shall appeyre an othre rich white rose, vnto whome
so being togedre all othre floures shall lowte and evidently yeue suffrantie."
Though cleverly inflected here for the sake of the roses of Lancaster and
York, the device of the growing roses is one that had probably been
perfected in performances of the Plasterers' Play of Creation, in which the
text clearly implies that in response to God's commandment, herbs, flowers,
and trees appear from a previously barren earth. The bowing of the other
flowers to the roses is probably derived from the Fullers' Play of Adam and
Eve. At the beginning of that play, God explains to Adam and Eve that
"Erbes, spyce, frute on tree . . . Shall bowe to you," and after explaining
at length that he has made man sovereign over all creatures, he again
promises that "All creatours shall to the bowe." [17] The text of the Fullers'
Play clearly invites the kind of device that is clearly made explicit in
the York *House Book* for the pageant at Micklegate Bar: by some mechanical device, the flowers are made to bow to the sovereign roses. Again,
the pageant has cleverly adjusted a ready-made motif from the York cycle.
After the flowers have bowed, a crown descends from a cloud to the
roses. Henry would undoubtedly have preferred that the appearance of
the white rose had been delayed until the general obeisance and crown
had been secured by the red rose alone, but York's choice of the theme
of unification was natural. Although it was a theme which Henry deliberately de-emphasized—indeed, the complete failure of the *Memory*
to speak of this ingenious garden raises the suspicion that it may have
been the victim of advance court censorship for precisely this reason—
it was nevertheless one which seized the general imagination more per-
manently than his alternatives. Two generations later, when Elizabeth
made her first royal entry into London, the first pageant greeting her
emphasized the Tudor right, not with a reference to Henry VII's providential victory in battle, nor with a description of his ancestry, but with
a representation of the union of the red rose with the white.

After the crowning of the roses, according to the York *House Book,*

shall appeir a citie with citisyns with the begynner of the same callid Ebrauk
which shall salute the king with wordes folowing in prose, and thervpon
present vnto the king the keys of the Citie, being thenheritaunce of the saide

17. *York Plays,* ed. Lucy Toulmin Smith (New York, 1963), pp. 18, 20, reprint
of 1885 ed.; for Plasterers' Play, see pp. 10–11.

Ebrauk, yelding his title and his crowne vnto the king as moost glad of hym above al othre.[18]

The appearance was probably by sudden disclosure, the movement of a curtain, revealing a stylized city (not unlikely one which had formerly been Jerusalem in cycle plays) with its mythical founder and its citizen-representatives (perhaps the "dyuers personages" of the *Memory*). The speech of King Ebraucus is of a generally conventional sort, consisting of four stanzas of alliterative rhyme royal (which is called "prose" in the York *House Book,* possibly by analogy with the liturgical use of that term) in which he introduces himself as king of Britain and founder of York, submits his "citie kee and coroune" to Henry, and asks his favor for the ruined city, assuring him that York never fought against his life but on the contrary suffered much in his behalf and now greets him with appropriate joy. The conventional key was undoubtedly presented to Henry, and the wording suggests that perhaps Ebraucus' crown was handed over too—visible emblems of the completeness of York's welcome and submission, enacted by a figure whose speech defines him as the symbol of sovereignty over York. Considering the reasons Henry had to be concerned about the loyalty of this city, it was sound diplomatic strategy to build into the welcoming speech not merely the ordinary assurances of submission and joy but explicit disclaimers of other allegiances and even of anti-Henrician activity prior to Bosworth Field—all the more important in that it was flatly untrue. On the day that the city's officers had received the proclamation of Henry VII from the apprehensive Sir Roger Cotam, they had also decided what wages they would pay the eighty soldiers conscripted to fight for Richard III.[19] But this, after all, was not a trial but a formal civic demonstration. What Ebraucus meant was the kind of thing Henry had come to hear; if the present and official disposition of York could not be adequately symbolized by accurate history, some distortion was appropriate. The King is not likely to have been deceived by the fiction and may have been pleased that York felt obliged to invent it.

Thus greeted, Henry and his elegant train passed on into the city of York. The traditional route to the next station was hung with cloth, according to the prescription of the common council; the junctions with

18. *YCR,* p. 156; *LMS,* p. 388.
19. *YCR,* p. 120.

Skeldergate and North Street were closed off with rich hangings, transforming the road into a corridor of cloth and tapestry. The council had ordained a shower of rose water as Henry passed from Micklegate Bar to Ouse Bridge, weather permitting, but the *Memory* does not reveal whether this worked out, for the reporter moves abruptly from the end of Ebraucus' speech to the pageant at Ouse Bridge. His silence means little. He would not necessarily have remarked (or even have been in a position to observe) the sprinkling of rose water by those near the King, and the practice of hanging the streets with cloths was too common in civic receptions to warrant his particular notice—indeed, neither he nor the York *House Book* bothers to mention the great display of heraldic banners for which the city paid more than two pounds. Such elements of civic pomp were simply taken for granted.[20]

The second pageant, according to the York *House Book,* was designed to begin with a council of kings:

on the hight of Ouse brigge a rioall troyne and therin sodanely appering set togidder in counsail sex kinges crouned betokining the sex Henries which after the sight had of the king with certaine conuenient laisour avisidly shall commyt a ceptour vnto Salamon cledd as king, which Salamon shall thervpon taking that ceptour and saying the wordes folowing vnto the king in prose yelde vnto him the saide ceptour in tokining that in hym is wisdome and iustice.[21]

The rubric "sodanely appering" suggests again the use of a curtain of some sort controlling a discovery space on the huge throne which seems to have served as a stage for the scene. It is possible that the six Henries were identified by labels placed either on them or on the pageant (neither practice was uncommon in civic shows); it was, at any rate, important that the spectator know who they were, and it is not clear that the technique with which they arrived at their decision included speeches in which they might identify themselves. The phrase "after the sight had of the king" is ambiguous and may refer to time allotted for the royal visitor to view the scene before the action began (a courtesy commonly allowed for pageants of intricate visual organization), but it is more probable that

20. *Ibid.,* p. 159, citing the Chamberlain's Rolls. Heraldic banners and street hangings probably appeared in subsequent receptions of the progress, even though the *Memory* does not notice them.

21. *YCR,* p. 157; *LMS,* pp. 390–391.

it refers to the six Henries' discovery of Henry VII, which then becomes the occasion of their deliberation and commission.[22]

The council of the six Henries is an interesting rudimentary development in the ancestry of the English history play, and it is curious that the *Memory* takes no notice of it, putting in its place a description of a motif unmentioned in the scenario copied into the York *House Book*: "another paiaunt garnysshede with shippes and botez in euery side in tokenyng of the kinges landing at Milforde Havyn and Salamon in his habite roiall crownede hadde this speche . . ."[23] The obvious inference is that at a later stage of planning, the ships replaced the six Henries, who were then entirely omitted in the presentation of the show. It is, however, more probable that the ships were simply added and that the Henries remained, the silence of the *Memory* notwithstanding, for Solomon's first stanza makes clear allusion to them:

> Moost prudent prynce of provid provisioun,
> Ther [*var*. Theiz] premordiall princes of this principalitie
> Hath preparate your reign the vij by successioun
> Remytting this reame as right to your roialtie.
> Ther of [*var*. Theiz ar] kinges conding of your consanguinitie.[24]

Furthermore, a fourth stanza which appears in the *Memory* (having been omitted from the York *House Book* by accident, most probably) returns to the six Henries: "Thies your noble progenitors recordeth the assistence Of this citie, to the assufferayn in yche tyme and place."[25] A considerable portion of Solomon's speech would be unintelligible without the prefatory council of kings, for Solomon acts as their spokesman both before he submits remarks of his own (establishing the historical and constitutional aspects of the new King's title before turning to the moral) and after (as he intercedes for York).

The use of Solomon as spokesman is decidedly clever, even if it is

---

22. Compare the reaction of the citizens in the castle pageant near the Guildhall: "after a sight of the king and remembrance of hyme," they demonstrate their affection for the King (*YCR*, p. 158; *LMS*, p. 393).

23. *Memory*, fol. 11; (1774), p. 188; *LMS*, pp. 390–391.

24. *Memory*, fol. 11; (1774), pp. 188–189; *LMS*, p. 391. The cited variants are of course from the York *House Book* (*YCR*, p. 157; *LMS*, p. 391), and suggest that the readings in the *Memory* derive from the copyist's mistaking of *iz* for *r*.

25. *Memory*, fol. 11ᵛ; (1774), p. 189; *LMS*, p. 392.

generally conventional. He defines himself, in accordance with common-place convention, as a type or "patrone" of wisdom, particularly of judicial wisdom. As such, he can commend the wisdom with which Henry had conducted himself prior to his coronation, acknowledge the utter justice of his claim to the throne, and direct him to continue to rule with wisdom and judicial prudence under the same influence of providential grace by which King Solomon earned his own distinguished reputation. In token of this Solomonic future, Henry is handed the speaker's "scepter of sapience." The transferred scepter thus becomes both an emblem of Henry's political right through the providence of legal succession (the meaning with which the council of Henries had endowed it) and his providential establishment by God as an inspired successor to Solomon's wisdom. Any misgivings Henry may have had about the role of the red rose at Micklegate Bar must have been set to rest by the deferential gift of Solomon and the Henries. And having thus satisfied the expectations of their royal visitor, the people of York manage to slip in a final stanza which gently urges their own deserving. Solomon now beseeches Henry to support York "with subsidie of your grace," pointing out that the first six Henries can bear witness to the devoted loyalty of the city which now receives their successor in the same tradition. All in all, the speech displays a clever exploitation of the elements of the show and a deft thrust of York's diplomacy as well: Solomon has enlarged upon the themes of an earlier letter from York to the King, in which a plea for relief was argued on the grounds that York had suffered greatly for its uncompromising loyalty to Henry VI—an argument for which Henry VII himself had given the cue.[26]

There is some question about the next stage of the entertainment. The council had ordained an unspecified "shew" beyond Ouse Bridge, where the procession turned left into Cony Street, with a hail of comfits to go with it. At the same spot, the *Memory* reports "a paiant of thassumpcon of oure Lady," and gives the speech which the council had ordained to

26. *YCR*, pp. 135–136. York was working with a precedent already established by the King, whose proclamation of pardon for Richard's supporters in the northern parts of England invoked their costly loyalty to Henry VI as one of the occasions of his mercy (*Tudor Royal Proclamations*, ed. Hughes and Larkin, I, 3–4; the proclamation was copied into the York *House Book* on 8 October 1485—see *YCR*, pp. 125–126).

be spoken by Mary in the final pageant near the entrance to the York Minster.[27] Either the York authorities had unaccountably shifted the Marian pageant from its most appropriate location to a position that breaks the sequence of the first three shows or the *Memory* reporter has erred. The latter hypothesis seems the more reasonable and is more easily defended than the former—but the issue is not sufficiently important to warrant its being argued here.

Both accounts are agreed, at any rate, that the next show was by the Guildhall, at the end of Cony Street, and that the key figure was David. The *Memory* merely reports that "King Dauide stode armede and crownede having a nakede swerde in his hand"; the York *House Book,* while silent about the armor and crown (which are nevertheless probable enough), adds that David appeared in a strong castle filled with citizens "which after a sight of the king and remembrance of hyme with gude countenaunce shall appeir in clothing of white and greyne shewing ther trueth and hertly affeccioun vnto the kinge."[28] Besides being a fine dramatic device, this engagement of the citizen-characters with the royal audience is an appropriate thematic motif: after receiving an enacted recognition from the founder and symbolic sovereign of York, from his own royal ancestors, and from his political patron saint, Henry VII now receives an enactment of the hearty welcome which has all along been attributed to the city (and which all the pageants of course manifest in a fundamental way). David submits to Henry his sword of victory, as Ebraucus had given his crown and keys and Solomon his scepter. By God's will, Henry is the successor of David too. David then continues with a neat explanation of his presence in York (being naturally disinclined to admit that the chief reason is that he was a stock character in civic receptions): he is a contemporary of that King Ebraucus who built York to commemorate his triumph over the French. As he submits this unvanquished city to Henry, David concludes—as his contemporary Ebraucus and his son Solomon had done before him—with a plea on behalf of the city of York, wounded for Henry's sake:

> To this youre enheritaunce take gracious complacence
> Sith that it [is] youre citie not filede with dissaveaunce,
> True and bolde to your bloode, not dreding perturbaunce

27. *Memory*, fol. 11ᵛ; (1774), pp. 189–190; *LMS*, pp. 393–394.
28. *Memory*, fol. 12; (1774), p. 190; *LMS*, p. 395. *YCR*, p. 158; *LMS*, p. 393.

> Whiche causede moost this citie to bee desolate
> Now reviuyng in comforte to atteigne youre astate.[29]

After the pattern of greetings and displays by Ebraucus, Solomon, and David, the planners of these shows thought fit to place near the Minster a final pageant, from whose heaven Mary would descend for a speech before ascending again "with angell sang and ther schall it snaw by craft to be made of waffrons in maner of snaw." [30] The ending (aside from the snow of wafers, another conventional device) is superficially akin to an Assumption, and indeed the city had rented the pageant designed for the Weavers' Assumption play—it is easy to understand why the *Memory* reporter thought of it as "a pageant of the Assumption of Our Lady." [31] But the speech is wholly unrelated to the matter of the Assumption, except insofar as Mary's remarks to Thomas about the power of her intercession, which form her final words in the Weavers' Play, are paralleled here in her final address to King Henry. After recognizing that Henry has been elected to office by Christ and reminding him that the downtrodden people of York have consistently shown great devotion to both Christ and herself, she promises that the power of her intercession will be used in his behalf—subtly reminding the King that he needs it, after all, and that her graciousness to him is partially the result of the devotion of the people of poor York. The plea is made by indirection, through mere juxtaposition of motifs, but the point is clear. The pattern of the three previous shows is here preserved as the interceding figure, after receiving Henry as worthy and rightful king and granting him some power by which his kingship may be further strengthened, closes with a gentle request for the city of York. Mary ascends back into heaven while the angels sing and the wafers snow down a hint of grace from above. The dignified and tactful civic reception is over. Henry VII, king by hereditary right, divine election, providential victory, personal virtue, and popular assent, passes into the York Minster for the offices of piety—hopefully, both gratified and mollified; hopefully, with his suspicions allayed and his charitable disposition toward the city of York at its maximum.

29. *Memory*, fol. 12ᵛ; (1774), p. 190; *LMS*, p. 396.
30. *YCR*, p. 158; *LMS*, p. 394.
31. *Memory*, fol. 11ᵛ; (1774), p. 189; *LMS*, p. 394. Among the payments listed for these shows in the Chamberlain's Rolls is one for four shillings for the Weavers' pageant; see *YCR*, p. 159.

II

Yet despite the apparent success of his visit to York, Henry's mind could not rest. The reports of the activities of Lovell and Stafford continued to arrive, and he could no longer afford the skepticism he had shown initially at Lincoln. As soon as he was received and settled in York, says Hall,

it was bruted, and openly shewed to the kyng him selfe that Fraunces lorde Louell was at hand with a strong and mightie powre of men, and would with all diligence inuade the cytie: also that the forenamed Homfrey Stafford & Thomas his brother were in worcestre shyre and there had raysed a great bande of rude and rusticall people, & had cast lottes what parte should assaute the gates, what menne should scale the walles of the cytie of Worcestre, & who should kepe the passages for lettyng of reskewes and aiders.[32]

The King "was afflicted with no small feare." His immediately available force was smaller than he might wish, but he could not wait while the rebels capitalized on the instability of loyalties in those parts of England. The Duke of Bedford was sent off to confront Lovell's army, at the head of a band of inadequately armed troops. As it turned out, the most important weapon was the power to pardon. When Bedford's heralds proclaimed the King's forgiveness for all who submitted immediately, Lovell fled and his troops surrendered. Humphrey Stafford, hearing of Lovell's flight, gave up his own assault and sought sanctuary. Henry knew the importance of seizing his advantage: he set out for Worcester, pausing in Nottingham long enough to commission a court that would sit in Worcester to investigate and determine the instances of treasonous activity in Worcestershire.[33]

The author of the *Memory* had left York after St. George's Day—

32. Hall, p. 427.

33. Some writers maintain that the Lovell incident took place before Henry arrived in York. Busch, for instance (*England under the Tudors,* p. 30), flatly rejects the order followed by Polydore Vergil and Hall, which I have retained here; but he gives no reason, and his own chronology seems dubious (his date of 22 April for Henry's entry into York can scarcely be reconciled with the *Memory*). For the present purposes, however, it matters little which order is adopted. For the commissioning of the court, see *Calendar of Patent Rolls* (1 Henry VII), pp. 106–107.

possibly, if we accept the chronology of Polydore Vergil and Hall, to take part in Bedford's move against Lovell (perhaps as one of the pardon-bearing heralds)—and rejoined the King some three weeks later in Worcester. Worcester had in the meantime received Henry, but more modestly than York: for although welcoming speeches and pageants had been prepared, for some reason they were not performed. Our chronicler nevertheless managed to secure copies of two of the prepared texts and wrote them into his account. The first is a long passage, sixteen stanzas of rhyme royal, headed simply "KH vjth"; the second is a seven-stanza speech headed "Loquitur Ianitor ad Ianuam."

Despite its position in the *Memory,* the latter was undoubtedly designed to be given first. It is a speech of recognition and greeting at the gate of the city, and at its end the speaker was to present Henry with the keys, as Ebraucus had done in the first pageant at York. The speaker himself, unlike those of the other shows in this progress, has no identity apart from his function as spokesman for the city. He speaks his own prologue—consisting of a reverent reference to the King, a self-identification, a statement of purpose, and an apology for his incapacity—and strikes the pose of bemusement demanded by the rest of the speech. The technique of the stanzas that follow is an interesting and fairly imaginative variant of the Nine-Worthies strategy. The speaker mistakes Henry for a wide variety of heroes:

> Quis est ille qui venit, so great of price
> I thought Noe whiche came late from the flodde
> Or it is Iason with the golden flece . . .

After offering hypothetical identifications with Noah, Jason, and Julius Caesar—each choice supported by some cited parallel between the hero in question and King Henry—he drops the provisional framework and speaks directly:

> Welcome Abraham whiche went from his kynnerede
> Of al this lande to take possession
> Welcome Ysaac that sumtyme shulde have be dedde
> And now is heire to his fader by succession.[34]

Welcome Jacob, welcome Joseph, welcome David, welcome Scipio. Each of the selected worthies offers a parallel by which the speaker cleverly

34. *Memory,* fol. 16; (1774), p. 195.

drives home the triumph, virtue, rightful succession, divine favor, and
providential accession enjoyed by Henry VII. These were all favorite
themes of Henry's own propaganda, as was the last on the list: Arthur,
"the very Britain kyng," defender of England, "Cadwaladers blodde
lynyally descending." With this final example, the most characteristically
Early Tudor of the lot, the speaker makes a graceful transition from the
centrifugal association of Henry with various worthies to Henry himself,
precisely as the Arthur *redivivus* whom ancient prophecy had foretold:

> Longe hath bee towlde of such a prince commyng
> Wherfore frendez if that I shalnot lye
> This same is the fulfiller of the profecye.
> Whiche he is this more playnely to expresse
> Henry the vij chosen by grace and chaunce . . .[35]

With this, the speaker moves into his peroration, expressing the welcome
of the city and its long desire to see him, and presents him with the keys
—apparently an afterthought, since the line corresponding to the presentation of the keys is an unrhyming one, thrust between the lines of the
couplet closing the stanza.

The speech of the Worcester gatekeeper is in general a fairly clever
performance, wittily designed and gracefully executed. But the other
Worcester show is far more clever and complex—and far more poorly
understood. It is not the conventional greeting it may seem to be. Its matter
is urgent.

The urgency is not apparent at first. The speaker, who presents himself
as Henry VI, begins in that character with "Welcome nevew, welcome
my cousyn dere, Next of my blood descended by alyaunce," and assures
Henry that by virtue of both legitimate succession and divine election,
the whole title of Henry VI has now descended to him, "wherfore I am
right glad." Then, after speaking briefly of his own reign and martyr's
death, Henry VI comes to one of the main themes of his address to his
royal kinsman:

> Mek and mercifull was I euermore,
> From crueltie refreynyng and from vengeaunce.
> God hath me rewardede largely therfore.
> And gentil cosyn sith thou hast this chaunce
> To be myn heire, vse wele my gouernaunce.

35. *Memory,* fol. 16ᵛ; (1774), p. 196.

Pytie with mercy haue alwey in thy cure
For by meknesse thou shalt lengest endure.

This is followed by another entire stanza on the subject of mercy—its importance in the Gospel, its primacy among the works of God, its importance in the future government of Henry VII.[36]

Under the guise of Henry VI, the speaker has adopted a complex pose. He speaks as a kinsman to his heir, as a king giving advice on successful government, and as a martyr and quasi-saint (a role sympathetic to Henry VII, who attempted to advance the canonization of Henry VI) giving advice on true Christian conduct and its terrestrial as well as celestial fruits. His stance is ingratiating, and he uses its advantage to insist on the theme of mercy as a quality of God, of saints, of true Christians, of good governors—a quality which wins the divine favor and the divine aid. After the thematic variety and balance of the York pageants, this single-mindedness about mercy seems peculiar. It is, however, a calculated and purposeful peculiarity. The next stanza reveals its rationale: "This poore citie with humble reverence A poore bill haue put into myn hande," and in his mercy, Henry VI has consented to intercede for the city and read the plea. The next four stanzas apparently constitute the quoted bill, and in them one can finally see the urgency and delicacy of the problem to which the show is addressed: Worcester, stained by complicity with recent treasonous activities, is pleading for its life.

Humbly besechith your high and noble grace
Your poore subiectes liegmen and oratours
Wher late befell a lamentable case:
A gentilman detected with riottours
Making suggestyon agenst you and youres
Contryved falsely by his informacon
Shewing so largely by his communicacon

That of your grace he had grauntede his perdon
By great charter of lif goodes and landes
Desiring hedere to come for his devocon
To offre at oure Lady where that she standeth.
By ignorance thus bee they brought in bandes
Beseching you moost mekely or ye passe,
Graciously pardon theym this trespasse.

36. *Memory*, fol. 14; (1774), pp. 192–193.

> For greatly greven theym both more and lasse
> So many men by oon to be deceyuede.
> Your oune citie that neuer pollutede was
> Is now defiled for she hath hym receyuede.
> Your saide subgettes that al this hath perceyuede
> Enclyne theymsilfes and to youre mercy calle . . .[37]

It is gingerly and oblique, but it presented no evasive obscurity to Henry VII. This was why he had come to Worcester and why he had commissioned a court to sit there at Worcester and deal with recent treason. Humphrey Stafford, attainted in Henry's first Parliament, had subsequently operated under the cover of a forged pardon to instigate a sedition in Worcestershire. However innocently, Worcester had in fact admitted the rebels within its gates. The matter was serious enough to draw an indictment of the bailiff and commonalty of Worcester. The offense was rank and recent: Stafford had just fled to Culham and would shortly be taken forcibly and brought before the court at Worcester while Henry was still there.[38] York had been able to wink at its own past and pretend a long-standing loyalty to Henry VII, but no such course was open to Worcester. Only two pleas were possible. The bill presented by the figure of Henry VI pressed the claim of innocent victimization as far as it would go, under the circumstances; beyond that, the only alternative was to beg for mercy. That is what this show is about, and its author did a splendid job of engineering the maximum effect of his central theme. Having presented the abject apology of the city, Henry VI concludes:

> And now swete Henry doo somewhat for me.
> I stod for vj. and now ye stande for vij.
> Fauer thoos folk that fele adversitie.
> God wille rewarde the therfor high in heven.
> Now as myghty lyon bere the even

---

37. *Memory,* fols. 14ᵛ–15; (1774), p. 193. The last word of the first quoted stanza is perhaps doubtful. In the MS, the last five letters are written out and are preceded by an abbreviation whose radical seems to be *Coi.* I have expanded according to an essentially identical abbreviation form in Cappelli, *Dizionario di abbreviature* (6th ed.), p. 57.

38. See the Year Book for 1 Henry VII (*Les Reports des Cases* [London, 1679], pp. 22–23, 25–26) and the account, richly documented from the Public Record Office, in C. H. Williams, "The Rebellion of Humphrey Stafford in 1486," *English Historical Review,* XLIII (1928), 181–189.

> Whose noble angre in his cruell rage
> To prostrate people never wolde doo damage.[39]

It may be that the pageant was to include a literal representation of the prostrate people of Worcester, who "enclyne theymsilfes and to youre mercy calle."[40] This would, at any rate, be the appropriate local counterpart of the joyful citizens in David's castle at York.

After this follows a stanza which vaguely imitates the structure of the confiteor: Henry VI beseeches the Holy Trinity and the Blessed Virgin

> And ye, both seintes of myn affynytie
> Oswolde and Wolstan right holy confessours
> Pray for my good sone King Henry at al houres.[41]

The final four stanzas are simply three prayers to the Trinity—begging power, wisdom, grace, peace, virtue, long life, and eternal bliss for Henry VII—and a last address to the King himself, advising him once more to follow the way of mercy. These stanzas have previously been regarded as the rest of the speech of Henry VI, but in fact the designer of this show was much more clever. The first eleven stanzas are linked, the final rhyme of each becoming the initial rhyme of the next; the "confiteor" stanza is the last of the series, and contains the final words of Henry VI. The next two stanzas are spoken not by him but by Oswald and Wulstan. It is a judicious strategy: as patron saints and former bishops of Worcester, Oswald and Wulstan occupy in the spiritual order essentially the same position taken politically, in the York reception, by King Ebraucus. As representatives of the city's spirit, they enact with their prayers what had just been promised in the city's bill:

> And youre saide oratours promysse to pray for euer
> For your noble estate and prosperitie
> Long to contynue in ioye and felicitie.[42]

And, of course, if Henry is kind to Worcester, the city's patron saints will presumably be all the more zealous in their prayers for him.

The third prayer, following in ascending order the pattern implied in the final words of Henry VI, is that of Mary:

39. *Memory*, fol. 15; (1774), p. 194.
40. *Memory*, fol. 15; (1774), p. 193.
41. *Memory*, fol. 15; (1774), p. 194.
42. *Memory*, fol. 15; (1774), p. 194.

Fader and Sonne and Holy Goost ful preste
Beholde the hande maide whiche they iij haue wrought
And namely thou my sone whiche soke my breste
Henry the vij preserue at my requeste . . .[43]

It is impossible to say just where she would have been placed on the pageant—possibly on one side, with Oswald and Wulstan together on the other, or perhaps on a second level—but there can be no doubt that she was intended to be there.

The rest of the lines follow the logic of Henry VI's final stanza: they are spoken by the Trinity, who would undoubtedly have been placed above the rest of the speakers on an upper scaffold. Despite its brevity, the speech of the Trinity is a masterful final statement on the themes of this show. Henry is reminded of the dependence of his throne on divine election, admonished to secure himself in the divine favor by the exercise of mercy, recommended to the patronage and example of his holy and merciful predecessor Henry VI, and promised that his mercy will draw rewards on earth and in heaven:

O Henry moche art thou beholde to vs
That thee haue reysede by our oune eleccon.
Bee thou therfore mercifull and graciouse
For mercye pleasith moost oure affeccon.
Folow King Henry whiche is thy proteccon
As welle in worke as in sanguinitie

And in this worlde it wille rewarded bee/Right welle
If thou serue God in love and drede
Hauyng compassion of theym that hath nede
Euerlasting ioye shalbe thy mede
In heven aboue where al seints dwelle.[44]

It is a pity that such a splendid piece of civic pageantry, so deftly contrived on such short and pressing notice, was never performed. Were the undelivered speeches subsequently shown to the King? It would surely be fitting if they had something to do with Worcester's ultimate rehabilitation in the royal favor and with a document among the Worcester manuscripts, dated shortly after Henry's return from his first progress,

43. *Memory*, fol. 15ᵛ; (1774), p. 194.
44. *Memory*, fols. 15ᵛ–16; (1774), p. 195. The virgule separating the seventh line from the bob-line "Right welle" is in the original.

which the Historical Manuscripts Commission described as a "Pardon of Henry VII. to prior and convent for diverse transgressions." [45]

III

Henry stayed in Worcester only a few days. On the Monday after Whitsun, he set out for Hereford. He was met by the mayor of Hereford and his horsemen well outside the town, then by a procession of friars, then by processions from the Hereford parish churches "as accustumed," says the *Memory*, "with great multitude of people of the countrey whiche in reioysing of the kinges commyng cried King Henry, King Henry, and holding up ther handez blessed and prayde God to preserue owre king"— a touching sight, undoubtedly arranged in advance by the common council, as its parallel in York had been. [46]

Hereford had prepared three pageants. With neither the dramatic sophistication of York nor the urgent occasion of Worcester, the Hereford shows are comparatively flat and ordinary, examples not of local ingenuity but of the conventions generally served by civic welcomes. The first was at the gate leading into the city, a pageant of St. George killing the dragon. George's brief speech establishes a parallel between himself and King Henry, and between the dragon and the King's enemies; just as God aids George to slay the dragon, so George will help Henry vanquish those who oppose him, "with the helpe of that blessed virgyn, The whiche loveth you right wele I dare playnly it say." It is not a very distinguished piece; yet its magnification of Henry as "Supporter of truth, confounder of wikkednesse" must have been moderately satisfying to the King, especially in view of the speech's hint that his victory over Richard III was an important step in the confounding of wickedness. [47]

45. Historical Manuscripts Commission, *Fourteenth Report, Appendix,* Part VIII (1895), p. 199.

46. *Memory,* fol. 17; (1774) p. 197.

47. *Memory,* fol. 17ᵛ; (1774), p. 197. This characterization of Richard, echoed in Worcester's parallel between Henry/Richard and David/Goliath (*Memory,* fol. 16), was understandably absent from the pageant at York, where David declines to mention his most famous victim and presents Henry with a sword rather than a sling. It was, however, a theme of earliest Tudor propaganda. The pardon proclaimed at York on 8 October 1485 includes a reference to Richard as the nameless

St. George sped the King on his way to the market place, where he came upon the second pageant, which presented King Ethelbert being censed by two bishops. Ethelbert was a happy choice, since as King of Kent and one of the patron saints of the Hereford cathedral, he combines the offices of Ebraucus and the saintly bishops of Worcester: Ethelbert can speak for Hereford as both a political and a religious spokesman. But aside from a bit of subtle didactic praise in his opening lines ("Moost vertuouse prince and gracious in gouernaunce, Not rigours but mercifull as Dauid in his juggement"),[48] Ethelbert is given little to do other than identifying himself, welcoming the King, and sending him on to the final pageant of the Blessed Virgin.

Mary's pageant stood at the entrance to the cathedral, of which both she and Ethelbert were patrons. She was surrounded by "many virgins merveolous and richely besene," for the court which attends her in the Wilton diptych is typical of street pageants too. These virgins seem to have been essentially decorative, which is the normal practice: the dramatic use made of pageantic supers in the York shows is extraordinary and a tribute to the York dramatic tradition. The main point of Mary's brief speech is merely to usher Henry into the cathedral, but she manages also to thank Henry for his support of her (and possibly, though the wording is obscure, of the local foundation) and to assure him that her intercession will make his heavenly reward certain.[49]

The theatrical artistry of York and the impassioned eloquence of Worcester make the perfunctory shows and speeches of the Hereford pageants seem drab and anticlimactic. They are not egregious; they are, in fact, rather good examples of a satisfactory handling of a conventional situation, the kind of pageants that one might expect any city to throw together to welcome a distinguished visitor. But on this progress, they seem not merely undistinguished but crude. Too much talent had been spent in York and Worcester to permit us to feel otherwise about the Hereford shows. When Henry arrived a few days later at the next major stage of his progress, Gloucester, he was met by the usual sequence of

---

"advarsarye of us, enemy of nature and of all puplique wele" (*YCR*, p. 125). The text printed in *Tudor Royal Proclamations*, ed. Hughes and Larkin, I, 3–4, gives a plural, "enemies," but the idea was apparently clear enough.

48. *Memory*, fol. 17ᵛ; (1774), p. 197.

49. *Memory*, fol. 18; (1774), p. 198.

processions (the mayor and others on horseback, well outside the town; the friars closer in; the parish churches), but "in that towne ther was no pageaunt nor speche ordeynede." [50] This was perhaps less thoroughly hospitable, but may have been a wise decision as well as a convenient one. If they had nothing important to say to their new King, processions could be considered adequate. Besides, the next stop was Bristol, and Bristol was taking the opportunity seriously.

IV

The journey to the Bristol gates went almost predictably: the mayor, sheriffs, and citizens on horseback met the King some three miles out of town, and the recorder spoke a welcome; within the suburbs, they were joined by a procession of friars; shortly thereafter, they were greeted by the processions of the parish churches. At the actual gate of the city "was ordeigned a pageaunt with great melodie and singing." When the King was in position the songs ceased, and King Bremmius (the Bristol counterpart of King Ebraucus of York) welcomed King Henry as a man sent by God

> To reforme thinges that be contrarious
> Vnto the comen wele with a myghty hande.
> I am right gladde ye be welcome to this lande
> Namely to this towne whiche I Bremmyus king
> Whilom bildede with her wallez olde
> And called it Bristow.

After another stanza describing the abundant and joyous prosperity of Bristol in its earliest days, Bremmius reveals why he has characterized Henry as a reformer. Since those golden days, it seems,

> Bristow is fallen into decaye
> Irrecuparable withoute that a due remedy
> By you, there hertes hope and comfort in this distresse,
> Prouede bee at your leysere convenyently
> To your navy and cloth making wherby I gesse
> The wele of this towne standeth in sikernesse.

50. *Memory,* fol. 18; (1774), p. 198.

However clumsy, this has at least the virtue of practical clarity. It is followed by a final stanza in which the plea is urged as variously as one can imagine: Henry is addressed as "cosyn," called "wele of bountie," reminded of the fidelity of his Bristol subjects, and asked to provide—in charity, for Mary's sake—the indispensable remedy, for which God will reward him.[51] It is, of course, an undisguised lobby, organized on an appropriate fiction and reinforced with convenient mythology as well as a good deal of court holy water. But even its bluntness has a certain charm when we realize that King Bremmius is pleading for the life of Bristol as surely (albeit in another key) as Henry VI had begged for Worcester.

Henry moved on into the center of town. At the high cross was erected "a pageaunt ful of maydyn childern richely besene," from which Prudence spoke. After the customary welcome, she assured Henry that he had the constant prayers of the inhabitants of Bristol and the love and fear appropriately inspired by a monarch: "The good fame of your renoume so fer dooth sprede That al youre saide subiectes both loue you and drede." She then praised Henry for his success in keeping his subjects in peace, quiet, and unity. Was there a touch of special pleading in "Ye yef not credence to lightly Too feyned tales that make myght discencon"? It would be interesting to know whether Bristol had good private reason to be grateful for Henry's resistance to invidious rumors. But Prudence does not elaborate. She merely sends the King further on his way, with a prayer for his guidance and success and especially for his prudence. Such were the delicate tactics of instruction by praise and prayer when a city spoke to a king. The next speech was much the same, and employed a similar abstract morality-character. On St. John's Gate, through which Henry passed on his way out of town, Justitia among her court of maiden children welcomed the King to "youre owne towne," described her own kinship to God and her earthly offices, and praised Henry for his administration of true justice, praying that he persevere.[52]

That was the end of the pageantic speeches in Bristol. The King passed on his way, past a speechless but hopeful "Shipwrightes pageaunt" toward St. Austin's Abbey. A little further on he encountered the last recorded example of his entertainment in the provinces. It is a beautiful specimen

51. *Memory*, fol. 19; (1774), pp. 199–200.
52. *Memory*, fols. 19ᵛ–20; (1774), pp. 200–201.

of the kind of aesthetic order which the popular imagination might normally produce in a civic reception and therefore a useful touchstone for the evaluation of the shows performed elsewhere on this progress:

There was anothere pageaunt of an Olifaunte with a castell on his bakk curiously wrought, the Resurreccon of oure Lorde in the highest tower of the same with certeyne imagerye smytyng bellis and al went by vices merveolously wele done.[53]

Marvelously well done indeed! Though quite innocent of the unity of design that prevailed at York and of the finesse of the speeches at Worcester, the forthrightness of the first Bristol pageant and the variety of the last are no less characteristic of civic shows than their more sophisticated counterparts. Even London would still be capable of producing such a pageantic gallimaufry a century later. If one relaxes aesthetic severity enough to empathize with the compilers of Bristol's elephant, it becomes an unusually rich amalgam of the techniques of heraldic imagery, religious symbolism, and mechanical ingenuity which had in various ways provided much of the standard fare of the displays all along the route. Bristol had a right to be pleased with its reception of the King and even to be hopeful that its shows might be effective as well as entertaining; and, in fact, its hopes were soon to be rewarded.

The following Thursday was the feast of Corpus Christi. The King went in procession to the great green where he was met by the processions from the town, presumably with appropriate ecclesiastical pomp. A pulpit was set up in the middle of the green, and the Bishop of Worcester preached.[54] The *Memory* does not mention the substance of his sermon, but it is not difficult to guess: at every important stage of the progress from Worcester on, the subject had been the proclamation of the papal bull which had just arrived in England, giving the official blessing of the Church to Henry's marriage.[55] The bull was beautifully drawn to Henry's interests, for it not only commended the harmonizing by marriage of the two warring houses but explicitly recognized Henry's right to the crown by natural succession, by conquest, and by popular acclaim and gave the

53. *Memory*, fols. 20–20ᵛ; (1774), pp. 201–202.
54. *Memory*, fol. 20ᵛ; (1774), p. 202.
55. *Memory*, fols. 17 (Worcester), 18 (Hereford), 18ᵛ (Gloucester). The original bull is dated 27 March 1486.

Church's curse to all who might rebel against him.[56] It was a useful instrument for the stabilizing of loyalties, but of course it really contained little that was new. Its themes were those of the King's own propaganda, and had already been echoed in the civic pageants of York, Worcester, Hereford, and Bristol.

After evensong came the answer to Bristol's prayers and pageants. Henry called for the mayor, the sheriffs, and a representation of the wealthier citizenry

and demaunded theym the cause of there pouertie and they shewde his grace fore the great losse of shippes and goodes that they had loost within v. yeres. The king comforted theym that they shulde sett on and make new shippes and to exercise there marchandise as they were wonte for to doon and his grace shulde so helpe theym by dyuers means like as he shewde vnto theym that the meyre of the towne towlde me they harde not this hundred yeres of noo king so good a comfort, wherfor they thanked Almighty God that hath sent theym soo good and graciouse a souueraigne lord.[57]

The officers of Bristol, whose pageants had commended the prudence of Henry VII, presumably knew that there was more to the King's gesture than generous whim. Yet they also knew that he was indeed being generous and appreciative, and that what he was giving them was precisely what their pageantic spokesman had requested at the gates of Bristol and what the Shipwrights' Pageant had more quietly solicited as he was leaving the town. The King's visit is not likely to have diminished their faith in the possibilities of civic shows.

Nor is the progress as a whole likely to disappoint the historian of English drama. For aside from the light it throws on such matters as York stage mechanics and the early dramatic employment of historical characters; aside from its reminder of the importance of elegant processional pomp and of the useful license that a dramatic fiction afforded; apart even from its manifestation of a richness of dramatic motifs in a popular culture that was later to generate from them dramatic entertainments of far greater distinction, the first progress of Henry VII discloses the remarkable vitality of dramatic modes long before the greatest period of the English drama. From the pageantic platforms of these cities were articulated the present needs, anxieties, beliefs, and wisdom of the English

56. See the abstract in *Tudor Royal Proclamations,* I, 6–7.
57. *Memory,* fols. 20ᵛ–21; (1774), p. 202.

people, for all the formal conventionality in which they are expressed. In the confrontation between these civic quasi-theaters and their royal audience, the foundations of the Tudor dynasty were symbolized and strengthened, and what was expressed in dramatic terms was then reabsorbed into the life from which it had come. When the mayor of Bristol and his fellows left the presence of the King, he had made their dream come true —but only after it had been objectified in the Bristol shows. And if the King, after this final recorded act of his first progress, paused to look back over his three-month tour, he must have felt that his objectives had been beautifully realized. His dream of the consolidation of English loyalties was on its way to truth, and as he settled in for his last night near Bristol, he may have reflected with some satisfaction, however tempered by critical irony, that it was not entirely a private dream, its lineaments having been shown to him in the solemn processions and the not altogether insubstantial pageants of his own cities.

"And on the morne the king departede to London warde," his first progress a considerable success, assured of the strength of his command over the fortunes and hearts of his people, having endured their praise, pleading, precepts, prayers, and pageantry—off to Londonward, to be met near Westminster by the mayor of London and his brethren, with great and expected pomp.

Lyly's Static Drama

MICHAEL R. BEST

I N THE EPILOGUE to *Sapho and Phao*, Lyly apologizes to his audience for the inconclusive plot: "Wee feare we haue lead you all this while in a Labyrinth of conceites, diuerse times hearing one deuice, & haue now brought you to an end, where we first beganne."[1] It is a characteristic of Lyly's plays that there is an almost complete lack of action and that the basic situation remains virtually unchanged throughout. This is most obvious in those of his plays which were based on a situation politically complimentary to Queen Elizabeth; in *Campaspe*, Alexander is placed in a situation of temptation, thus providing the dramatic tension of the play; but although he resists the temptation as a monarch should, he suggests in the final lines of the play that the situation has not really changed:

ALEXANDER
. . . And good *Hephestion*, when al the world is woone, and euery countrey is thine and mine, either find me out an other to subdue, or of my word I wil fall in loue.

(V.iv.153–155)

---

1. All citations from Lyly in my text are from *The Complete Works of John Lyly*, ed. R. W. Bond (Oxford, 1902).

In the same way, not only does *Sapho and Phao* remain static, ending where it began, but *Endimion* begins and ends with the same complimentary situation, the courtly lover hopelessly in love with the goddess, who graciously permits the love.

Normally, in play or novel, we witness what we might call the dramatic equation; motivation leads to a situation of conflict which is resolved in action, the consequences of which decide whether the plot is tragic or comic. It is the progression from motivation to action which defines character; complex character may be revealed by a complex reaction (which may include nonaction, as for example with Hamlet) to a complex motivation. Although some of Lyly's dramatis personae have complete dramatic equations, we also find, seemingly arbitrarily, a complex motivation leading to nothing and action without apparent or adequate motivation. We cannot therefore discuss Lyly's plays in normal critical terms; Endimion's motivation, for example, is complex enough, but he never resolves action, with the result that we cannot think of him as a character. This is surely one reason why there have been so many interpretations of *Endimion* using the equally unsatisfactory tool of allegory—we clearly do not have a character, so perhaps we have an abstraction.[2] There may be a political reason for the lack of action in these plays, for to involve a figure likely to be associated with the Queen in direct dramatic action might be to invite misinterpretation by the court audience, accustomed as it was to "applying pastimes," interpreting plays topically.[3]

But in Lyly's pastoral plays, which we may assume were relatively free from the political pressure of direct compliment, we find the same tendency. *Gallathea,* the earliest and simplest of his pastoral plays, presents two main threads of action: the love between two girls disguised as boys and a debate between Chastity and Love—Diana and Cupid-Venus. The

2. See, for an interpretation of the political allegory, among others, Bond, III, 81–103; A. Feuillerat, *John Lyly* (Cambridge, 1910), pp. 141–190; J. W. Bennett, "Oxford and *Endimion*," *PMLA*, LVII (1942), 354–369. For moral allegory see P. W. Long, "The Purport of Lyly's *Endimion*," *PMLA*, XXIV (1909), 164–184, and "Lyly's *Endimion*, an Addendum," *MP*, VIII (1910–1911), 599–605; B. F. Huppé, "Allegory of Love in Lyly's Court Comedies," *ELH*, XIV (1947), 93–113. For the modern view see J. A. Bryant, Jr., "The Nature of the Allegory in Lyly's *Endimion*," *Renaissance Papers* (1956), pp. 4–11; G. K. Hunter, *John Lyly: The Humanist as Courtier* (London, 1962), pp. 184–193.

3. See the Prologue to *Endimion*, l. 7.

debate theme is left entirely unresolved, each goddess being as convinced of her rightness at the end of the play as at the beginning, though the love of the two girls silently suggests (like Spenser's Amoretta [4]) that married fidelity can combine both qualities. Nor does the love of Gallathea and Phillida itself develop, except in the increasing bewilderment of the girls, and it is left to a convenient sex change after the play to resolve their predicament. Even this is deliberately left as vague as possible, as we are not told which of the girls is to be changed and thereby which has the more assertive character. What we have is not a play of character but a static study of the paradoxical phenomenon of love.

It is possible, I think, to see the difference between Lyly's approach and the more usual dramatic equation in terms of a musical analogy. An identical harmonically complex chord may be found in, say, Liszt and Debussy, but it will be treated in quite different ways: to Liszt a given chord was part of a logical harmonic progression; it was either resolved or further complicated, whereas Debussy would suspend the same chord as an end in itself, leaving it unresolved and exploring its inherent sonorities by his characteristically lucid orchestration.[5] Lyly was far more interested in the situation of conflict than in the action resulting from it; he explored the possibilities of varied stresses within a static state of mind, rather than concerning himself with its resolution.

The paradox is at the center of Lyly's view of life, from the relatively crude "in paynted pottes is hidden the deadlyest poyson . . . in the greenest grasse is the greatest Serpent . . . in the cleerest water the vglyest Toade" (*Euphues,* in Bond, I, 202) to the sophisticated thesis of *The Woman in the Moon* that *"Nature* workes her will from contraries"* (I.i.29). What we have in his plays is the exploitation of dramatic situations equivalent to paradox. The paradox is a picture, a frozen or suspended condition of contradiction, and Lyly's plays present a series of

4. *The Faerie Queene,* Book III, Canto vi.

5. An equally valid comparison could be made with composers nearer Lyly's time; the contrapuntal logic of Byrd or Palestrina may be compared with the static use of modal harmony for effects of resonance by, for example, Clement Jannequin—notably in *La Battaile de Marignan,* with its limited harmony and repetitive nonsense syllables. Musical analogies have often been used in the discussion of Lyly's plays, written as they were for choirboys. See, for example, M. C. Bradbrook, *The Growth and Structure of Elizabethan Comedy* (London, 1955), p. 65, and Hunter, *John Lyly,* p. 159.

tableaux exploring paradoxical states of mind, particularly those of love, "A heate full of coldnesse, a sweet full of bitternesse, a paine ful of pleasantnesse" (*Gallathea*, I.ii.16–17), and jealousy, that "strange effect of loue, to worke such an extreame hate" (*Endimion*, V.iii.93). It is my intention to demonstrate the usefulness of this critical approach to Lyly by discussing two of his most interesting plays, the later pastorals *Love's Metamorphosis* and *The Woman in the Moon*, one concerned with the paradox of love, the other with the paradox of jealousy.[6]

The pastoral plot of *Love's Metamorphosis* is concerned with the selfish love of three foresters and the equally selfish rejection of their love by the nymphs of Ceres. The love of the foresters is shallow and cynical:

[RAMIS]

I cannot see, *Montanus,* why it is fain'd by the Poets, that Loue sat vpon the Chaos and created the world; since in the world there is so little loue. . . .

SILUESTRIS

I doe not thinke Loue hath any sparke of Diuinitie in him; since the end of his being is earthly. . . .

RAMIS

. . . since it will aske longer labour and studie to subdue the powers of our bloud to the rule of the soule, then to satisfie them with the fruition of our loues, let vs bee constant in the worlds errours, and seeke our owne torments.

(I.i.1–3, 9–10, 17–20)

The foresters despise their own desires but accept them because it would be harder to overcome them. There is no differentiation made between the three foresters; they are alike in the shallowness of their love, the aim of which is physical gratification. After each has pursued his nymph and tried, without success, to persuade her to yield to love, the foresters go to Cupid to ask for revenge on their mistresses.

The nymphs, similarly, are sterile; frigid, not chaste. The characteristics which lead to this frigidity are clearly and appropriately differentiated; Nisa is stupid, Celia is proud, and Niobe is inconstant. For their refusal to love, Cupid transforms them to a rock, a rose, and a bird respectively. These metamorphoses are so appropriate that the situation remains virtually unchanged—there has been no dramatic movement

6. See Paul E. Parnell, "Moral Allegory in Lyly's *Love's Metamorphosis,*" *SP,* LII (1955), 1–16. Much of what follows was stimulated by this article, together with the chapter "The Plays" in Hunter, *John Lyly*. Hunter was the first critic to look outside normal critical terms to describe the static, diversified unity of Lyly's plays.

apart from the expression of the foresters' spite. In one of those touches that stamp Lyly as a writer of ideas, not clichés, the nymphs, upon regaining their shapes as a result of the intercession of Ceres, decide that metamorphosis into objects so appropriate is better than yielding to the indignity of love. The stone was safe from "the importunities of men, whose open flatteries make way to their secret lustes" (V.iv.69–70); the rose, which "distilled with fire, yeeldeth sweete water" (V.iv.81–82), is better off than love, which "in extremities, kindles iealousies" (V.iv.82–83); the bird of paradise saw in the heavens "an orderly course, in the earth nothing but disorderly loue, and pieuishnesse" (V.iv.97–98). It is only when Cupid threatens to turn them into monsters loathsome to themselves and others—to force a violent change from the established tableau—that the nymphs capitulate. Before they do so, however, they emphasize that the dramatic movement will be minimal and that their natures will not change. The foresters accept this with the same cynicism as they showed towards love at the beginning of the play:

RAMIS
O, my sweete *Nisa!* bee what thou wilt, and let all thy imperfections bee excused by me, so thou but say thou louest me. . . .
MONTANUS
Let me bleed euerie minute with the prickles of the Rose, so I may enioy but one hower the sauour . . .
SILUESTRIS
My sweete *Niobe!* flie whither thou wilt all day, so I may find thee in my nest at night, I will loue thee . . .

(V.iv.136–137, 144–145, 154–155)

The only change that has taken place is that the nymphs and foresters have consented to accept a state of imperfection in order to achieve some happiness.

The same shortcomings appear in extreme forms in two fringe figures, Fidelia and Erisicthon. Fidelia, metamorphosed to a tree to avoid the lust of a satyr, withdraws completely from sex, and Erisicthon, chopping down Fidelia's tree, symbolically represents the extreme of physical lust which culminates in rape; the nymphs' rejection of love becomes complete in Fidelia, and the foresters' cynically physical attitude to the fruits of love becomes the physical violence of Erisicthon. The evocative symbolism of this episode becomes even more striking when the goddess of fruition sends Famine to gnaw at the vitals of Erisicthon—the inevitable increase of an appetite fed by violence or lust. By contrast, the fruits of the rape, appropriately, are fresh flowers (V.i.36).

Parallel to the plot of the nymphs and foresters is the story of Protea and Petulius. Just as the love of Gallathea and Phillida made an implied comment on the debate in the pastoral plot of *Gallathea,* so the love of Protea and Petulius illuminates the attitudes to love expressed by the nymphs and foresters. The love of Protea and Petulius is far from perfect, but it is warm and positive. Protea at some time prior to the play was seduced (willingly, one gathers) by Neptune, who, in gratitude, changed her first to a fisherman, to avoid the Merchant, and later to Ulysses to save Petulius from the clutches of the Siren. The Merchant, it seems, is prepared to make commercial use of Protea, by prostitution I suppose, but he is foiled in his attempt (off stage) by Protea's disguise as a fisherman. This could perhaps be interpreted as an ironical *double entendre;* the Merchant, desirous of becoming a fishmonger, speaks to a fisherman about the one that got away. Protea's preplay lapse is duplicated by Petulius' on-stage near-seduction by the Siren, another fish figure, and probably a symbol for a prostitute (see, for example, *Euphues,* Bond, I, 189, 255). Petulius is saved by the fact that Protea has been unfaithful, has become experienced, and therefore is able to become Ulysses; their love is made possible by the fact that they are warm and prepared to yield to love, even though this leads to a different kind of imperfection which must be accepted. In this way they make a powerful contrast to the nymphs and foresters, who achieve happiness only because their desires are shallow; Petulius and Protea achieve happiness because their capacity for love is sufficient for them to accept and forgive imperfection. Again, the only dramatic movement in this part of the play is the discovery and acceptance of imperfection.

Lyly has inverted the conventional attitude towards love (an attitude strongly expressed in his own earlier works) that the love associated with chastity and with the nonattainment of its object is most to be desired and admired. Lyly demonstrates that chastity is sterile and frigid and that warm love, although it may lead to excesses and technical unfaithfulness, is fruitful and satisfying. The play is thus an exposition of a double paradox of love in two separate tableaux presided over by the divinities Ceres, who embodies the conflict between the two opposed qualities of ideal love, chastity and fruitfulness, and Cupid, who demonstrates that the phenomenon of love, as well as creating the paradox, can resolve the conflict either by blind acceptance of imperfection or by its warmer power of forgiveness. Cupid has perhaps the most impressive speech in the play, defending specifically the compatibility of love and chastity:

CUPID

Why, *Ceres,* doe you thinke that lust followeth loue? *Ceres,* louers are chast: for what is loue, diuine loue, but the quintescens of chastitie, and affections binding by heauenly motions, that cannot bee vndone by earthly meanes, and must not be comptrolled by any man?

(II.i.122–126)

The only dramatic movement in *Love's Metamorphosis* is the acceptance of imperfection by the various couples, for widely different reasons, yet the ideas expressed are both complex and intellectually satisfying, though Lyly creates neither character nor specific allegory. The theme of imperfection in love also appears in *Endimion,* where the couples assembled on stage at the end of the play are a most oddly assorted group of misfits, from Sir Tophas, prepared to accept Bagoa as a substitute for his earlier love Dipsas ("Turne her to a true loue or false, so shee be a wench I care not" [V.iii.279–280]), to Tellus, blackmailed by Cynthia into accepting Corsites as a substitute for Endimion. Lyly's interest in Tellus' jealousy (she has almost as much to say as the flattering Endimion) anticipates the almost tragic passion of Stesias in *The Woman in the Moon,* his last play.

The Woman in the Moon is a rather puzzling play. It was probably written for adult actors rather than the choirboys who acted in Lyly's other plays.[7] This may explain its use of a rather rigid blank verse instead of the flexible dramatic prose which Lyly had developed in his earlier works, but I do not think that we can look for such external changes to explain its unusual form and particularly its uncharacteristic ending.

The play is Lyly's version of the last act of Genesis, the creation of woman, here Pandora rather than Eve, but plainly possessing some attributes of both. In an opening scene overtly allegorical and rather masque-like, four Utopian shepherds ask Nature to give them a mate of pleasure

7. The date and character of the play are discussed in E. K. Chambers, *The Elizabethan Stage* (Oxford, 1923), III, 416–417; H. N. Hillebrand, *The Child Actors* (Urbana, 1926), p. 142; and Hunter, *John Lyly,* pp. 81 ff.

to complete their happiness. Nature agrees and calls upon Concord to assemble the best parts of all the gods and goddesses into one being, then on Discord to give it speech. At this stage it looks as though we are being prepared for an Eve rather than a Pandora, for Nature remarks of the gift of a tongue: ". . . from that roote will many mischiefes growe, / If once she spot her state of innocence" (I.i.85–86). But the trouble comes from a different source, for the seven planets, Saturn, Mars, Jupiter, Sol, Venus, Mercury, and Luna enter, envious of this new creation which is supposed to surpass them in wit and beauty, and decide to influence her maliciously, each in turn, to upset Nature's plan for perfection.

There follows a series of situations in which the effect on the shepherds of Pandora's variously influenced attitudes is studied. Each of these situations, as we might expect, is basically a static tableau, the only movement connecting them being the gradually increasing experience of the four shepherds.

The gods, then, intervene in the innocence of the Utopian world through jealousy. The original Pandora brought misery through her curiosity, Eve through pride, but in Lyly's genesis the original sin is envy, with Pandora and the Utopian swains the innocent victims of the gods. Saturn begins the process of destroying Pandora's innocence by making her sullen, Jupiter makes her proud, and Mars makes her "a vixen Martialist" (II.i.180). The swains respond appropriately, though with some bewilderment, treating her melancholy (ineffectively) with music, her pride with respect and adoration, her viciousness by turning the other cheek. Of these the most interesting and extended episode involves Jupiter, who at first is overcome by Pandora's beauty, and, despite Juno's jealousy, tries to add her to his list of conquests. (The loves of Jupiter always seemed to Lyly to be an archetype of the improper interference of the gods—see, for example, *Euphues,* Bond, I, 236; *Campaspe,* III.iii.10–20; *Sapho and Phao,* I.i.36–37; *Midas,* I.i.77–79, II.i.12–18, IV.i.47–48.) Ironically, Jupiter is defeated by the effects of his own influence over Pandora, for she accepts his homage but proudly refuses to accede to his desires. The themes of jealousy and interference are specifically treated in this one passage of the play where Pandora is shown other than in the company of her clown-servant Gunophilus and the shepherds. Her rejection of Jupiter foreshadows the final stand by Stesias.

At no time is Pandora a character. Rather, as something of an anticipation of Ben Jonson, she epitomizes in turn various humors for the sake of confusing the shepherds (she actually uses the word "humor" to describe one of her moods [II.i.111]). Of the four shepherds it is Stesias who gradually becomes of increasing importance. He is wounded by Pandora in her martial mood and accepts his hurt with dignity and humility, in words which recall the paradoxical nature of love:

> Her hardest words are but a gentle winde:
> Her greatest wound is but a pleasing harme:
> Death at her hands is but a second life.
>
> (II.i.233–235)

Sol brings a seemingly beneficent humor to Pandora; she becomes kind and loving and makes amends to the wounded Stesias by promising him her hand, plighting him her "spotles fayth" (III.i.57). Stesias sees the earlier trouble as a preparation for his delight and a trial of his faithfulness:

> Blest be the hand that made so happy wound,
> For in my sufferance haue I wonne thy loue;
> And blessed thou, that hauing tryed my faith,
> Hast giuen admittance to my harts desert:
> Now all is well, and all my hurt is whole,
> And I in paradise of my delight.
>
> (III.i.72–77)

Stesias sees Pandora's behavior as a continuum, whereas her humors, separate and unconnected, make her in effect a series of different people. The fact that Stesias, however, remains unchanged means that he is capable of dramatic movement in a way that Pandora is not; he has achieved the perfect happiness originally asked of Nature. All this would be a pretty parable illustrating the way to gain perfection in love—through understanding, sympathy, respect, valor, humility, and sufferance—but before Stesias can enjoy his love, complication ensues as Venus takes over from Sol.

From this point the play becomes less masquelike, as a net of intrigues is woven by Pandora to keep the four shepherds on a string. Pandora moves from wantonness under Venus to spiteful, ingenious deception under Mercury and finally to incoherence under Luna. Despite the busy nature of the plot, Pandora's whole object is to ensure that nothing decisive happens at all, and in this she succeeds, for the tableaux are basically

as static as those under the earlier influences. Stesias remains convinced
that Pandora is faithful to him, until the other shepherds, seeing that
Pandora has finally run lunatic, reject all hope of obtaining her and the
higher happiness she represents:

> LEARCHUS
> Fret, *Stesias,* fret; while we daunce on the playne.
> MELOS
> Such fortune happen to incredulus swaines.
> IPHICLES
> Sweete is a single life; *Stesias* farewell.
>
> (V.i.240–242)

Accordingly, they tell Stesias of Pandora's duplicity. It is not possible for
Stesias to return to the sweetness of the single life, since he has briefly
experienced the perfection of mutual love, so he determines to assuage his
jealousy by killing Pandora. At this point Stesias achieves a breathing
passion not found anywhere else in Lyly's work:

> Let wild bores with their tuskes plow vp my lawnes,
> Deuouring Wolues come shake my tender lambes,
> Driue vp my goates vnto some steepy rocke,
> And let them fall downe headlong in the sea.
>
> (V.i.245–248)

At the critical moment, the seven planets enter and restore Pandora to her
right mind.

At this point we might expect a happy ending. However, just as in
Love's Metamorphosis the nymphs refused to cooperate at the last moment, Stesias refuses to be reconciled to Pandora. The gods, and later
Nature, descend from their machines but are unable to manipulate a
happy ending. To make amends for the interference of the gods, Nature
places Pandora on their level—in Luna's sphere, after some envious com-
petition amongst the gods for the privilege. Stesias continues to reject
Pandora, though he cannot now kill her. His passion, stimulated by the
envy of the gods for Pandora, has become transcendent, and, since he will
not recant, he is immortalized in hate as Pandora's attendant. He plucks
the hawthorn bush which Gunophilus had been changed into, intent still
on revenge: "if eare she looke but backe, / Ile scratch her face that was
so false to me" (V.i.318–319). This act of defiance, in which Stesias refuses

to accept the imperfection of Pandora's love, is the one action which the gods could not control; Stesias asserts his independence at the expense of a bitter immortality. He is perpetuated as the paradoxical figure of the jealous lover, hating in proportion to the depth of his original love, a kind of reverse to the image of the lovers seen by Keats on the Grecian urn. The conclusion of the play is a static tableau of Discord.

Lyly's point is not so much that the original sin was envy, because Pandora herself is not guilty of it; rather it is that for earthly happiness the acceptance of imperfection is necessary—a point he had already made in *Love's Metamorphosis*—and, further, that heroic nonacceptance of the human condition of imperfection will lead to disillusionment, though it may also lead to immortality. It might be possible to interpret the play as a study in character, with Stesias, who, for Lyly, has a remarkably complete dramatic equation, the protagonist; or it might be possible to find in it a political allegory—Nature, the Queen, thwarted by her governors and unable to give justice to her people, Lyly particularly, perhaps —or an allegory of the artist subservient to his Muse. Lyly may also be making an interesting comment on humanistic thought; Stesias shares the fate of those who assert against the gods the perfectibility of humanity. But I feel that interpretations of this kind would impose on the play an arbitrary standard which it would not live up to consistently and which would rob it of much of its meaning.

Once we accept Lyly's basically static technique, it becomes clear that he was interested in investigating human attitudes, particularly those concerned with love, in depth but not in movement. In *Love's Metamorphosis* and *The Woman in the Moon* we have complementary views of the same human predicament, the imperfection of love: in *Love's Metamorphosis* imperfection is accepted, and any moral difference to be made between the sets of lovers is measured by warmth or coldness in love, rather than chastity; in *The Woman in the Moon* imperfection is rejected, perhaps because perfection has been experienced, and the result is a bitter immortality. The ideas Lyly expressed in these plays differ widely not only from those of his earlier works, but from the attitudes of his contemporaries. *The Woman in the Moon* would have been written at about the same time as *A Midsummer-Night's Dream* and may even have been influenced by it, yet Shakespeare's attitude to love, though at times satiri-

cal, and even cynical, is basically more conventional. There is in Lyly's
later plays an intellectual toughness and consistency which I find strongly
at variance with the accepted image of Lyly as a gentle and rather effete
dramatist. His brittle and artful style and the lack of action in his plays
have obscured the fact that he explores ideas of complexity and humanity.

The Triumph of Chastity: Form and Meaning in The Arraignment of Paris

ANDREW VON HENDY

IN SPITE OF ITS CHARM, *The Arraignment of Paris* is usually dismissed by criticism as either disorganized or trivial.[1] This treatment is understandable if the play is judged by standards appropriate to more mimetic forms of drama. It appears both significant and well-designed, however, if we recognize how strongly it has been affected by the conventions of masques and entertainments. Peele responded to a specific occasion with a beautiful compliment to the Queen. This compliment is the formal intention of his play. He constructs *The Arraignment* to culminate, as masques do, in a scene which will absorb the audience into its imaginary

1. For typical complaints about the play's formlessness see Paul Reyher, *Les Masques anglais* (Paris, 1909), pp. 135–138; Enid Welsford, *The Court Masque* (Cambridge, Eng., 1927), pp. 277–278; Tucker Brooke in *A Literary History of England* (New York, 1948), pp. 455–456. Dismissals of the play as frivolous are generally connected with eighteenth- and nineteenth-century assumptions about the essentially frivolous nature of masque and pastoral. See, for example, W. W. Greg's discussion of the play in *Pastoral Poetry and Pastoral Drama* (London, 1906), pp. 216–224. The only commentary I know which recognizes both the "moral earnestness . . . at all times characteristic of Peele's work" and his "constructive dramatic skill" is Thorleif Larsen's in "The Early Years of George Peele, Dramatist, 1558–1588," *Transactions of the Royal Society of Canada* (1928), pp. 294–311.

world. The plot inclines us to accept the moral and political ideals with which the climactic moment invests the Queen. When she resolves the pastoral dilemma within the play, we witness a formal "triumph," the triumph of chastity over moral and political subversion.

The resemblance of the play to a masque is indicated on the title page of the 1584 quarto.[2] There *The Arraignment* is called a "pastorall." Our literary historians find the essence of Renaissance pastoral in the self-conscious contrast between the natural and the artificial.[3] The poet withdraws from the world to contemplate the problems of his everyday existence. Spenser and Milton meditated in a form which encouraged the projection of their ideal aspirations. I think both masque and pastoral are species of what Northrop Frye calls "romance," a mood in literature of dreamlike wish fulfillment.[4] Romance moves away from mimetic representation of the "real" world. The unfulfilled wish usually appears as the goal of a quest, and romance plots in general have a way of suggesting allegory. The characters are general types, sometimes clearly fragments of a single personality. Their actions are often absurd or puzzling by realistic standards. A psychologist might call their behavior "compulsive." The setting of romance is nearly always remote in time and space, a magic world where suspension of the natural laws is taken for granted. Romantic narrative is apt to seem sporadic, since the author is never far from his besetting abstractions. He introduces meditations on matters like fortune

2. We have no satisfactory edition of *The Arraignment of Paris*. Except for modernizing spelling for consistency with other editions from which I quote, I have followed throughout the text of the 1584 quarto, ed. H. H. Child (Malone Society Reprints; London, 1910). Child, however, follows previous modern editors in numbering lines according to altered divisions of act and scene. I have consulted for line numbering, therefore, the edition of the play in *English Drama 1580–1642*, ed. C. F. T. Brooke and H. B. Paradise (New York, 1933), which is unusual in honoring the divisions of the quarto.

3. See, for example, William Empson, *Some Versions of Pastoral* (London, 1935), especially his first two chapters; Frank Kermode's introduction to *English Pastoral Poetry from the Beginnings to Marvell* (London, 1952); Hallett Smith, *Elizabethan Poetry* (Cambridge, Mass., 1952), pp. 1–63; Edward Tayler, *Nature and Art in Renaissance Literature* (New York, 1964).

4. *Anatomy of Criticism* (Princeton, 1957), especially pp. 36–37, 186–203, 304–307. My description of the form is based on Frye but considerably modified by my own opinions. If "romance" is understood in its wide signification, pastoral and masque are species of this kind of narrative fiction.

and justice or explicit debates, as between love and honor. Finally, to borrow a term from current politics, romance is radically conservative; it contrasts an ideal society that never was or will be to the actual society in which the writer lives.

The Arraignment opens with a prologue best explained, I think, by the political implications of romance. Ate introduces the gold ball which will cause the goddesses' quarrel. But her appearance is in unexplained contrast to the mood of the scenes which follow. Enid Welsford describes the problem in *The Court Masque:* "The appearance of Ate 'from lowest hell' should surely prelude the 'tragedy of Troy,' instead of leading to a piece of extravagant flattery written in pastoral style" (p. 278). This objection seems to me valid if we see no connection between the appearance of Ate and the "extravagant flattery" which follows it. I think we do find such a connection, however, in the political implications of *The Arraignment*'s romantic plot. We can recognize these implications by recalling some commonplaces of Elizabethan literature. First, Tudor history identified Trojan Brute as the founder of England and London as Troynovant. The "tale of Troy" had nationalistic consequences. Second, the poets inherited from antiquity an association of the pastoral world with the Golden Age of Saturn's reign. Third, Elizabeth was frequently identified with Astraea, goddess of justice, who fled the world at the end of the Golden Age. The famous line in Virgil's fourth eclogue, *"iam redit et Virgo, redeunt Saturnia regna,"* is obviously ready for application to the Virgin Queen. Fourth, political unrest was often represented as an anti-Olympian principle of evil. The Titans frequently appear, for example, in the role Ate takes in *The Arraignment.*

These four considerations are associated with each other in various combinations in Peele's nondramatic works, especially in *The Tale of Troy, The Device of the Pageant Borne Before Wolstan Dixi, Descensus Astraeae,* and *Anglorum Feriae.* In the most elaborate grouping, *Descensus Astraeae,* the Lord Mayor's Pageant of 1591, "Astraea with hir sheephook on the top of the pageant" is identified with the Queen.[5] Euphrosyne, guarding Astraea with the other Graces, explains the device:

5. For *Descensus Astraeae* see *The Life and Minor Works of George Peele,* ed. David H. Horne (New Haven, 1952), pp. 214–219. I cite in the text lines as numbered in this edition. The Web in the pageant is a play on the name of the new Lord Mayor, Sir William Webbe.

> Whilom when Saturnes golden raigne did cease,
> and yron age had kindled cruel warres:
> Envie in wrath, perturbing common peace,
> engendring cancred hate and bloody jarres:
> Lo then Olympus king, the thundring Jove,
> raught hence this gracious nymph Astraea faire,
> Now once again he sands hir from above.
>
> (ll. 66–72)

Astraea is threatened by "malecontents" who "strive and cannot strike." Elizabeth is preserved by miracle from the mortal condition. *"In the hinder part of the Pageant did sit a Child, representing Nature, holding in her hand a distaffe, and spinning a Web, which passed through the hand of Fortune and was wheeled up by Time . . ."* (p. 218).

> And Time and Kinde
> Produce hir yeares to make them numberlesse
> While Fortune for hir service and hir sake,
> With golden hands doth strengthen and enrich
> The Web that they for faire Astraea weave.
>
> (ll. 33–37)

Thus, in *The Arraignment,* Ate provokes a whole cycle of war and injustice, but she fails to disturb seriously the order of the gods, and she cannot affect at all a nymph served by the Fates themselves. *The Arraignment* follows the pattern of political myth summarized in Euphrosyne's speech.

The prologue, then, stands in much the same relationship to the scenes which follow it as an antimasque does to the masque proper. That is why Peele considers it decorous to change so abruptly from Ate to an ideal landscape across which the gods move in formal progress. (Their procession resembles a summer pageant greeting the Queen on the grounds of an estate.) Though the reign of Saturn is past, the Iron Age has not yet come and will not come till Ate prevails. Death and unrequited love have already appeared "even in Arcadia," but the natural world still keeps about it some of its unfallen glory. The setting of the first four scenes derives obviously from the *locus amoenus* of medieval dream vision, the earthly paradise just below the moon. The minor deities bring their gifts as Diana's vassals, but these gifts also signify the abundance of nature in the paradisal garden.[6] This traditional mode of symbolism shows most clearly, perhaps, in Flora's lovely catalogue of her jewels (I.iii.17–32). This ordered nature, governed by Diana, will become especially significant in the fifth act.

The procession of minor deities culminates in a spectacular burst of song and dance. A "quier within" responds antiphonally to a choir outside, that is, off stage. The latter is composed of the country gods, whereas the former, we are told, consists of the Muses themselves. This suggests again how far we are from a fallen world. The three goddesses march in "like to the pompe of heaven above" (l. 85), but as they exchange compliments we discover they have a further goal. They leave the stage moving toward a meeting with Diana herself. This procession will not reach its goal, however, until the last act. Its movement is interrupted by the disturbances that comprise the center of the play.

Act I concludes ominously with an interview between Paris and Oenone. The scene is superficially idyllic. Before the famous roundelay, "Faire and fayre and twise so faire," Paris assures Oenone that their music is "figure of the love that growes twixt thee and me" (I.iii.54). But Oenone is worried. In deciding what he should play, Paris has raised sinister topics:

> How Saturne did devide his kingdome . . .
> How mightie men made foule succesles warre,
> Against the gods and state of Jupiter.
>
> (I.v.19–22)

This catalogue proceeds (as the play does) from political rebellion to "love offence." Peele foreshadows the fate of Paris in terms of Ovid moralized. Paris' repertoire, both political and amatory, consists of tales of infidelity later corrected by justice. Oenone wisely invokes Cupid's curse: "They that do chaunge olde love for new, pray gods they chaunge for worse."

Act II opens *ex abrupto,* as the stage direction has it, with a fight among the goddesses on their way to Diana. Nothing in the first act has pre-

6. For a good exposition of this symbolism see J. A. W. Bennett, *The Parlement of Foules* (Oxford, 1957), especially pp. 140–142. See also E. R. Curtius, *European Literature and the Latin Middle Ages* (New York, 1953), pp. 183–202. Curtius shows explicitly that this topic was still a commonplace to Shakespeare.

pared us for the low tone and diction of the participants. Discord has invaded even the society of the gods. Its personification, Ate, appears in a thunderstorm and places before the goddesses the fatal apple, to be given "to the fayrest." They agree only to make the next person who appears "umpier in this controversie," and in walks Paris.

His judgment had long been a popular topic for moral allegory. In Montemayor's *Diana*, for example, "Delia and Andronius spend the greater part of a night arguing the question whether Paris gave the apple to the right goddess or not and whether the inscription on it referred to physical or mental beauty."[7] In England the topic had even been applied traditionally to royal compliment. "The Paris story was a common subject of the pageants—for Queen Margaret at Edinburgh in 1503, for the coronation of Anne Boleyn in 1533, and at a marriage masque in 1566."[8] I would guess that the topic was common on such occasions not only because Paris made the most famous pastoral choice but also because of the connection of Troy with the Tudor political myth.

Paris' three temptations are symbolized in the elaborate "shows" with which each goddess accompanies her claim. Juno offers gold and empire, Pallas wisdom and martial glory. Venus offers both herself and Helen, whom she introduces with a significant change of diction as

> A gallant girle, a lustie minion trull,
> That can give sporte to thee thy bellyfull,
> To ravish all thy beating vaines with joye.
>
> (II.ii.75–77)

Helen's song is itself a relevant piece of wit. Its language recalls the great Tuscan celebrators of courtly love, but it is a song against Diana as the personification of chastity. Diana, as Helen sings, is the goddess of a love

7. Hallett Smith, *Elizabethan Poetry*, p. 6. Smith discusses Peele's play on pp. 3–9, primarily in connection with the significance of Paris' pastoral choice.

8. *Ibid.*, p. 7. Smith follows T. S. Graves, *"The Arraignment of Paris and Sixteenth Century Flattery," MLN*, XXVIII (1913), 48–49. As Graves points out, the pageant at Anne's coronation is especially significant, for Elizabeth's mother also received the gold ball from the goddesses. In "The Source of Peele's 'Arraignment of Paris,'" *MLN*, VIII (1893), pp. 206–207, Felix Schelling shows that the topic is applied to Elizabeth in the works of Gascoigne, including an unacted pageant at Kenilworth in 1575. Larsen, in "The Early Years of George Peele," pp. 298–299, adds to the evidence a Latin epigraph addressed to Elizabeth in Lyly's *Euphues His England*. As Larsen observes, it is unlikely that Peele knew none of these allusions.

very different in kind from Helen's. As queen of nymphs and flowers, woodland and forest, Diana deals death to shepherds. But as queen of hell she comforts the damned who died for love, and as queen of heaven she tenders light to weary hearts. She is a goddess of the Platonic ladder. Helen, however, calls herself a "Diana" who can make war with her very glances on this triple goddess of chastity. And Paris gives Venus the ball.

Now, it is quite possible to argue that Paris makes the correct pastoral choice. Paris himself makes this claim in his speech before the Council of the Gods. Hallett Smith summarizes his argument:

The simplicity of the shepherd's conditions makes for an invulnerability to appeals in the name of wealth or of chivalry. It is only beauty, of the three ideals represented by the goddesses, which has any significant power in a pastoral life.[9]

The structure of the play, however, frames this bold assertion in an ironic moral perspective. Helen's song clarifies the issue. All three of the goddesses represent forms of beauty; Paris chooses the lowest form. At the end of Act II he exits with Venus, but Act III consists almost entirely of choral commentary on his lack of wisdom. At the end of Act II Ate has succeeded in making the goddesses forget their purpose; the Diana against whom Helen sings is the very goal of their progress. From now on, however, the rift widens between gods and men in the post-Saturnian world. After Paris has been arraigned and judged, the gods will remember Diana.

The contrast between "the two loves" determines, I think, Peele's famous plagiarism at the beginning of Act III where he introduces a cast of characters out of *The Shepherd's Calendar.* As Peele conceives their conduct, it resembles the behavior of Lyly's lovers, the behavior Shakespeare remembered with a certain irony in *A Midsummer-Night's Dream* and *As You Like It.* "As all is mortall in nature, so is all nature in love, mortall in folly." Love is midsummer madness, lunacy induced by the elixir of a flower called "Love in idlenesse." Lyly's treatment of the theme in *Endymion* is especially appropriate for comparison with *The Arraignment;* in it, too, the presence of the Queen at the performance actually affects the meaning of the play. And Lyly, as usual, makes his antitheses crystal clear. Cynthia is the Moon, chaste affection, true friendship, and Elizabeth. Tellus is the Earth, physical sex, perfidy, and (perhaps) Mary,

9. Smith, *Elizabethan Poetry,* p. 8.

Queen of Scots. Eumenides must decide between the two extremes. He must choose between love and honor, attaining his lady, Semele, or freeing Endymion from his fatal sleep. Of course he elects honor: "Vertue shall subdue affections, wisedome lust, friendship beautie." Eumenides has to make the so-called choice of Hercules prominent in medieval and Renaissance iconography.

Paris' choice in *The Arraignment* is built on a similar dichotomy, although the presence of three alternatives rather obscures the two contraries. Montemayor's characters see the Platonic dualism when they dispute whether the inscription on the apple refers to physical or mental beauty. In his narrative poem, *The Tale of Troy,* Peele himself reduced the three possibilities to two:

> Ah Paris, hadst thou had but equall eyes,
> Indifferent in bestowing of the pryze,
> Thy humaine wits might have discerned well,
> Where the true beautie of the mind did dwell.
> But men must erre, because but men they bee.
> And men with love yblinded may not see.[10]

Act III demonstrates the folly of Paris' blindness to "true beautie of the mind" and the consequences of his erring choice.

It opens with Colin himself exhibiting his famous wares. He sings a medieval "complaint" which will soon be matched by Oenone's venture in the same form. Hobinol, Digon, and Thenot, who succeed Colin on stage, make the connection between his fate and Oenone's. Paris' choice offends all true lovers: "Poore *Colin,* that is ill for thee, that art as true in trust / To thy sweete smerte, as to his Nymphe *Paris* hath bin unjust" (III.iii.19–20). When Mercury enters to summon Paris, Oenone imagines "th'unpertiall skyes" have answered her prayer.[11] She does not realize that he comes at the partial behests of Juno, Pallas, and Vulcan and that injustice seems now to prevail above as below.

10. Horne, *Life and Minor Works,* pp. 187–188. These are ll. 113–118.

11. *Mercu. entr. with Vulcans Cyclops.* The Cyclops have no speaking role. They are apparently an iconographic representation for Peele of Vulcan's jealousy. In the fragment of Peele's *The Hunting of Cupid* anthologized in *Englands Parnassus,* the last two lines read, "Fourth, Jealousie in basest mindes doth dwell,/ This mettall Vulcans Cyclops sent from hell" (Horne, *Life and Minor Works,* p. 208). Within the play, Venus' scornful remark about *"Chimnysweepers"* seems to suggest the same sort of thing (III.vi.29–30).

This state of affairs is reiterated in the curious scene which follows. A group of shepherds begs Venus for revenge on Thestylis. She has finally murdered Colin by her disdain. Venus promises justice for Paris' sake. She blames her son "that ever love was blinde." Paris has been listening quietly, but now he objects. If Venus would handle Cupid's bow, justice could be done in love. Venus immediately counterattacks by asking Paris if he has ever been in love. In reply to his evasive answer, "Lady, a little once," she seems to insist that true lovers, unlike wantons, will their own condition and cannot be cured by external causes. Paris is worried. Can Venus and Cupid excuse a slight past offence? Venus replies sardonically with a description of the torments false lovers suffer in hell. Paris is astounded: "Is Venus and her sonne so full of justice and severytye" (III.v.31)? The answer sounds even more like something out of a medieval dream vision. Venus explains that her son is not only a boy but also a "mighty god." He is, in fact, the Eros of classical tradition: "His shafts keepe heaven and earth in awe" (l. 38). Paris, however, sees the fallacy (ll. 39–44):

> PARIS
> And hathe he reason to mantayne why Colin died for love.
> VENUS
> Yea, reason good I warrant thee, in right it might beehove.
> PARIS
> Then be the name of love adored, his bow is full of mighte,
> His woundes are all but for desert, his lawes are all but right:
> well for this once me lyst apply my speeches to thy sense,
> And *Thestilis* shall feele the paine for loves supposed offence.[12]

Venus' reply is analogous to the traditional Christian explanation of evil as God's will. Cupid's "right" can only seem like "might" to a mere mortal. Venus shrugs off Paris' sarcasm. This one time she will take a position he can understand; she will punish Thestylis according to Paris' standard.

The rest of the scene marks the working of her justice. The chant of the shepherds bearing Colin's hearse is matched by Thestylis' singing of "an olde songe called the woing of Colman" and of the complaint which fol-

---

12. I assume, with modern editors, that ll. 43 and 44 belong to Venus. Does the lower case opening of l. 43 indicate some larger typographical confusion about the beginning of this line?

lows it. The shepherds pick up the refrain of the complaint, "the grace of this song" being, as Peele says in his stage direction, "in the Shepherds Ecco to her verse." In other words, everyone sympathizes with her suffering, even Paris. Or perhaps I should say especially Paris. He has discovered that romantic love is a lord of terrible aspect. There is an undercurrent of threat in Venus' relationship with Paris. When he pities Thestylis aloud, Venus says, "Her fortune not unlyke to his whome cruell thow hast slaine" (l. 57).[13] She had only been toying with him, then, when she asked if he had ever been in love. Paris is already plunged in melancholy when Mercury enters. And when he sees Venus' fury he realizes at last that his folly is an instrument of destiny: "The angrye heavens for this fatall jar, / Name me the instrument of dire and deadly war" (III.vi.39–40).

The scenes of low humor which open Act IV parody in the usual manner the serious plot. Diana's nymph repulses Vulcan who thinks he can "treade awry as well as *Venus* doth" (IV.ii.2). At least this country jig quickly gives way to the Assembly of the Gods. I use Lydgate's title deliberately, to emphasize the medieval tradition behind this scene. The cosmological implications have their sources probably in the late Latin encyclopedists. They were popular in European literature at least from the time of the twelfth-century school of Chartres. The Olympians are not in this scene merely the gods Peele found in his Latin school texts. They are the planetary powers these deities had come to represent in the Middle Ages. In medieval literature they frequently pass judgment upon changeable men from a realm of changeless values. E. M. W. Tillyard describes this convention in speaking of the descent of the gods in *The Testament of Cresseid*:

The Middle Ages looked on the stars as an organic part of God's creation and as the perpetual instruments and diffusers of his will. . . . When Henryson used the planets as the instruments of Cresseid's punishment he . . . implied that her punishment was by God's will.[14]

13. I accept the logic of modern editors who change "his" to "hers," but it is possible that Venus refers not to Oenone but to Colin. The shepherds have pointed out that Paris is unjust to all true lovers, and only Colin at this point is literally dead.

14. E. M. W. Tillyard, *Five Poems 1470–1870* (London, 1948), pp. 20–21. The essay on Henryson's poem contains the best basic exposition I know of "the Assembly of the Gods." See especially pp. 19–22.

Peele's point is no more explicitly Christian, of course, than Henryson's, or Spenser's in the Mutability Cantos. Peele's gods, like Spenser's, convene in a place like the Garden of Eden, an earthly paradise presided over by the goddess Natura, who is called Diana in Peele's play.

The arraignment itself is modeled on the form of the law case, which was nearly as popular for literary analogies as the parliament. Peele probably considered "Paris oration to the Councell of the gods" the major setpiece of the play. It is marked by the specious argument, the handsome elaboration of topics customary in traditional rhetoric. Paris defends himself principally by pleading, as Smith points out, that he made the correct choice for a shepherd. He excuses his moral blindness: "beauties blaze" is physical for him. Peele, however, does not excuse it any more than the Spenser of *Four Hymns* would. After Paris has withdrawn to await the verdict, the gods concur that by his own standards he is innocent. Juno merely pouts, but Pallas comes up with the crucial distinction of the play: "Whether the man be guiltie yea or noe, / That doth not hinder our appeale, I troe" (IV.iv.141–142). The choice of an erring mortal has not decided, and indeed could not decide, which is the greatest sort of beauty.

The sequence of events immediately following the oration has been frequently disregarded. It is crucial, however, to the unity of the plot and to the moral significance of the play. Paris is recalled and dismissed, but the gods do not imagine that in dismissing him they approve his argument. They send him forth to the fate his nature guarantees, to what Apollo calls "his never-dying payne." Paris' choice is its own punishment. Venus will stand by her promise of "luck in love," but Paris is now aware that he has made a tragic error, destined somehow to cause the destruction of his city: "My lucke is losse, howe ere my love do speede" (l. 166). Paris is shut out of the Garden forever. But in the pastoral world of man's fulfilled wish the gods can still triumph. Discord has darkened their counsel, but Apollo, the god of poetry and prophecy, restores them to light. Jurisdiction in the appeal belongs, he says, to Diana, in whose realm the affair took place. As in the Mutability Cantos, the threat of disorder above the moon is to be handled by the goddess of nature. Apollo recalls the gods to their festal progress toward Diana. As they "rise and goe foorth," the processional movement of the play resumes, proceeding brilliantly now toward a goal off stage.

Act V is a single scene. After Diana receives the goddesses' pledges to support her decision, she *"describeth the Nymphe Eliza a figure of the Queene."* The goddesses agree; Elizabeth combines their wisdom, charm, and majesty. It happens to be the time of year when the Fates, the true "unpartiall dames" of Oenone's world, pay "their yearely due" to Elizabeth. So the goddesses follow them before the Queen, and Diana delivers, amid general acclaim, the ball of gold.

If this scene really strikes us as inconsequential "extravagant flattery," then Peele has failed to lure us sufficiently inside the masquelike mood and structure of the play. By "masque" I mean a spectacular, romantic form of drama which culminates in a dance integrating actors with audience. Masque is spectacular in its use of a full range of auditory and visual effects. It is romantic in plot (what Peele called the "device," Jonson the "hinge"). Its dancing leads to the exaltation of the audience who have been from the beginning the goal of the dancers' processional movement. Both their unmasking and selection of partners are meant to be gestures toward union. The successful masque must somehow incorporate the audience into its imaginary world.[15] The masque usually attempts a compliment which will equate the social harmony of its ideal world with the actual hierarchy of the court. In *The Arraignment* Peele wants Elizabeth to share for a golden moment of fantasy the pastoral world of the goddesses. Even granted the Tudor appetite for flattery, a moment of this sort would be indecorous if the mood were not perfect. The mood of an actual dramatic performance is as irrevocable as the mood of a dream, and this is particularly true of a masquelike play written for a specific occasion. But perhaps we can remind ourselves abstractly of the importance of mood in *The Arraignment* by considering briefly a masque in which Ben Jonson actually allegorizes the psychology of the revels.

A Vision of Delight opens with the arrival of Delight "accompanied with *Grace, Love, Harmonie, Revell, Sport, Laughter.* WONDER *following"* (ll. 4–6).[16] Delight represents the determination of the court to

15. My attempt to define "masque" owes much to E. K. Chambers' discussion of the form in *The Elizabethan Stage* (Oxford, 1923), I, pp. 149–212, and to Northrop Frye's comments on masque in *The Anatomy of Criticism,* pp. 287–293. For an interpretation of some of Jonson's masques which uses as an aesthetic criterion the success of the "hinge" in joining actors and audience, see Stephen Orgel's *The Jonsonian Masque* (Cambridge, Mass., 1965).

16. For the text of *A Vision of Delight* see Ben Jonson, *Works,* ed. C. H. Herford and P. and E. Simpson, 11 vols. (Oxford, 1925–1952), VII, 463–471.

enjoy itself within the form of the revels. He announces directly (ll. 9–12) that the performance to follow is intended to unite the Christmas festivities of the court with the pastoral atmosphere of the masque. The occasion, even the time of day, must be special. Delight dismisses the clowns of the first antimasque as "all sowre and sullen looks away / that are the servants of the day" (ll. 26–27). He summons up Night instead, "to help the vision of DELIGHT" (l. 31) by keeping "all awake with *Phantomes*" (l. 40). And Night, to accomplish this, conjures up "Phant'sie" while the "Quire" invokes her mood:

> Yet let it like an odour rise
>   to all the Sences here,
> And fall like sleep upon their eies,
>   or musick in their eare.

(ll. 51–54)

These lines express the intention behind the successive regressions from the "real" world. Phant'sie, so to speak, is the audience's willing participation in the "hinge" of the poet. After she first breaks forth with a tumultuous speech, a second antimasque "of Phantasmes" portrays the mental dangers of Night which correspond to the "sowre and sullen looks" of Day. Fancy can be dangerous, even lunatic, if not controlled by the decorum of the occasion. Phant'sie herself dismisses her phantasms and produces a new scene. "The gold-haird *Houre*" descends, to the song of Peace, bringing with her "*the Bower of* Zephyrus." The speech of Wonder which follows praises in descriptive detail this new marvel of Art and Nature. Wonder represents the willingness of the courtiers to exclaim over the spectacular sets. When she concludes, Phant'sie remarks significantly, "How better then they are, are all things made / By WONDER!" (ll. 166–167). Phant'sie, however, immediately surpasses her previous achievement. "*Here (to a loud musicke) the Bower opens, and the Maskers [are] discovered, as the glories of the Spring*" (ll. 170–171). Wonder marvels over the details of this scene as she did the preceding one, concluding, "Whose power is this? what God?" (l. 199). And Phant'sie replies, "Behold a King / Whose presence maketh this perpetuall *Spring*" (ll. 201–202). After the Quire confirms her assertion, the maskers advance, singing and dancing "*their entry*" and "*their maine Dance.*" Then "*they Danc'd with Ladies, and the whole Revells followed*" (l. 232). While the "gold-haird Houre" lasts King James does make, in the vision of delight, "perpetuall Spring." But Night and the Moone descend and Aurora appears "to bid you come away." As the maskers dance their *"going off"* the Quire sings, "They yield to Time, and so must all" (l. 244). Only the excited interplay of Phant'sie and Wonder could evoke a vision of a garden court where King James reigns in a timeless world. Our revels now are ended, and the mood melts into air, into thin air.

We can see by comparison that Peele's play is not a proper masque. Its spectacle, though plentiful, is relatively incidental; it does not end in formal dance; and its romantic plot is too rich in action and even in character development. We can also see, however, that it is constructed like a masque to induce the willing suspension of disbelief necessary to the compliment. Act V of *The Arraignment* is in no sense merely tacked on for the occasion; rather, the occasion shapes the play. The festive social conventions affect the literary ones. To resolve the action Elizabeth must be taken into the pastoral as queen of the triumphing gods.

In the forms of Renaissance romance where a social compliment of this type is intended, political allegory nearly always suggests itself. The works I have mentioned because of their relevance to the conventions of *The Arraignment* all have political implications. Even Spenser's generalized allegory in the Mutability Cantos contains the archetypal pattern of revolt which haunted the Elizabethan mind. Spenser's mythopoeic use of the traditional Platonic cosmology implies a highly conservative politics. The same is true of Jonson's masques, where the favorite themes, as in medieval dream vision, are the triumph of reason over sensuality and of order over disorder. These are the explicit themes, too, of Lyly's *Endymion,* yet Tellus is suspected of being someone like Mary, Queen of Scots in contrast to Cynthia's Elizabeth. One might almost say that the presence of the Queen attracts a political application.

In fact, I believe we can safely reverse the causal relationship and say that where we find this masquelike theme, the presence of the Queen is probable. I have referred, in connection with "Love in idlenesse," to the famous "faire Vestall, throned by the West" passage in *A Midsummer-Night's Dream* (II.i.148–169). The allegory in this passage closely resembles that in both *Endymion* and *The Arraignment,* which we know were affected by the Queen's presence. Cupid, flying between earth and moon, thinks he shoots at an appropriate sublunary target. But the time, the person, and his aim are all misjudged. The song of a mysterious mermaid enraptures nature, and in this brief restoration of the Golden Age the "imperiall Votresse" to Diana walks in a realm apart. Cupid's arrow is analogous to Ate's golden ball. Among fallen mortals it produces the maddening moral blindness called "Love in idlenesse," but Elizabeth is above the sting of sensuality as she is above every assault from below. She passes on, "in maiden meditation, fancy free." Recognition of this theme will not help to resolve the voluminous controversy about the occasion for the first composition of *A Midsummer-Night's Dream* or the occasion alluded to in the passage above, but I think it does support the probability that the play was written for a performance at which the Queen presided.

So in the case of *The Arraignment,* the intention to compliment the Queen seems to draw Peele to a plot with political overtones. He may have chosen the story of Paris for his "device" because it combined with its choice-of-Hercules parable some specific associations with Tudor history. As Tillyard finds in Shakespeare's history plays a kind of secularized mystery cycle, we can find in *The Arraignment* suggestions of a political analogue to the Fall and the Redemption. Paris is the first parent of England. His choice of the lesser good inaugurates a cycle of history in the fallen world which will lead to Brute's settlement of England and to the establishment of the Tudors on the throne after a century of civil broils. Elizabeth's reign in the New Troy restores at last the social harmony and justice which Paris lost. This restoration is symbolized in the play by the course of the golden ball from the hand of Ate to the hand of Elizabeth. Ate first rises at the bidding of Tellus. Whether or not Tellus represents Mary, Queen of Scots as she is sometimes said to do in *Endymion,* Ate does represent the recurrent threat of political chaos in postlapsarian society. But evil is dreamlike in romance. The malcontents are powerless to strike. The revolt of the disordered passions cannot touch a Queen enthroned in the sphere of the moon, changeable like mortals, but changeless like the gods. Peele saw chastity, the predominant virtue of romance, as the symbol not only of the Queen's majesty in general, but of her political stability in particular. And I like to think that by the time the full effect of his beautiful "device" had worked upon her, the old Queen could rest for a moment in the fiction that she *had* restored the order of the world, and deserved the poet's golden ball.

The Helmingham Hall Manuscript of Sidney's The Lady of May: A Commentary and Transcription

ROBERT KIMBROUGH

PHILIP MURPHY

IN 1962 WILLIAM RINGLER announced in his preface to *The Poems of Sir Philip Sidney*[1] the discovery by Miss Jean Robertson in the previous year of a manuscript version of *The Lady of May* which is unique and which contains a conclusion to the entertainment that is lacking in the only other substantive text, that printed at the end of the 1598 collected works. As Professor Ringler indicated then, the new manuscript is "a substantive text of fundamental importance," especially because the new conclusion attempts to invalidate what had been a clear allegorical intention of the entertainment proper. For these reasons we wish to present a commentary on and transcription of the version of *The Lady of May* found in the Helmingham Hall manuscript, now owned by Arthur A. Houghton, Jr.[2]

1. *The Poems of Sir Philip Sidney* (Oxford, 1962).

2. We are deeply grateful to Mr. Houghton for making the Hm manuscript available to us and for permitting the following transcription. The whole MS contains the *Old Arcadia*, with some leaves wanting, and *The Lady of May*, fols. 154ᵛ–158, separated from the *Old Arcadia* by blank fols. 153–154 (see *The Poems of Sir Philip Sidney*, ed. Ringler, pp. x–xii for a full description). We should like particularly to thank our colleague Professor Standish Henning for his generous help at all stages.

I

The Lady of May, Sidney's first public, nonacademic literary gesture, probably was written for the visit of Elizabeth in May of 1578 to Wanstead,[3] the manor house near Greenwich which was a gift of hers, as Kenilworth had been, to Robert Dudley, the Earl of Leicester. Sidney had been present at Kenilworth in 1575 when Leicester had entertained and flattered the Queen through a series of varied pseudo-dramatic pageants. These showed him what was expected in royal entertainment, and George Gascoigne's "farewell" to the Queen may have provided him with a suggestion for theme and characterization. But in addition to having the same kind of "spontaneous" quality and ultimate purpose as Gascoigne's, Sidney's entertainment shows as well his reliance on academic training in his adaptation of the *commedia rusticale.*

Sidney while on his grand tour may well have watched performances of this popular kind of farce which is derived from the *contrasto* (a debate between suitors and lovers, or husbands and wives) and the *maggio* (a play of spring).[4] By genre and heritage, *le commedie rusticali* are not pastoral because they do not invite the audience into their world. Rather, as befits their predominance in the north of Italy in the sixteenth century, rustic comedies present "folk" who take themselves quite seriously while performing before a gentle, learned audience—one thinks of Bottom the Weaver and his troop, but with differences. As a result, the basic appeal lies in satire. But Sidney's adaptation of the form is elaborated. Going beyond simple *contrasti,* he introduced a pastoral motif through a singing match, which Ringler suggests is the first in English, and exploited a traditional topic—the active versus the contemplative life—in a debate shaped to be an appeal on behalf of Leicester for a gesture from the Queen signifying her favor.

The two extant versions are both without title and simply begin with a description of what actually took place: as the Queen was walking through a garden at Wanstead "there came sodenly amonge the trayne one ap-

---

3. See *The Poems of Sir Philip Sidney,* ed. Ringler, pp. 361–362.

4. See Marvin T. Herrick, "Italian Farce," *Italian Comedy in the Renaissance* (Urbana, 1960), pp. 26–59.

parelled Like an honeste mans wyf of the Countrie," who, crying out for justice, is brought kneeling before Her Majesty. The plot of the entertainment—one hesitates, in spite of Stephen Orgel's recent argument, to use the term masque[5]—is simple enough: the woman has a daughter, whom the local folk have crowned as the Lady of the month of May and who cannot choose between the two men who are wooing her—Espilus, a rich shepherd of "smale Desertes and no faultes," and Therion, a forester of "manie Desertes and manie faultes." But such a plot was all that Sidney needed to carry out his basic purpose: to entertain by presenting a variety of rustic types in speech, song, and dance and to flatter by having each rustic acknowledge the majesty of Elizabeth without "knowing" that she was Her Majesty, as well as by leaving the choice of suitors up to her.

The ultimate purpose of the entertainment lies in this final choice, for the active Therion is clearly a Leicester-figure, as were Sylvanus and Deep-Desire, the speakers in Gascoigne's "farewell." As a result, the singing match between the two suitors and the debate between their followers are clearly weighted in favor of Therion-Leicester. In answer to the richer Espilus who conservatively and traditionally defends the quiet, productive life of the shepherd and invites his lady to come live with him and share his wealth, Therion offers a free life in the forest where the only wealth will be the lady herself. Then, the argument which follows between the shepherds and foresters over who sang the better drifts into the traditional debate, between Dorcas, a shepherd, and Rixus, a forester, over the contemplative life versus the active—but with this major difference: Dorcas' defense of an innocent world implies a stagnant life, whereas Rixus tries to show that his world has the benefits of the pastoral and more, "for ours besides the quiet parte doth both strengthen the bodie and raise of the mynde with this gallante sorte of activitie."

Still, at the end, when the May Lady asked Queen Elizabeth to judge "whether [of] theis tooe be moste worthie of me or whether I worthie of them, and this I will saie that in Iudinge me you Iudge more then me in yt," Elizabeth chose the shepherd Espilus, a choice which probably came as a surprise to few. Surely Leicester and Sidney were disappointed; they must have hoped to coax a nod of approval from the Queen for her Earl, still a favorite, but now in the dangerous position of secretly courting Essex's widow.

5. *The Jonsonian Masque* (Cambridge, Mass., 1965), pp. 44-56.

This last address to the Queen, just quoted, contains two requests: to judge between the suitors, and to judge the Lady in judging whom "you Iudge more then me in yt," which is, of course, merely a reminder to the Queen of what must have been obvious to her, that she was the Lady of the *maggio*. Naturally, she chose to ignore this second charge, and when she chose the shepherd, Orgel and David Kalstone believe that the Queen had not been paying attention to the developing logic of the presentation.[6] Her choice proves just the opposite; like Caesar, she knew what kind of men she wanted around her, as her consistent treatment of the Sidneys, father and son, bears witness.

To be safe, Sidney had provided a final song of triumph which was sufficiently ambiguous that it could be sung by either suitor. The first of three stanzas tells of Sylvanus, the god of forests, who sounds and acts like a shepherd; the second is about Pan, the god of shepherds, who sounds and acts like a forester; and the third has four lines of joy and two lines of lament so general that either suitor could sing either part. Furthermore, Sidney had an "epilogue" prepared against the chance that the Queen might make this "wrong" choice.

After the May Lady makes an appropriate farewell to the Queen in both versions of *The Lady of May,* the Helmingham (or Hm) manuscript continues with Rombus stepping forward to address the Queen in a speech which makes clearer the fact that Leicester was seeking a favorable gesture from the Queen. But the emphasis must be on the relative —clear*er.* First of all, no one ever addressed the Queen directly without endangering his standing, as Sidney was reminded the next year. Moreover, the speech is spoken by Rombus, that typical product of the academically oriented Northern Renaissance: the pedagogue who wallows in complicated syntax using his little Latin and less Greek to coin impossible inkhorn terms in what he thinks is a grand display of method and learning. A final difficulty lies in the fact that by the time the scribe had finished copying the *Old Arcadia* and started on *The Lady of May,* he was getting tired and anxious to finish, so that one cannot tell here whether or not some of Rombus' errors are intentional or only scribal.

This much may be deduced: he starts his speech with a castigation of the "obscure barbarous *per fidem perfide,"* that is, the departing for-

6. Kalstone, *Sidney's Poetry: Contexts and Interpretations* (Cambridge, Mass., 1965), pp. 42–47.

esters, who, he says, deserve to be "vapilated" (i.e., vapulated, thrashed), thus divorcing Leicester from Therion. Then he turns to the Queen to present her with some round agates which have been strung to resemble a rosary. They are a gift of the Earl, whom he calls familiarly Master Robert, an honest and generous man, falsely accused of Romish leanings (a rumor which, with some justice with regard to appearances, Leicester's rivals periodically renewed). The truth is, he says, that although the Earl has some *"papisticorum Bedorus,"* he uses them only to say "and [an] Elizabeth as many Lynes [times?] as theare be beades on this stringe," which he then presents with a pseudo-legal flourish (*"Quamobrem* I saie *secundum,"* etc.) to the Queen. In his farewell, the bad Latin is his, but the plea is obviously that of Leicester: *"me vt facias ama* that is to loue me much better then you were wounte [wont]."

When *The Lady of May* was printed in 1598 this "epilogue" was dropped, not simply because the allusions were dated, private, and slightly damaging to the name of Leicester but mainly because Rombus' speech is an anticlimax.

The Hm manuscript, written throughout in a single sixteenth-century secretary hand, is in good condition. Although *The Lady of May* is riddled with errors, many obviously the result of carelessness and haste, the manuscript version contains a number of substantive readings superior to the 1598 version, as well as, of course, the "epilogue" discussed above.

The following is a *literatim* transcription with certain exceptions. Abbreviated and contracted forms, save the familiar *Mr* and *&,* have been expanded; superior letters have been lowered; and virgules, often used simply as decorations to accompany full stops, have been transcribed only when they are functional. Scribal errors, however, have been retained.[7]

II

Her most excellente Maiestie walkinge in wansted garden as she passed owne into the grove there came sodenly amonge the trayne one apparelled Like an honeste mans wyf of the Countrie where crienge oute for Iustice and desieringe all the Lordes and gentlemen to speake a good

7. Mr. Murphy is preparing a critical edition of *The Lady of May* under the direction of Professor Henning.

woorde for her, she was broughte to the presence of her maiestie to whome vppon her knees she offered a Supplicacion & vsed this speeche /

The Suitor

Most faire Ladie for other your titles of state, stalier person shall geue you, and thus muche my owne eyes are wytnes of. Take here the complaynt of me poore wretch as Deeplie plonnged in myserie, as I wishe to you the higheste poynte of happines One only Dawghter I haue, in whome I had placed all the hope of my happe so well had she with her good parts, Recompenced my payne of bearinge her & care of bringinge her vp. But now alasse, that she is come to the tyme I should Reape my full comeforte of her, so is she trobled with that notable matter of *Matrimonie* as I cannot chuse but feare the losse of her wyttes, at leaste of her honestie. other weomen thincke theie may be vnhappie with one housbande, my poore dawghter is oppressed with tooe both lovinge her, both equally liked of her, both strivinge to deserve her, but nowe lastely as this Ielosy forsooth is a vilde matter, eache hauinge broughte theire partakers with them and are at this present withoute your presence redresse yt in some blouddie controversie, my poore child is amonge them. now sweete Ladie helpe. your owne way guides you to the place where they encomber her, I dare staie no longer, for our owne men saye heere in the Countrye, the sighte of you is infectious.

And wyth that shee wente away a good pace Leavinge the supplicacion with her maiestie which very formally conteyned this.

Supplicacion

Most gracious Soueraigne
To one whoes state is Raysed over all
whose face doth ofte the bravest sorte enchaunte
whose mynde is suche, as wysest myndes appale
whoe in one self theis divers giftes can plante.

How dare I wretche seeke there my woas to Reste
where eares be burnte Eyes dazeled harte oppreste.

your state is greate, your greatnes is your shilde.
your face hurtes ofte but still yt doth delighte

your mynde is wyse, your wisdome makes you mylde
such planted guiftes, enrich even beggers sighte
So dare I wretche my bashfull feare subdewe.
and feed myne eyes, myne eares, myne harte on you

Herewith the woman suitor beinge gon, ther was hard in the woodes a confused noise and fourthwith there came oute sixe shepheardes, with as many fosters halinge and pullinge, to whether side they should Drawe the Ladie of maye, whoe seemed to enclyne, nether to the one nor other side, Amonge whome was mr *Rombus* A Scoole mr of a village, therby, whoe beinge fully perswaded of his owne Learned wysdome, came thither with his Awthoritie to parte the fraye. where for an answer he receaved, many vnlearned blowes. But the Quene cominge to the place, where she was seene of them, though they knew not her estate yet some thinge ther was which made them startle aside and gaze vppon her, Till owlde fathe *Lalus* (one of the substantialst Shepheardes) and makinge a Leg or too saide theis few woordes.

Lalus the owld shephearde

May yt please your benignitie to geue alitle superfluous intelligence to that which wyth openinge my mouth my tonge and teeth will deliuer vnto you. So yt is righte worshipfull audience that a certeyne she creature which we shepheardes call a woman of an innsicall countenance but by my white Lambe not three quarters so beautious as your self disanulled the brayne pan of twoe of our fittioust younge men / And will you wott how by my mothers Kittes sowle with a certeyne fransicall malladie they cale Love, when I was ayonge man they called yt flatt folly, But here is a substanciall scoole mr can better disnounce the whole foundacion of the matter, althouge forsooth for all his Loquence owr yonge men were nothinge Dutious to his clarckeship. Come on come on mr scoole mr be not so basheles, we saie that the fayrest are ever the gentlest, tell the whole case for you can much better vent the poynte of yt then I can.

Then came forwarde mr *Rombus* and wyth many speciall graces made this Learned Oratioun

Rombus

Now the thundrie thumppinge *Ioue* trannssende his dotes into your excellent formositie, which with your resplendannte beames this segregated the Enmyty of theis Rurall animalls I am *potentissma:* a scoole mr, that is to saye a *pedagoge* one not a litle versed in the Disciplinatinge of the iuuentall frye wherin (to my laude I saie yt) I vse such *geometricall* proportion as nether wanteth mansuetude nor correction for so yt is described,

parcere Subiectos et debillire Superbos.

yet hath not the pulcretude of my vertues protected me from the contamynatinge handes of theis *pliebeians* for cominge *solumodo* to haue parted theire sanguinolet fray they yelde me no more Reuerence then yf I had byn some *pecorus Asinus* I even I that am whoe I am! *Dixi verbus Sapiento Satum est* but what said that *Troian Æneas* when he soiorned in the surginge sulkes of the sandiferous seas. *Hec olim memonasse iubebit* well well and pro*positos reuertebo* The puritie of the veritie is that a certeyne *pulcra puella profecto* ellected and constituted by the integrated determination of all this *Topograficall* Region as the soueraigned Ladie of this Dame *Maias* moneth hath bynne *Quodamodo* hunted as you wolde say pursued, by tooe, a brace, a cupple, a caste of younge men to whome the craftie coward *Cupid* had *Inquam* deliuerd his dire Dolefull, Diginge, Dignifienge Darte.

But here the may Ladie interrupted him

Maie Ladie

Awaie away you tedious foole, your eyes are not worthie to looke to yonder princely sighte, muche Lesse your foolish tonge to troble her wyse eares

At which mr *Rombus* in greate chafe cried oute.

Rombus:

O tempori o moribus in profession a childe, in dignitie a woman in yeres a Ladie in *ceteris* a mayde, should thus turpofy the reputacion of my

Doctryne with the which superscription of a foole, *o tempori o moribus.*
But here againe the may Ladie saienge vnto him

Maie Ladie

Leave good *Latin* foole and let me satisfie the long desier I haue had to
feed myne eyes with the onely sighte this adge hath grannted to the
worlde.

The poore scoole mr wente his way backe and the ladie kneelinge
downe said in this manner

Maie Ladie

Do not thincke sweete and gallante Ladie that I do abase my self this
much vnto you because of your gaye apparrell, for what is so brave as the
naturall beautie of the flowers nor because a certeyne gentleman heere by
seekes to do you all the honor he can in his house that is not the matter
he is but our neighbour and theis be our owne groves, nor yet because of
your greate estate since no estate can be compared to be the ladie of the
sole month of maye as I am so that since both this place and this tyme are
my servantes, you maye be suer I wolde looke for reuerence at your handes
yf I did not see some thinge in your face which makes my yeelde to you,
the troth is you excell me in all thinges wherin I desier most to excell, and
that makes me geve this homage vnto you as to the beautifullest Ladie
theis woodes haue ever receaved, but now as oulde father *Lalus* directed
me I will tell you my fortune that you may be iudge of my myshapps
and others worthines. Indeede so yt is that I am a faire wench or ells I
am deceaved, and therfore by the consent of all our neighbours haue byn
chosen for the absolute Ladie of this merry moneth with me haue byn
(alasse I am ashamed to tell yt) tooe younge men the one a Foster named
Therion the other *Espilus* a shephearde verye Longe even in love forsooth, I like them both and love nether, *Espilus* is the richer but *Therion*
is the Livelier, *Therion* doth me manie pleasures, and stelinge me venison
out of theis Forestes and manie other such like prettie and prettier services, but with all he growes to suche Rage, as some tymes he strikes me
and some tyme he Rayles at me: This shepheard *Espilus* of a mylde disposition, as his fortune hath not byn to do me greate services so hath he

never donne me anie wronge, but feedinge his sheepe sittinge vnder some sweete bushe, some tymes they saie he Recordes my name in dolefull verses. Now the Question I am to aske of you fayre Ladie is whether the manie Desertes and manie faultes of *Therion* or the smale Desertes and no faultes *Espilus* be to be preferred. but before you geve your Iudgemente most excellente Ladie you shall heere what each of them can say for them selves in theire Rurall songes.

There vppon *Therion* challanged *Espilus* to singe wyth him speakinge theis sixe verses.

Therion:
Come *Espilus* come now declare thie skill
Shew how thou canste deserve so brave desier
warme well thie wittes yf thou wilte wyn her will
for water coulde did never promisse fier
 Greate suer is she on whome our hopes do live
 greater is she whoe muste the iudgemente geve.

But *Espilus* as yf he had byn enspired with *muses* began forth with to singe wherto his fellow sheppheardes sett in with theire *Recordes* which they bare in theire bages like pipes and so on *Therions* side did the fosters with the cornettes they ware aboute theire neckes like hunntinge hornes in Bowdrikes

Espilus
Tune vp my voyce a hier note I yelde
to hie Conceites the songe muste needes be hie
more hie then starres, more fyrme then flintie feilde
are all my thoughtes, in which I Live or Die /
 Sweete sowle to whome I vowed am A Slave
 Let not wilde woodes so great a treasure have
Therion:
The highest note come of from baseste mynde
as shallowe brookes do yeelde the greateste sounde
Seeke other thoughtes thy self or death to fynde
Thie starre be falen plowde is the flyntie grounde

Sweete sowle let not a wretche that serveth shepe
among his flocke so sweete a treasure kepe

Espilus

Tooe thowsande sheepe I haue as white as milke
thoughe not so white as is thie Lovely face
The pasture Ritche the wolle as softe as silke
All this I geue let me possesse thie grace
 But still take heede leste thou thie self submitte
 To one that hath no welth and wantes his witte

Therion

Twoe Thowsande Deere in wildest woodes I haue
Them can I take but you I cannot howlde /
he is not poore whoe can his freedome save
Bounde but to you no welth but you I woulde /
 But take this beaste of beastes you feare to mysse
 For of his beastes the greateste beaste he is /
 Espilus knelinge to the Queene /
Iudge you to whome all beauties force is Lente

Therion

Iudge you of Love, to whome all love is bente.

But as theie wayted for Iudgemente her majestie sholde geue of theire Desertes, the sheppherdes and foresters grewe to a greate contention whether of theire fellowes had songe beste, or whether the estate of shepheardes or Fosters were the more worshipfull, The spekers were *Dorcas* and an owlde shepheardes one *Rixus* A younge foster betwene whome the scoole mr *Rombus* came in as a moderator.

Dorcas the shepheard /

Now all the blessinges of myne owlde grandame lylly *Esipus* lighte vpon thie showlders for this honnycombe singinge of thine, now of myne honestie all the belles in the Towne coulde not haue songe better, yf the prowd harte of a harlotry be not downe to thee nowe, the sheeps rotte ketch her, that A fayer woman, hath not her fayrenes to let yt growe Ruryshe /

Rixus the Foster.

O Midas whie arte thou not alive now to Lend thine eares to this Drivell by the pretious bones of a huntesman he knowes not the bleinge of A calfe from the songe of A nightingale but yf yonder greate gentlewoman be as wyse as she is faire *Therion* thou shalte haue the price and thou olde *Dorcas* with younge mr *Espilus* shall remayne tame fooles as you be.

Dorcas.

And with cap and knee be yt spoken is it your pleasure neighbor *Rixus* to be A wylde foole.

Rixus

Rather then a sheepish Dolte.

Dorcas.

Yt is muche refresshinge for my Bowells you haue made your choyse for my share, I will bestowe your leavinges vppon one of your fellowes /

Rixus

And arte thou not ashamed owld foole to liken *Espilus* a shepherd to *Therion* of the noble vocation of hunters in the presens of suche a one as even with her eye can geue the punishmente.

Dorcas.

Howlde thie peace I will nether medle with her nor her eyes they saine in our Towne they are Daungerous both nether will I liken *Therion* to my boy *Espilus* since one is a theevishe proler, and the other is as quiet as a Lambe that newe came from suckinge.

Rombus the Scoole mr

Hem eheu hei Inciputem Insatium vulgorum et populorum whie you brute Nebulones haue you had my corpusculum all this while amonge you & cannot yet tell how to edifie an argumente? attend and throw your ears to me, for I am gravidated with child till I haue indoctrinated your ploumbeous cerebrosities, firste you muste Divisionate your poynte *Quasi* you should cutte a chees in tooe particles for thus muste I vniforme my speech to your obtuse conceptions for *prima diuidendum oratio* and then *definiendum exemplum gratia* eyther *Therion* must conquer this Dame *Maias nymphe* or *Espilus* muste overthrow her and that *secundum* their Dignitie which must also be subdivisionated in tooe equall members eythr accordinge to the ponetranncie of theire singinge or the melioritie of theire functions or lastely the superanncy of their Merites Do singe *satis* nuc are you to Argumentate of the quallifienge of the estate firste and then whether hath more infernally I meane Deepely deserved /

Dorcas /

O poore *Dorcas* poore *Dorcas* that I was not set in my younge daies to scoole that I mighte haue purchased the vnderstondinge of mr *Rombus* mysterious speeches, but yet this muche my capatcitie doth conceave of him that I muste geue vp from the Botome of my stomack what my conscience doth fynde in the behalfe of shepheardes, O sweete honny mylken Lambes and is theire anie so flynten a harte that can fynd aboute him to speake againste them that haue the chardge of suche good sowles as you be amonge whome theris no envie but all obedience / where yt is Lawfull for a man to be good yf he liste and hath noe owtewarde cause to with Draw him from yt where the eye may be busied in consideringe godes workes and the harte quietly reioysed in the honest vsinge them yf contemplacion as clarckes saie be most excellente, which is so fitte a life for a Templer as ours is? which is nether subiecte to violente oppression nor servile flattery how many courtiers (thincke you) I haue hard vnder our somer bushes make theire wofull complayntes some of the greatenes of theire mistris estate, which dazeled theire eyes and yet burned theire hartes some of the extremytie of her beautie cupled wyth extreme creweltie some of to much witte which mad all these theire Lovinge Labors folly O how often haue I hard one name sounde in many mouthes makinge our valleyes wytnesses of theire dolefull Agonies so that with longe loste Labor fyndinge theyre thoughte bere no other wolle but Dispaire, of you courtiers they grewe owlde shepheardes well sweete Lambes I will ende with you as I began, he that can open his mouth againe suche innocente sowles let him be hated as muche as A filthie foxe Let the taste of him be worse then musty cheese the sound of him more terrybelle then the howlinge of A woolf his sighte more odible then a wadde in ones porrage.

Rixus

your life in deed hath some goodnes

Rombus the scoole mr

O tace tace, or all the fatte is ignified firste let me dilucidate the very intricall mariebone of the matter he doth vse a certene rethoricall Invasion into the poynte as yf indeed he had conference with his Lambes but the trothe is he doth equitate you in the meane tyme, but this he saith the sheep are good *Ergo* the shepheard is good an *Enthimeme A Loco contigentibus* as my finger and my thombe are contigentes, lyke wyse he saies whoe lives well is good, but shepheardes live well *Ergo* theie are good *sillogisme in Darius* Kinge of *Persia,* a coniugatis as you wold saie a man cuppled to his wyfe tooe bodies but one sowle but do you acquiescate to my exortacion and you shall extinguishe him, tell him his maior is a knave his minor a foole and his conclusion a foole

Rixus

I was saieinge the shepheardes life had some goodnes in yt because yt borowed of the countrie quietnes some thinge like ours but that is not all for ours besides the quiet parte doth both strengthen the bodie and raise of the mynde with this gallante sorte of activitie o sweete contentacion to see the longe life of the hurteles trees to see how in streighte growinge vp though never so hie they hinder not their fellowes, those onely enviously troble, which are crookedly bente what life is to be compared to ours where the very growinge thinges are example of goodnes, we haue no hopes but we may quickely goe aboute them and goinge aboute them wee soone obteyne them not Like those that hauinge longe followed one in troth excellente chase, do now at length perceaue she wold neuer be taken, but that yf she staide at anie tyme neere the pursuers yt was never mente to tary with them but only to take breath to fly further from them he therefore that doutes that our life doth not farre excell all others, lett him also doute that the well strivinge and exercisinge and painefull *Therion* is not to be preferred before the idle *Espilus* which is even as muche to saie as that the Roes are not swyfter then shepe nor the stagges more goodly then goates.

Rombus:

Bene bene nuc de questione propsitus that is as much to say as well well nowe of the purposde Questione that was whether the manie greate services and many greate faultes of *Therion* or the fewe smale services and noe faultes of *Espilus* be to be preferred incepted or accepted the former.

The Ladie May.

No noe your ordinarie braynes shall not deale in that matter I have alreadye submitted yt to one whoes sweete spiritte hath passed throughe greate difficulties neyther will I that your blocke heades Lye in her waie. Therfore o Ladie worthy to see the accomplishemente of your desiers, since all your desiers be most worthie of you, vouchesafe our eares suche happines, and me that particuler favor as that you will iudge whether theis tooe be moste worthie of me or whether I worthie of them, and this I will saie that in Iudinge me you Iudge more then me in yt.

This beinge saide yt pleased her Maiestie to Iudge yt *Espilus* did the better deserve her, but what woordes and Reasons she vsed for yt this paper which carryeth so base names is not worthie to conteyne, sufficeth yt that vppon the Iudgemente geven the sheppheardes and fosters made a full consorte of theire Cornettes and Recorders, and then did *Espilus* singe this songe tendinge to the greatenes of his Ioyes, and yet to the comeforte of the other side, since they were overthrowne by a wyse woorthie Ladie the songe conteyned tooe shorte Tales and this yt was.

> Silvanus longe in Love and longe in vayne
> at length obtained the poynte of his Desier
> when beinge axte, now that he did obtayne
> his wyshed weale what more he could Requier
> > Nothinge saide he for most I ioy in this
> > That goddes myne my blessed beinge sees.

> when wanton Pan deceaved with Lions skyn
> came to the bed, whe wounde for kysse he gotte
> To woa and shame the wretche did enter in
> Till this he tooke for comefor of his lotte
> > Poore *pan* he saide although thou beaten be
> > It is no shame since Hercules was he

> This Ioyfull I in ioyfull tvnes Reioyce
> that such a one is wittnes of my harte
> whoes cleerest eyes I blisse and sweete of voyce
> That see my good and iudgeth my deserte
> > This wofull I in woe this salve doe fynde
> > my fowle my happe came yet from fayrest mynde.

The musicke fullie ended the may Ladie tooke her leave in this sort Ladie your self for other titles doe rather diminishe then ad vnto you, I and my litle Companie muste nowe leave you, I shoulde do you wronge yf I shoulde beseche to take our follies well since your bountie is such as to pardon greate faultes therfore I will wyshe you good nyghte, prayenge to god accordinge to the title I professe that as hither to yt hath excellentely don so hence forward the florishinge of maie May Longe Remayne in you.

And so they parted leavinge Mr *Rombus* whoe presented her Maiestie with a chayne of Round Aggates somethinge like beades firste beginninge in a chafe.

Videre theis obscure barbarous *per fidem perfide.* you were well served to be vapilated Relinquishinge my Dignitie before I haue *valedixed* this *Nymphes* serenitie well aliss I will be *vindicated,* But to you *Iuno Venus pallas & profecto plus* I haue to ostend a Mellifluous fruite of my fidelitie *sic est* so yt is that in this our sittie we haue acerteyne neighbour they cale him mr Roberte of wansteed, he is counted an honeste man, and one that Loves vs doctified men *pro vita* and when he comes to his *Edicle* he distributes *Oves boves et pecores campi* Largely amonge the *populorum* but so states the case that he is fowlly commaculated with the papisticall enormitie *O Heu Æstipus Æcastor* the bonus *vir* is a huge *Catholicam* wherwith my conscience beinge Replenished coulde no Longer Refrayne yt from you *proba dominus doctor probo Inveni* I haue founde *vnum par* a payre *papisticorum Bedorus* of papistion Beades *cum quos* with the which *omnium dierum* every daie nexte after his pater noster he *semper* saith and Elizabeth as many Lynes as theare be beades on this stringe *Quamobrem* I saie *secundum* the civill Lawe nine houndereth *paragroper of the Iustinian* Code in the greate Turke Iustinians Library that he hath deparded all his Iuriousdiction and yt is forfayted *tibi dominorum domina* accipe therfore for he will never be so audacious to reclamat yt againe, beinge *Iure Gentiorum* this manumissor, well *vale vale Felissima et me vt facias ama* that is to loue me much better then you were wounte and so *iterum valeamus & plaudiatmus plauditamus & valeamus.*

To Make Boards to Speak: Inigo Jones's Stage and the Jonsonian Masque

STEPHEN ORGEL

Oh, to make Boardes to speake! There is a taske
Painting & Carpentry are y° Soule of Masque.

J ONSON'S COUPLET[1] is intended sarcastically, but it glances at a complex truth. The soul of masque has always lain in large measure in the eye of the beholder, whether poet, architect, spectator, or critic. Jonson's court productions display enough variety over the twenty-five years of their development to make definitions difficult and render generalizations unrewarding; still, certain elements are clearly basic to the form as he conceived it. On the practical level, as a celebration of the court, the masque was an entertainment that included its audience, both figuratively, by allegorizing its noble spectators and their milieu, and literally, by culminating in the revels—social dancing between spectators and the courtly masquers. On the theoretical or philosophical level certain concepts are equally basic. The masque is always about the resolution of discord, and antitheses, paradoxes, and the movement from disorder to order are central to its nature. Jonson does not devise a full-fledged antimasque until *The Masque of Queens* in 1609, though *The Haddington*

1. *An Expostulation with Inigo Jones,* quoted in Ben Jonson, *Works,* ed. C. H. Herford and P. and E. Simpson, 11 vols. (Oxford, 1925–1952), VIII, 404, ll. 49–50. This edition of Jonson is hereafter cited as *"Works."*

Masque of the previous year does include a relatively brief "antimasque of boyes," which fulfills all the requirements of the genre. Nevertheless, these antimasques are merely ways of giving theatrical expression to an idea that has been inherent in Jonson's work from the beginning, in *The Masque of Blackness* and indeed in the form as he received it from his Elizabethan predecessors.

But Jonson's conception of the masque is only part of my concern here; for much as he succeeded in making of the ephemeral courtly entertainment a viable literary form, the text of a masque is not the thing itself. In production, the central relation between antimasque and masque is expressed not only rhetorically and dramatically, but in terms of spectacle, choreography, and music; and the fact that Jonson's idea of a masque did not invariably coincide with that of at least one of his collaborators hardly needs documentation. Still, the quarrel with Inigo Jones is only part of the story, and for most of their collaboration, the scene designer and the poet did work together to produce a form of remarkable consistency, with its own principles of decorum and concepts of unity. Jones's stagecraft, insofar as we can recover it from descriptions and designs, is in its own way a statement about the nature and form of the masque and is moreover in the most direct sense an interpretation of Jonson's text. Indeed, the development of the form is inseparable from the development of the stage on which it was produced. Jonson's complaints about the tyranny of painting and carpentry must be weighed against his increasing reliance on the resources of the complex theater that Jones was providing for him.

It is this interaction between the inventions of the poet and of the designer that I wish to consider here. Much valuable discussion has been directed toward their quarrel, too little toward their joint achievement.[2] Jones's stage, which is essentially that of the modern theater, was invented for the Jonsonian masque; and it opened up, in turn, a range of unimagined possibilities for the poet's creation. My subject is the process by which these two came into a real and fruitful coincidence, and I shall concentrate in particular upon that period between 1610 and 1618 when the collaboration achieved its most striking successes.

2. The most detailed and useful study of the quarrel is that of D. J. Gordon, "Poet and Architect: The Intellectual Setting of the Quarrel between Ben Jonson and Inigo Jones," *Journal of the Warburg and Courtauld Institutes,* XII (1949), 152–178.

In the earliest masques, text and production tend to be curiously independent of each other. Jonson provides admiring descriptions of costumes and scenic devices in the masques of *Blackness* and *Beauty,* but
these are in effect pauses in the text; the poet is simply giving the designer
his due. In production the stage became at these moments essentially a
dramatic entity, which by itself provided the "action" of the masque:

This *Throne,* (as the whole *Iland* mou'd forward, on the water,) had a
circular motion of it owne, imitating that which wee call *Motum mundi,*
from the *East* to the *West,* or the right to the left side. . . . The steps, whereon
the *Cupids* sate, had a motion contrary, with *Analogy, ad motum Planetarum,*
from the *West* to the *East:* both which turned with their seuerall lights. And
with these three varied *Motions,* at once, the whole *Scene* shot it selfe to the
land.

Aboue which, the *Moone* was seene in a *Siluer* Chariot, drawne by *Virgins,*
to ride in the clouds, and hold them greater light: with the *Signe Scorpio,*
and the *Character,* plac'd before her.[3]

In *Hymenaei,* what must have been the outstanding moment of the
masque in production barely finds a place in Jonson's text: *"Here out of a*
Microcosme, or Globe, *(figuring Man) with a kind of contentious
Musique, issued forth the first* Masque, *of eight men"* (213:109–111).
    This was a spectacular device and would have commanded a good
deal of the audience's attention. There is no point in looking for jealousies
in the curtness of Jonson's description; the effect simply is not part of the
masque-as-poem. At this moment in the work what is important to Jonson
is not that the scene was breathtaking but that it represented a microcosm.
Later the poet devotes over a hundred lines to summarizing the magnificence of the scenes and costumes, and here at last, out of context, the
great globe machine is described and praised:

No lesse to be admir'd, for the grace, and greatnesse, was the whole *Machine* of the *Spectacle,* from whence they came: the first part of which was a
ΜΙΚΡΟΚΟΣΜΟΣ, or *Globe,* fill'd with *Countreys,* and those gilded; where
the *Sea* was exprest, heightned with siluer waues. This stood, or rather hung
(for no *Axell* was seene to support it) and turning softly, discouered the first
Masque (as wee haue before, but too runningly declared) which was of the
men, sitting in faire *composition,* within a *mine* of seuerall metals: To which,

3. *The Masque of Beauty,* 189: 256 ff. *Beauty* was not designed by Jones, but the
production was strictly in his style. Page and line references are to the text of the
masques in *Works,* Vol. VII.

the lights were so placed, as no one was seene; but seemed, as if onely REA-
SON, with the splendor of her crowne, illumin'd the whole Grot.

(231:631 ff.)

Clearly the poet's text and the architect's stage are different phenomena.

But both artists appear to have had a notion of unity in the form; and
despite their quarrel, what they produce does imply an increasing ability
to think in each other's terms. In *The Masque of Queens,* Jonson makes
the stage machine genuinely integral to the dramatic structure of the
masque. His antimasque figures are *"Haggs,* or Witches, sustayning the
persons of *Ignorance, Suspicion, Credulity,* &c. the opposites to good
Fame" (282:17–19)—they are devised, that is, as the abstract antitheses to
the virtues represented by the queens of the main masque. So conceived,
the worlds of antimasque and revels are mutually exclusive, and no confrontation between them is possible. The moral victory, the triumph of
virtue, is therefore achieved not through drama, the ordinary means of the
poet and playwright, but through Inigo Jones's machinery, which Jonson
is employing to make a symbolic statement about the world of his masque:

In the heate of they' *Daunce,* on the sodayne, was heard a sound of loud
Musique, as if many Instruments had giuen one blast. W'h w'h, not only the
Hagges themselues, but they' *Hell,* into w'h they ranne, quite vanishd; and
the whole face of the *Scene* alterd; scarse suffring the memory of any such
thing: But, in the place of it appear'd a glorious and magnificent Building,
figuring the *House of Fame.*

(301:354 ff.)

The structure of the masque does not simply allow for this spectacular
machine; it requires it.

In such a structure as this, the transition from antimasque to masque
is a metamorphosis, and the theatrical machine is crucial to its accom-
plishment. Symbolically the total disappearance of the hags and their hell
demonstrates a basic assumption of the universe Jonson has created: the
world of evil is not real. It exists at all only in relation to the world of
ideals, which are the norms of the masque's universe. So the antimasque
is physically ugly, threatening but in fact dramatically powerless and
ultimately—when the transition takes place—without status even as a
concept, "scarse suffring the memory of any such thing." This last is, of
course, a moral statement, not a literal description of the spectators' experience, but it illustrates the extent to which Jonson was willing to use

the theatrical realities as the metaphors of his text. In fact, as the form takes on more consistency in the years after 1609, the stage and its devices appear less and less as separate phenomena and more as integral parts of a unified whole. *Queens* is the last of the great spectacular masques, and both artists show a steady and deliberate movement away from the sorts of devices it embodies. Though the masques of the next decade are various enough to defy easy categorization, they all reveal a new attitude toward the function of the scene and its machinery, and, more specifically, they reveal what we might call an anti-spectacular bias. The culmination of this movement is in the masques produced by Jonson and Jones between 1615 and 1618—*The Golden Age Restored, Mercury Vindicated from the Alchemists at Court, The Vision of Delight,* and *Pleasure Reconciled to Virtue.*

I wish here to consider the nature of the new developments and to suggest some reasons for them. On the surface, the move away from spectacle in the masque, however justified by formal considerations, would appear to have been self-defeating: spectators during the second decade of the seventeenth century complained regularly of the poverty of both the scenic and poetic inventions. This should give us pause. Surely there is no genre in Renaissance literature more directly involved with the demands and expectations of its audience than the court masque. Traditional explanations for what happened to the Jonsonian form after 1610 observe this fact without really taking it into account. For example, Enid Welsford, writing on *The Vision of Delight* (1617), adduces as primary sources for its form an Italian production of 1608 and, more significantly, a French ballet of 1606.[4] For Miss Welsford, the combination of bright ideas from the continent and audiences' demands for foreign pleasures produces a viable theory about the genesis of *The Vision of Delight:*

> All . . . masques written at this time by writers other than Ben Jonson show the increasing popularity of the antimasque and the tendency to multiply the grotesque dances and to emulate the bizarre inconsequence of the French ballet-masquerade; they help us to realise how strenuously Ben Jonson was resisting popular pressure in his attempt to keep the antimasque in a subordinate position. Gradually, however, even Ben was forced to give way, and the masques prepared by him in the year 1617 mark a fresh stage in his submission to foreign influence. . . . The introduction of two antimasques in the

4. *The Court Masque* (Cambridge, Eng., 1927), p. 202.

Vision shows that Jonson was having to accommodate himself to the prevailing fashion, and compose his masques *à la mode de France*. He resented the necessity.[5]

The trouble with this is that after making the masques slavishly responsive to public taste, the theory has no way of accounting for their striking unpopularity. Miss Welsford is particularly hard on *The Vision*'s first antimasque, which is "obviously an imitation of the first part of the *Ballet de la Foire St.-Germain.*" [6] She notes that the masque was unpopular and concurs with contemporary court opinion, explaining that "The first antimasque is certainly rather unattractive and pointless," and concludes that "it must have filled up quite a considerable part of the performance, and may perhaps have altered and marred the balance of the whole piece." [7]

All this illustrates the dangers of treating influences as explanations. Miss Welsford's dissatisfaction with the antimasque she mentions is justified by observing that it has been imported from a French source in deference to popular tastes. In Miss Welsford's own terms, this ought at the very least to rank as a startling miscalculation on Jonson's part, since what was allegedly designed solely to please the public is here being held solely responsible for its displeasure. Moreover, in the following year Jonson produced *Pleasure Reconciled to Virtue,* a masque with many of the same characteristics, and even more unpopular. But on the other hand, if one argued, as I intend presently to do, that the antimasque in question is by no means pointless but both beautifully apt and structurally necessary, it would follow that the form of the work was determined not by influences and demands—pressures outside Jonson—but by the force of the poet's own creative intelligence. For surely artists *select* their influences, which are, properly speaking, aspects of their invention; and the relation between an audience's expectations and the artist's creation is far more complex than Miss Welsford allows. It is too simple to think merely in terms of the tyranny of the spectators' demands. For it must also be true that Jonson is educating his audiences and employing his knowledge of their expectations as he employed conventions and traditions: as the tools and devices of his art.

5. *Ibid.,* pp. 198–203.
6. *Ibid.,* p. 202.
7. *Ibid.,* p. 254.

I am equally concerned with Inigo Jones's development during this period; for contemporaries ascribed the faults of the productions to him as well as to Jonson. "Mr. Inigo Jones hath lost in his reputacion," wrote Sir Edward Sherburne after *Pleasure Reconciled to Virtue* in 1618, "in regard some extraordinary devise was looked for . . . and a poorer one was never sene." [8] In this case, it was presumably the spectacular scenic effects of *Hymenaei* and *Queens* that the audiences missed; nevertheless, Jones throughout the period ignored the expectation. Again, traditional explanations for this are confused, but Jonson is usually held to be somehow liable. For example, Allardyce Nicoll observes that in the masques of this decade Jones introduced nothing new and cites, approvingly, the comment of Sherburne quoted above.[9] The difficulties of interpretation are compounded by lack of information, but here the poet's aged malice becomes the culprit: "'The scene chang'd' in Jonson's *The Golden Age Restored,* but by this time the crabbed old author was being very parsimonious in his notices of scenic display." [10] "The crabbed old author" was forty-two in 1615; he is present only because Professor Nicoll assumes that there is something sinister about the lack of scenic detail in Jonson's text. Behind this is the assumption that more ought to have been going on in Jones's theater than we find there and that perhaps something is even being concealed from us.

I see no reason to make any of these assumptions. My sense of what happens to the Jonsonian masque between 1610 and 1618 is that poet and architect are moving toward a significant redefinition of the form. The movement is somewhat tentative, and the two artists are not always in perfect accord; but throughout the period a central idea is always in view, and it is specifically a structural idea. Behind this claim are two assumptions of my own: that Jonson, unlike most of his contemporaries, took the masque seriously as a form; and that Inigo Jones's concept of theater was throughout his career dynamic and coherent. Considering the texts with these assumptions in mind, we might wish to suggest that Jonson does not pause to describe scenery because the masque has become for him a unified form and the text a work of literature. The machines

---

8. Quoted by G. E. Bentley, *The Jacobean and Caroline Stage* (Oxford, 1941–1956), IV, 670.

9. *Stuart Masques and the Renaissance Stage* (London, 1937), pp. 82–84.

10. *Ibid.,* p. 82.

and devices of the stage no longer constitute a separate entity but have become an integral part of that form. If this is true, it is as much the architect's doing as the poet's.

The new structural idea involved primarily the relation of antimasque to masque or to the revels. We have observed that from the very beginning the concept of the antimasque was a defining feature of the form for Jonson, though it was a feature that he was not always able to express through the dramatic action of the masque. The fact that his career opens with the antithetical and complementary worlds of *Blackness* and *Beauty* [11] is evidence enough that the antimasque idea was essentially abstract and philosophical to him and only incidentally involved with the traditional grotesquerie of the "antic masque." Jonson's own description of the witches' scene in *Queens,* "a foyle, or false masque," is misleading if we place the emphasis on "foyle" and therefore assume that it is structurally insignificant. Its falseness explains the truth of the revels, for through the antimasque we comprehend in what way the masque's ideal world is real. At the same time, the crucial action of the form, the actual transition from disorder to order—from blackness to beauty or vice to virtue—is one that is omitted entirely from Jonson's first masque and its sequel and can only be indicated and described by the text of *Queens.* After 1609, Jonson begins to conceive of the antimasque not as a simple antithesis to the world of the revels but essentially as another aspect of that world, and therefore ultimately capable of being accommodated to and even in-cluded in the ideals of the main masque. The productions of the second decade, starting with *Oberon* (1611), begin to represent the transition less as a single moment of transformation than as a gradual process of re-finement. This process, for the courtly audience, is an education in the meaning of the revels.

The brief antimasque of boys in *The Haddington Masque* is a rudi-mentary version of this concept. The boys, *"most antickly attyr'd . . . represented the sports, and prettie lightnesses, that accompanie* Loue" (254:159–160). Though they disappear after their dance is over, the quali-ties they embody are not banished from the masque but are summoned up and included in the final epithalamion:

> *Loues* common wealth consists of toyes;
> His councell are those *antique* boyes,

11. *Beauty* was not produced, however, till 1608.

> *Games, laughter⟨s⟩, sports, delights,*
> That triumph with him on these nights.
>
> (262:404–407)

Wedding masques can hardly reject the delights of love. Jonson's purpose is to place those delights in their proper perspective, to move them from the capriciousness of their first appearance to the larger order implied by words like "common wealth" and "councell."

In *Oberon,* Jonson first fully conceives of the transition from antimasque to revels as the ordering and redirecting of a vital energy that is both essential and good. The antimasque of satyrs is in every sense a part of the world of Oberon, and during the course of the masque the satyrs are converted from their games to the Prince's service. All this is accomplished in what is dramatically the most completely realized masque Jonson composed. Its very coherence caused difficulties, chiefly at the moment when the action had to break through the boundaries of the stage and move outward to include the King and court.[12] This crucial movement would naturally be less problematical in works with a less solid dramatic form, and Jonson in the following decade experiments significantly with non-dramatic masques, such as *The Golden Age Restored* and *The Vision of Delight.*

Let us consider what kind of theater Inigo Jones was providing for the masque.[13] In the early years it was heavily dependent on machinery, from simple devices like pageant cars (e.g., the floating island in *Blackness*) to wave and cloud machines and the great *machina versatilis,* the turning machine, of *Hymenaei,* used again the following year in *The Haddington Masque.* This last device, combined with carefully planned lighting that was reflected as it turned, seems to have produced the most striking effects of the early productions. Late in Jones's career, he was to describe the masque as "nothing else but pictures with Light and Motion,"[14] and the combination of these elements was indeed essential to

12. See the detailed discussion in my study, *The Jonsonian Masque* (Cambridge, Mass., 1965), pp. 82 ff.

13. The most useful general discussions of the subject are Richard Southern, *Changeable Scenery* (London, 1952), pp. 17–106; Nicoll, *Stuart Masques;* and Lily B. Campbell, *Scenes and Machines on the English Stage* (Cambridge, Eng., 1923), pp. 164 ff.

14. E. K. Chambers, ed., *Aurelian Townshend's Poems and Masks* (Oxford, 1912), p. 83.

his stage from the beginning. Control over lighting was, of course, minimal by modern standards; the hall could not be darkened, but Jones made full use of mirrors and magnifiers, colored lamps, and metallic or sequined costumes. Bacon was describing the architect's practice when in 1625, in the essay *Of Masques and Triumphs,* he wrote, "Let the scenes abound with light, specially coloured and varied."

Jones's early stages are designed to operate as much on the vertical axis as on the horizontal. *Blackness* opens with a seascape, in which the realistic properties of perspective are clearly of much importance. But by the middle of the masque, the action has moved upward:

The Moone *was discouered in the vpper part of the house, triumphant in a* Siluer *throne . . . & crown'd with a* Luminarie, *or* Sphere *of light. . . . The heauen, about her, was vaulted with blue silke, and set with starres of* Siluer, *which had in them their seuerall lights burning.*

(175:212 ff.)

The seascape had included "an obscure and cloudy nightpiece," presumably painted on a curtain at the rear of the stage. When this was removed, the moon, the heavens, and a whole new dimension of action were revealed above.

The stages of the next few productions make little use of the realistic illusions of perspective and almost abandon the horizontal assumptions of the normal stage entirely. In fact, what Jones provides for *Hymenaei* and *The Haddington Masque* are, properly speaking, not settings at all, but symbolic pageants; that is, they are not the scenes in which actions take place: they are themselves the actions. The scenery is concentrated on the center of the stage, forming, in *Hymenaei,* a series of theatrical emblems—an altar with a mystic inscription, which is interpreted by the characters; the microcosm; Juno on her throne surrounded by appropriate symbols. "The scene" for *The Haddington Masque* "was a high, steepe, red cliffe, aduancing it selfe into the cloudes, figuring the place, from whence . . . the honourable family of the RADCLIFFES first tooke their name" (250:23 ff.). Onto this emblematic mountain Venus and the graces descend from above, and it finally opens to reveal the turning machine, the great globe, surrounded by the masquers, each representing a sign of the zodiac. *The Masque of Beauty,* produced a month earlier, though not designed by Jones, exhibits the same notion of the function of settings through an even more elaborate *machina versatilis.* Jonson's description of the floating island bearing its symbolic throne forward with "three varied motions, at once," has already been quoted.

After all this, what is striking about *Queens* is not its machinery but how much better coordinated its symbolic stage is with Jonson's text; or, to put it another way, how much more significance the text has in the action of the masque. Again, there is little here that resembles a normal dramatic stage, either Jacobean or Italian; and both texts and settings throughout this period serve to remind us that the masque was providing a radically different sort of theatrical experience from even the most elaborate private playhouses. The axis of the stage is still as much vertical as horizontal, and the action still tends to be grouped around a series of central symbols. The witches enter from hell by rising through trap doors and disappear by the same route. For the antimasque, the symbolic setting is for once the whole stage, rather than a single pavilion, or machine, or pageant, and Jones uses fire and smoke as well as scenery to create his hell. But with the transition to the main masque, we are back in the theater of emblems:

In the place of it appear'd a glorious and magnificent Building, figuring the *House of Fame,* in the vpper part of w°h were discouered the twelue *Masquers* sitting vpon a Throne triumphall, erected in forme of a *Pyramide,* and circled w'h all store of light.

(301:359 ff.)

The full metamorphosis is accomplished by the turning machine, which by now has a relatively minor function in the spectacle: "Here, the Throne wherein they sate, being *Machina versatilis,* sodaynely chang'd; and in the Place of it appeard *Fama bona*" (305:446 ff.).

It is the movement toward drama in the development of the masque that should surprise us, not the move away from it. The solidly realized world of *Oberon* is something new and marks a turning point for both poet and architect. Much of the action of the masques before 1611 is concerned with elucidating the emblems of their stages; but the action of *Oberon* is dramatic and requires a different kind of theater. Instead of pageant cars and the *machina versatilis,* Jones began to devise settings that could serve as the media for action of some complexity. It is a mistake to assume that this is something Jonson has forced on the architect or that Jones's settings have suddenly become subservient to the poet's texts. Jonson from the beginning was "the inventor," and Jones's machines were, at least till the final years of the collaboration, realizations of Jonson's poetic symbols. What is new is that the machinery has become integrated with the action and that *Oberon* thus has a new sort of unity.

For *Oberon*, Jones turned his attention to the *scena ductilis*, the "tractable scene," a device he had occasionally used before. Basically this was a series of flats set in grooves in the stage, which could be swiftly and quietly drawn aside into the wings to reveal the setting behind them. Since the number of scene changes with this device was limited only by the number of grooves the platform could contain, the flexibility of the masque stage became, through the *scena ductilis,* almost infinite. And while the *machina versatilis* could turn, say, a cave into a temple, only the *scena ductilis* could wholly transform the entire stage. This was presumably the device in *Queens* by which "the whole face of the Scene alterd; scarse suffring the memory of any such thing."

Oberon opens in a wilderness:

The first face of the Scene *appeared all obscure, & nothing perceiu'd but a darke Rocke, with trees beyond it; and all wildnesse, that could be presented: Till, at one corner of the cliffe, aboue the* Horizon, *the* Moone *began to shew, and rising, a* Satyre *was seene (by her light) to put forth his head, and call.*

(341:1-5)

The satyrs are unruly but good natured; their pleasures, indeed, are courtly ones: dancing and drinking. They are presided over by Silenus, the exemplar of wisdom, and under his tutelage they are educated to the virtues of reason and decorum and led to submit to Oberon, the fairy prince. This is accomplished in verse of wonderful delicacy and variety, which constantly controls and directs the energy of the antimasque.

Jones's designs for *Oberon* have been preserved,[15] and the setting he creates for this scene provides an interesting parallel.[16] Jonson's direction (or is it his description?) calls for "all wildnesse, that could be presented," but in fact the rocky landscape, like the figures it contains, is clearly controlled by principles of decorum, balanced and symmetrical (see Figure 1). This was presumably painted on one or more pairs of shutters. Halfway through the antimasque, Silenus observes the *scena ductilis* in action: "See, the rocke begins to ope."

15. See P. Simpson and C. F. Bell, *Designs by Inigo Jones for Masques and Plays at Court* (Oxford, 1924), Nos. 40–55.

16. No. 40 in Simpson and Bell, *Designs by Inigo Jones.*

FIGURE 1. *Oberon,* first scene: "all wildnesse, that could be presented." From the Chatsworth collection. Reproduced by permission of the trustees of the Chatsworth settlement.

There the whole Scene *opened, and within was discouer'd the* Frontispice *of a bright and glorious* Palace, *whose gates and walls were transparent.*

(346:135 ff.)

The removal of the front panels has not only transformed the face of the scene; it has moved the action farther back on the stage and farther into the perspective. That is, the spectators' sense of the reality that the theatrical illusion is providing has been, literally, deepened. In Jones's design for the second scene,[17] the stage is now framed by high rocks—the outermost panels from the first scene have not been removed—and the palace

FIGURE 2. *Oberon,* second scene: façade of Oberon's palace. From the Chatsworth collection. Reproduced by permission of the trustees of the Chatsworth settlement.

itself is a curious combination of rustication and elegance, a medieval fortress with a Palladian balustrade and pediment, surmounted by a very Italian dome (see Figure 2). Here as in the action of the masque, the ideal is classic order, attained (again, literally) by gradual stages.

Like the opening landscape, the front of the palace must be a pair of flats set in grooves, constituting essentially a backdrop for the action of the second scene. But not entirely, because the "gates and walls were trans-

17. No. 42 in Simpson and Bell, *Designs by Inigo Jones.*

parent," and this implies to a spectator that more is behind the scene, that the action extends somehow beyond the background. It is not until the next, and final, transformation that the full depth of the stage appears:

There the whole palace open'd, and the nation of Faies *were discouer'd, . . . and within a farre off in perspectiue, the knights masquers sitting in their seuerall sieges: At the further end of all,* OBERON, *in a chariot.*

(351:291 ff.)

What the spectator sees now is the inside of the palace (see Figure 3). Jones's drawing [18] is a little difficult to interpret; it seems to show only the central portion of the setting. It is a pavilion from the emblematic theater of earlier masques, a Renaissance classical temple; but we see through it and beyond it down the whole length of a perspective setting. It is from the depths of this image of order, now fully realized, that Oberon's chariot comes "as far forth as the face of the scene" and that the masquers at last move out into the Renaissance classical world of the audience, the columned and galleried Banqueting House at Whitehall.[19]

We may observe that what the stage presents in this masque is radically different from anything Jones has conceived up to this time. The axis of the stage is now entirely horizontal, with the single exception of the appearance at the end of "Phosphorus, the day-starre," presumably in the heavens. The setting is the medium for action, and unlike the microcosm of *The Haddington Masque* or the House of Fame in *Queens,* it has no independent existence. It is wholly coordinated with Jonson's text and indeed may be considered an aspect of it. More than this, the world it represents, however idealized, is a version of the spectators' own world, and scenic realism has become a prerequisite of symbolic glory. Visually the masque is a triumph of elegance and taste; it is significantly less spectacular than any of the Jonsonian productions preceding it.

We must now turn to a problem of evidence. What happens to the masque stage between 1611 and 1615 is very unclear. Jonson's texts include almost no scenic detail whatever and do not mention Inigo Jones. This is

18. I take Simpson and Bell's No. 45 (Plate VIII) to be the design for this scene. It is probably related, however, not to the medieval palace but to the alternative version of that scene (No. 44, Plate VII), which it closely resembles.

19. The predecessor to the present Banqueting House, built in 1608, was supported by two tiers of Doric and Ionic columns. See Per Palme, *The Triumph of Peace* (London, 1957), pp. 115–118.

FIGURE 3. *Oberon,* third scene: interior of Oberon's palace. From the Chatsworth collection. Reproduced by permission of the trustees of the Chatsworth settlement.

usually taken to be a result of the quarrel between poet and architect, and indeed Professor Nicoll accuses Jonson of being "churlish" in the meagerness of his descriptions.[20] The masques in question are *Love Freed from Ignorance and Folly* (1611), *Love Restored* (1612), *A Challenge at Tilt* (1613/14), and *The Irish Masque at Court* (1613). Information about

20. *Stuart Masques,* p. 72.

settings begins to reappear in Jonson's texts with *The Golden Age Restored* (1615), though not fully enough to satisfy most critics.

Let us consider what evidence we have. *Love Freed* was prepared at the same time as *Oberon;* it was the Queen's masque for Christmas 1610/11, as *Oberon* was the Prince's. If the lack of stage description in *Love Freed* is due to Jonson's quarrel with Jones, how are we to explain the simultaneous inclusion of all the scenic detail in *Oberon?* Clearly it is *Love Freed* that is the anomaly here, and I have only a makeshift explanation for it. It is the most thoroughly literary of Jonson's masques, requiring a running marginal commentary to explain its action. Jonson might reasonably have felt that in a text addressed so completely to the reader, details of the staging were superfluous. But in any case, it cannot be used as evidence of anything; moreover, it seems to me the only one of the four masques to pose any problem. As for the other three, there is no indication that Jones had anything to do with any of them. He was in Italy at Christmas 1613/14, when *The Challenge at Tilt* and *The Irish Masque* were presented, and his name is nowhere mentioned in connection with *Love Restored,* nor are payments to him for it recorded. (The accounts, it should be added, are very incomplete, and no payments are recorded to Jonson either.) The cost of *Love Restored,* £280 8s. 9d., is unusually low and may suggest that Jones's machinery was being spared at Christmas: a month later he was employed on the sumptuous production of Campion's *Lords' Masque* for the wedding of King James's daughter Elizabeth.

The existence of the quarrel is evident enough from Jonson's failure to acknowledge his collaborator, but this is essentially peripheral to my concerns here. On the whole, Jonson provides much more in the way of scenic detail when he is working with Jones than with anyone else, and the settings—to judge from the texts alone—are, with a single anomalous exception, clearly important to him. Our consideration of the collaboration must skip the works between *Oberon* and *The Golden Age Restored,* and in the latter, as we have observed, the scenic machine is once again in evidence. Its presence is even more strongly felt in the masques of the next three years, *Mercury Vindicated* (1616), *The Vision of Delight* (1617), and *Pleasure Reconciled to Virtue* (1618).

During this period what Jones appears to be creating is an efficient machine wholly integrated with the dramatic action. Like Jonson, that

is, he sees the masque as essentially a unified form. And the properties
of the stage that he is most interested in developing have only incidentally
to do with spectacular effects. He is primarily concerned with the control
of realistic visual illusions. The stage becomes a total picture, working
inward and backward from a proscenium arch, and his devices now more
and more involve the manipulation of shutters and *periaktoi* for instan-
taneous changes of complex perspectives. It would be a mistake not to see
this development as the joint responsibility of both poet and architect, and
Jonson's relative silence about scenic effects may testify more than anything else to their efficiency.

Contemporary accounts, on the other hand, testify with remarkable
unanimity to general dissatisfaction with the new developments. Of *The
Golden Age Restored,* John Chamberlain reports that "neither in deuise
nor shew was there any thing extraordinarie but only excellent dauncing." [21] Of *The Vision of Delight,* he writes, "I haue heard no great speach
nor commendations of the maske neither before nor since." [22] And Sir
Edward Sherburne's observation that because of *Pleasure Reconciled to
Virtue,* "Mr. Inigo Jones hath lost in his reputacion," is one of many in
the same vein. It is evident that a radical transformation of the masque,
at least to the contemporary spectator's eye, was in progress and that the
result was less than satisfactory. The complaints rarely cite anything more
specific than lack of invention, or simply dullness. But one comment of
Chamberlain's on Campion's *Lords' Masque* (1613) makes an interesting
attempt at explaining the general displeasure. The effects that Jones
created for this production comprise almost an anthology of scenic machinery of the time; reading Campion's descriptions, one would think the
success of the spectacle would have been assured. Chamberlain reports,
however, that he hears "no great commendation" of the production, "save
only for riches, their devices being long and tedious, and more like a play
than a mask." [23] To a modern reader there is little about Campion's text
that suggests drama, and "like a play" may only mean that Chamberlain
finds the speeches too long; but it is worth noting that a masque in 1613
was not expected to be "like a play." Moreover, though "devices" can refer
only to the dialogue, the spectacle of Inigo Jones's machinery falls under

21. Quoted in *Works,* X, 553.
22. *Ibid.,* p. 568.
23. Quoted by E. K. Chambers, *The Elizabethan Stage* (Oxford, 1923), III, 243.

the general curse. At the very least, it is doing nothing to relieve the work from the onus of being like a play. Perhaps there is simply not enough of it in proportion to the speeches, or perhaps its very integration with action and speech is felt to be inappropriate.

Whatever Chamberlain meant by "like a play," it is apparent that from the time of *Oberon* on, and especially after Inigo Jones's return from Italy in 1614, masques began to look a good deal more like what we, at least, conceive plays to be. Perspective was the basic scenic device in the masques of the period, and all the action, until the crucial move off the stage and onto the dancing floor, was separated from the audience by a proscenium wall. This would not, of course, have been recognized by a contemporary English spectator as being like a play. On the contrary, dramatic stages that employed proscenia, perspective, and attendant machinery did not appear until more than twenty years later and then were imitating the masque.[24] Indeed, the physical embodiment of both masque and drama, the theater, is undergoing an important transformation in this era. The continuing charge that masques were dull implies not so much that Jones was introducing nothing new as that English audiences were not yet educated to appreciate what he *was* doing. Italian observers were much more alive to the ingenuity of the scenes. For example, *The Lords' Masque,* which for Chamberlain was too much like a play, was called "very beautiful" by the Venetian ambassador, who particularly admired its three changes of setting.[25] And at *Pleasure Reconciled to Virtue* (1618), another admiring Venetian observer is at some pains to account for the mechanics of the scenic effects:

Si aprì il Monte con il girar di due porte, et si uide frà' monticelli sorger l'Aurora, in capo d'una prospettiua lontana, sendoui poste dai lati alcune finte colonne d'oro per far maḡg. il sfondro.[26]

[The mountain opened by the turning of two doors, and dawn was seen to break between small hills above a distant perspective, some false gilded columns being placed along the sides to make the distance seem greater.]

To an English audience this sort of theater was relatively unfamiliar and unspectacular enough for the ingenuity of its devices to pass unno-

24. See Irwin Smith, *Shakespeare's Blackfriars Playhouse* (New York, 1964), pp. 269 ff.

25. Chambers, *The Elizabethan Stage,* III, 244.

26. Quoted in *Works,* X, 582.

ticed. Glynne Wickham even argues that in 1606 the average London theatergoer "would not have been aware of many material differences between the stage conventions that met his gaze" at court masques and those he saw at public and private playhouses and that this would still have been true over twenty years later.[27] It is difficult to see why this should have been so, but the point must be granted on documentary evidence alone: insofar as contemporary English observers take note of the new devices at all, they do so merely to declare their lack of interest in them. Yet Jones is starting to conceive the stage as a unified machine, not as a series of individual effects; this is a revolutionary idea in the English theater, and the Italian visitors recognize it as worthy of comment.

Moreover, Inigo Jones's masque settings are making the most far-reaching statements about the nature of the theatrical illusion; for a realistic scene implies that seeing—not hearing, or understanding—is believing. Jonson's famous *Expostulation* shows the process fairly well completed in 1631:

> O Showes! Showes! Mighty Showes!
> The Eloquence of Masques! What need of prose
> Or Verse, or Sense t'express Immortall you?
> You are y° Spectacles of State! . . .
> You aske noe more then certeyne politique Eyes,
> Eyes y^t can pierce into y° Misteryes
> Of many Coulors!
>
> (VIII, 403–404: 39–47)

We shall consider the implications of this development presently. Here, it is sufficient to remark that the integration of setting with text in the masques of the second decade of the century is amply indicated by the fact that descriptions of the stage, however desirable they may be for the theatrical historian, are no longer *necessary* for the masque to express its meaning. But ironically, this is also the first step toward the poet's becoming superfluous. We may find a curious correspondence between the beginning and end of Jonson's and Jones's collaboration. In 1605, the court saw the emblems of *Blackness,* crystallizations of pure meaning requiring Jonson's prose for explication; in 1631, it saw the perspectives of *Love's Triumph through Callipolis,* in which sight has so overwhelmed sense that Jonson must prefix to it an essay entitled "To make the Spectators

27. *Early English Stages* (London, 1963), II, Part 1, 7–8.

vnderstanders." In both cases, though in very different ways, the meaning is somewhere outside the courtly entertainment, finally available not to an audience but only to a reader. That spirit and sense did, for a time, unite is the particular triumph of a few works from this uneasy coalition.

The Golden Age Restored is Jonson's first masque with Jones after the latter's return from Italy. In most respects it is a wholly new departure, abandoning the drama of *Oberon* for an essentially lyric and musical mode. But drama had proved a dubious virtue in the masque, both for playwright and spectator, and here it is poetry that dictates the form of the work and establishes its values. *The Golden Age* is a series of lyric poems. There is no way of knowing how much of it was set to music, but Jonson's preference in it for stanzaic verse, rather than declamation, and the use of duets, a quartet, and a choir strongly suggest that music played a large part in it. Its plot—the banishment of the Iron Age by Pallas and the return to earth of Astraea and the Golden Age—is roughly that of *The Masque of Queens,* but the difference in the handling of the antimasque and the realization of the ideal world show us that the Jonsonian form has entered a new phase. To begin with, this antimasque is presided over by Pallas: as in *Oberon,* wisdom opens the masque and pervades it. James's pacifism is celebrated in verse whose clarity and order establish from the outset the controlling principles of this world:

> Looke, looke! reioyce, and wonder!
>   That you offending mortalls are,
>   (For all your crimes) so much the care
> Of him, that beares the thunder!
>
> IOVE can endure no longer,
>   Your great ones should your lesse inuade,
>   Or, that your weake, though bad, be made
> A prey vnto the stronger.
>
> And therefore, meanes to settle
>   ASTRAEA in her seat againe;
>   And let downe in his golden chaine
> The age of better mettle.
>
>   (421:1–12)

As the Iron Age and his antimasquers appear, Pallas withdraws, not because wisdom is threatened, but in order to establish a moral point:

> Hide me, soft cloud, from their prophaner eyes,
>   Till insolent rebellion take the field,

> And as their spirits, with their counsels, rise,
> I frustrate all, with shewing but my shield.
>
> (422:25–28)

Still later, routing the antimasque, she points the moral further: " 'Twas time t⟨o⟩'appeare, and let their follies see / 'Gainst whom they fought, and with what destinee" (423:73–74).

The antimasque itself has much in common with that of *Queens;* but given the new context, its effect is quite different. The antimasquers, like the witches of 1609, personify all the evils of a fallen world—Avarice, Fraud, Slander, and so forth. But here they are summoned up in an invocation of only thirty-five lines, and their function in the masque is limited to their dance, accompanied, to strengthen the point, by "a confusion of martiall musique." The moment analogous to the sudden blast of many instruments that overthrew the hags in *Queens* is here provided by Pallas showing her shield; and Jonson's remark about the transformation of hell "scarse suffring the memory of any such thing" now becomes explicitly part of the moral and dramatic structure of the masque, enunciated by Pallas as a concomitant to her action:

> So change, and perish, scarcely knowing, how,
> That 'gainst the gods doe take so vaine a vow.
>
> (423:69–70)

The resolution is accomplished and the Golden Age is established literally by poetry: Chaucer, Gower, Lydgate, and Spenser are summoned, "the Scene of light discouered" (425:140), the darkness of night and the cold of winter are banished, and Astraea returns to earth.

Stage directions for this production are given extremely briefly and, for the most part, marginally. Indeed, this is the text that prompted Professor Nicoll to charge Jonson with parsimony, complaining that when the poet says " 'The scene chang'd' . . . , we have no means now of knowing what the two sets represented." [28] We have no means of knowing if we read only the stage directions; and doubtless it was ungracious of Jonson not to provide more marginal information. Nevertheless, what the two sets represented is amply indicated in the text. Pallas descends in her chariot, perceives a "tumult from yond' caue" (422:21), and hides behind a cloud (422:25). Then "the scene chang'd," and shortly afterward

28. *Stuart Masques,* p. 82.

she is indicating "yonder soules, set far within the shade, / And in *Elysian bowres*" (425:126–127). For the third setting, "the Scene of light [is] discouered" (425:140). There is quite enough information here to show that the stage of *The Golden Age Restored* is very much like that of *Oberon,* with the addition of machines for descending and ascending—Pallas, the Golden Age, Astraea, and the poets all descend to enter, though only Pallas reascends, leaving the rest in a world of Elysian bowers and light. Such a conclusion is, on the whole, justified by the realities of Jacobean history: the King has, after all, banished war from the realm and given poetry a real place at his court.

The sort of reality that Inigo Jones's settings provide for the truths of Jonson's fiction is worth considering. Perspective stages establish their particular kind of reality by depending on a set of assumptions that the English spectator was not, on the whole, used to exercising in the theater. These assumptions are not moral ones, such as that beauty is better than blackness or that man is a microcosm, but empirical ones, involving not what we believe but how we perceive our world. Actions on such a stage begin necessarily to take on the quality of empirical data: the abstract vices and virtues of *Queens* gradually become the exemplary figures of *Pleasure Reconciled to Virtue;* and in part, the increasing appearance of dramatic characters in the masque, rather than symbolic figures, is an aspect of this movement. The transition obviously was neither immediate nor self-conscious, and nothing in *The Golden Age Restored* suggests that Jonson was aware of the implications of his collaborator's stage. But the very lack of commentary in the text reflects the character of the new theater: symbols must be explained, but facts are self-evident. Surely this bears also on the movement of the later antimasques toward comedy, with its empirical assumptions and basic and worldly realities. This is an organic movement, part of the joint development of poet and architect. It grows directly and logically out of the new stage and Jonson's response to its nature and possibilities. It can hardly be seen as an instance of the tyranny of the audience's tastes.

With these considerations in mind, we may re-examine the general modern critical attitude toward Jonson's later productions with their comic antimasques. "The elaboration of the antimasque begins with this piece," write the Oxford editors of *For the Honor of Wales;* "it leads in the later masques to a lack of balance, but it suited the taste of the Court for which

the dances alone were important and a comic induction was tolerable." [29]
Presumably the texts, comic or otherwise, were more than tolerable to
somebody, because Jonson received steady employment from the court for
twenty years. But for our purposes, the significant assumption has to do
with comic antimasques producing a "lack of balance." "The element of
comedy," Herford and Simpson observe again, "at this period encroaches
more and more on the antimasque." [30] Comedy, then (we are asked to
believe), is inappropriate to antimasques, and the proportionate relation
between antimasque and masque is a fixed one which, when violated,
results in a lack of balance. What norms these assumptions derive from
are never stated; needless to say, they are not Jonson's norms. The nature
of the antimasque and its relation to the main masque are continually
changing throughout Jonson's career, but both elements are essential from
the beginning. It would be strange to find the author of *Volpone* and
Bartholomew Fair disapproving of comedy and writing it only because
he is forced to do so by the low tastes of his courtly employers: obviously
the notion that comedy has no place in the masque is not Jonson's. All
claims that the poet's true interests lay with the main masque must con-
tend with the evident and pervasive vitality and inventiveness of the antimasque, whether grotesque, comic, or satiric. The great achievement of
the last period is *The Gipsies Metamorphosed,* that vast triumph of
vulgarity and wit, crudity and finesse, tastelessness and grace. It was the
King's favorite masque, and the court's. It is difficult to believe that it was
not Jonson's favorite as well.

Far from dictating the tone or structure of the masques, the audience
at best followed the inventors' lead and often enough lagged very far
behind. "Neither in devise nor shew was there anything extraordinary"
in *The Golden Age Restored.* John Chamberlain did not like being made
to *listen* to a masque—Campion's had been too much like a play—and
moreover was not interested in what he saw. There was, however,
"excellent dauncing"; his pleasure derived from the courtly realities. In
fact, the first masque for which we have evidence of any more general
approbation was not produced until three years later. It is *For the Honor
of Wales,* the revised version of the most unpopular *Pleasure Reconciled
to Virtue.* The nature of the revision is worth considering carefully, since

29. *Works,* X, 590.
30. *Ibid.,* p. 635.

this is the only instance in Jonson's entire career of his rewriting an unpopular masque. The complaints are, as usual, about dullness, but there are two that make more specific charges. The first has to do with what Jonson had called, in *The Masque of Queens,* "the Nobilyty of the Inuention." Edward Sherburne (as already noted) reported discontent with the poverty of the device, "it being the Prince [Charles] his first mask." [31] The second is even more pertinent, being King James's own reaction to the performance. An Italian observer reports that the King, finding the dances too brief, angrily shouted, "Perche non si balla, à che fine m'hauete fatto uenir qua? che'l Diauolo ui porti quanti, che sete, ballate." [32] ("Why don't they dance? What did you make me come here for? The devil take all of you, dance!") Now if Jonson were really concerned with his audience's demands, the masque's second version would surely be an instance to demonstrate the fact. But *For the Honor of Wales* does not undertake to meet either objection. Its comic Welshmen and goats hardly make the masque more appropriate for the Prince's debut; and if the production included more dancing than *Pleasure Reconciled to Virtue,* the additions find no place in Jonson's text.

Moreover, even with the revision Chamberlain was unimpressed: "the Princes mask for twelf-night was represented again wth some few alterations and additions, but little bettered." But another correspondent, Sir Gerard Herbert, writes that "it was much better liked then twelveth night; by reason of the newe Conceites & ante maskes & pleasant merry speeches made to the kinge, by such as Counterfeyted wels men." Nathaniel Brent is less approving, but nevertheless responsive to the work: "The princes maske was shewed againe . . . with som few additions of Goats and welshe speeches sufficient to make an English man laugh and a welshman cholerique, without deserving so great honour as to be sent to y^r L°." [33] Leaving questions of taste aside, we may observe that this appears to be the first masque in many years to which the court responded with interest of any kind. Its success must in part be due to the crudeness of its humor—dialect jokes were always good for a laugh—but it seems to me that the real point of the joke has been missed by modern commenta-

31. *Ibid.,* p. 576.
32. *Works,* X, 583. For a fuller discussion of the incident and its implications see Orgel, *The Jonsonian Masque,* pp. 70–71, 183.
33. All are quoted in *Works,* X, 576–577.

tors. The Welshmen are attacking *Pleasure Reconciled to Virtue;* they complain that the masque was irrelevant and inept: "there was neither Poetries, nor Architectures, nor designes in that bellie-god; nor a note of musicks about him" (503:197–198). This is a parody of court opinion—indeed, of the court opinion of the preceding five years—and its wit lies in the way it makes dramatic capital out of the failure of the Twelfth-night production. *For the Honor of Wales* was a Jacobean in-group joke, and it shows Jonson using in a new way the realities of court life as part of the substance of his invention.

For the Honor of Wales establishes a norm for the late Jonsonian masque. From this time till the death of King James in 1625, the anti-masque was a scene from comedy, unified and dramatic. The 1618 production carries the logic of the realistic stage to an extreme, dispensing entirely with scenic illusions and in effect denying that it is theater. Jonson had used this kind of antimasque only once before, in *The Irish Masque* of 1613, but he was to employ it again in four of the eight remaining masques presented before King James. Apparently a new departure, this was in fact only an extension of a very familiar idea: for Jonson, one of the most compelling aspects of Jones's theater was the way it could make the stage's illusion merge with the court's reality, and we may view the group of works between *The Golden Age Restored* and *For the Honor of Wales* as studies in the potentialities of this idea.

All masques are, of course, about the court and conclude by uniting spectator and masquer; but these masques often seem to be about masques themselves, about the function of poetry and the uses of art in the world of the court. We have seen how poetry in the persons of Chaucer, Gower, Lydgate, and Spenser is essential to the establishment of James's golden age. *Mercury Vindicated from the Alchemists at Court,* in the next year, is about false and true artists and the proper use to which Mercury—wit and learning—may be put. *The Vision of Delight* is almost an anatomy of the devices and conventions of masques and undertakes to define the true nature of their courtly pleasures. And *Pleasure Reconciled to Virtue* considers the whole concept of revelry, banishing the riots of Comus in favor of the art of Daedalus, through whom poetry, song, and dance become the means by which princes are educated to virtue. *For the Honor of Wales,* with its ironic critique of *Pleasure Reconciled to Virtue,* is an appropriate end to the sequence.

Relating these texts to their stages reveals something interesting about the progress of the masque idea. For *The Golden Age Restored* we have seen that Inigo Jones employed a stage that was essentially that of *Oberon*, with the addition of some machinery. *Mercury Vindicated* undertakes something quite new to masques. The scene opens in *"a laboratory, or Alchymists workehouse"*; Vulcan is *"looking to the Registers,"* a cyclops is *"tending the fire."* When Mercury appears, he does so *"thrusting out his head, and afterward his body, at the Tunnell of the middle furnace."* The last phrase suggests at least two more furnaces, one on either side, and the amount of elaboration and particularity in this setting reveals how far Jones has come from the emblems of *Hymenaei*, on the one hand, and the generalized façades and landscapes of *Oberon*, on the other. The anti-masque of *Mercury Vindicated* is conceived as a tiny comic drama. Jonson's earlier experiments with the same device—in *Love Restored* (1612) and *The Irish Masque at Court* (1613)—appear to have employed no settings at all; and even *Oberon* had required essentially only a series of backdrops. But *Mercury Vindicated* opens on something we would recognize as a full dramatic stage. Its very consistency and realism would have been part of the masque's point for the audience at Whitehall: the alchemists are practicing below stairs at court. The transformation, when it comes, is from naturalism to Nature: *"At which the whole Scene changed to a glorious bowre, wherein* Nature *was placed, with* Prometheus *at her feete; And the twelue Masquers, standing about them"* (415:196 ff.). Professor Nicoll thinks that the laboratory was "almost certainly shown by means of front flats" and that these were drawn aside to reveal the bower.[34] But the transformation of a "middle furnace" to a central bower sounds more like the work of the *machina versatilis*, here combined with the side flats of the *scena ductilis*, which completed the change. This sophistication of an old device is an ingenious solution to the problems of a new kind of text and suggests the extent to which Jones and Jonson were genuinely responsive to each other's ideas.

Mercury Vindicated is conceived around the relatively simple antithesis of artifice and nature, the worlds of Vulcan and Prometheus. *The Vision of Delight*, in the following year, is structurally quite different, presenting a series of scenes and a gradual progression from antimasque to revels. It is perhaps Jonson's most eclectic masque, and its continental aspects

34. *Stuart Masques*, p. 81.

would have been apparent at once to the spectator. The scene opens on a formal theatrical prospect, "A Street in perspective of faire building discovered." Into this Serlian setting "DELIGHT Is seene to come as afarre off"; she announces the masque's subject at once:

> Let us play, and dance, and sing,
>   let us now turne every sort
> O' the pleasures of the Spring,
>   to the graces of a Court,
>
> From ayre, from cloud, from dreams, from toyes,
>   to sounds, to sence, to love, to joyes.
>
> (463:9–14)

The masque is to find suitable devices for celebrating the court and defining the proper nature of courtly pleasures. What follows is a series of presentations, visions summoned by Delight, that increase in substance, relevance, and rationality. First appears *"A she Monster delivered of sixe* Burratines, *that dance with sixe* Pantalones" (464:22–23). The masque's pleasures begin on a preverbal level as a grotesque comic figure gives birth, appropriately enough in the conventional Italian comic scene, to stock characters from the *commedia dell' arte*. This is the "antic masque" in its purest and most traditional form. But then under the tutelage of Delight, the antimasque moves beyond the familiar world of grotesque comedy; the daytime setting dissolves; Night and the Moon are summoned, and in their turn they call up Fantasy. *"The* Scene *here changed to Cloud, and* Phant'sie *breaking forth, spake"* (465:55–56). The delusively rational "perspective of faire building" disappears, and the antimasque now offers a new vision of delight. In a cloudy setting, Fantasy brilliantly puts forth the claims of gluttony and lechery, describing a series of surrealistic emblems conceived in the manner of Brueghel or Bosch. These are then realized in a second antimasque dance of phantasms.

But the dreams of Fantasy too pass as the night proceeds, and when one of the gold-haired "Houres" descends, *"the whole Scene changed to the Bower of* Zephyrus" (467:126–127). Delight is finally established within the world of nature and an idealized court. Even winter is banished on this Twelfth-night; *"the Bower opens, and the Maskers ⟨are⟩ discovered, as the glories of the Spring"* (469:170–171), with King James identified as the god who makes the idealization possible. As the revels conclude, Aurora appears, and the masque leads into a new day.

Inigo Jones's stage for *The Vision of Delight* is far more flexible than that for *Mercury Vindicated,* and its settings are clearly an important part of the masque's meaning. The scene moves from a perspective street to a cloudy dream world to a pastoral bower; from afternoon to night to dawn; from winter to spring. Part of this is accomplished illusionistically, part (such as the change from night to morning) symbolically. Jones was able to use the conventions of both emblematic and realistic theaters without feeling a sense of strain. By contrast, when a month later Lord Hay presented Jonson's *Lovers Made Men* for the entertainment of the French ambassador, the setting conceived by Nicholas Lanier was a single and unchanging perspective landscape.

The masque for 1618 was *Pleasure Reconciled to Virtue.* In Jonson's moral fable, Hercules is the courtly hero; he banishes the pleasures of Comus—gluttony, drunkenness, riot—in favor of the rational delights of song and formal dancing.[35] For this production, Jones provides a central symbol, Mount Atlas, the embodiment of wisdom. This device commands the scene throughout the performance. Jonson describes the mountain: "His top ending in y° figure of an old Man, his head & beard all hoary & frost: as if his sholders were couerd wth snow" (479:1–3). English observers were as usual unimpressed; so is Professor Nicoll, who remarks that "the central mountain was by now an old device."[36] However, our Venetian correspondent was delighted with the setting and adds the information that it "giraua gli occhi, et se stessa, con assai bell' artificio"[37] ("rolled its eyes and moved itself with wonderful cunning"). The action begins in an ivy grove at the foot of the mountain; when Comus is banished, "the whole *Groue* vanisheth, and the whole *Musiq[ue]* is discouered, sitting at y° foote of y° *Mountaine,* w^th *Pleasure* & *Vertue* seated aboue y^em" (483:115–118). Presently the masquers are called forth from the lap of the mountain—the Italian visitor's description of the opening of the device has already been quoted. It then remains open during the dances and revels, and finally, to conclude the masque, the performers

35. For a detailed study of the work, see Orgel, *The Jonsonian Masque,* pp. 150–185.

36. *Stuart Masques,* p. 84.

37. Quoted in *Works,* X, 582.

"returne into ye Scene: wch closeth, and is a Mountaine againe, as before" (491:350–351).

There is nothing particularly spectacular about this setting, but (as the Venetian observer realized) it is a beautiful machine; moreover, it is designed to supply a principle of coherence for a work whose action tends to be diffuse. Everything in the masque proceeds from the mountain or disappears into it. Always in view, it serves as both symbol and locale and provides both unity of place and unity of action. There are few masques in which the imagination of the architect is so thoroughly in touch with the nature and special requirements of the poet's text.

The attenuation of structure in *The Vision of Delight* and *Pleasure Reconciled to Virtue* is unusual only according to Jonson's own practice. Other productions of the period (e.g., Campion's Somerset masque of 1613) are far more shapeless, and all the problems that had become central for Jonson, involving the unification of the form and its transformation into literature, hardly exist for any of his contemporaries. *For the Honor of Wales,* the revised masque of 1618, will seem a less radical departure if we remember that Jonson was constantly experimenting with a form that was, in large measure, his to define. Its conventions were those of its function—the adulation of the king, the inclusion of disguised courtiers, the accommodation of a great deal of dancing. By contrast, its form was and had always been infinitely mutable; indeed in the masque, novelty and variety were in themselves virtues. This means that we must be wary of treating any of these works as normative and that we can speak of their "development" (at least once the basic problems have been solved) only in a limited sense. To conceive the development of Elizabethan drama is relatively easy, for powerful though possibly specious reasons: Shakespeare is so clearly its greatest playwright that we tend, whether rightly or wrongly, to see every play from *Gorboduc* forward in terms of the way it leads toward Shakespearean drama. But the masque requires a different sort of critical perspective. The crucial problem for Jonson was the unity and integrity of the form, and his solution was to treat the form fully as literature, to give moral and poetic life to its occasional elements, just as to its symbols and action. One might, then, be persuaded that a masque like *Lovers Made Men* is "better" than *The Masque of Queens* because it is more integrated and thus more successful by Jonson's own standards, but nevertheless one might continue to prefer *Queens* on less exclusive grounds, its superior poetry, for example.

Any solution to the problems of so dynamic a form was necessarily a temporary one, and Jones was developing his own ideas about what was essential to a court masque. If allegory, myth, metaphor, and drama were central qualities of the masque-as-poem, it was nevertheless natural that the designer should have conceived these qualities in terms of spectacle and machinery and not of language. By the time of the Caroline masque, as the title pages of *Love's Triumph* and *Chloridia* proclaim, the architect has at last firmly taken his place beside the poet as inventor. Jonson's *Expostulation,* however, makes clear that his own sense of the form is no longer the operative one:

> And I haue mett w'h those
> That doe cry vp y° Machine, & y° Showes!
> The majesty of Iuno in y° Cloudes,
> And peering forth of Iris in y° Shrowdes!
> Th' ascent of Lady Fame which none could spy
> Not they that sided her, Dame Poetry,
> Dame History, Dame Architecture too,
> And Goody Sculpture, brought w'h much adoe
> To hold her vp.
>
> (VIII, 403: 31–39)

These are the goddesses that had appeared in *Chloridia;* for Jonson the masque's allegorical figures are no longer poetry but stagecraft. "Painting and Carpentry are the Soule of Masque."

This will seem less prejudicial to Jones if we recall that they were about to become the soul of drama too. Here is Antony à Wood's account of the production of William Strode's play *The Floating Island* before the King and Queen at Oxford in 1636:

It was acted on a goodly stage reaching from the upper end of the Hall almost to the hearth place, and had on it three or four openings on each side thereof, and partitions between them, much resembling the desks or studies in a Library, out of which the Actors issued forth. The said partitions they could draw in and out at their pleasure upon a sudden, and thrust out new in their places according to the nature of the Screen, whereon were represented Churches, Dwelling-houses, Palaces, &c. which for its variety bred very great admiration. Over all was delicate painting, resembling the Sky, Clouds, &c. At the upper end a great fair shut [i.e. shutter] of two leaves that opened and shut without any visible help. Within which was set forth the emblem of the whole Play in a mysterious manner. Therein was the perfect resemblance of the billows of the Sea rolling, and an artificial Island, with Churches and Houses waving up and down and floating, as also rocks, trees and hills. Many other fine pieces of work and Landscapes did also appear at sundry openings thereof, and a Chair was also seen to come gliding on the Stage without any visible help. All these representations, being the first . . . that were used on the English stage.[38]

Jonson might have observed, vindictively, that Wood scarcely sees the play for the scenery. But for us, at least, the old collaborators cannot be so easily dissociated. Wood's description represents the end product of a unique coalition in the history of the English stage, which in great measure determined the course of English drama for the next three hundred years. Its triumph, though Jonson would probably be loath to acknowledge it, properly belongs as much to him as to the architect.

38. *Jonson*, X, 410–411.

Jonson's Early Entertainments: New Information from Hatfield House

SCOTT McMILLIN

J ONSON'S EARLY ENTERTAINMENTS, slight pieces in themselves, were useful occupations for a poet who was about to become famous for his court masques. The entertainments at Althorp and Highgate preceded Jonson's first important venture—*The Masque of Blackness* (1605) —in the court of James I and Queen Anne. A year later he provided *Hymenaei* for the marriage of the Earl of Essex and Lady Frances Howard, but thereafter two years were to elapse before his next court spectacle (*The Masque of Beauty* in January 1608), and in the interval he maintained his literary connections with the aristocracy by dressing out two entertainments for royal visits to the Earl of Salisbury's estate at Theobalds. These brief elaborations of noble flattery hardly engaged much of Jonson's creative strength—an entertainment stands to a masque about as an epigram does to an ode—but through the entertainments he maintained contact with those sources of wealth that could be tapped by graceful compliment, and through them too he practiced the techniques of adjusting dramatic poetry to the conditions of tact and display which aristocratic entertainment demanded. Today we recognize the masques as a major part of Jonson's artistry; and while in comparison the entertainments seem frail, we should respect their connection with Jonson's more important work, especially when new information becomes available.

153

What has come to light in recent months is a set of documents which provide information about Jonson's entertainments for the Earl of Salisbury. The documents, consisting of expense accounts, bills, and inventory lists, are included in the vast collection of Cecil papers now stored in the archives at Hatfield House. No textual material is included in these particular manuscripts; their importance lies in the pieces of theatrical and historical information which they reveal through an accountant's care. They indicate, for example, that Jonson prepared two entertainments for Salisbury which have been generally unknown to us: one for performance before the King in the library of Salisbury House in 1608; and the other for the opening of Britain's Burse (later to be known as the New Exchange) in 1609. The documents also name Inigo Jones as Jonson's collaborator in all four entertainments for Salisbury (the two at Theobalds in addition to the 1608 and 1609 pieces), and they suggest that Edward Alleyn was the leading actor in the 1608 Entertainment. Other professional actors are named, details of costuming and staging abound, and the rewards paid to Jonson, Jones, and some of the players are made quite distinct.

My purpose here is to call attention to the most significant pieces of information which the Hatfield documents reveal, first discussing the dates and occasions of the four entertainments and then collecting items under three other headings: Actors' Names; Payments to Jonson and Jones; and Staging and Costumes. Since my transcript will receive a final checking against the manuscripts before publication, all quotations below should be regarded as tentative. To avoid a complicated editorial apparatus in this article, I have silently expanded a few abbreviations.[1]

I Four Entertainments: Dates and Occasions

1606. Entertainment at Theobalds for James I and Christian IV of Denmark

James I and Christian IV of Denmark stayed at Theobalds from 24 to 28 July 1606, and the festivities in their honor ranged from the brief wel-

1. I am indebted to Lord Salisbury for permission to quote from the Hatfield manuscripts and to Miss Clare Talbot, Librarian at Hatfield House, for valuable assistance in working with the documents.

coming addresses which Jonson printed in the 1616 Folio to the de-
bauched evening show, *Solomon and the Queen of Sheba,* which Sir
John Harington described in his famous sardonic letter.[2]

Among the Cecil Papers 119/162 there is a summary of expenses incurred during the royal visit. One brief section of this summary list is
headed "Chardges of yᵉ Showe at Theoballs." No other papers for this
entertainment have been found. The brief list of charges includes a payment of £23 to "Inigo Iones the painter for his chardges & paines" and
another of £13 6s. 8d. to "Ben: Iohnson the Poett." Both payments seem
too large for the brief welcoming speeches which Jonson later printed,
and we should probably suspect that he and Jones participated in other
phases of the four-day revelry. Possibly there was more to the welcoming
speeches than Jonson chose to publish in the Folio. The anonymous account of the welcome, published in 1606 as *The King of Denmarkes welcome . . . ,* alludes to "verie learned, delicate, and significant showes and
deuises," suggesting that something beyond the Folio's eight lines of
welcome and sundry Latin inscriptions graced the approach of the two
kings.[3] On the other hand, the possibility exists that Jonson and Jones had
some share in preparing the disastrous *Solomon and the Queen of Sheba.*
Unfortunately, the Hatfield documents do not specify the shows for which
Jonson and Jones were rewarded, and the possibility that they were associated with the evening masque remains a matter of speculation.

1607. Entertainment at Theobalds for James I

Jonson published the full text of this entertainment in the 1616 Folio.
It was presented on 22 May 1607 to celebrate the transfer of the Theobalds
estate from the Cecil family to the King. Among the Cecil household bills
for 1607 (Family Papers—Bills 386) there is one pertinent item, a partial
inventory of materials used in the entertainment. Its references to actors
and its information about costuming will be discussed below. One item
in the inventory—"Mᵣ Iones hath all the waxe lightes torches and candle-
stickes"—suggests that Inigo was again Jonson's collaborator.

2. *The Letters and Epigrams of Sir John Harington,* ed. N. E. McClure (Phila-
delphia, 1930), pp. 118–121.

3. Quoted in Ben Jonson, *Works,* ed. C. H. Herford and P. and E. Simpson, 11
vols. (Oxford, 1925–1952), X, 400–401. All Jonson references pertain to this edition,
hereafter cited as *"Works."*

1608. Entertainment at Salisbury House in the Strand for James I

Jonson published no text for this entertainment, and no other references to it seem to exist. The Cecil household bills for 1608 (Family Papers—Bills 22) contain nine invoices for the show. One of these, which is partly written in Salisbury's own hand, lists rewards of £20 each to "Iohnson," "Alyn," and "Iones," along with a payment of £10 to the "Iuggler." The other eight bills are: Inigo Jones's signed receipt for his reward; Jones's bill for "wagies for yᵉ Painters" and for material expenses; Jones's bill for wages paid to the "Smyth, the taillor & others for worcke donne about the shewe"; a list of rewards given to royal musicians and attendants; a list of rewards given to other musicians; the joiner's bill for "worck donn in the librarie about the shewe"; a bill for costume material; and a bill for various items "towerds setting forth the showe and adorning the lybrary against the Kings cominge thether."

The invoices indicate that the entertainment was held in early May, but the precise date is hard to determine. The costume invoice states that material was delivered on 5 May. The same date appears on the heading of the joiner's bill, which implies that carpentry work taking "4 dayes & 4 nightes" was finished by then. Jones's receipt for his reward is dated 10 May, and he was reimbursed for his expenses on the 11th. The performance day, then, must have fallen between 5 and 11 May. The entertainment was held in the library of Salisbury House (the Cecil family's Westminster residence), and although the occasion for royal celebration is not mentioned in the documents, it probably had some connection with Salisbury's appointment to the position of Lord Treasurer on 4 May.

1609. Entertainment at Britain's Burse for James I

Another Jonson-Jones entertainment for which there is no text figures in the Cecil Family Papers for 1609. The central document is a summary account of expenses for the show (Family Papers—Accounts 160/161), which lists rewards of £13 6s. 8d. for both "Inigo Iohnes" and "Iohnson the Poett," along with lesser payments to "Feild," "Ostler the player," and Ostler's boy (see discussion of actors, below). Most of the items in this summary account are supported by individual bills and receipts (Family Papers—Bills 35), including Jones's bill for workmen and material, an invoice for the hiring of costumes, a list of payments to performers, and two bills for "Toyes" which were given to the spectators.

The occasion was a visit of the royal family to the newly-built Britain's Burse (the New Exchange). The date was 11 April, when the building was named.[4] A description of this affair, worth quoting in part, appears in the Venetian ambassador's dispatch of 6 May of the same year (O.S. 26 April):

Hard by the Court, the Earl of Salisbury has built two great galleries, decorated, especially outside, with much carving and sculpture. Inside each of these galleries, on either hand, are rows of shops for the sale of all kinds of goods. These will bring in an immense revenue. Last week he took the King, the Queen, and the Princes to see them. He has fitted up one of the shops very beautifully, and over it ran the motto: "All other places give for money, here all is given for love." To the King he gave a Cabinet, to the Queen a silver plaque of the Annunciation worth, they say, four thousand crowns. To the Prince he gave a horse's trappings of great value, nor was there any one of the Suite who did not receive at the very least a gold ring. The King named the place Britain's Burse.[5]

In the various documents for 1609, which are discussed in detail in the section below entitled "Actors' Names," three roles are made distinct for this entertainment: a shopkeeper, his apprentice, and a keykeeper. Clearly Jonson and Jones responded to this particularly mercantile occasion at Britain's Burse by preparing a particularly mercantile show.[6] It is worth recalling, without hinting at literal connections, that about a year after this entertainment Jonson wrote his brilliant comedy about roguery and the London commercial life, *The Alchemist*. To celebrate the endeavors of shopkeeping at Britain's Burse, with the royal family assembled near a sign which said "all other places give for money, here all is given for

4. John Nichols, *The Progresses of James I*, 4 vols. (London, 1828), II, 248. See also Lawrence Stone, "Inigo Jones and the New Exchange," *Archaeological Journal*, CXIV (1957), 116, where the 1609 Entertainment and some of the Hatfield documents are mentioned.

5. *Calendar of State Papers, Venetian*, XI, No. 497. The ambassador states that the royal visit occurred "last week," which would have been later than 11 April, but this should probably be taken as a casual reference.

6. See also the discussion of Thomas Wilson's manuscript synopsis of this entertainment in Lawrence Stone, "Inigo Jones and the New Exchange," p. 116.

love," might have seemed inimical to a poet who always disliked cant as readily as he eventually disliked the Earl of Salisbury.[7] Perhaps the satirical impulse which produced *The Alchemist* a year later began to form in April of 1609.

II *Actors' Names*

Apart from the 1606 Entertainment, the Hatfield documents are fairly explicit in mentioning the names of players. It is clear that professional and boy actors were called upon to perform these shows before the King, and if my identifications are correct some well-known figures were involved: particularly Edward Alleyn, Nathan Field, and William Ostler. To provide an accurate view of the evidence, which is tantalizing on a few points, I shall quote the documentary readings for the performers of each entertainment before going on to offer my own interpretations.

1606 Entertainment at Theobalds

No actors are named.

1607 Entertainment at Theobalds

In the partial inventory of materials, the following are mentioned (probably as actors): "dover," "m^r kendall," "Thomas hunt," and "the . . . boaye Iobson." Another phrase, "for the boyes," shows that more than one child actor was involved. These names customarily appear in connection with costume material received, and the inventory is unusually explicit in identifying the roles for which costumes were to be tailored. Thus typical entries read:

> delivered to m^r kendall 5 yardes of yewlowe tyncell for Ieniuse
> delivered more to dover one ell and 3 quarters of blewe tafyta for
>   Mercurie
> More to m^r kendall 2 yards of watchet cheny tafyta for a scarfe

The Folio text has five speaking roles: Mercury, The Genius, and the Three Parcae. Good Event, a boy, has no lines.

---

7. Jonson's opinions of Salisbury appear in *Conversations with Drummond* (*Works*, I, 141–142).

In the inventory, the participants' names (with some variation in form) can be sorted in this way: "dover" appears four times, always in connection with material for Mercury; "m^r kendall" appears thirteen times, once in connection with material for Lachesis, thrice in connection with material for The Genius, and nine times in connection with material for which no role is mentioned; "Thomas hunt" appears once, in connection with material for The Genius; "Iobson" is named once, as are "the boyes," in connection with material for which no roles are mentioned.

1608 Entertainment at Salisbury House

There is no text. The name "m^r Allen" or "Alyn" occurs seven times in the bills for this entertainment. Four items in the list of materials pertain to his costume, and twice his name is associated with the high reward of £20. The seventh appearance of the name occurs in an unusual item: "spent upon Allen Iones & Iohnson before they came to diett in my lords [Salisbury's] house."[8]

Other references to actors are not very precise. "Iobson," named as a boy in the 1607 inventory, appears twice in the 1608 costume list. "The Iugler" occurs three times, once in connection with a reward of £10, indicating that his role was important. The "Coniurer" is mentioned once, and unnamed boy actors have several references, including "the Flying Boye" and "the 2 boyes that played fancy & Barahon."

1609 Entertainment at Britain's Burse

There is no text. In the summary list of expenses three performers are named: "Ostler the player," "his Boye," and "Feild the key keeper." The separate bill of payments to performers lists these three as "Ostler the shoppkeeper," "ye boy in ye shopp," and "feld the key keeper." The bill for costume rental names three roles: "the Key keeper," "the Shop M^r," and "the Prentise." Putting these three listings together yields the following assignment of roles:

> Ostler—the shopkeeper
> Ostler's boy—the apprentice
> Field—the keykeeper

Ostler's boy, according to a receipt on the bill of payments to performers,

---

8. This may have been the occasion for Jonson's discontent over conditions at the Earl of Salisbury's table. See *Works,* I, 141.

was "Gilles Gary." There are no clear references to other actors or other roles.

From these various pieces of evidence we derive the personal names of eight performers. These are listed below in alphabetical order, according to the identifications with known actors which seem most plausible to me.[9]

ALLEYN, EDWARD "Alyn" or "m^r Allen" was clearly the leading performer in the 1608 Entertainment at Salisbury House. His reward was £20 (the same amount paid to both Jonson and Jones), he was invited to dine with the Earl of Salisbury (again, along with Jonson and Jones), and his costume included a robe of crimson taffeta for which the material cost £3 10s. Of the several "Allens" in the acting tradition, only Edward Alleyn would have received such bestowals.

By 1608 Alleyn had ended his famous career on the public stage; but he had taken part in the coronation procession for James in 1604, and as late as 1611 he was a servant to Prince Henry, who attended the 1608 Entertainment.

DOVER The name "dover" appears four times in the partial inventory for the 1607 Entertainment at Theobalds. In each case, he is mentioned as receiving costume material for the role of Mercury. If "dover" was the actor who played the role of Mercury, then he remains unidentified.

If, however, he was serving as wardrobe keeper for the production, a tentative identification becomes possible. In 1634 one Anthony Dover was a wardrobe keeper for the King's Revels Company. Nothing further is known of this man, and to assume that he was the "dover" of 1607 is to stretch a similarity of names over a long period of time. What makes this possibility intriguing, however, is that Anthony Dover's fellow as wardrobe keeper for the King's Revels Company in 1634 was Richard Kendall. In the 1607 inventory list, "m^r kendall" is busy with costume material, along with "dover." My interpretation is that "m^r kendall" stands for the actor William Kendall (q.v.) rather than the later wardrobe keeper Rich-

---

9. Fuller information on these actors will be found in E. K. Chambers, *The Elizabethan Stage* (Oxford, 1923), II, 295–350; G. E. Bentley, *The Jacobean and Caroline Stage* (Oxford, 1941–1956), II, *passim;* and Edwin Nungezer, *A Dictionary of Actors* (New Haven, 1929), *passim.*

ard Kendall, and hence I take "dover" as an unidentified actor. But the Richard Kendall–Anthony Dover relationship should be kept in mind as a possible explanation for the 1607 names.

In 1634 Richard Kendall's age was "50 or upwards." [10] Hence he would have been in his mid-twenties at the time of the 1607 Entertainment. Nothing is known of Anthony Dover's age.

FIELD, NATHAN Various items in the 1609 documents combine to show that an actor named "Feild" or "feld," received £4 for playing a key-keeper in the entertainment at Britain's Burse. These references point to Nathan Field, since no other actor of the name (or a name like it) is on record in the early Jacobean period. The identification is especially apt in view of Jonson's statement that Ned Field was once his scholar. [11] And if being Jonson's protégé allowed Field to perform in an entertainment before the King, it might also have entailed more pedantic tasks. One of the 1609 bills refers to "feld that satt up all night [writing] the speeches songes & inscriptions."

In 1609 Field belonged to the Children of the Queen's Revels, with whom he appeared in *Epicoene* in the same year. In 1613 he became a leader of the newly-enlarged Lady Elizabeth's men, which included other names from these documents: Giles Gary and Thomas Hunt (*q.v.*).

GARY, GILES Among the documents for the 1609 Entertainment at Britain's Burse is a receipt for a "reward given by my Mr Willm Ostler" and signed "Gilles Gary." Other items make it clear that Ostler's "Boye" played an apprentice and was rewarded £2.

In 1609 Giles Gary (or Cary) belonged to the Children of the Queen's Revels, with whom he played in *Epicoene*. By 1611 he was with Lady Elizabeth's men. His career thus paralleled Field's (*q.v.*).

HUNT, THOMAS The full name appears once in the inventory of costume material for the 1607 Entertainment. It clearly refers to the Thomas Hunt who had acted minor roles for the Admiral's men in the late 1590's. By 1607, if he had remained with the same company, he would have belonged

10. Information on Richard Kendall comes from *Crosfield's Diary*, quoted in Bentley, *Jacobean and Caroline Stage*, II, 688.
11. *Conversations with Drummond* (*Works*, I, 137).

to Prince Henry's men, which succeeded the Admiral's men in 1603. In 1611 he was with Lady Elizabeth's men (see GARY and FIELD).

JOBSON   A "boaye Iobson" is mentioned in the inventory of costume material for the 1607 Entertainment, and his name occurs twice in a similar list for the 1608 Entertainment. The name seems to be unknown in other theatrical records.

KENDALL, WILLIAM   "m^r kendall" is mentioned thirteen times in the 1607 inventory as receiving costume material for at least two different roles. Because of the clear identification of Thomas Hunt in the same inventory (see above), I take "m^r kendall" to stand for Hunt's fellow actor in the earlier Admiral's men, William Kendall. Little is known of Kendall or of Hunt in 1607, but possibly they were minor actors in Prince Henry's men, the successors to the Admiral's men.

For the possibility that Richard Kendall might be involved in this identification, see DOVER above.

OSTLER, WILLIAM   The documents for the 1609 Entertainment at Britain's Burse show that Ostler played a shopkeeper, receiving a reward of £5. His "Boye," who played an apprentice, was Giles Gary (*q.v.*). There can be little question that this is William Ostler.

Ostler had earlier belonged to the Children of the Queen's Revels, performing in *The Poetaster* in 1601. By 1610 he had joined the King's men, with whom he acted in *The Alchemist*.

The coincidence of Field, Ostler, and Giles Gary in the 1609 Entertainment deserves a word of comment, for possibly all three belonged at that time to one acting company, the Children of the Queen's Revels (sometimes called the Children of the Blackfriars). For Field and Gary there is no question: both acted in *Epicoene* for the Revels in 1609. Ostler had begun his career in the same company a decade before, but since he is not named in the *Epicoene* list, and since he had joined the King's men by 1610, his affiliation in 1609 is uncertain. His designation as Gary's "master" in the Hatfield documents for 1609 suggests, however, that he was still with the Revels company, perhaps as an adult manager or instructor. If that is so, then it becomes likely that Jonson and Jones turned to the Revels company in casting the 1609 Entertainment at Britain's Burse.

III. Payments to Jonson and Jones

The Hatfield documents offer some information about the over-all expenses of two entertainments, against which the payments to Jonson and Jones can be measured. For the 1609 Entertainment the summary account of expenses seems to be complete. It comes to a total of nearly £180. For the 1608 Entertainment, although here we cannot be certain that all bills are included, the cost is nearly the same: just over £170. As will be made clear in the next section, these two entertainments were dissimilar in emphasis, but since the documents for both of them include costs for all normal phases of production, we can take them as the most typical guide we have. A properly cautious conclusion would be that the Earl of Salisbury was not inclined to spend over £200 in arranging a theatrical display for his King. The average cost of a Jacobean court masque has been calculated at £2,000.[12] Hence the entertainments for Salisbury amounted to only about one-tenth of the cost of the average court masque.

It would seem, in that light, that Jonson and Jones were handsomely paid for their efforts in the entertainments. Each was rewarded £20 in 1608 and £13 6s. 8d. in 1609. For the 1606 Entertainment Jonson received £13 6s. 8d. and Jones probably earned the same amount.[13] If the Earl of Salisbury's bounty bears on such matters, the soul and the body of the entertainments were viewed as equals. It is in comparison to their rewards for court masques that Jonson and Jones seem well paid for the smaller entertainments. The few payments which are recorded for their court spectacles run between £40 and £50.[14] To receive nearly half that amount for a comparatively slight effort in 1608, or nearly one-third of that amount in 1609, must have seemed to both men ample recompense. And for a poet who complained that he had not £200 for all of his plays together, a reward of up to £20 for gracing a royal visit to the Earl of Salisbury must have arrived as a welcome overpayment.

12. Chambers, *Elizabethan Stage*, I, 211.

13. The entry for Jones in 1606 combines his expenses and his reward for a total of £23. By analogy with the entries for other entertainments, I assume that his reward equaled Jonson's (£13 6s. 8d.) with his expenses coming to just under £10.

14. See Chambers, *Elizabethan Stage*, I, 210. Only for *The Lord's Masque, Love Freed from Ignorance and Folly,* and *Oberon* are figures for Jonson and Jones available.

IV *Staging and Costumes*

Jonson's earliest entertainments were not so much stage pieces as out-door pleasantries. Following the Elizabethan tradition in this form of compliment, the entertainments at Althorp and Highgate both consist of several encounters between royalty and the figures of a pastoral land-scape, and the encounters normally occur in the pastoral landscape itself. It is the garden and the park, rather than the stage, which provide loca-tions for these dramatic addresses to royalty.

In the entertainments at Theobalds, however, with Inigo Jones serving as Jonson's collaborator, a change begins to occur. In the first (1606), as far as we can tell from the printed speeches of welcome, the outdoor con-vention still operates. Yet the high rewards paid to Jonson and Jones, as explained above, hint that a show more substantial than the printed welcome may have been offered. Unfortunately, the 1606 document fails to give further clues, beyond listing an expenditure of £20 for costume silks and "other necessaries for the showe."

It is in the 1607 Entertainment at Theobalds that a change toward a fully staged performance becomes clear. The printed text is particularly helpful here. The show was put on in the gallery after dinner. At first *"there was seene nothing but a trauerse of white, acrosse the roome: which sodainely drawne, was discouered a gloomie obscure place, hung all with black silkes, and in it only one light, which the GENIUS of the house held, sadly attir'd."* [15] The Hatfield inventory of costume material shows that this sad attire was made of purple rich taffeta, yellow taffeta, and yellow tinsel.

A moment later the scene changes suddenly, and we sense the first strong influence of Jones upon Jonson's early entertainments:

And withall, the black vanishing, was discouered a glorious place, figuring the Lararium *. . . erected with Columnes and Architrabe, Freeze, and Coro-nice, in which were placed diuers Diaphanall glasses, fill'd with seuerall wa-ters, that shew'd like so many stones, of orient and transparent hiewes. Within, as farder off, in* **Landtschap**, *were seene clouds riding.*[16]

15. *Works*, VII, 154.
16. *Ibid.*, VII, 155.

Three features of Jones's technique are evident in this passage: the construction of a monumental stage property; lighting that property by the special technique of *"Diaphanall glasses"* which gave off a jewel-like illumination; and creating behind the monumental property, *"as farder off,"* a view of distant perspective.[17] Clearly in 1607 the entertainment had moved indoors to a stage location, and the pastoral setting was now more a matter of art than of nature.

This tendency toward stage design seems to continue in the 1608 Entertainment, although in this case no printed text is available and we must depend upon inferences from the Hatfield documents. Jones's expenses for material and workmen come to more than £30. Some of this cost—as items for "Coolers," "Goulde," and "Sillver" indicate—would have concerned costumes, but a payment of over £9 to "y° Painters" suggests that ample work was performed on scenic devices. An entry "for Glasses for y° Rokke" shows that the method of lighting by diaphanous glasses was again employed for a scenic property, additional lighting effects being provided by "26 waxe lightes waying 36¹¹." We cannot be certain that a special stage was constructed; the joiner's bill refers to "twoe men that wrought uppon the shewe . . . 4 dayes & 4 nightes," but possibly they were constructing scaffolding for the audience or altering the library in which the entertainment was held. Whether or not a raised platform was built, two curtains were hung from rings, and over thirty pulleys were purchased. The costumes must have been splendid. Alleyn's robe was made from five ells of "Ell broad crimson Rich Taffaty," the material costing £3 10s., his open sleeves were of white sarcenet, his girdle of white taffeta. The "Blew Rich Taffaty" for the Juggler's costume came to £3 3s., and special expenses were incurred for skin coats and cloven feet, suggesting that the show may have been satyrical. In all, the documents indicate that the 1608 Entertainment, like the show at Theobalds a year before, employed striking effects of scenery, costuming, and lighting.

The 1609 Entertainment at Britain's Burse, however, seems to have possessed far less theatricality than the two preceding shows. Jones's expenses for materials and workmen are listed at only £9 12s. (compared to over £30 the year before). Other documents contain no references to curtains or to special lighting devices, and instead of an inventory of costume ma-

17. See Allardyce Nicoll, *Stuart Masques and the Renaissance Stage* (London, 1937), pp. 54–137; and *Works*, X, 406–420.

terial we find a bill for the hiring of outfits for the three leading roles. In fact, the documents make it clear that in 1609 the staging of the entertainment was financially less important than the sharing of exotic gifts among the royal retinue and spectators. Over £96, or more than half the total cost of the royal visit, was spent on various Indian commodities, China commodities, and gold rings with poesies in them, all to be "given awaye at the naming of Brittains Burss." It would seem that Jonson's plot about a shopkeeper, an apprentice, and a keykeeper was little more than the focal point for a display of international gift-giving at Westminster's new center of commercialism.

If that is so, we are reminded that entertainments, like masques on a much larger scale, were essentially at the service of political, economic, and diplomatic authority. The theatrical fullness of the 1607 and 1608 entertainments is worth noting as we study the careers of Jonson and Jones and the development of Jacobean masquing technique. That such theatrical fullness gives way to expensive gratuities in 1609 comes as no surprise in a form of dramatic courtesy which represents the interests of the Earl of Salisbury and the King at least as directly as it does the artistry of Jonson and Jones. For the poet and the designer, high cash rewards and growing fame were probably the chief benefits of the entertainments; and the absence of the 1608 and 1609 pieces from Jonson's Folio indicates the extent of his concern for their literary posterity. Our concern today is different from his. For us, the entertainments are part of the intrigue of theatrical history, particularly because we know so little about them. The Hatfield documents, once they are published in full, will fill in some of the pieces, and perhaps a host of information exists in similar archives to complete our understanding of the connections between aristocratic entertainments and the extraordinary milieu of early Jacobean drama.

The Emblematic Nature of
English Civic Pageantry

DAVID M. BERGERON

ENGLISHMEN of the late sixteenth and early seventeenth centuries, as is well-known, took great delight in emblem books, and these books profoundly influenced many poets—Spenser and Herbert, to name but two. Emblem literature had been popular on the continent long before the first English emblem book, Geoffrey Whitney's *A Choice of Emblems,* appeared in 1586. This was but the first of a long line of such books in England, a subject very ably discussed by Rosemary Freeman.[1] We have long been aware of Ben Jonson's indebtedness to emblem books, especially the Italian ones, in his court masques.[2] It is only natural to assume that the books also had a rather direct bearing on civic pageantry, the less sophisticated counterpart of the masque. Though some writers have noticed a relationship between emblem and pageant, the subject has not been dealt with extensively. I propose here to make some initial suggestions about the connection between emblems and civic pageantry in England during the period 1558–1640.

Both the emblem and the pageant were obviously drawing upon a common iconographical tradition; and although no one can say with final

1. *English Emblem Books* (London, 1948).
2. See Allan H. Gilbert, *The Symbolic Persons in the Masques of Ben Jonson* (Durham, 1948).

167

certainty that a particular emblem influenced a specific pageant, we can at least make the parallels and state the possibility of a relationship. In so doing, we demonstrate how iconography could leap the bounds of the printed page and assume dramatic form in a civic entertainment.

The typical emblem is essentially tripartite in arrangement. It must have a picture—usually allegorical, symbolic, or mythological in content. Frequently there is an accompanying "word" or "motto," a brief epigraphic summary of the meaning of the illustration. Verses which attempt to bring the picture and motto together and make clear the meaning of the drawing constitute the third element of the emblem. The verses leave no room for doubt as to the meaning of the emblem.

Francis Quarles, who was chiefly a religious emblematist, says in the "To the Reader" section of his emblem book that

An Embleme is but a silent Parable. . . . Before the knowledge of letters, God was knowne by *Hierogliphicks;* And, indeed, what are the Heavens, the Earth, nay every Creature, *Hierogliphicks* and *Emblemes* of His Glory? I have no more to say.[3]

Quarles emphasizes the instructional nature of the emblems; this is of course in keeping with their allegorical expression. Civic pageantry certainly shares this didactic function.

Geoffrey Whitney usefully categorizes the different types of emblems.

. . . all Emblemes for the most part, maie be reduced into these three kindes, which is *Historicall, Naturall,* & *Morall. Historicall,* as representing the actes of some noble persons, being matter of historie. *Naturall,* as in expressing the natures of creatures, for example, the loue of the yonge Storkes, to the oulde, or of suche like. *Morall,* pertaining to vertue and instruction of life, which is the chiefe of the three, and the other two maye bee in some sorte drawen into this head. For, all doe tende vnto discipline, and morall preceptes of liuing.[4]

We might add the category of mythology to Whitney's list, but perhaps he intended that one of his divisions would subsume mythology, for he certainly uses mythological figures in his own book.

Emblem books, at least in England, look backward in the allegorical tradition toward the morality drama, and it is possible that they drew some of their inspiration from the medieval theater. Miss Freeman notes:

3. Francis Quarles, *Emblemes* (London, 1635), sig. A3.
4. Geoffrey Whitney, *A Choice of Emblemes* (Leyden, 1586), "To the Reader." All quotations will be from this edition.

Emblem books depended for their existence upon the validity of these allegorical ways of thinking; they depended also upon a close interrelation between the arts of poetry and painting. While poetry was regarded as "a speaking picture" and painting as "dumb poetry," the emblem convention, in which poem and picture were complementary to each other, could flourish.[5]

The same may be said for civic pageantry. Indeed the individual pageants are frequently animated emblems.

When I speak of civic pageantry, I refer to three different styles of entertainments current in Tudor and Stuart England. One type was the "royal entry" of the sovereign into a city. Elizabeth and James both had very elaborate pageants presented for them as each made his respective coronation passage through the city of London. Various allegorical *tableaux vivants* were placed throughout the city, each with instructional purpose. The sovereigns also made many summer progresses which of course included visits at the estates of noblemen where the royalty was elaborately entertained. The Lord Mayor's Show, an institution which began in the mid-sixteenth century and flourished most opulently during the reigns of James I and Charles I, is yet another type of pageantry. Each year on the 29th of October when the new mayor of London was installed, his trade guild would present pageants located at various places in the city, pageants which were similar in their nature to the royal entry entertainment in the use of allegorical presentations.

In her comparative study of Middleton's 1613 Lord Mayor's Show and Heywood's 1631 show, Sheila Williams has rightly noted the relationship between emblem and pageant. She says:

Certain tableaux devised by several other pageant-poets had all three elements —picture, motto, and verses—and usually the motto was placed above or before the tableau in emblem-book fashion. If we allow that the essence of the emblem was a picture plus a verbal explanation, and accept either the motto or the verses as fulfilling the second function, then the normal method of the pageant-poets was the same as that of the emblem-writer.[6]

To cite more than a few examples from the pageants to illustrate their emblematic nature would be supererogatory since the method is used consistently by the pageant writers.

5. Freeman, *English Emblem Books*, pp. 4–5.
6. Sheila Williams, "Two Seventeenth Century Semi-Dramatic Allegories of Truth the Daughter of Time," *The Guildhall Miscellany* (October 1963), II, No. 5, 220.

A convenient and altogether appropriate place to begin is with Queen Elizabeth's coronation passage through London on 14 January 1559, the first civic pageant of the chronological period I have selected. Any one of the several tableaux stationed throughout the city would suffice to suggest the emblematic technique. For example, at the device at Soper-lane on a scaffold arrangement were eight children representing the eight Beatitudes, "eche hauing the proper name of the blessing, that they did represent, writen in a table and placed aboue their heades." [7] In addition, "Euerie of these children wer appointed & apparelled according vnto the blessing which he did represent" (p. 41). This, then, is the "picture" of the typical emblem.

The name or "motto" of the pageant was inscribed on the forefront— "The eight beatitudes expressed in the. v. chapter of the gospel of S. Mathew, applyed to our soueraigne Ladie Quene Elizabeth" (p. 41). "And all voide places in the pageant wer furnished with prety sayings, cōmending and touching yᵉ meaning of the said pageant, which was the promises & blessinges of almightie god made to his people" (pp. 41–42). Some of these additional sentences were in Latin, all enhancing the theme of the pageant.

When the Queen arrived, one of the children stepped forth and spoke the verses:

> Thou hast been . viii. times blest, o quene of worthy fame
> By mekenes of thy spirite, when care did thee besette
> By mourning in thy griefe, by mildnes in thy blame
> By hunger and by thyrst, and iustice couldst none gette.
>
> By mercy shewed, not felt, by cleanes of thyne harte
> By seking peace alwayes, by persecucion wrong.
> Therfore trust thou in god, since he hath helpt thy smart
> That as his promis is, so he will make thee strong.
>
> (p. 42)

The pageant-emblem is thus complete, and the observer has been duly instructed. From this pageant one could easily construct a corresponding emblem.

The emblematic technique is duplicated frequently in the Lord Mayor's

7. *The Quenes Maiesties Passage through the Citie of London to Westminster the Day before her Coronacion,* ed. James M. Osborn (New Haven, 1960), p. 41. All quotations will be from this edition.

Shows. I cite two instances from the pageants of Anthony Munday, whom I choose only arbitrarily, for though he is the most prolific of the writers of Lord Mayor's Shows, he is neither more nor less "emblematic" than the others. In the 1616 show which Munday called *Chrysanaleia* he depicted, among other things, a pelican. The bird is located near a lemon tree— "Neere to the stocke or roote thereof, a goodly *Pellicane* hath built her nest, with all her tender brood about her." [8] After giving the necessary "picture," Munday then states the common interpretations of the symbolic meaning of the bird, all of which fit Whitney's category of the "Naturall" emblem. Munday makes the application of the pelican to the new mayor:

An excellent type of gouernment in a Magistrate, who, at his meere entrance into his yeares Office, becommeth a nursing father of the Family. . . .

If his loue and delight be such to the Commonwealth, as that of the *Pellican* to her young ones, by broken sleeps, daily and nightly cares, that the very lest harm should not happē to his charge: then doth he iustly answere to our Embleme. . . .

(sig. B2)

In the presentation of the various devices Munday has the figure representing William Walworth give a speech in which he makes clear the meaning of the different tableaux; this fulfills the function of the verses of an emblem. I think it noteworthy that Munday uses the term "emblem," for he quite obviously understands the tradition.

Similar techniques are employed by Munday in his 1618 Lord Mayor's Show, *Sidero-Thriambos*. He uses a number of allegorical figures, and the speeches in the pageant explain their meaning. Munday, in effect, speaks to the issue of the emblem method near the end of the pamphlet where he says:

For better vnderstanding the true morality of this deuise, the personages haue all Emblemes and Properties in their hands, & so neere them, that the weakest capacity may take knowledge of thē; which course in such solemne Triumphes hath alwaies beene allowed of best obseruation: both for auoiding trouble to the Magistrate, by tedious and impertinent speeches, and deuouring the time, which craueth diligent expedition. [9]

8. Anthony Munday, *Chrysanaleia: The Golden Fishing* (London, 1616), sig. B2. All citations are to this quarto edition.

9. Anthony Munday, *Sidero-Thriambos or Steele and Iron Triumphing* (London, 1618), sig. C1ᵛ.

Munday suggests that the method of the emblem books is both universal in practice and efficacious in achieving the desired result.

These examples are sufficient to establish that the method of the emblem book and the civic pageant is fundamentally the same. We might further consider the relationship between emblem and pageant by showing that certain figures depicted in the books are also used by the pageant writers— in other words, by citing specific parallel instances. This is not to suggest that Munday, for example, was influenced by Whitney—that could not be established—but the common ground between both forms is clearly demonstrable. Two emblem books, Whitney's *A Choice of Emblems* (1586), a highly derivative one, and Henry Peacham's *Minerva Britanna* (1612), will illustrate my point.

One of the first emblems in Whitney's book portrays Time and his daughter Truth (see Figure 4). The motto is "Veritas temporis filia." Time with wings at his back and carrying a scythe is in the process of rescuing Truth, who has been incarcerated by Envy, Slander, and Strife. The concluding lines of the verses offer hope:

> Yet Time will comme, and take this ladies parte,
> And breake her bandes, and bring her foes to foile.
>   Dispaire not then, thoughe truthe be hidden ofte,
>   Bycause at lengthe, shee shall bee sett alofte.

(p. 4)

The association of Time and Truth is of course an old one, and Whitney is but continuing the tradition.[10]

Time and Truth were also linked by writers of civic pageants. In Elizabeth's coronation progress through London (1559) we have such a presentation. Here is obviously a case where Whitney, some twenty-seven years later, could have had no influence; it is at least remotely possible that the influence flowed the other way. Nevertheless, the point is the similarity in representation, not the indebtedness.

At the Little Conduit in Cheapside two hills were erected—one representing a decaying and the other a flourishing commonwealth. Each was

---

10. See Erwin Panofsky, *Studies in Iconology* (New York, 1962), Chap. 3; and D. J. Gordon, "'Veritas Filia Temporis': Hadrianus Junius and Geoffrey Whitney," *Journal of the Warburg and Courtauld Institutes,* III (1939–1940), Nos. 3–4, 228–240.

THREE furies fell, which turne the worlde to ruthe,
  Both Enuie, Strife, and Slaunder, heare appeare,
In dungeon darke they longe inclofed truthe,
But Time at lengthe, did loofe his daughter deare,
    And fetts alofte, that facred ladie brighte,
    Whoe things longe hidd, reueales, and bringes to lighte.

Thoughe ftrife make fier, thoughe Enuie eate hir harte,
The innocent though Slaunder rente, and fpoile:
Yet Time will comme, and take this ladies parte,
And breake her bandes, and bring her foes to foile.
    Difpaire not then, thoughe truthe be hidden ofte,
    Bycaufe at lengthe, fhee fhall bee fett alofte.

FIGURE 4. Time and Truth. From Geoffrey Whitney, *A Choice of Emblemes* (Leyden, 1586). Reproduced by courtesy of the Folger Shakespeare Library, Washington, D.C.

decorated to enhance its allegorical message, and between these hills was a cave out of which Time came forth,

apparaylled as an olde man with a Sythe in his hande, hauynge wynges artificiallye made, leading a personage of lesser stature then himselfe, which was fynely and well apparaylled, all cladde in whyte silke, and directlye ouer her head was set her name and tytle in latin and Englyshe, *Temporis filia,* the daughter of Tyme.

(p. 47)

Whitney, we recall, also depicts Time as leading Truth out of some sort of cave or dungeon. In case there is any doubt, Truth in the pageant wears the title *Veritas* across her breast; she also carries the word of Truth, the Bible, and presents it to Elizabeth. A child delivers appropriate verses which elucidate the allegorical meaning of this pageant-emblem.

Thomas Middleton brings the two figures together in the Lord Mayor's Show of 1613, *The Triumphs of Truth;* but here, though Time is appropriately costumed, he is only of subsidiary importance and appears but briefly, mainly to urge the new mayor to follow Truth. The similarity between Thomas Heywood's treatment of Time and Truth in the 1631 show, *London's Ius Honorarium,* and the civic pageant of 1559 has been noted by Mrs. Williams, in an article cited earlier. Heywood uses a hill designated as symbolic of a "City well governed," on which there are various sentences which specify the qualities which make for good government. And "At the foot of the Hill sitteth old Time, and by him his daughter Truth, with this inscription; *Veritas est Temporis Filia. . . ."* [11] In a long moralizing speech delivered to the new mayor, Time asks him to note the beautiful hill, the trees, the flowers, "All Emblems of a City governd well; / Which must be now your charge" (sig. B3). He also asks the mayor to defend his daughter Truth. At one point in the speech he pauses, picks up a leafless and withered branch, and makes the emblematic application: "See you this withered branch, by *Time* o're growne / A Cities Symbole, ruind, and trod downe. / A Tree that bare bad fruit . . ." (sig. B3ʳ). Time then enumerates the vices which can lead to the decay of a city. This fulfills the emblematic function of the hill which represented the decaying commonwealth in the earlier 1559 pageant. One sees in these two pageants an excellent example of the continuity of the

11. Thomas Heywood, *London's Ius Honorarium* (London, 1631), sig. B2ʳ.

allegorical-emblematic technique, a similarity which is striking in pageants separated by some seventy-two years.[12]

In addition to showing Time and Truth together, Whitney also has an emblem in which he shows Time alone. Here Time seems to be descending from a cloud; he is naked, carries a scythe, and has wings at his back. Two people seem to be trying to escape the presence of Time, but this is futile, as Whitney observes. On the contrary, he urges, we must use our brief span as well as possible:

> And since, by proofe I knowe, you [Thomas Wilbraham] hourde
>   not vp your store;
> Whose gate, is open to your frende: and purce, vnto the pore:
> And spend vnto your praise, what GOD dothe largely lende:
> I chiefly made my choice of this, which I to you commende.
>
> (p. 199)

In this emblem Whitney commends his friend Wilbraham for his wise use of time.

When Elizabeth made one of her last progresses, she visited Harefield (1602) and was greeted by the personage of Time in appropriate garb; and he also appears several times in the Lord Mayor's Shows dressed in the traditional habit. Munday assigns important dramatic and speaking roles to Time in his pageants of 1611 and 1615. John Taylor's treatment of Time in the civic pageant of 1634 is typical. Early in the entertainment Time addresses the mayor and commends him for loving his daughter Truth: "I doe command her, still with you t' abide, / Doe you defend her, she shall be your guide: / For truth-sake *Time* shall be your servant still."[13] At the conclusion of the pageant Time once again speaks to the mayor, bids him to follow virtue, to use his moments wisely:

> Tis truly said, that man that rules his passions,
> Doth conquer more, than he that conquers Nations.

12. Mrs. Williams suggests that at the time Heywood devised this pageant of 1631, he was "interested in pageantry and acquainted with this particular Elizabethan procession. *Englands Elizabeth,* his account of the reign of the great queen, was licensed to be printed on April 26th, 1631" (p. 218). I would also add that the ending of Heywood's play, *If You Know Not Me* (Part I), reveals his acquaintance with Elizabeth's coronation procession. At the end of this play Elizabeth is welcomed to the city by the mayor, who presents a purse and Bible to her. She kisses the Bible just as she had done in the actual event.

13. John Taylor, *The Trivmphs of Fame and Honovr* (London, 1634), sig. A7.

> As you have rul'd your selfe, let it appeare
> In ruling London this ensuing yeare. . . .
>
> (sig. B4)

Like Whitney, Taylor directs the message of Time to an individual, but all may share in the wisdom.

Truth also has devoted to her an entire emblem in which Peacham depicts her as naked with one foot resting on a globe (see Figure 5).[14] In her right hand is a sunburst, in the left an open book and palm branch. Peacham interprets the meaning of her presentation:

> Her nakednes beseemes simplicitie:
> The Sunne, how she is greatest frend to light:
> Her booke, the strength she holds by historie:
> The Palme, her triumphes over Tyranrs [*sic*] spite:
> The world she treads on, how in heaven she dwels,
> And here beneath all earthly thing excells.

As is usually the case, Peacham is not original in his representation of Truth; he has before him a long history of similar portrayals.

In three of his Lord Mayor's Shows Middleton presents the figure of Truth. The most elaborate description is in the 1613 pageant, *The Triumphs of Truth,* in which he duplicates but also embellishes Peacham's picture. She wears a "close garment of white satin, which makes her appear thin and naked, figuring thereby her simplicity . . . ," has a sun in her right hand and in her left, "a fan, filled all with stars . . . with which she parts darkness, and strikes away the vapours of ignorance."[15] In Middleton's portrayal Truth treads upon serpents "in that she treads down all subtlety and fraud." It is interesting to note that Peacham's picture of Truth is framed by a border of two serpents intertwined. Peacham may have intended the border merely as decoration; nevertheless, it squares with Middleton's association of snakes and Truth. Furthermore Middleton adds to Truth a diadem of stars, a white dove atop her head, a robe filled with the eyes of eagles, "showing her deep insight and height of wisdom," and on her breast "a pure round crystal, showing the brightness of her thoughts and actions." In the Lord Mayor's pageant of 1617, Middleton places Truth among other allegorical figures at the Castle

14. Henry Peacham, *Minerva Britanna* (London, 1612), p. 134. All quotations will be from this edition.

15. *The Works of Thomas Middleton,* ed. A. H. Bullen (Boston, 1886), VII, 244. All quotations from Middleton will be from this edition.

A BEAVTEOVS maide, in comly wife doth ftand:
Who on the Sunnes bright globe, doth caft her eie:
An opened booke, fhe holdeth in her hand,
withall the Palme, in figne of victorie;
 Her right foote treadeth downe the world belowe:
 Her name is T R V T H, of old depainted fo.

Her nakednes befeemes fimplicitie:
The Sunne, how fhe is greateft frend to light:
Her booke, the ftrength fhe holds by * hiftorie:
The Palme, her triumphes over Tyrants fpite:
 The world fhe treads on, how in heaven fhe dwels,
 And here beneath all earthly thing excells.

FIGURE 5. Truth. From Henry Peacham, *Minerva Brittanna* (London, 1612).
Reproduced by courtesy of the Folger Shakespeare Library, Washington, D.C.

of Fame; she holds "in her right hand a sun, in the other a fan of stars . . ."
(VII, 304). In 1621 Middleton says simply that Truth carries the emblem
of a "fan of stars, with which she chases away Error . . ." (VII, 348).
These brief descriptions in 1617 and 1621 may merely be a type of short-

hand; that is, Middleton may just be assuming the other usual accouter-
ments of the figure Truth.

In his emblem portraying Time and Truth Whitney also includes the
person of Envy, who is one of the forces that has imprisoned Truth. In
the picture Envy is shown as eating her heart, and her head is covered
with serpents. Whitney has another emblem devoted exclusively to Envy
in which she is especially unattractive (see Figure 6). She is eating snakes
—"that poysoned thoughtes, bee euermore her foode" (p. 94)—and there
are snakes atop her head, "the fruite that springes, of such a venomed
braine." Whitney suggests that her heart is filled with gall, and her tongue
"with stinges doth swell."

At the triumphal arch constructed at Fleet Street King James I could
see the figure of Envy, among others, during his coronation passage
through London on 15 March 1604. Thomas Dekker describes Envy as
being "vnhandsomely attirde all in blacke, her haire of the same colour,
filletted about with snakes." [16] Having had this experience with presenting
Envy, Dekker uses her again, this time in his first Lord Mayor's Show,
Troia-Nova Triumphans (1612). She is an important figure, for she is
set in direct opposition to Virtue, and she serves as commandress of the
Forlorn Castle. Her description reveals the traditional portrait: "her haire
full of Snakes, her countenance pallid, meagre and leane, her body naked,
in her hand a knot of Snakes, crawling and writhen about her arme"
(III, 238). Middleton perhaps drew some inspiration from Dekker for
his depiction of Envy in the Lord Mayor's pageant of 1613; but he in-
tensifies the picture. Envy accompanies Error; she is shown as "eating of a
human heart, mounted on a rhinoceros, attired in red silk, suitable to the
bloodiness of her manners! her left pap bare, where a snake fastens; her
arms half naked; holding in her right hand a dart tincted in blood"
(VII, 241). Middleton has recovered the detail used by Whitney of Envy
eating a heart. In the civic entertainment presented for Prince Henry in
Chester on St. George's Day in 1610, Envy, along with others, rode by on
horseback. She had a "wreath of snakes about her head; another in her
hand, her face and armes besmeared with blood." [17] In a speech Peace

16. *The Dramatic Works of Thomas Dekker,* ed. Fredson Bowers (Cambridge,
1955), II, 295. All quotations from Dekker are from this edition.

17. John Nichols, *The Progresses . . . of King James the First* (London, 1828),
II, 295. Future references to this source will be cited in the text as *PJI*.

VV ʜᴀᴛ hideous hagge with visage sterne appeares?
Whose feeble limmes, can scarce the bodie staie:
This, Enuie is: leane, pale, and full of yeares,
Who with the blisse of other pines awaie.
　　And what declares, her eating vipers broode?
　　That poysoned thoughtes, bee euermore her foode.

What meanes her eies? so bleared, sore, and redd:
Her mourninge still, to see an others gaine.
And what is mentë by snakes vpon her head?
The fruite that springes, of such a venomed braine.
　　But whie, her harte shee rentes within her brest?
　　It shewes her selfe, doth worke her owne vnrest.

Whie lookes shee wronge? bicause shee woulde not see,
An happie wight, which is to her a hell:
What other partes within this furie bee?
Her harte, with gall: her tonge, with stinges doth swell.
　　And laste of all, her staffe with prickes aboundes:
　　Which showes her wordes, wherewith the good shee woundes.

Fertilior seges est alienis semper in agris,
Vicinumq́; pecus grandius vber habet.

Figure 6. Envy. From Geoffrey Whitney, *A Choice of Emblemes* (Leyden, 1586). Reproduced by courtesy of the Folger Shakespeare Library, Washington, D.C.

indicates that she will "send pale Envie downe to hell with speed, / Where she upon her snakes shall only feed . . ." (*PJI*, II, 302). The figure of Joy speaks last and bids Envy be gone. Again as with the emblem books verbal commentary is added to the visual portrayal of the allegorical figure.

Peacham brings together the qualities of Virtue and Fame in a single emblem designed to honor Sir Thomas Chaloner (p. 35). Virtue unfolds a scroll and seeks the services of Fame to publish abroad the reputation of the gentleman. Fame stands to the left in the illustration; she is dressed in a robe decorated with eyes, she has wings at her back, and she blows a trumpet (see Figure 7). This traditional portrayal is likewise used by pageant writers.

It is especially interesting to note that at least two of the pageant dramatists bring Virtue and Fame together. Dekker was the first to make the association in the Lord Mayor's Show presented in the very year Peacham's book was printed—1612. Dekker describes Virtue much more elaborately than Peacham had pictured her; for Dekker, Virtue wears a diadem of stars, "her roabes are rich, her mantle white (figuring *Innocency*) and powdred with starres of gold, as an *Embleme* that she puts vpon *Men,* the garments of eternity" (III, 235). Virtue successfully brings the mayor past Envy and the Forlorn Castle, and having done this, "the next and highest honour shee can bring him to, is to make him ariue at the house of *Fame* . . ." (p. 240). Dekker says of Fame that she is "crowned in rich attire, a Trumpet in her hand, &c." Perhaps he does not feel it necessary to add further description. Fame delivers a long speech instructing the mayor to follow Virtue, thus fulfilling the function of the verses in the typical emblem. In quite similar fashion Fame is one of the chief residents in the Tower of Virtue in Middleton's 1621 Lord Mayor's Show, *The Sun in Aries.* Fame addresses the mayor and explains the meaning of the tower.

More frequently, Fame appeared by herself in the pageants. For example, at the arch at Soper-lane King James could see as one of the main representations the figure of Fame whom Dekker describes as a "Woman in a Watchet Roabe, thickly set with open Eyes, and Tongues, a payre of large golden Winges at her backe, a Trumpet in her hand . . ." (II, 276). Munday uses as one device in his 1618 Lord Mayor's Show the Mount of Fame where she occupies the most eminent place, "seeming as

Est hac almus honor.
Thomas Chalonerus.

HEERE Virtue ſtandes, and doth impart a ſcroule,
   To living fame, to publiſh farre and neere :
The man whoſe name, ſhe did within enroule,
And kept to view, vnſeene this many yeare,
   That erſt me thought, ſhe ſeemed to envie,
   The world his worth, his fame, and memorie.

But ſince ſhe ſees, the Muſe is left forlorne,
And fortune fawning, on the worthles wight,
And eke her ſelfe, not cheriſht as beſorne.
She bringes Mœcenas once againe to light:
   The man (if any elſe) a frend to Artes,
   And good rewarder, of all beſt deſertes.

FIGURE 7. Virtue and Fame. From Henry Peacham, *Minerva Brittanna* (London, 1612). Reproduced by courtesy of the Folger Shakespeare Library, Washington, D.C.

if shee sounded her Golden Trumpet, the Banner whereof, is plentifully powdred with Tongues, Eyes and Eares: implying, that all tongues should be silent, all eyes and eares wide open, when *Fame* filleth the world with her sacred memories" (sig. B4). Fame assists in pointing the way to good government for the new magistrate. John Taylor presents Fame in the 1634 Lord Mayor's entertainment, this time with a silver trumpet. Here at her monument Fame sounds forth the praises of former Lord Mayors, "and inforceth *Time* to revive their noble Memory, encouraging his Lordship to follow them in all their Honourable actions . . ." (sig. B3). Fame teaches partly through citing notable people of the past; in a sense this fits the "historical" category which Whitney suggested in analyzing the emblems.

Peacham includes an emblem celebrating the virtue of Zeal, especially religious zeal. Though there are two or three pageants in which Zeal appears, I find no fundamental correspondence in the portrayal of the quality.[18] Furthermore, I believe the above examples are sufficient to demonstrate the essential similarity between the treatment of certain allegorical figures in the still life of the emblem book and the dramatic animation of the civic pageants. We have explored, as it were, the "moral" emblem as Whitney conceived it and have seen its parallel expression in pageantry.

Even as there are many mythological personages represented in emblem books, so are they plentiful in civic pageantry. As noted above, Whitney does not have a category for these figures, unless he means to include them in the "historical" section. I will be presumptuous enough to do that. In the first few pages of his book Whitney depicts Ulysses tied to the mast in a boat (see Figure 8); he is being enticed with the music of the sirens—

18. Much the same could be said of the figure of Learning. She is portrayed by Peacham in an emblem on p. 26 in which she is seated with an open book on her lap, her arms outstretched, bearing in one hand a scepter, at the top of which is a sunburst; a gentle rain from heaven falls upon her. Peacham interprets the picture:

> Her out spread Armes, and booke her readines,
> T' imbrace all men, and entertaine their loue:
> The shower, those sacred graces doth expresse
> By Science, that do flow from heauen aboue.
> Her age declares the studie, and the paine;
> Of many yeares, ere we our knowledge gaine.

Though Learning makes an appearance in several civic pageants, she is never treated fully. Dekker in the 1628 show groups her with other allegorical personages and merely notes that she carries a book.

WITHE pleafaunte tunes, the SYRENES did allure
Vliffes wife, to liften theire fonge:
But nothinge could his manlie harte procure,
Hee failde awaie, and fcap'd their charming ftronge,
    The face, he lik'de: the nether parte, did loathe:
    For womans fhape, and fifhes had they bothe.

Which fhewes to vs, when Bewtie feekes to fnare
The careleffe man, whoe dothe no daunger dreede,
That he fhoulde flie, and fhoulde in time beware,
And not on lookes, his fickle fancie feede:
    Suche Mairemaides liue, that promife onelie ioyes:
    But hee that yeldes, at lengthe him felffe diftroies.

    Hæc Venus ad mufes: Venerem exhorrefcite Nimphæ,
      In vos armatus aut amor infiliet.
    Cui contrà mufæ, verba hæc age dicito marti:
      Aliger huc ad nos non volat ille puer.

FIGURE 8. Ulysses. From Geoffrey Whitney, *A Choice of Emblemes*
(Leyden, 1586). Reproduced by courtesy of the Folger Shakespeare
Library, Washington, D.C.

"WITHE pleasaunte tunes, the SYRENES did allure / Vlisses wise, to listen theire songe . . ." (p. 10). Whitney makes clear the moral meaning of this incident from mythology:

> Which shewes to vs, when Bewtie seekes to snare
> The carelesse man, whoe dothe no daunger dreede,
> That he shoulde flie, and should in time beware,
> And not on lookes, his fickle fancie feede:
> Suche Mairemaides liue, that promise onelie ioyes:
> But hee that yeldes, at lengthe him selffe distroies.

In Heywood's 1631 Lord Mayor's Show we encounter a strikingly parallel presentation. As the new mayor made his voyage on the Thames to Westminster, he was entertained on the river with a scene depicting the dangers of any voyage; there were broken vessels scattered about, and the dangers of Scylla and Charybdis were present as well. In addition, "Vpon these Rocks are placed the *Syrens,* excellent both in voyce and Instrument . . . The morrall intended by the Poets, that whosoever shall lend an attentive eare to their musicke, is in great danger to perish; but he that can warily avoyd it by stopping his eares against their inchantment, shall not onely secure themselves, but bee their ruine . . ." (sig. B1). Ulysses is present and addresses the mayor, interpreting the pageant scene in true emblematic fashion. He warns the mayor of all the dangers and especially of the sirens:

> But though their tones be sweete, and shrill their notes,
> They come from foule brests, and inpostum'd throats,
> Sea monsters they be stiled, but much (nay more,
> 'Tis to be doubted,) they frequent the shoare.
>   Yet like *Vlisses,* doe but stop your eare
> To their inchantments, with an heart sincere;
> They fayling to indanger your estate,
> Will from the rocks themselves precipitate.

(sig. B2)

Thus Ulysses, in whom Heywood personates "a wise and discreete Magistrate," has made his own experience relevant to the current mayor; the message is not greatly different from Whitney's.

Peacham has an emblem which shows Ulysses in the company of Pallas (Minerva), who is dressed in a warrior's garb and is leading Ulysses by the hand, "That he aright, might in his Iourney treade, / And shunne the traine of Error, everywhere . . ." (p. 69). The subject of Pallas, the traditional embodiment of Wisdom, must somehow have fascinated Peacham, for he has no less than four emblems which include her. In one the forces of Mars and Pallas are balanced on a set of scales held in a hand extended from the sky; here Pallas, symbolized by the bay and a golden pen, outweighs the cannon, symbol of Mars; and Peacham concludes: "Yet wiser PALLAS guides his [Mars's] arme aright, / And best at home preventes all future harmes . . ." (p. 44). Yet another emblem shows the birth of Pallas, springing from the forehead of Jove. In the fourth, Pallas is shown trapped in a net by Money and Dissimulation, and the emblematist draws a fitting moral. One of Whitney's emblems shows the Judgment of Paris which, of course, involves Pallas. Indeed Whitney goes so far as to disagree with Paris' decision and concludes: "But yet the wise this iudgement rashe deride, / And sentence giue on prudent PALLAS side" (p. 83).

In Dekker's 1628 Lord Mayor's Show, *Brittannia's Honor,* Pallas joins other figures around the Tree of Honor. Dekker calls her "Inuentresse and Patronesse of Artes, Handy-crafts, and Trades"; she has "Ornaments proper to her quality . . ." (IV, 86). Located near her is Bellona, "goddesse of Warre, in a Martiall habit. . . ." Dekker joins these two much as Peacham had done in one of his emblems, though Dekker's interpretation is somewhat different: "both *Artes* and *Armes,* are (in a high degree and fulnesse of honor), nurc'd vp and maintain'd by and in the City." A speech by London at this tree indicates the necessity of making room for both Pallas and Bellona. Heywood in 1635 brings together Juno, Pallas, and Venus as Whitney had done in his emblem. For Heywood, Pallas represents *Armes* and *Artes,* and she has with her some owls, a detail not used by the two emblem writers. Venus in a speech explains the meaning:

> . . . you must watch even as they wake:
> For all such as the management of state
> Shall undergoe, rise earlie, and bed late,
> So Wisedome is begot; from Wisedome Love. . . .[19]

Pageant and emblem writers agree with the common interpretation that Pallas, as a representative of wisdom, serves as a useful guide to all who govern.[20]

19. Thomas Heywood, *Londini Sinus Salutis* in *The Dramatic Works of Thomas Heywood* (London, 1874), IV, 289.

20. Venus and Cupid are favorite subjects of both embelmatists. Whitney has

Mercury is portrayed in two emblems by Whitney. In the first he is sitting by a roadside, wearing a winged helmet and carrying a caduceus. His function is to point the way to the traveling man; and having been shown the way by Mercury, man "neuer went awrie, / But to his wishe, his iorneys ende did gaine / In happie howre, by his direction plaine" (p. 2). Whitney likens this guidance to God's providence. Mercury is similarly costumed in the second emblem that Whitney devoted to him, in which he is busy stringing a lute, "Which being tun'de, such Harmonie did lende, / That Poettes write, the trees theire toppes did bende" (p. 92).

When Elizabeth made her progress to Norwich in 1578, she was greeted by a figure personating Mercury in the traditional costume. Similarly, Charles I in his coronation passage through Edinburgh in 1633 encountered Mercury. And in the Lord Mayor's Shows of 1612, 1633, and 1634, Mercury made an appearance, each time dressed appropriately. Heywood in 1633 calls Mercury the "Patrone of all Trade," and in such a role he addresses the mayor. For John Taylor in the entertainment of 1634, Mercury has "his Caduceus or charming rod in his hand, with wings on his head to signifie quickness of Invention, Acutenesse of wit, and Volubility of tongue with Eloquence of speech. He hath also wings on his feet to signifie his swiftnesse; as Messenger to the Gods" (sig. A6ᵛ). Time, who accompanies Mercury, speaks of Mercury's function: he

> Hath brought the Poet wit, and Eloquence;
> And quick Invention, likewise he Inflam'd
> Into the Artists that these pageants fram'd,
> That for your future Honour, this may be
> A day of well Compos'd Variety. . . .

(sig. A7)

---

three emblems which depict either Venus and Cupid together or Cupid alone (pp. 63, 147, 148); Peacham includes two emblems of Cupid (pp. 73, 195) both of which celebrate the power of Venus' child (he is at one point likened to Hercules in strength). In each picture Cupid is presented in the garb traditionally associated with him. Though one or both of the figures appear in several of the civic entertainments, they seldom have significant roles in the pageants. Cupid, for example, accompanies Venus in Heywood's 1635 Lord Mayor's Show; Heywood says that they represent Love. Dekker presents Cupid in his usual array in the 1629 show—he has curled yellow hair, carries a bow and quiver, and has wings at his back. But these figures are present almost incidentally.

One cannot get more immediate than to have Mercury inspire the very poet devising the pageant. Thus the guidance of which Whitney had written may take different manifestations, but Mercury inspires whether he guides the traveler or coaxes harmony out of nature or assists the pageant poet.

In one emblem Whitney portrays Apollo dressed in a robe and holding a lute in his right hand, in the company of Bacchus (p. 146). Whitney views them as two necessary forces in life; he does not place one above the other. In yet another emblem Apollo is shown playing on the lute, and Whitney's four brief lines explain the scene:

> Presvmptvovs PAN, did striue APOLLOS skill to passe:
> But MIDAS gaue the palme to PAN: wherefore the eares of asse
> APOLLO gaue the Iudge: which doth all Iudges teache;
> To iudge with knowledge, and aduise, in matters paste their reache?
>
> (p. 218)

Here Whitney makes the traditional association of Apollo with music and harmony.

Among the various entertainments presented to honor the newly married Prince Frederick, Count Palatine, and Princess Elizabeth, daughter of James I, was the procession in the tiltyard at Heidelberg in mid-June 1613. Interestingly, Apollo and Bacchus came into the tiltyard together as Whitney had earlier arranged them. Midas also appeared, "sitting on an *Asse,* hee himselfe hauing *Asses* eares for comparing *Pan,* to *Apollo:* and next him, miserable *Marsyas,* and a *Saytire,* fleaing of his skin, because he durst cõtend with *Apollo,* in musicke." [21] There are no verses to explain the pageant-emblem, but perhaps none were needed. John Squire in the Lord Mayor's Show of 1620, *The Triumphs of Peace,* presents Apollo with the Muses on Mount Parnassus. They also appear this way in the coronation procession for Charles I in Edinburgh. The pamphlet writer observes: "*Apollo* sitting in the midst of them was clad in Crimson taffeta, covered with some purle of gold, . . . his head was crowned with Laurell, with locks long and like gold; hee presented the King with a booke." [22] With a slight alteration Dekker presented Apollo with the Seven Liberal

21. John Stow, *The Annales, or General Chronicle of England* (London, 1615), p. 922.

22. *The Entertainment of the High and Mighty Monarch Charles . . . Into his auncient and royall City of Edinbvrgh* (Edinburgh, 1633), p. 15.

NO mortall foe. fo full of poyſoned ſpite,
  As man, to man, when miſchiefe he pretendes:.
The monſters huge, as diuers aucthors write,
Yea Lions wilde, and fiſhes weare his frendes:
  And when their deathe, by frendes ſuppoſʹd was ſought,
  They kindneſſe ſhewʹd, and them from daunger brought..

ARION lo, who gained ſtore of goulde,
In countries farre: with harpe, and pleaſant voice:
Did ſhipping take, and to CORINTHVS woulde,
And to his wiſhe, of pilottes made his choiſe:
  Who robʹd the man, and threwe him to the ſea,
  A Dolphin, lo, did beare him ſafe awaie.

  Quis neſcit vaſtas olim delphina per vndas,
    Leſbida cum ſacro vate tuliſſe lyram?

FIGURE 9. Arion. From Geoffrey Whitney, *A Choice of Emblemes* (Leyden,
1586). Reproduced by courtesy of the Folger Shakespeare Library, Washington, D.C.

Sciences in *London's Tempe* (1629). Apollo, "on his head a garland of bayes" and in "his hand a Lute," occupied the chief position (IV, 111) and advised the new mayor: "Go on in your full glories: whilst *Apollo,* and these Mistresses of the Learned Sciences, waft you to that Honourable shore, whither Time bids you hasten to arriue" (IV, 112). As is frequently the case in the civic pageants, the mythological figure here offers support and moral guidance.

Another figure associated with music is Arion, who was miraculously saved by a dolphin when some sailors threw him overboard. Whitney recounts the story in picture and verse, and he is especially distressed at man's inhumanity to man as epitomized in the Arion incident. The picture shows a turbulent sea, the sailors throwing Arion into the water, and a dolphin coming to his rescue (see Figure 9). The seamen "rob'd the man, and threwe him to the sea, / A Dolphin, lo, did beare him safe awaie" (p. 144). It is, of course, Arion's beautiful music that attracts the dolphin to him.

Arion came floating forth on a mechanical dolphin and sang to Elizabeth as part of the entertainment provided for her during the prolonged stay at Kenilworth Castle in 1575. In honor of the new mayor and especially the Fishmongers' Company, Munday presented Arion, "a famous Musicion and Poet," riding on a dolphin's back, "being saued so from death, when Robbers and Pirates on the Seas, would maliciously haue drowned him" (sig. B1ʳ), in the Lord Mayor's pageant of 1616. A speech later in the day explains the emblematic significance of Arion. The most extensive treatment came in Heywood's civic entertainment for 1632, *Londini Artium & Scientiarum Scaturigo* in which he recounts the traditional story. Arion, "with his Harpe in his hand, riding vpon the backe of a Dolphin," greets the mayor in a pageant on the Thames.[23] He also gives the concluding speech of the day where he fulfills the function of the verses of an emblem by explaining the allegorical significance of all that the mayor has seen. He closes: ". . . you are the Spring and Fountaine made / To water euery Science, Art, and Trade; / Obseruing those, your Honour shall shine bright . . ." (sig. C2). The didactic function of the civic pageant, like that of an emblem, is thus fulfilled.[24]

23. Thomas Heywood, *Londini Artium & Scientiarum Scaturigo* (London, 1632), sig. A4ᵛ.

24. The figure Hercules appeared in two or three entertainments in which Arion

The music of Orpheus has a soothing power in nature, and it is in this traditional role that Whitney depicts him (see Figure 10). Orpheus is the dominant figure in a circular arrangement; he is seated and carries his harp and is surrounded by all sorts of animals. Perhaps Whitney has chosen the circular pattern to underscore the sense of harmony which Orpheus conveys. Besides being able to calm the savage kind of the animal world, Orpheus

> . . . could with sweetenes of his tonge, all sortes of men suffice.
> And those that weare most rude, and knewe no good at all:
> And weare of fierce, and cruell mindes, the worlde did brutishe call.
> Yet with persuasions sounde, hee made their hartes relente,
> That meeke, and milde they did become, and followed where he wente.
>
> (p. 186)

Whitney suggests that man can be like Orpheus if he but seeks to be harmonious.

The view of the pageant writers toward Orpheus parallels that of Whitney. Orpheus addresses the new mayor in Middleton's Lord Mayor's Show of 1619, *The Triumphs of Love and Antiquity*. He explains the device stationed in Paul's Churchyard and says of the beasts represented there in a thicket:

> . . . by fair example, musical grace,
> Harmonious government of the man in place,
> Of fair integrity and wisdom fram'd,
> They stand as mine do, ravish'd, charm'd, and tam'd:
> Every wise magistrate that governs thus,
> May well be call'd a powerful Orpheus.
>
> (VII, 320)

---

had also been used. Whitney has two emblems devoted to portraying Hercules (pp. 16, 40). In both, Hercules is shown with his traditional club. In the emblem on p. 40 Hercules is involved with making a choice between virtue and vice, and of course he chooses virtue. Peacham also presents Hercules in an emblem (p. 36). Hercules carries his club in one hand and three golden apples in the other. Peacham says of him—"The Lions skinne, about his shoulders stretcht, / Notes fortitude, his Clubbe the crabbed paine, / To braue atcheiuements, ere we can attaine." Though Hercules has this relative popularity in these two emblem books, he is never a principal character in the pageants. He does greet Queen Elizabeth upon her arrival at Kenilworth Castle in 1575, is submissive to her, and surrenders his club and keys to the sovereign. But the other references to Hercules—the tiltyard entertainment at Heidelberg in 1613, the Lord Mayor's Shows of 1615, 1621, and 1623—mention only his presence; he does not speak.

·186   *Orphei Musica.*
           Ad eundem.

L O, O R P H E V S with his harpe, that fauage kinde did tame:
    The Lions fierce,and Leopardes wilde,and birdes about him came.
For, with his muficke fweete, their natures hee fubdu'de:
But if wee thinke his playe fo wroughte, our felues wee doe delude.
For why? befides his fkill, hee learned was, and wife:
And coulde with fweetenes of his tonge, all fortes of men fuffice.
And thofe that weare moft rude, and knewe no good at all:
And weare of fierce, and cruell mindes, the worlde did brutifhe call.
Yet with perfuafions founde, hee made their hartes relente,
That meeke,and milde they did become, and followed where he wente.
Lo thefe, the Lions fierce, thefe,Beares, and Tigers weare:
The trees, and rockes, that lefte their roomes, his muficke for to heare.
But, you are happie moft, who in fuche place doe ftaye: [playe.
You neede not T H R A C I A feeke, to heare fome impe of O R P H E V S
Since, that fo neare your home , Apollos darlinge dwelles;
Who L I N V S,& A M P H I O N ftaynes, and O R P H E V S farre excelles.
For, hartes like marble harde, his harmonie dothe pierce:
And makes them yeelding paffions feele, that are by nature fierce.
But, if his muficke faile: his curtefie is fuche,
That none fo rude, and bafe of minde,but hee reclaimes them muche.
Nowe fince you, by deferte, for both, commended are:
I choofe you, for a Iudge herein, if truthe I doe declare.
And if you finde I doe, then ofte therefore reioyce:
And thinke,I woulde fuche neighbour haue,if I might make my choice.

FIGURE 10. Orpheus. From Geoffrey Whitney, *A Choice of Emblemes* (Leyden, 1586). Reproduced by courtesy of the Folger Shakespeare Library, Washington, D.C.

Anyone who can govern discordant elements is entitled to the name
Orpheus; Whitney had implied much the same thing. Heywood's treatment of Orpheus in the 1639 Lord Mayor's entertainment, *Londini Status
Pacatus,* is virtually a reissue of Whitney's emblem. Orpheus with his
harp is "seated in a faire Plat-forme, beautified with pleasant Trees, upon
which are pearcht severall Birds, and below Beasts of all sorts," all of
whom are attentive to Orpheus' music.[25] He addresses the mayor in words
strongly reminiscent of Middleton's:

> You are that *Orpheus* who can do all these:
> If any streame beyond its bounds shall swell,
> You beare the *Trident* that such rage can quell.
> When beasts of Rapine (trusting to their power)
> Would any of your harmelesse flocks devoure:
> Yours is the sword that can such violence stay. . . .
>
>   (V, 367)

It is a didactic imperative which Whitney, Middleton, and Heywood
enunciate: appropriate the qualities of Orpheus and be a wise man, a
harmonious ruler.

As a means of separating the two parts of his book, Whitney introduces
an emblem of Janus, depicted as a warrior with the customary two faces
looking in opposite directions. In one hand he holds what may be a
scepter or a key and in the other an object which seems to be a mirror
(it is difficult to tell from the drawing). Whitney suggests that Janus
bids us review the past year in order to make amends for the coming year.
Whitney says further:

> This Image had his rites, and temple faire,
> And call'd the GOD of warre, and peace, bicause
> In warres, hee warn'de of peace not to dispaire:
> And warn'de in peace, to practise martiall lawes:
>   And furthermore, his lookes did teache this somme;
>   To beare in minde, time past, and time to comme.
>
>   (p. 108)

In the coronation entertainment for King James in 1604 a device called the
Temple of Janus was situated at Temple Bar. It is interesting to note that
Peace is the principal figure at the temple; and beneath her feet lies Mars.

25. *Dramatic Works of Thomas Heywood,* V, 365.

Though the device is dedicated to Janus, he apparently is not depicted as an actual figure. But in Heywood's show of 1639, Janus is present in traditional emblematic garb. At the first pageant on land Janus is the chief figure and is accompanied by persons representing the four seasons. Heywood, in the pamphlet, briefly traces the history and the meaning of Janus:

He holdeth in his hand a golden Key to shut up the yeare past, as never more to come; and open to the yeare future: it may also be an Embleme of noble policy to unbosome and bring to light their trecherous devises and stratagems, who seeke to undermine and supplant the prosperity of a faire & flourishing Common-weale.[26]

Janus addresses the mayor, resigns the seasons to his charge, and bids him to "spend the *Houres* to inrich future story, / Both for your owne grace and the Cities glory" because "none knowes better than your selfe (Grave Lord) / What *Mercy* is: or when to use the Sword" (V, 365). For Whitney and Heywood Janus is a symbolic reminder of the need for an attitude of watchfulness both in private lives and in the body politic.

In an emblem which truly belongs in the "historical" category Whitney celebrates the glories of Sir Francis Drake (see Figure 11). This, incidentally, is an emblem which we know to be of Whitney's own devising. In the picture a hand reaching down from a cloud holds a rope which is attached to a boat perched atop a globe. The motto is: *Auxilio diuino* (p. 203). Whitney begins the verses by speaking of the accomplishments of Jason, "Who throughe the watchfull dragons pass'd, to win the fleece of goulde." He did this *"By help of power deuine."* Then Whitney likens Drake to Jason.

> But, hee, of whome I write, this noble minded DRAKE,
> Did bringe away his goulden fleece, when thousand eies did wake.
> . . . .
> Geue praise to them, that passe the waues, to doe their countrie good.
> Before which sorte, as chiefe: in tempeste, and in calme,
> Sir FRANCIS DRAKE, by due deserte, may weare the goulden palme.

It is small wonder that Whitney writing in 1586 should speak with such adulation of Drake; the comparison to Jason is a natural one.

26. *Ibid.,* p. 364.

To RICHARD DRAKE *Esquier, in praise of*
Sir FRANCIS DRAKE *Knight.*

Throvghe ſcorchinge heate, throughe coulde, in ſtormes, and
    tempeſts-force,
By ragged rocks, by ſhelſes,& ſandes: this Knighte did keepe his courſe.
By gapinge gulſes hee paſſ'd, by monſters of the flood,
By pirattes, theeues, and cruell foes, that long'd to ſpill his blood.
That wonder greate to ſcape: but, GOD was on his ſide,
And throughe them all, in ſpite of all, his ſhaken ſhippe did guide.
And, to requite his paines: *By helpe of power deuine.*
His happe, at lengthe did aunſwere hope, to finde the goulden mine.
Let GRÆCIA then forbeare, to praiſe her IASON boulde?
Who throughe the watchfull dragons paſſ'd, to win the fleece of goulde.
Since by MEDEAS helpe, they weare inchaunted all,
And IASON without perrilles, paſſ'de: the conqueſte therfore ſmall?
But, hee, of whome I write, this noble minded DRAKE,
Did bringe away his goulden fleece, when thouſand eies did wake.
Wherefore, yee woorthie wightes, that ſeeke for forreine landes:
Yf that you can, come alwaiſe home, by GANGES goulden ſandes.
And you, that liue at home, and can not brooke the flood,
Geue praiſe to them, that paſſe the waues, to doe their countrie good.
Before which ſorte, as chiefe: in tempeſte, and in calme,
Sir FRANCIS DRAKE, by due deſerte, may weare the goulden palme.

FIGURE 11. Sir Francis Drake. From Geoffrey Whitney, *A Choice of
Emblemes* (Leyden, 1586). Reproduced by courtesy of the Folger Shakespeare Library, Washington, D.C.

Drake appears as a figure only once in the civic pageantry of the period, in Webster's 1624 Lord Mayor's Show where he sat with six other famous navigators on a globe. But he was alluded to several times, all reminiscent, at least to me, of Whitney's emblem. In both 1621 and 1623, Middleton presents some sort of pageant which includes a list of famous members of the Drapers' Company, and the list indicates why these men are remembered. Of Drake, Middleton says in 1621—"the son of Fame, who in two years and ten months, did cast a girdle about the world . . ." (VII, 342). He repeats the idea in 1623. The 1626 Lord Mayor's pageant, again by Middleton, makes the comparison of Drake and Jason. One of the devices in the entertainment is the "Sanctuary of Prosperity" on

the top arch of which hangs the Golden Fleece; which raises the worthy memory of that most famous and renowned brother of this company, Sir Francis Drake, who in two years and ten months did encompass the whole world, deserving an eminent remembrance in this sanctuary, who never returned to his country without the golden fleece of honour and victory. . . .

(VII, 406)

A speech delivered in the "Sanctuary" makes the association clear:

> If Jason, with the noble hopes of Greece,
> Who did from Colchis fetcht the golden fleece,
> Deserve a story of immortal fame, . . .
> What honour, celebration, and renown,
> In virtue's right, ought justly to be shown
> To the fair memory of Sir Francis Drake,
> England's true Jason. . . .

(VII, 406)

The speech concludes by likening the mayor's year in office to a perilous voyage on the sea. He is, by implication, to draw instruction from the noble example of Drake. I would not want to press the case of Middleton's debt to Whitney, but it is at least remotely possible. In any event, emblematist and pageant writer are dwelling on common ground.

While Whitney could celebrate Drake, Peacham chose another "son of Fame"—Prince Henry, elder son of King James. In fact, his emblem book is dedicated to the Prince, and one of the first emblems shows the Prince suited out in his armor complete with lance astride a charger. The adulatory verses conclude with suggesting that "thy Trophees may be more, / Then all the HENRIES euer liu'd before" (p. 17). It is something of the ultimate of compliments to speculate that the Prince might be greater than all the previous Henries of English history when one recalls how revered were such men as Henry V and Henry VII.

In Dekker's Lord Mayor's Show of 1612 Henry was securely ensconced in a device called the House of Fame to which the new mayor was led by Virtue. A special place was reserved for the Prince because some five years earlier he had accepted the freedom of the Merchant Taylors who were responsible for this particular pageant. But more than that, the gesture was essentially one of praise for the eighteen-year-old Henry who was already carving out his niche in the House of Fame. Though he had planned to attend the show, Henry was unable to come because of illness, and within a week of the pageant he was dead. The most fulsome treatment of Prince Henry in a civic pageant comes twelve years after his death in John Webster's Lord Mayor's Show for that year, *Monuments of Honor* (1624). In the final device of the entertainment, the Monument of Gratitude, Prince Henry stands on a pedestal of gold surrounded by allegorical figures, each representing some aspect of his character—Liberality, Unanimity, Industry, Justice, Peace, Obedience. These personified figures with their symbolic properties all demonstrating Henry's several virtues constitute a grand compliment to the dead Prince. Should the meaning not be clear, Webster has a figure named Amade le Graunde deliver a closing speech in which Henry's virtues are reviewed (this, of course, fulfills the function of the verses of the typical emblem). The speaker takes special note that the Prince leaves "a most Cleere and Eminent Fame behind." [27] It is obvious that the lessons and examples of history are echoed in emblem and pageant alike.

Much earlier in this paper I referred to Munday's use of the pelican in the 1616 Lord Mayor's Show, and I suggested that this constituted a "natural" emblem. This is further supported by Whitney's use of precisely such an emblem. He shows the bird with her young and writes verses which elucidate the symbolic meaning:

> The Pellican, for to reuiue her younge,
> Doth peirce her brest, and geue them of her blood:

27. *The Complete Works of John Webster,* ed. F. L. Lucas (London, 1927), III, 327.

> Then searche your breste, and as yow haue with tonge,
> With penne proceede to doe our countrie good:
>   Your Zeale is great, your learning is profounde,
>   Then helpe our wantes, with that you doe abounde.
>
>   (p. 87)

These words would be most appropriate to a new mayor. And Munday certainly captured their spirit in his likening of the mayor to the pelican.

Another natural emblem which Whitney uses is the picture of a thorny thicket in which a lily struggles to survive. Whitney clearly views this as the age-old struggle between vice and virtue: "The wicked sorte to wounde the good, are glad: / And vices thrust at vertue, all their stinges . . ." (p. 221). But hope is expressed in the presence of the lily which is able to bloom despite the adverse circumstances. Whitney is persuaded that the good will be preserved. Middleton in the 1619 show presents a similar thicket and has the figure of Orpheus explain the meaning to the mayor:

> The rude and thorny ways thy care must clear;
> Such are the vices in a city sprung,
> As are yon thickets that grow close and strong; . . .
> Just such a wilderness is a commonwealth
> That is undrest, unprun'd, wild in her health. . . .
>
>   (VII, 319–320)

It is incumbent upon the mayor to clear out the vices and let the virtues of the city blossom forth. This garden metaphor is, of course, one of Shakespeare's favorite ways of speaking of the commonwealth.

Did the pageant dramatists draw some of their inspiration from the emblem books? I do not know for certain; I am convinced that they could have. I know of no telling argument against the possibility. The emblematists could also have been influenced by the pageant writers. I think I have established that the method of the emblem and the pageant is fundamentally the same and that in many instances there are specific parallels between the presentation of certain figures and ideas in both emblem and pageant. Both artistic forms are of course drawing upon a rich common inheritance, and they assist in transmitting this iconographical tradition to us.

One can in fantasy imagine that the inveterate pageant-goer, who also happened to be educated, took his place on a street corner in London regularly each 29th of October to see the Lord Mayor's Show and perhaps carried with him his well-thumbed copy of Whitney's *Choice of Emblemes*. I like to think of it that way.[28]

28. I am greatly indebted to the Folger Shakespeare Library for a summer fellowship which provided the opportunity and the materials for much of the research for this paper.

Form and Themes in Henri II's Entry into Rouen

MARGARET M. McGOWAN

ENAISSANCE ROYAL ENTRIES have a twofold significance. As products of
a particular view of kingship they are embedded in the political realities of their time, on the one hand reflecting the achievements of
princes and on the other setting forth the hopes and expectations of the
people. Moreover, their complex form required the services of architects,
painters, sculptors, poets, and engineers, who worked together introducing
ingenuity and variety into each new entry they tackled. Henri II's entry
into Rouen in 1550 provides a good example of the range of talent needed
when the civic authorities decided to combine local artistic traditions with
the re-enactment of a Roman triumph. The study of this entry illustrates
how the revival of an ancient ceremonial corresponded exactly to the
political situation in which Henri II found himself at the beginning of his
reign. It further demonstrates how artistic elements, the personal taste of
the King, and the political and religious wishes of his people constantly
interplayed to produce a form of art whose size and complexity made this
royal entry one of the most important of all sixteenth-century public
spectacles.

"Le dernier iour de Mars, presage certes memorable,"[1] Henri II suc-

1. From the prose account of Henri II's entry into Rouen, Q,iii^v. There are three
main sources for this entry: 1) *C'est la Deduction du sumptueux ordre plaisantz*

199

ceeded to the throne of France. The significance seen in the date of Henri's accession is explained by the close parallel which exists between the traditional martial temperament of the month of March ("Mars— dieu des batailles") and that of the new King. Observers at the French court had often remarked upon his warlike abilities, "on le croirait *tout fait de muscles*," Matteo Dandolo, the Venetian ambassador, had declared in 1542.[2] He was of the same opinion five years later when he set down, at some length, Henri's addiction to sports, which made great physical demands, and his indefatigable attention to exercise with arms:

tout plein de valeur, très-courageux et entreprenant; il recherche le jeu de paume au point de n'y jamais manquer un jour, à moins de pluie, car il joue à ciel ouvert, et quelquefois même après avoir couru à tout train un ou deux cerfs, exercice des plus fatigants, comme le savent Vos Excellences. Le même jour, après avoir accompli de telles manoeuvres, il fera des jeux d'armes durant deux ou trois heures, et il y est des plus fameux.[3]

---

spectacles et magnifiques theatres dresses, et exhibes par les citoiens de Rouen ville Metropolitaine du pays de Normandie, A la sacree Maiesté du Tres Christian Roy de France, Henry second, leur soverain Seigneur, Et à Tres illustre dame, ma Dame Katharine de Medicis ... Rouen chez Robert le Hoy, Robert et Iehan dictz du Gord ... 1551. This account, which will be referred to throughout as *"La Deduction,"* is the most complete of the three sources. 2) Robert Masselin, *L'Entrée du Roy nostre sire faicte en sa ville de Rouen* (Paris, 1550); referred to throughout as "Masselin." This account gives a summary of the shows and differs in many places from *La Deduction;* its detail accords more readily with 3) *L'Entrée du tres Magnanime tres Puissant et victorieux Roy de France Henry deuxisme de ce nom en sa noble cité de Rouen ... en rithme francoyse.* MS at Bibliothèque Municipale, Rouen, Press mark M⁸ Y28 (1268), referred to throughout as *"L'Entrée."* About two-thirds of the verses contained in this manuscript were printed in Jean Dugort, *Les Poutres et figures du sumptueux ordre plaisantz spectacles, et magnifiques theatres, dressés et exhibés par les citoiens de Rouen* ... (Paris, 1557), along with the original engravings from *La Deduction.* S. de Merval published a useful anno- tated edition of the poetry version for the Société des Bibliophiles Normands (Rouen, 1868). Many literary historians have referred to Henri II's entry. Twice, attempts have been made to discuss it in detail. A. Pottier's account in the *Revue de Rouen* (1835), pp. 29-43, 86-108, is virtually useless. J. Chartrou's analysis in *Les Entrées solennelles et triomphantes à la Renaissance* (Paris, 1928) is illuminating and suggested some ideas for this article.

2. Armand Baschet, *La Diplomatie vénetienne* (Paris, 1862), p. 430; hereafter cited as "Baschet."

3. *Ibid.,* p. 433.

Dandolo's successors, Marino Cavalli and Lorenzo Contarini, add further details to this bellicose picture, stressing Henri's prowess as jouster, wrestler, archer, tennis player, and horseman—at all these sports, he was acknowledged to be unbeatable.[4]

With such a robust temperament, it is hardly surprising that Henri began his reign with a tremendous burst of activity. As soon as his father's funeral had been ceremoniously disposed of, Henri prepared himself for his coronation (April 1547), greeting that event with great seriousness and fervor.[5] Already he had shown himself worthy of the title "Fils aîné de l'Eglise," supporting the Catholic faith against the intrusions of the heretics by banning the import of books from Germany.[6] Directly after his coronation, he confirmed the nomination of Mathieu Orry as inquisitor [7] and listened with approval to deputies from Paris who sought authority to hunt for those suspected of heresy and to condemn those found guilty. Henri graciously granted their demands, signing an edict which brought into being the infamous Chambre Ardente which was to meet eighty-four times within the space of a year and condemn 176 people. The King's attention was soon drawn to requests for aid from the Dowager French Queen of Scotland, whose authority was under direct attack with the success of Somerset's troops (Pinkie Cleugh had fallen to the English in September 1547, and Haddington in April 1548). Henri lost no time; he dispatched at once the Maréchal d'Essé in charge of six thousand troops, sent MM. de Brézé and de Villegaignon to rescue the six-year-old Mary, Queen of Scots, and on her arrival in France betrothed her forthwith to his son François.[8]

4. *Ibid.,* pp. 430 ff. Brantôme confirms these facts in his account of Henri II whom he describes as "tout marcial, et nay tel, il ayma à faire la guerre, et ne s'y espargna non plus que le moindre soldats des siens," *Mémoires,* 12 vols. (Paris, 1864–1896), III, 249; hereafter cited as "Brantôme."

5. Dandolo was particularly impressed by the devotion with which Henri received the crown. He had stated "Que si la couronne qu'il allait prendre promettait un bon gouvernement et assurait le salut de ses peuples, Dieu lui fît la grâce de la lui laisser pour longtemps, qu'autrement il la lui prît bien vite." Baschet, p. 434.

6. Auguste de Thou, *Histoire de France,* 3 vols. (Paris, 1659), I, 159; hereafter cited as "de Thou."

7. Pierre Champion, *Paganisme et réforme* (Paris, 1936), p. 173.

8. A detailed account of the Scottish campaign was written by J. de Beaugué, *Histoire de la guerre d'Ecosse* (Paris, 1556); most historians borrow from this source. Information can also be found in Jean Bouchet, *Annales d'Aquitaine*

Thus, having satisfactorily taken the affairs of the Church and of Scotland in hand, Henri resolved upon a tour of his kingdom, "considérant qu'il n'y ha rien, qui tant meintienne un Peuple en obeissance et fidelité, que la vue de son souverain Prince, et naturel Seigneur." [9] Political convenience was perhaps only partially responsible for this decision. Flickering thoughts of personal prestige might well have passed through Henri's mind as he remembered that the last triumphant march through France had been not by a French king but by the all-conquering Emperor Charles V in 1539–1540, and as he also pondered upon the royal progress Prince Philip, son of that emperor, was at that moment about to enjoy on his way from Spain through parts of Italy to the Low Countries. [10] The French King undoubtedly wished to establish his own authority and was eager for acclaim to be made to him personally. But solid political necessity also guided his plans, and his first concern was to see for himself that the frontiers of his country were safe, insuring that the towns were well-protected and their forts mended or even rebuilt. His next concern was to make a triumphant visit to his states in Italy, where he was joyously received by all his subjects.

While Henri was enjoying acclaim in the Piedmont, his subjects in the South West of France were proving less reverent of royal authority. Their revolt against the financial demands of the salt tax collectors culminated in June 1548 with the murder of M. de Monneins, president of the Bordeaux Parlement. His body was pulled to pieces by the mob and made to endure all kinds of indignities. [11] Henri, in retaliation, briskly

---

(Poictiers, 1557), p. 333 (hereafter cited as "Bouchet"). George Buchanan's account seems very prejudiced—*History of Scotland* (London, 1690), pp. 100 ff. De Thou has the most balanced and reasoned account, based on Beaugué's details and Buchanan's diatribes against the French (I, 167–174, 285–296).

9. G. Paradin, *Histoire de nostre temps* (Lyons, 1558), p. 610; hereafter cited as "Paradin."

10. The parallel is drawn by Brantôme, III, 258: "Lorsque toutes ces belles magnificences se faisoient, et que nostre grand roy alloit ainsy triumphant parmi les entrées des belles villes de son royaume, quasy en mesmes temps, comm'il est aysé à computer, le prince d'Espagne, depuis roy, en faisoit de mesmes en ses belles villes de Flandres."

11. For details on the Bordeaux uprisings, see Bouchet, pp. 329 ff.; Paradin, p. 660; de Thou, pp. 276–277; and Maréchal de Vieilleville, *Mémoires*, 2 vols. (Paris, 1757), I, 437 ff. (hereafter cited as "Vieilleville").

dispatched forces to the area under the command of the redoubtable *connétable,* who speedily, and cruelly, restored order; "il fut executé plus de sept vingt personnes à mort en diverses sortes de supplices, comme de pendus, decapitez, rouez, empellez, desmembrez à 4 chevaux, et bruslez." [12]

While the *connétable* punished the rebels in the West, Henri awaited his triumphant entry into Lyons where his favorite, the Governor of the Lyonnais, the Maréchal de S. André, who excelled in organizing ingenious and erudite shows,[13] and the poet Maurice Scève, were busy with splendid preparations. The King made his entry on 23 September 1548,[14] accompanied by his Queen, Catherine de Médicis, and a host of nobles, prelates, ambassadors, and strangers. The program had been arranged to give pleasure and amusement to the royal couple: gladiators showing their skill at diverse sorts of arms, galleons fighting on the Saône, and water combats of many kinds were especially designed to content the vigorous temperament of Henri II, while magnificent theater spectacles greeted his delighted Italian wife.

The royal progress then continued through France where Henri, "fut vu, et receu, non seulement comme vray Roy, mais aussi comme Pere, et seul restaurateur de la République, et auteur de tranquilité, vindicateur de notre Sainte Foy, et seul espoir d'asseurance publique." [15] Hopes were indeed high for a King who had shown firmness and resolution and whose measures were already bearing fruit. The South West of France was subdued, French arms in Scotland were victorious, the frontiers of the kingdom were safe—with the one exception of the English possession of Boulogne. As Henri made his journey towards Paris in May and June 1549 he planned his attack on this town; tournaments were arranged not only to bring his Paris entry (June 1549) to a magnificent conclusion but

12. Vieilleville, I, 437.

13. De Thou furnishes this detail (I, 285): "tout cela se fit par les ordres du Maréchal de S. André, Gouverneur de la Province, qui estoit ingénieux et sçavant en ces sortes de magnificences."

14. There are two principal accounts of this entry: 1) *La Magnificence de la superbe et triumphante entrée de la noble & antique Cité de Lyon* ... (Lyons, 1549), and 2) *La Magnifica et triumphale entrata* ... (Lyons, 1548), which is more detailed. They, together with details from the municipal archives, were published by Georges Guigue in 1928. V. L. Saulnier has discussed this entry at length in *Maurice Scève* (Paris, 1948), Chap. XV.

15. Paradin, p. 611.

also to prepare French knights for an impending war. Henri could hardly wait, and he curtailed the festivities in his haste to get to Boulogne.[16]

During his stay in Paris, however preoccupied Henri might have been, he could not miss a spectacle of another sort: "il vit en s'en retournant aux Tournelles, le supplice de quelques personnes que l'on brusloit, pour avoir esté convaincus d'adherer à la doctrine de Luther."[17] Inspired by such zealots as Jean Morin and Pierre Lizet, the Chambre Ardente had all too willingly pursued Protestants, turning justice into its opposite, "Son parement estoit d'escarlatte sanglante / Qui goutte sans repos"; the Châtelet in Paris was known as "le palais, le fort / De l'inquisition, le logis de la mort."[18] Ecclesiastical courts were both jealous and appalled at the public scandal of increasing numbers of deaths ordered by the inquisitorial commission of the Parlement of Paris. The King promised to repeal his former edict, putting judgment of the heretics' cause in the hands of ecclesiastical courts.[19] Having acceded to the pressures of his religious advisers, Henri could at last turn his thoughts to military action. With characteristic flourish, he descended on the country surrounding Boulogne, swiftly besieged and overcame the forts encircling the town, and laid siege to the city itself. While he waited for the town to fall, he enjoyed the privilege of having those he had captured process before him,

Les vaincus passans en grand desolacion devant le Roy, de trois en trois, luy faisoient la reverence, luy rendant graces de ce qu'il leur avoit laissé leurs vies

---

16. Edouard de la Barre du Parcq, *Histoire de Henri II* (Paris, 1887), p. 14, wrote: "Henri II avait hâte que tout cela fût fini à cause de l'entreprise qu'il méditait contre Boulogne"; Vieilleville also refers to Henri's speed (II, 64). The official account of the Paris entry, *C'est l'ordre qui a este tenu a la nouvelle et joyeuse entree ...* was published in 1549; V. L. Saulnier has examined the themes of this entry in *Fêtes de la Renaissance* (Paris, 1956), I, 31 ff.

17. De Thou, I, 311.

18. Quoted from Agrippa d'Aubigné's *Les Tragiques,* Bk. III, "La Chambre Dorée." For further details on the Chambre Ardente see V. L. Saulnier, "Pantagruel au large de Ganabin," *BHR,* XVI (1954), 58–81.

19. The complaints of the ecclesiastical courts must have been loud and vigorous, since all contemporary historians discuss this problem at some length. Cf. Bouchet, p. 345ᵛ; Nicole Gilles, *Annales* (Paris, 1551), fol. xliiiᵛ, fol. xliij (hereafter cited as "Gilles"); Paradin, pp. 638–641; de Thou, I, 316 ff. In spite of Henri's new edict, the Chambre Ardente was reinstated in 1553.

sauves. Les aulcuns desquels estoient ou moitié bruslés, les aultres ung braz en escharpe, les aultres boiteux, les aultres n'avoient que la moitié d'une chemise, et les autres tous nuds.[20]

But matters did not fall out according to the French King's desires. A misguided storm came to the rescue of the besieged. It destroyed tents and fortifications, disrupted Henri's army, and forced him into retreat, though not before he had indubitably manifested his superior strength and dogged determination. The English were quick to see both these factors, and, since they also had to admit several defeats in Scotland, they hurriedly negotiated an ignominious peace; the treaty which handed Boulogne over to the French at the price of 400,000 *livres tournois* was finally signed in April 1550.[21]

Flushed with the joy of victory and acquisition, Henri continued his journey through France, contemplating his next war—to be fought this time against the Emperor. Passing triumphantly through Meulanc, Mantes, Vernon, and Louviers, he seemed to fulfill Cavalli's prediction that he would be "le plus digne roi qu'elle [La France] ait eu depuis deux cents ans." [22] On 25 September 1550 he arrived before Rouen, where the citizens were anxious to greet him, though, as preparations for his entry were not quite perfect, Henri decided to pass some days at a convent outside the town.

I *Henri II's Entry into Rouen*

Rouen was renowned for its generosity in providing magnificent welcoming shows to greet its dukes and monarchs. A long tradition of such entertainments stretched back to the fourteenth century, giving substance to the praise that Pierre Grognet recorded in 1533:

> Les gens de Rouen sont honnestes
> Grans entrepreneurs dedifices

20. Bouchet, p. 335.
21. Details on the Boulogne campaign can be found in Bouchet, pp. 333 ff.; Gilles, fol. xliiij^v; Paradin, pp. 645–646; de Thou, I, 312–314; Vieilleville, II, 73–86.
22. Quoted in Baschet, p. 430.

De theatres et artifices
Es entrees des grans seigneurs.[23]

In planning Henri II's entry, the Town Council debated for a long time
on the manner of their welcome; the members of the council knew this
would necessitate "de longue execution, et de grande entreprise" and
therefore started their deliberations on 12 June 1550. First, practical details
had to be settled. Although they stipulated that any "bourgeois notoire-
ment riches" would be severely punished for refusal to take part in the
entry, some councilors declined to take part, pleading their age as an
excuse (though no doubt the expense involved was the real reason for
their dissent). Others, however, took charge of the most difficult quarters
of the city, which like S. Hilaire were notoriously reluctant to contribute
their share of cost and labor.[24] Most citizens were eager to show their
loyalty; according to the fullest official account of the entry, "Tous
liberallement s'offrirent d'y employer leurs biens et personnes," [25] although
they did not offer their services and their wealth without disturbance, to
judge from the municipal archives, which are full of complaints, appeals,
and suits concerning matters of precedence.

Everything was prepared with the utmost care and method. The work
was divided among the councilors, each according to his knowledge and
capacity. No shows of any kind were to be privately arranged. All intentions and ideas had to be submitted to the town councilors for their
approval, so that, if necessary, these could be fitted into a general plan.[26]
While carpenters, painters, sculptors, and poets put the last minute touches
to their ingenious inventions, the streets along the processional route were

23. The final lines of Grognet's poem *Description et louenge des excellences de
la noble cité de Rouen capitalle de toute Normandie* (n.p., 1533). For evidence of
other entries and festivals at Rouen, see T. Godefroy, *Le Cérémonial françois,* 2 vols.
(Paris, 1649); hereafter cited as "Godefroy."

24. Charles Robillard de Beaupaire, *Documents historiques* (Rouen, 1891),
records that "Guillaume Auber, Sr Delahaye ... est septuagénaire et plus ... et supplie
estre tenu pour excusé" (p. 36), and that "M. du Couldray, sr de Tréville, non
obstant la difficulté" took charge of the "quartier Sainct-Hilaire" (p. 42). Both these
comments are drawn from local archives.

25. *La Deduction,* B,i.

26. For details see L. Roche, *Claude Chappuys* (Paris, 1929), p. 56.

barricaded, strewn with one foot of sand to hide the dirt, and hung with tapestries.

The city itself was crowded for this remarkable event. The Dowager Queen of Scotland was in residence, with a considerable concourse of rowdy Scottish noblemen, who indulged in "such brawling, chiding and fighting . . . for their lodgings, and others' quarrels, as though they had lately come from some new Conquest." [27] The King had brought with him a substantial household, fit to impress any city, and thus found himself surrounded by cardinals, bishops, and priests, ambassadors from the Pope, Spain, Germany, Venice, England, Portugal, and other foreign states. Rouen was thronged with people who had come in from the surrounding country; their infinite number was

respandu sur les eschauffaulx, galleries, appuys, fenestraiges, carreaulx, goutieres, festes des maisons, et clochers, iusques a rompre paroys, et cloisons . . . Et tellement estoit la forme des edifices umbragée de spectateurs, que le tout ensemble se monstroit estre une seulle masse de corps humains tasses l'un sur l'autre.[28]

The visitors' first sight, at 7 A.M. on 1 October 1550, must have been the mounted archers who lined the processional route, protecting those townspeople who had made their way to the meeting place on the meadow of S. Catherine de Grandmont's priory. There, four large pavilions had been erected: three were spacious, circular tents decorated with rich tapestries and flying King Henri's device, the crescent moon, and one was an immense square tent carrying the town's crest. Under these four roofs, set out as imposingly as on a battlefield, the townspeople assembled in their order, closely following the instructions of the twelve masters of ceremony who had been appointed for the occasion.

It was not until midday that the King took up his position in the double gallery which had been provided.[29] Richly decorated with the

27. Sir John Mason, quoted in P. F. Tytler, *England Under the Reigns of Edward VI and Mary* (London, 1839), pp. 325 ff. (hereafter cited as "Tytler"). The Scottish had cause for rejoicing, having just returned from successful wars against the English.

28. *La Deduction,* Q,i.

29. Some kind of "loge" was always built for the King on these occasions; see C. F. Menestrier, *Réflexions et des remarques sur la pratique et les usages des*

King's device and hung with tapestries, this gallery, built on Ionic pillars, formed the focal point of the first part of the ceremonies. On one side, within its shelter, the King sat on a throne which stood on a carpet of cloth of gold; from the other side, the members of his court could view the entire procession unfolding, before it passed beneath the broad arch separating the two galleries. First came the clergy singing psalms. Then followed the merchants on horseback: twenty-four "Mesureurs de Grain," twenty-four "courtiers de vin," forty "courtiers aulneurs de draps," twelve "vendeurs de Poisson et Aulneurs de toille," dressed flatteringly in the King's colors (black and white) [30] and trimmed in gold and silver. Tax officials, numbering around fifty, came next; clothed in satin and velvet of the King's colors, they preceded fifty crossbowmen. These, dazzling with riches of gold and silver woven into their black and white garments, came mounted on fine horses; their trappings carried the arms of Rouen intricately worked in silver and gold thread. Pressing from behind were forty "sergentz de la ville," anxious to show the warrior King, whose colors they also wore, their skill at horsemanship. Two mace bearers brought up the rear, followed by more tax collectors.

It was now the turn of the men at law. The grand figure of the "Lieutenant general du Bailly de Rouen," [31] accompanied by counselors, lawyers, clerks, and innumerable lackeys, and followed by two hundred of the most worthy citizens of Rouen, made his way towards the King. As he arrived in front of Henri II the procession came to a stop. All stood silent while the lieutenant delivered a speech, acknowledging the authority and expectations of the King but also stressing the power and hopes of the citizens who did him homage. They welcomed their monarch loyally and magnificently, but they expected favors in return, such as the confirmation of the privileges received by the town from earlier monarchs. When the King showed himself pleased to accept both their show of welcome and

---

décorations (Grenoble, 1701), p. 136. Published by Leber in *Coll. des meilleurs dissertations* (Paris, 1826–1838), Vol. XIII. A double gallery is shown quite clearly in the prose account; the manuscript miniatures, however, show a single gallery, with no arch.

30. Henri probably wore these colors for the first time in 1545 at the tournament held for the baptism of Elizabeth de France; see Godefroy, II, 148.

31. The lieutenant was Jacques de Brévedent; he had held this office since 1547; see *L'Entrée*, p. 3, n. 30.

their demands, "[étaient] joyeux et asseurez lesdictz Lieutenant et Conseillers Eschevins voyantz leur intention sortir à bon et proffitable effect qui estoit le but ou ils et chacun d'eulx tendoit." [32]

After this interlude, the procession continued on its way. All trades were represented: "porteurs de Sel et Bled," "Visiteurs Courtiers de cuyr, de Laine," "Crieurs de Vins, Des Chargeurs et Trieurs de Fruicts," "Questeurs de Vins" walked together with their officials. The civil law followed in large number, dressed in scarlet, their garments decorated with all manner of riches. A sumptuous company of three hundred crossbowmen was then seen, their golden, jeweled helmets and scarlet tunics glistening in the sun. Fifes and drums regulated their march, which was interrupted from time to time with the sound of cannon fire. The appearance and behavior of the crossbowmen were immaculate, "dignes de servir a quelque bonne affaire, leur souverain seigneur et Roy;" it was to them the King must look if he needed more resources for his wars. Their glory seemed surpassed, however, by the fifteen hundred soldiers who followed. These were the rich "enfants de la ville," divided into three companies, wearing different colors, vying with each other in the richness of their jewels and decorations, but all carrying the royal standard woven in the King's device, and with his "chiffres qui sont deux D entrelassez, et une H. couronnée." Eighteen experienced men of war brought up the rear; dressed in antique Roman fashion, carrying two-handed swords, they fought among themselves with such dexterity that they recalled the skill of ancient Roman gladiators. They also, no doubt, reminded Henri of the two superb displays of martial skill he had seen in Lyons in 1548, when warriors dressed as gladiators had entertained the company for over an hour.[33]

A regiment of fifty captains quickly followed; their standard, displaying the King's device, was imprinted with the arms of Normandy and scattered with the eyes and tongues of military vigilance and renown. They came to remind the King, and the townspeople, of the large part that the province of Normandy had always played in the "deffence de la

---

32. The procession is colorfully described in *La Deduction,* C,ii–iv[v].

33. *Le Grand Triumphe faict à l'entrée* ... (Lyons, 1548). Describing the combat, the author says "Lequel passetemps fut le Ier et celluy, qui, aye donné autant de satisfaction à la Magesté, comme d'une nouvelle mode de combatre et si dangereuse, en sorte qu'il la voulut encor revoir 6 jours apres son entrée."

République françoyse." [34] Rouen's show of strength was over, and the first movement of the entry had come to an end. The second movement was to be an elaborate re-enactment of the King's recent military victories; for if Fabius—a pagan—had been given a triumphant entry into Rome,

> Pourquoy ne doit plain triumphe Rouen
> Au treschristian, qui festins et Tournoys,
> Arriere a mis, pour plus grande entreprise
> Executer, premier que s'en advise,
> Son ennemy. Car sans froisser harnoys
> A l'instant prit, cinq forts en Boullonnoys,
> Puis en sa main fut Boullongne remise. [35]

Four white-winged horses drew the first triumphal chariot; [36] enriched with moldings and friezes displaying battles, piled high with the spoils of war, it carried two dead soldiers, who lay at the feet of a representation of Death. This last figure—a skeleton—was in chains, held by the goddess of Fame. [37] She sat enthroned, dominating all, her wings spread with the eyes and tongues of many nations, a trumpet held to her lips. She herself explained her presence to Henri,

> Moy Renommée, ô hault Roy très christian,
> Du ciel en terre, a ton loz estendue,
> I'ay sur la mort, au feu Roy pere tien,
> Donne triumphe, et gloire à toy bien dëue,
> Les Vertueulx, que Vertu perpetue,
> Touiours vivantz, ie represente en moy,
> Pour ce ROUEN, pour ta vertu congneüe,
> Sur mort te donne, immortel nom de ROY. [38]

34. *La Deduction*, D,iii.

35. *Ibid.*, A,iv^v.

36. The sources do not agree on who or what drew the first chariot along. Masselin says they were unicorns, *L'Entrée* says elephants. "Chars de triomphe" were often used in indoor festivals during banquets, and there are several examples of their use in earlier French entries: Rouen (1532), Rennes (1532), Lyons (1533), where they appeared on a frieze, and Paris (1548). Since the titles of these entries are inordinately long, and since there are two very convenient bibliographical sources, I refer readers to Godefroy, *Le Cérémonial*, and G. Kernodle, *From Art to Theatre* (Chicago, 1944), pp. 220 ff.

37. Fame, or *la Renommée*, an essential ingredient for success in the sixteenth century, was a popular figure in royal entries. She had appeared at the Rouen entry in 1531.

38. *La Deduction*, D,iv^r.

She had the power to perceive Henri's worth, the authority of the citizens of Rouen to grant him the title of King, and through her role as guardian of the reputation of the kings of France, she would disseminate the knowledge of his virtues throughout the world. The prose text, as yet, makes no specific reference to Henri's recent victories; the homage is to a virtuous monarch worthy of his ancestors, one who can maintain his kingdom in peace and prosperity. The verse account, however, immediately says of Renommée,

> C'est celle là qui a rendu notoire
> Par l'univers l'heur de ta grant victoire,
> C'est celle là qui publie Angleterre
> Avoir ceddé à la françoise guerre.[39]

The more general point made about the virtues of French kings is confirmed by the arrival of Henri's fifty-seven ancestors, splendidly attired, mounted on horseback and wearing golden crowns.[40] They are present at this triumph as much to offer advice and example to the reigning monarch "par leur magnanime vertu et solide prudence, et pénétrâte providence," as to add to its magnificence. The departure of these august personages was signaled by the sound of trumpets, which also served to introduce the second triumphal chariot (see Figure 12).

This ingenious structure, decorated with stories from history, with statues and moldings, was drawn by two unicorns, their trappings embossed with the device of Henri II. Men in turbans accompanied the chariot, which carried five beautiful, rich, and variedly dressed ladies. Seated conspicuously in the throne of honor was Vesta, goddess of Religion. In her hands she supported the model of a church, "reduict au petit pied, autant bien taillé, proportionné et assouvy d'ouvrage d'orfaverie, pour son volume qu'en peult souffrir l'art d'architecture."[41] The ladies seated at her side represented Royal Majesty and Virtue Victorious; two

39. *L'Entrée*, p. IX. It is amusing to note that Simon Renard, the Imperial ambassador, declared that some thirty Spaniards appropriately accompanied the Chariot of Fame. *Calendar of State Papers, Spanish, Edward VI: 1550–1552*, p. 181; hereafter cited as "*CSP*."

40. Ancestors were a common feature of royal entries; they had walked in procession at Rheims (1484), Rouen (1484), Paris (1498), and so on.

41. *La Deduction*, E,iv^v. The prose and verse accounts differ on this chariot. *L'Entrée* replaces the *Char de religion* by a *Char de victoire*, opposite p. IX^v, thus giving more emphasis to the political interpretation.

FIGURE 12. From *C'est la Deduction ...* (Rouen, 1551).

more ladies—denoting Reverence and Fear—sat at the front of the chariot. Together they performed a song in five parts, "Louenge et gloire, en action de grace, / Chantons à Dieu, de la Paix vray autheur." [42] Again the implications are neither specific nor personal to Henri II. The inventor of the pageant was mainly concerned with expressing his thoughts on peace and maintenance of order. The church held prominently aloft signified, according to the prose account, the union of Christendom. Only God can be its author; but since the kings of France are "dieu-donné," they are inspired with zeal and fervor, "à debeller les adversaires de la foy catholique, et extirper toutes erreurs, affin de maintenir en paix et union leglise chrestienne." [43] In the past, the endeavors of the kings had earned for them the titles Very Christian King and First Son of the Church; their virtue and their filial reverence towards God had always insured victory for the Church whose preservation must be a constant goal. Henri no doubt felt very satisfied as he contemplated his own religious achievements: his prompt dealings with the Protestants, who continued to be burned every day in spite of the temporary relaxations; the religious fervor he demonstrated by going to mass regularly and providing his people with a worthy example; and finally his generosity to the rapacious financial needs of the Church—he had recently donated a silver statue of the Virgin

42. The music to these verses is printed at the end of *La Deduction*.
43. *Ibid.*, F,i^v.

Mary to the Cathedral at Boulogne. This gift had been especially calculated to please the citizens of Rouen, who had a long tradition of devotion to the Virgin, and the King's liberality was recorded for posterity in an image of the Virgin carried behind the Chariot of Religion for all to see.

Six bands of military men wearing Henri's device followed Religion. The first of these carried models of the forts Henri had won at Boulogne; [44] "abondance de tous biens" was represented by the large vases which the second group carried. Festive circlets of laurel were held aloft by the next group, who were followed by soldiers holding banners (see Figure 13) on which had been painted the country around Haddington which the King had won from the English.[45] Spoils of war were the proud posses-

44. The inventors were perhaps inspired by Louis XII's entry into Paris (1461), where his victory at Dieppe was depicted in detail at the pageant at the "Boucherie de Paris"; see Godefroy, I, 181 ff. The verse account actually details the forts in the following way, p. XIII^r:

> Voilà après, O race d'Ilyon
> La tour qui est lanterne d'Albyon
> Et ce qui plus l'anglois faict ses mains tordre
> De rage grant; c'est la haulte tour d'Ordre.
>   Voilà après, dont sont fort estourdiz,
> Par eulx construit le fort de Paradis.
> Ceulx qui y ont receu mainct coup de fer,
> Plus proprement l'ont appellé Enfer.
>   Ensuict après qui veilloit à double oeil
> Sur vos vaisseaulx l'un & l'autre Ambleteul.

45. I have adopted the suggestions of the verse account which are by far the most detailed and circumstantial. The prose account suggests Boulogne again here, but it is unlikely that two direct references to this victory would have been made, while there is no reference to the Scottish battles at all. The verse account reads, pp. XIV^v–XV:

> Voilà Dondy, Edimpton, Portugray,
> Où Termes prist & Essé le degré,
> Pour devenir chevalier de ton ordre.
> Tout le pays où avoit osé mordre
> Sur l'escossois la nation angloise
> Est recouvert par la force françoise
> Après avoir enduré mainctz travaulx.
>   Sire, voyez ceste Ysle des chevaulx,
> Voyez aussy le fort chasteau de Fargues.
> O quants assaulx, escarmouches & cargues
> On y a veu sans veoyr les françois las!

FIGURE 13. From *C'est la Deduction* ... (Rouen, 1551).

sions of the fifth group of these bands of military men, the last of which
carried live lambs, ready to be sacrificed. At least one person was very
displeased with this part of the triumph; Mason, the English ambassador,
was heard to say "when he saw it, that if it [Boulogne] had cost them
nothing, they might have had a triumph with good reason." [46]

> Voilà aussy le fort près de Donglas,
> Et plus deçà où est assis ce bourg
> Est le chasteau conquis de Rossebourg.

46. By the treaty with the English, April 1550, the French agreed to pay 400,000
livres tournois for Boulogne. The facts we quote are reported by the Imperial ambassador, *CSP,* p. 182.

Fifty redoubtable soldiers belonging to the King followed; they had taken part in his recent campaigns and deserved to walk in his triumph. In fact, they heralded his approach. But first, behind them, led by twelve men in turbans, came six elephants (see Figure 14), "aprochans si pres

FIGURE 14. From *C'est la Deduction* ... (Rouen, 1551).

du naturel, pour leur forme couleur et proportion de membres, que ceulx mesme qui en avoient veu en Affrique de vivantz, les eussent iugez à les veoir elephans non faintz." [47] Three elephants carried great antique bronze vases out of which leaped flames spreading pleasant odors through the

47. *La Deduction*, G,iii. In *L'Entrée* the elephants come after the *Char d'heureuse fortune,* as in Masselin.

crowd. Two had castle fortresses "reduitz au petit pied par bonne et iuste symmetrie," and the last one carried a ship, shattered and torn as though it had just survived some fateful sea battle. Observers do not agree about the meaning of these symbols carried by the elephants. The prose version suggests that the flames denoted joy at the triumph and remains silent on the rest; the Imperial ambassador thought that the flames were merely fireworks. It is in the verse account that one finds the most elaborate explanations of their meaning. The flames, carried only by the first elephant, signify "la clarté / Qui n'apartient qu'à ta grant maiesté" (a direct reference to Henri II). The second elephant supported a temple assuring all who saw it that Henri's Church would triumph. "Des bastiments et logis de plaisance" crowned the third, "Et le quart ou les chasteaulx et les forts Qui ont senty tes merveilleux efforts." Surmounting the fifth was a plan of Boulogne, and the ship on the sixth was a simple reminder of the ravages suffered by the English in their recent encounters with French galleons.[48] It will be seen that the various accounts not only disagree in meaning but are also at variance as far as the objects which the elephants carried are concerned. Both prose and verse accounts support their facts by reproducing the different details of the text in their engravings and illuminations. In view of the subsequent elements of the entry which refer directly to Boulogne and to the war in Scotland, one is tempted to give more credence to the verse account. In any event, neither of the two accounts contradicts the main tenor of the entry, whose implications become increasingly more precise.

A group of captives, sad of countenance and chained together, approach the King. Just as he enjoyed seeing the spoils of recent battles piled upon the chariot of Fame, so he rejoiced in the remembrance of a procession of captives, mournfully doing obeisance before him a year earlier in front of the town of Boulogne. Their trailing exit contrasts with the joyous noise of trumpet players. The rhythm of the procession accelerates. Flora and her nymphs come by, strewing flowers of celebration to show that the culminating point of the triumph is nigh.

Two strong horses with the device of Henri II appear drawing a triumphal chariot "d'exquis ouvrage" (see Figure 15). Fortune, rich and prosperous, spreading her peacock wings, is balanced on a wheel of silver.

48. *L'Entrée*, p. XII. The naval battles were fought for the French by Leon Strozzi and refer to 30 July 1547, and 1 August 1549.

FIGURE 15. From *C'est la Deduction* ... (Rouen, 1551).

Below her on a throne sits a second Henri II, "un beau et elegant personnage, aprochant de corsage et traict de visage, à la noble personne du Roy nostre Sire." [49] In his hands he holds the royal scepter and the palm of peace. Held high above his head, Fortune presents the Imperial crown, both to acknowledge Henri's victories and "pour declarer que la souveraine maiesté des Roys de France ne releve que de Dieu." Thus, once again, Henri's personal triumph is tempered with more general comment; but presented as he is, so lifelike, surrounded by four of his children, the real presence of the reigning monarch and his recent achievements is strongly felt. This impression is underlined in the words spoken by the living image of the King who praises the "incomparable Roy." Magnificently attired and riding a splendid horse, the Dauphin (similarly depicted by one of the prominent citizens of Rouen) speaks his personal homage to his father. Fifty more men at arms drawn from the province of Normandy, who had accompanied the King on all his successful military excursions, come to pay homage. They also come to receive their share of praise.

Their splendor is enhanced by the company of three hundred "enfants de la ville," attired in glorious military costume, some on horseback, others on foot, marching to the sound of pipes and drums. The magnificence of

49. *La Deduction,* H,iv^v. It seems to have been customary to show the King a living image of himself, as in the Rouen entry of 1485. The Imperial ambassador, Renard, *CSP,* p. 181, did not recognize the goddess Fortune.

their garments "d'incredible richesse" defied description. After several pages detailing jewels, rich stuffs, plumes, glittering weapons, and so on, the prose account grandly claims that "son excellence, exactement imprimée au cerveau des spectateurs, ne peust par laps de temps, de la memoire des Hommes aucunement estre effacée." [50] They wished not only to offer their riches to the King but also to show themselves worthy of the costume they wore. Before the astonished eyes of the citizens of Rouen, they performed great feats upon their steeds, making them "faire pannades, bondir, volleter, et redoubler le sault en l'air." This unusual sight brought the procession of the townspeople to an end.

It was now time for the third movement of Henri's entry—his own triumphal ride through the city. Announced by six trumpets, his household of two hundred gentlemen and officers set out. Monsieur de Boisy, "grand écuyer," led the King's "cheval de parade," closely followed by a hundred Swiss guards. Then came the Admiral of France and King Henri's favorites, M. de S. André and M. de la Marck. The ambassadors came behind with cardinals, bishops, and prelates; and finally, led by the Connétable de Montmorency carrying the sword of state, appeared the King himself.[51] Dressed simply in black velvet, trimmed with silver and jewels, he made a startling contrast to the glorious colors which surrounded him. A suite of princes of the royal blood and knights accompanied him.

As they approached the Seine they could see a most uncommon scene laid out before them. A meadow (two hundred feet long and thirty-five feet wide), planted with natural and artificial shrubs and trees, provided a home for exotic birds, for monkeys and squirrels, and for fifty naked Brazilian men and women who had been brought to France in the ships of Rouen merchants (see Figure 16).[52] At each end of the meadow primitive huts made of solid tree trunks had been erected. For a long time the royal visitors contemplated the activities in which these natives were

50. *Ibid.,* I,iv^v.

51. According to Renard, *CSP*, p. 182, "the king was seated on a wolf skin and rode a powerful Spanish horse."

52. According to the prose account the Brazilians numbered three hundred, with the addition of citizens of Rouen who had traveled to Brazil and understood the natives' speech and ways. Montaigne admired their behavior, as he recounts in "Les Cannibales," *Essais,* I, 31.

FIGURE 16. From *C'est la Deduction* ... (Rouen, 1551).

absorbed: running after monkeys, firing their arrows at birds, lazing in cotton hammocks strung from one tree to another, chopping wood and carrying it to the fort near the river, where French sailors would customarily trade with them (a French ship in full sail, flying the device of Henri II, was waiting in the Seine to give a sense of reality to the mimicry). Most alarming was the battle between two tribes—the Tabagerres and the Toupinaboux—which suddenly broke out. They fought furiously with arrows, clubs, and other warlike instruments until the Tabagerres were finally repulsed. The conquerors made good their victory by burning the homes of their opponents to the ground. The show was so arresting that even those who knew the country of Brazil were constrained to comment on its authenticity. From the scaffolding which had been built to give him the best possible view,[53] the King showed his enjoyment openly;

---

53. The Imperial ambassador reported that there were two scaffolds, one for the King, the other for the ambassadors. Probably the additional one for the King was in fact made for the Queen, so that she too could view the ceremonies.

he liked fights, and although the combat was a traditional part of any entry,[54] no town had yet produced anything so uncommon as this fight of two tribes, completely naked, "sans aucunement couvrir la partie que nature commande."[55]

The King and company made their way towards the bridge, where a huge rock, sixty feet wide and more than 150 feet high, seemed to bar their passage.[56] Within this structure, as in a grotto, Orpheus sat upon a marble throne playing his harp. Beside him were the nine Muses with their musical instruments, and above, stretched across the entrance to the cave, was a rainbow surmounted by a crescent moon. Strangely, in the opposite corner Hercules "s'occupoit, à couper les testes de l'hydre serpentine" which had emerged from some dark cavern in the rock (see Figure 17). A placard hung below on which were written the following explanatory verses,

> Ta maiesté royalle o tres chrestien Roy,
> Est au grand bien de tous, un Hercules sur terre,
> Qui met le fier aspic, de mars en dessaroy,
> Pour planter en honneur, la paix au lieu de guerre,
> L'arc du ciel en croissant, pour gage et divin arre,
> Comme un signe de paix, s'aparoit en tous lieux,
> En monstrant bon temps proche, et malheur mis en serre,
> S'esiouyssent les cieulx, les hommes et les dieux.[57]

54. There had been a prolonged fight of gladiators in the Lyons entry (see n. 33 above). Rabelais has an extremely amusing account of a sciamachy arranged by the Cardinal du Bellay in Rome to celebrate the birth of a son to Henri II (Louis, Duke of Orleans). It was first printed in 1549 and is given in full at the end of the Garnier 1962 edition of Rabelais, II, 579 ff. It was a very grand affair, much bigger in scope than anything attempted by the French at the same period, though it could be argued that this Roman sciamachy was really a very elaborate castle storming, and these were frequent enough in France. A particularly spectacular one had been arranged in 1389 for the banquet following Isabelle de Bavière's entry into Paris; see Godefroy, I, 637 ff. For earlier examples see Sydney Anglo's article in this volume, pp. 3–44.

55. The spectacle of the Brazilians was a point of departure for Ferdinand Denis' study, *Une Fête brésilienne célébrée à Rouen en 1550* (Paris, 1850).

56. This rock is incomprehensibly interpreted by the Imperial ambassador as being a desert!

57. *La Deduction*, L,j. *L'Entrée* changes the rhythm of the poetry; from this point on, its comment takes the form of an ode. Such odes were a feature of Roman triumphs; see Plutarch's account of Paulus Emilius, 1699 ed., II, 226.

FIGURE 17. From *C'est la Deduction* ... (Rouen, 1551).

After Henri's recent feats of arms no one would have thought of complaining that the parallel was inappropriate. Indeed, the figure of Hercules would probably come first to their minds, so familiar were his deeds to the sixteenth century. They had been embroidered into tapestries, expanded in the books of Raoul Le Fèvre and Jean Lemaire de Belges, and exploited in earlier royal entries—Paris (1517); Rouen (1531); Lyons (1533); and Paris (1549).[58] The rainbow, as well as standing for peace in this context, was the personal device of Catherine de Médicis.[59]

Henri now passed onto the bridge. Before he had gone many yards he was confronted by three marine creatures: Neptune, Palemon, and Glaucus, who darted out from a rock. The king of the seas saluted Henri, offering him dominion over the waves; and as soon as the King of France had accepted Neptune's trident, the three sea creatures leaped into the river, there performing marvelous acrobatics amid the crowd of marine life which had surfaced to greet the French monarch (see Figure 18). Dolphins, Arion and his lute, "une grandissime Balene: Laquelle vomissoit de grands poissons, fort bien escaillez, iusques au nombre de trente," [60] and other smaller whales, together with Tritons playing their instruments, surrounded Neptune as he reappeared, this time on his triumphal chariot, drawn by sea horses and decorated with the four winds. Behind him swam sirens, the three nymphs of Calliope, goddess of Rhetoric, playing their dulcimers with such effect that the crowd was enchanted; even the Queen, observing the triumph from a scaffold nearby, was so absorbed that she forgot to eat the sweetmeats provided for her. The meaning of this spectacle is obvious: the inhabitants of the seas perform a triumph to honor a victorious monarch from the earth. Neptune said as much when he offered his trident to Henri at the beginning of the show. And yet the Imperial ambassador misunderstood. Far from appreciating the acrobatics performed by Neptune and his companions, he states, "Three men jumped down from the bridge just over the cross into the water, and were supposed to be swallowed by the whale; but this part of the show did not come off

58. Raoul Le Fèvre, *Histoire de Troie* (Lyons, 1529); Jean Lemaire de Belges, *Illustrations des Gaules* (Paris, 1548). The vast complexities of the Hercules theme have been admirably studied by Marc-René Jung, *Hercule dans la littérature française du XVIe siècle* (Droz, 1966).

59. Claude Paradin, *Devises héroiques* (Lyons, 1557), pp. 37–38.

60. *La Deduction*, L,iv^v.

FIGURE 18. From *C'est la Deduction* ... (Rouen, 1551).

according to expectations."[61] So much for the intentions of the authors of this pageant and the powers of observation of a supposedly intelligent member of the admiring crowd!

The English ambassador and others fared no better; they failed to interpret the next show which took place on the other side of the bridge. Mason admits:

There was both the days [that is to say for the King's and Queen's entries] a fight upon the river between two ships, the one garnished with white crosses, and the other with red, and both the days the red crossed ship had the worst and was burned. Many thought, and so did I, at the beginning, the same had been made for an English ship; but it was afterwards known that it was a representation of a fight between the Portugals and the French about the old quarrel for the Isle of Brazil.[62]

61. *CSP*, p. 182.

62. Quoted in Tytler, p. 325 ff. The French-Portuguese struggle had lasted for some time; in 1546 Marino Cavalli writes: "Avec le Portugal il ne peut y avoir bonne intelligence, puisque une guerre sourde dure toujours entre les deux pays les Français prétendent naviguer vers la Guinée et le Brésil, ce que les Portugais

The ship which represented the Portuguese foundered under the force of cannon and grenades from the French vessel, and its sailors were forced to swim for their lives. The seriousness of their plight aroused much emotion in the crowd, even among the gondola-shaped boats assembled along the riverside to have a good view of the fight. It seems that Henri II was particularly fond of sea fights, or naumachiae. At every major entry he had made, some kind of sea battle had been arranged. There was one at his coronation entry into Rheims in 1547; [63] in Lyons (1548) he viewed the sea fight from the bucentaur, a castellated boat built specially for the purpose. At Paris (1549) a castle had been constructed on the Île de Louviers, which after a sea fight was stormed and destroyed by the sailors from the victorious side. [64] To salvos of cannon shot, Henri II made his way to the far end of the bridge, towards the first of the triumphal arches through which he would pass. On its summit two sibyls supported a large crescent moon on which stood the figure of Saturn, a tablet placed beneath him explaining, "Je suis l'aage d'or / D'honneur revestu." This triumphal arch, a relatively new feature to French entries, [65] officially marked the point where the King entered the town, bringing with him, through his deeds and virtues, a new age of abundance, of peace and prosperity. Such was the dream which not only accompanied Henri II's entry but permeated European idealism and imagery for more than a century. This theme cropped up everywhere, but it was especially popular in court festivals. It had been used in the Low Countries at the Emperor's entry into Bruges in 1515 and at Antwerp in 1520 and 1549; it would be echoed in Ronsard's *Bergerie,* created for the Fontainebleau Festival of 1564, [66] and it would

---

n'entendent pas du tout" (quoted in N. Tommaseo, *Relations des ambassadeurs vénitiens* [Paris, 1838], p. 293).

63. Godefroy, I, 303 ff.

64. A lengthy account is given by de Thou, I, 311. There had been such a battle at Louis XII's entry into Rouen in 1508 and at the baptism festivities for Henri's first son at Fontainebleau in 1543. See also Godefroy, II, 144, 146.

65. As Chartrou has shown, the *arc de triomphe* is an Italian invention which the French imitated from the early 1530's. It plays a less important role at Rouen than at other entries, such as Lyons (1533), Poitiers (1539), Rheims (1547), Lyons (1548), and Paris (1549).

66. "Si nous voyons le Siècle d'or refait, / C'est du bienfait / De la bergere Catherine . . ." *Bergerie,* in *Elegies et mascarades* (Paris, 1948), XIII, 79.

reappear in Charles IX's entry into Paris in 1571. The very frequency with which the arch was evoked and employed is important, for it expressed real hopes and desires for peace and it pointed to precise goals. Henri II could be in no doubt that his glorious progress throughout France was not just a means of obtaining the personal homage due his position and achievements, of getting his people to recognize his authority, but was also a way of finding out, however indirectly, what the expectations of his subjects were.

At this point of the itinerary four councilors awaited the King as they held the canopy of honor under which he was to ride during the rest of his triumph. Standing out against the rich red velvet cloth of the canopy were the embossed silver letters of the King's motto: "Donec totum impleat orbem." The aspirations contained in this phrase are freely translated by the prose account in the following way:

> Puisque Henry second du nom à pris
> Pour sa devise un celeste croissant
> Sans riens choisir du terrestre pourpris
> C'est bien raison quen bon heur soit croissant
> Tant que tout lorbe ait soubz sa main compris.[67]

Henri's motto sums up his character and his wishes; hopes for peace dim before the urgent desire for terrestrial expansion.

As the King continued on his way he passed Notre Dame de Rouen. Opposite the cathedral, on a platform held up by crouching Harpies, stood the proud figure of Hector, hero of Troy, clad in full armor. As soon as the King was in sight of the statue, which stood beneath a dense cloud, "tout à coup par subtil moyen, de l'endroit ou Hector avoit esté navré par Achilles, le sang s'esbullit, comme s'il fut exprimé d'une Seringue jusques dedans ladicte nuée, duquel sang, se forma lors un treple Croissant, proprement entrelassé." [68] The strangeness of this occurrence arrested everyone's attention, but few hesitated about its meaning, for triple crescents had adorned all the banners carried at the procession earlier in the afternoon. If there were any who were ignorant of its meaning, an explanation was appended below the statue, saying that Hector felt no distress at his fate since from his blood had sprung "un treple croissant / Qui

67. *La Deduction,* M,iii^v.
68. *Ibid.,* N,i.

remplira le monde." Thus the implications of Henri's motto are linked with his device.

In the sixteenth century everyone knew that the French race was descended from the illustrious Trojans. Raoul Le Fèvre had gone to great pains to detail this very complicated genealogy; Jean Lemaire de Belges had also explored the ancestors of Francus, and in the works of these men the names of Hector and Hercules occur on almost every page.[69] For decades, French royal entries had explored the theme in an almost continuous tradition—beginning in 1389 at the Paris entry of Isabelle de Bavière. It was woven into tapestries at Blois in 1501 and at Paris in 1517 and would continue to provide a source of inspiration for art and festivals well on into the seventeenth century.

After the grand pretensions of Hector's prophecy, the King was surprisingly confronted by a spectacle of another sort (see Figure 19). Blazing before him, high on the first level of a complicated arch structure, was the salamander, symbol of his father, François I. On a backcloth beyond, painted in accurate perspective, were Clotho and Atropos, goddesses of Fate, holding up the emblem of a serpent biting its tail. Although the ignorant Imperial ambassador could make nothing of this sign ". . . two children carrying a coiled snake. I have not been able to interpret the symbol," [70] he writes to the Emperor—had he taken the trouble to read the motto underneath, "Hoc est tempus," the meaning of the pageant might have become clear to him. It implies that François I has gained lasting renown from his years of kingship (the serpent eating its tail being the symbol of eternity), and that his son should learn from his experience. As the King stepped closer, the whole scene was transformed. It became enveloped by "un grand et spacieulx globe," around which licked flames of fire; suddenly the globe burst, and out of it sprang an artificial Pegasus moving "agillement les pieds, teste, aureilles, et yeulx, comme si nature luy eust lors communiqué l'usage de vie." [71] A winged Pegasus signifying "bonne renommé" had flown at the Paris entry of 1501; it had appeared

69. As usual, the Imperial ambassador sees imperfectly; he confuses Hector with Hercules and states baldly, "In the town itself there was set up a figure of the invincible Hercules Gallicus, with three crescents as his attributes, intended to represent the King." *CSP*, p. 182.

70. *Ibid.*, p. 183.

71. *La Deduction*, N,ii^r.

FIGURE 19. From *C'est la Deduction ...* (Rouen, 1551).

again with the same meaning a few months prior to the Rouen festival, at Henri's entry into Troyes.[72] At Rouen, however, it was given a much more complicated significance—"denotant, la constante promesse, d'heureuse et longue vie; divinement faicte, à la sacrée majesté de nostre Roy." This long life and prosperity, it was stressed, were not simply for Henri's own personal glory, but for the maintenance of the state, for the assurance of peace and of union within the Church, and for the support and encouragement of the arts which would bring France, and her King, fame throughout the world. High above Pegasus sat a lonely Triton. When the Triton sounded a fanfare on its trumpet, the globe which had produced Pegasus turned again, unfolded, and revealed a painted life image of Henri II. Below this image was written the simple word *Fides.* On such a solid foundation the King could enjoy the prospect of fruitful prosperity.

While he gazed at his picture, Henri saw that from his royal heart sprang a vine, whose luscious grapes tempted foreign nations who were anxious to partake of the sweetness of "amyable confederation et obeissance." His royal example of faith and justice, represented by the flowering sword held in his right hand, has brought all peoples into his subjection. Above his head, the King could see the whole array of heavenly planets lined up to give him their gifts, "sceptres tant modernes que antiques avec couronnes imperiales, royales et ducales." [73] The earlier prophecy of Hector is thus confirmed and given a kind of tangible reality in this latest spectacle. So complicated is the invention that the author of the prose account finds himself unable to express the full implications. He therefore tries to expand his thoughts in a long *cantique,* singing the praises of this King, so endowed with virtue that he can bring peace not only to his own kingdom but also to

> Nations estrangeres
> Sesgayent et font chere
> Et nont plus de soucy.[74]

72. For the Paris entry (1501), see Godefroy, II, 722 ff.; for Troyes (1548), see Bouchet, p. 320ᵛ.

73. The same seven planets had offered their services to Queen Eleanor at Lyons in 1533.

74. *La Deduction,* N,iv.

However extravagant these thoughts might seem, they cannot outdo the excited exhilaration of the verse account, whose last section is a sustained paean of praise, a long ode summarizing the political and religious achievements of Henri II.[75] Orpheus, Neptune, and Apollo are the chief spokesmen in this poem, and their prophecies are much more specific than the enthusiastic generalities of the prose account. Orpheus sings of the King's force and prudence. Neptune imagines the King, of Trojan ancestry and renown, on his way to conquer "le perfide Albion" and comes to assure him not only of fair winds and a safe passage but also of the support of Juno, Venus, Pallas, Apollo, and Jupiter—their anger against the Trojan race having been appeased by the persuasive words and deeds of "feu Francoys de Valoys." Attended by such deities, the King is compared successively to all the great warriors of history whose excellence he easily surpasses. Neptune shows him sailing triumphantly up the Thames, and Apollo comes to confirm this victory, expressing first the wish of joining England and France into one kingdom ("Faire je veulx de deux une couronne"), and then the certitude of "Henry second et Henry le neufiesme." Henri II of France becomes the natural successor to Henry VIII of England. To this victory, which brings back memories of the Norman conquest, must be added the French possession of Scotland, an acquisition which makes Henri II thrice King—a happy fact of wishful thinking symbolized throughout the entry into Rouen by the presence of the device of the triple crescent. The verse account ends

> Exaulcez-vous, O portes du grant temple,
> Pour recevoir ce grant Roy d'honneur ample,
> Exaulcez-vous longtemps à qu'il n'avint
> Qu'ung si grant Roy à vostre seuil parvint!
>   Honneur à Dieu qui tel Roy nous envoye!
> Salut au Roy qui de Dieu suict la voye![76]

The almost prayer-like quality of these lines sums up the main intention of the final pageant which was set up in the square commonly called the Pont de Rebec (see Figure 20). The place was made to resemble the Elysian fields, planted with shrubs, an abundance of fruit trees, and a

75. *L'Entrée*, pp. XVIII–XXVII. This long ode, which incorporates verse from the prose account, forms a kind of solid center around which the author embroiders his political hopes and wishes for Henri II.

76. *Ibid.*, p. XXVII.

FIGURE 20. From *C'est la Deduction* ... (Rouen, 1551).

thousand beautiful flowers;[77] there were trellises of vines and roses and formal gardens, and the entrances were surmounted by great crescent moons. Within reposed François I in the company of two ladies: Good Memory and Egeria. At their feet two figures, representing Nobility and Labor, lay sleeping. The first of the two nymphs held a book in her hand which commended the late King for his love of letters; the second, Egeria, was both a reminder of his generosity to the Muses and the cause of learning and a clear indication of the profit he himself had derived from those arts and sciences he had encouraged. Just as Roman Numa had sought advice from his wife Egeria in order to transform his barbarian subjects into virtuous men, so François had fruitfully sought the advice of his learned men of letters. Three placards hung down to spell out this significance to Henri II and his company. The first explained the nature of the place: "C'est le repotz, le paradis heureulx, / Des Roys qui sont des lettres amoureulx." The second pointed out the advantages and pleasure that letters could offer kings "apres guerre effrenée."[78] The third developed themes encouraging the practice of the virtues and of industry, explaining that after the pressures, the danger, and even the afflictions of this life, virtuous men of all degrees, "En fin de temps aurons fruition, / De doulx repotz d'ayse et ioye assouvye."[79]

Thus the triumphal entry of Henri II into Rouen ended on a note which raised men's thoughts above temporal considerations of war and peace, strong kingship, and good government, although these elements were the starting point for this final pageant and meditation. After this, it seemed natural for the King to make his way to the cathedral in order to give thanks to God for the honor and power with which he was endowed and for the devotion and show of obedience of his subjects.

On the steps of the cathedral awaited Claude Chappuys, "chantre d'icelluy college et orateur facond." He summarized all the themes of the entry, the moral, religious, and political intentions which lay behind the pageants, calling Henri's attention to the need to maintain the Catholic

77. There had been a similar *clos de repos* at the Paris entry of 1517 (Godefroy, I, 482, 756).

78. The Imperial ambassador understands the implications of this pageant, but thinks that one of the recumbent figures is the Cardinal of Lorraine; "on one side of him was the recumbent figure of the late Cardinal de Lorraine" (*CSP*, p. 182).

79. *La Deduction*, O,iii.

faith in riches and in doctrine, to protect the Church and his people from heretics and foreign invaders, to be worthy of eternal happiness through a just use of the Imperial crown which had been given to him by God, not for personal gain, but for the public good. Confident in being able to fulfill these hopes, the King passed into the cathedral where the *Te Deum* was sung and the festivities for that day came to an end.

On the following morning it was the Queen's turn to make her entry into the city. Accompanied by a grand concourse of ladies, brilliantly attired, she watched the citizens pass, this time wearing her colors, green and white. In his harangue, the Lord Lieutenant praised her virtues, her beauty, and especially her fecundity, so valuable "pour la force manutention et augmentation de ce royaulme." The same triumphal chariots swept before her, with one significant exception: all specific reference on banners to the acquisition of Boulogne, all representation of the town and its forts, had been omitted by command of the King.[80] Simon Renard reports this fact; when writing of the Queen's entry, he says, "the same shows were repeated in her honour, except the triumphs of Boulogne, as it was feared it might irritate the English." [81] There were a few other details which were modified for the Queen. As she crossed the bridge over the Seine, she was greeted not by Neptune but by his wife, the goddess Thetys, accompanied by her water nymphs. At the arch of the Golden Age, the prose account devotes more space to Catherine's device—the rainbow—which would help to heal the ills that have beset France, "Car soubz c'est arc, plain despoir, tout mal cesse." The last pageant, displayed as on the previous day, could not be fully appreciated "pour la nuict qui avancoit." [82] There was time, however, for the Queen to hear the wisdom of Claude Chappuys, who praised her virtues and her erudition and then developed the fruitful consequences of her fecundity,

---

80. The British ambassador reported: "Among sundry pageants that were represented therein, the plots [maps] of Boulogne, and all those pieces, were carried aloft upon long poles. The next day the Queen made her entry in the same sort thoroughly and with like solemnity as the King had done the day before; saving that by the commandment of the King, the representation of Boulogne was omitted"; printed in Tytler, pp. 325 ff.

81. *CSP*, p. 182.

82. Masselin states that the pageant at the Cross had also been modified, although the lengthier prose text does not suggest this.

La quelle posterité, de graces speciales prevenue, monstre la benediction de Dieu, L'amour de son espoux, L'espoir de son peuple, La reverence des es-trangers, La crainte des ennemys, l'asseurance du royaulme, et l'augmentation de la christianté.[83]

She then gave thanks to God and went on her way to the banquet which had been prepared for her and the King in the convent of S. Ouen.

The royal party stayed for almost a fortnight in Rouen, graciously re-ceiving presents from the citizens, attending to the "affaires serieuses du Royaume" (the King spent the whole day of 8 October hearing plaints of justice at the Parlement), enjoying more water festivities, playing tennis, and watching the antics of the Conards. Greatly pleased at his reception, the King then departed, determined to visit other towns in his province of Normandy—Dieppe, Fécamp, and Harfleur, but more particularly Le Havre, in order to inspect for himself the new ships which were being built for the French fleet. The triumphs that his subjects had prepared for him encouraged him all the more in his designs to come to blows with Emperor Charles V, and he was on his way to make all things ready.

II *Political and Religious Themes*

It would seem that the authors of the surviving descriptions of Henri II's entry into Rouen tried to maintain a judicious balance between praising the French King for his personal achievements, for "la grandeur de ses mérites," and reminding him of the public duties which were expected of a monarch. A very clear progression can be found in the treatment of political and religious themes in the King's entries. His entry into Lyons (1548) had been primarily concerned with efforts to amuse him; Paris (1549) had stressed his potential greatness and had encouraged prepara-tions for war. Rouen (1550) praised achievements and expressed hopes for consolidation and expansion. In this last entry Henri II's personal triumph is emphasized not only by the presence of his device—the crescent moon—which adorned every garment and every spectacle but also by specific ref-erences to his recent military successes, literally depicted before him. The King's own contributions to victory are described as legendary, "Par ses

83. *La Deduction,* Q,ii.

vertus et faits chevalereulx, / ... il surpasse aisement les neuf preux." [84]
Many of the shows, displays of physical skill, and sea battles were obviously designed to please his personal taste, but the good people of Rouen
did not extend their wish to please so far that ideas of kingship were
sacrificed in order that flattering compliments might be offered to the
Duchesse de Valentinois. The King's mistress had enjoyed public praise
at the Paris entry in 1549:

> Et celle-là qui en la court royalle
> Est en faveur, la grant Seneschalle,
> Doit-elle pas icy le renc tenir
> Où par vertu on la veoit parvenir.[85]

At Lyons in 1548 the spectacle "Diane à la chasse" had formed an integral
part of the triumph. At Rouen, however, the only mention of the duchess
in the official account is her presence in the suite of Catherine de Médicis,
playing a subdued but honorable role. We learn also that she was one of
the people honored with a present; she was given "2 bassins et 2 aiguieres
d'argent doré" in a private ceremony, when the town councilors came to
pay their respects to members of the court. The honor which they felt was
due her was of a private kind, not to be exposed to the gaze of the general public.[86]

Such careful treatment of the most important woman in the land gives
some idea of the seriousness with which the people of Rouen considered
this royal entry. On this occasion the King appeared not so much as a
person (although Rouen had done its best to praise his deeds), but rather
as the embodiment of kingship, a God-given personage whose primary
role was to preserve and extend his kingdom. Woven in and out of the
pageants were themes which stressed the religious and moral basis upon
which kingship grew and prospered; the chariot of religion precedes that
of the King's "Heureuse Fortune," for example; a line of ancestors extends
before him, teaching him the art of kingship, and legendary heroes fore-

84. *Ibid.*, R,ii[v].
85. Quoted by Contarini and printed by Baschet, p. 474.
86. For the details of the presents see Merval's introduction to *L'Entrée,* pp. 19–
20. It is remotely possible that Diane de Poitiers was the intended recipient of the
prose manuscript; more likely, given the content of the poem, it was destined for
Henri II, in spite of the bow, arrows, and quivers which adorn its margins.

tell future prosperity. The vision which remains with him, however, is that of his father, enjoying the fruits of his labors in Paradise, reminding his son that although he must persevere and work to maintain good government in his land, the final goal in life is a spiritual one.

Nevertheless, hopes that the territories of France might be considerably extended occur more than once. Towards the beginning of the verse account, for example, we read:

> Voicy le Roy, qui avec oraison
> Des ennemys se fera la raison:
> Et qui pourra ses limites estendre
> Tant qu'il vouldra, sans humain sang espandre
> Et touteffois de glaive furieux
> Quant il vouldra, les ennemys des dieux
> Il punira et prendra la querelle
> De nostre foy encontre le rebelle.[87]

These generalities, which serve to amplify Henri's personal motto, "Donec totum impleat orbem," are later given greater precision. It seems that Henri's domains will be extended in two directions; first to encompass England, then to encroach upon the lands of the Emperor Charles V. In 1550 there were good reasons to believe that both these hopes might be realized. Henri had shown his strength in three encounters with England (in Scotland, at Boulogne, and with naval victories). Furthermore, it was thought that the French King had rights upon the throne of England, a throne which had once belonged to France and should again—to rid the country of the foul disease of Protestantism. Feelings still ran high against England at this time: Henri himself in a letter to the Cardinal de Ferrare, dated 26 October 1549, referred to the English as "une si odieuse nation." [88] The hatred they aroused seemed mainly to stem from their religious beliefs, which the French thought were polluting Europe. Henri was a fervent Catholic, and so were the Rouennais; it was natural that they should express extreme belligerence against "perfide Albion" and hope fervently to conquer it. Such hopes might nevertheless seem extraordinarily idealistic when it is remembered that exactly the same wishes had been formulated on behalf of King Edward VI of England only three

---

87. *Ibid.*, pp. III[v]–IV.

88. G. Ribier, *Lettres et mémoires d'estat des roys, princes et ambassades, sous les règnes de François I, Henri II et François II,* 2 vols. (Paris, 1666), II, 248.

years before, in "A Ballet of the King's Majestie," sung at his coronation entry into London, where the following lines occur:

> Hee hath gotten already Boullen that goodly towne,
> and biddeth syng speedily up and downe;
> when he waxeth wight, and to manhood doth sprynge,
> He shalbe streight of iiij realmes the Kynge.[89]

This provides us with a sufficiently ironic comment on the enforced hollowness of political themes in court festivals, where writers are apt to adopt the grand tones traditionally expected of them in such a context and voice impossible ambitions. This was obviously the case at Edward's coronation entry, where even the most blind of political idealists could not help realizing that any military acquisitions for England were hardly likely to come from the personal intervention or contribution of their weak child king. The Rouen entry, on the other hand, is operating in a context where reality is continually intruding and providing a basis for the spectacle. A letter from Henri II, dated 27 September 1550, shows just how close the organizers of the entry were to his own personal wishes and expectations. He describes his satisfaction at the events of his reign so far:

J'ai pacifié le Royaume d'Ecosse que ie tiens et possede avec tel commandement et obéissance que i'ay en France, ausquels deux Royaumes, j'en ay joint et uny un autre, qui est Angleterre, dont par une perpetuelle union, alliance et confederation, ie puis disposer, comme de moy-mesme, du Roy, de ses subjets, et de ses facultez; de sorte que les dits trois Royaumes ensemble se peuvent maintenant estimer une mesme monarchie.[90]

It is also the very strength and number of the military companies that process before Henri II which inspires the authors of the verse account to write:

> Doresnavant que l'aigle ne prétende
> Monter si hault, il fault qu'elle descende
> Du hault en bas et qu'elle plane l'aesle
> Dessoubz le coq, qui sera sa tutelle.[91]

For some time it had been known that the King of France was contemplating war with the Emperor, who was in considerable difficulty with

89. *Literary Remains of King Edward the Sixth,* ed. John Gough Nichols, 2 vols. (London, 1857), I, ccxc.
90. Ribier, *Lettres et mémoires,* II, 288.
91. *L'Entrée,* p. X.

recalcitrant German Protestant nobles on the one hand and threatening Turks on the other. Many reasons are offered to explain the speed with which Henri wanted to set in motion his next military enterprise. Saulx de Tavannes, very critical of his monarch, suggests that the King's personal ambitions and those of his favorites inspired him with enthusiasm:

Sa Majesté desire guerre avec l'Empereur pour ses pretentions, et offences receües, ainsi pour l'heureux succez de Bologne desire de paroistre plus que son predecesseur, s'esleve par presomption, poussé par les desireux des nouvelletez, qui pirouettent plus qu'ils ne vouloient tenir; et par le connestable pour aggrandir sa maison.[92]

Whatever the reason, there is no doubt that the triumphs he had just witnessed at Rouen, which had published his military greatness to the representatives of many foreign nations, goaded the King who, given his martial spirits, needed little encouragement to seek further honors from war, this time against one of the keenest political leaders of his age.

III *The Artistic Significance of Henri II's Entry*

According to the author of the prose account of this entry, its excellence

excede autant les facultez de mon esprit, comme il s'est trouvé surmonter l'expectation du Roy et de toute sa court, et grandement surpasser tous autres precedentz triumphes de temps immemorial celebrez en France.[93]

These extravagant claims are corroborated by other contemporaries; by Gilles and, miraculously, by the English ambassador.[94] Indeed, they had some cause for admiration since they had just witnessed a highly devel-

92. Saulx-Tavannes, *Mémoires* (Paris, 1819), p. 127. Contarini also cites similar reasons but adds the practical point that the King needed plenty of land since he had so many children: "Sa majesté est magnanime, et on voit qu'elle désire l'agrandissement de son Etat; on la tient pour être inclinée aux guerres, tant par son ambition que pour la guerre même. . . . Il faut dire en outre que la multiplication d'enfants lui fait ambitioner l'acquisition d'Etats nouveaux, pour les laisser grands sans toucher aux choses de la Couronne" (Baschet, p. 434).

93. *La Deduction*, K,i[v].

94. "En verité c'estoit une chose tant bien inventée qu'impossible seroit à croire qui ne l'auroit veue car tout estoit si bien umbragé de richesses et excellences que l'oeil du vivant estoit tout ravy" (Gilles, p. cxlv). Mason is quoted by Tytler, pp. 325 ff.

oped example of a complex art form which included processions, combats, song, verse, architectural achievements, and water sports, horse displays, lavish tapestries, and paintings, together with mock triumphs and satirical farces.[95]

The principal aims of the inventors of this triumph seem to have been to produce a spectacle which would astonish by its variety and richness— and this they achieved not only in the pageants and the triumphal cars but also in the detail of the costume; to introduce elements unknown to other triumphs—for example, the presence of the exotic Brazilians and their activities; to flatter the personal taste of the monarch in water shows and combats; and finally to create as great an impression of authenticity as possible. The prose account is always careful to point out that the elephants looked as if they were real; that the Frenchmen playing at being Brazilians were so painted and made up that they were indistinguishable from the natives they imitated; that the exotic trees looked genuine; that even the difficult tricks of making Hector's blood form three crescents and producing three successive transformations at the pageant at the Cross were so managed that the spectator's illusion was not destroyed and what he saw appeared as "extraordinary but natural."

Ingenuity in the devising of a machine to startle the onlooker had always been one of the hallmarks of court entertainments, and the Rouennais were not disappointing. It is hard to see, in fact, how they managed Hector's blood and the sky above, unless they were painted—which apparently they were not. The successive changes of the spectacle at the Cross must have been achieved, in part, by a series of drop curtains, used in conjunction with a complex revolving globe mechanism. Such complexity was not uncommon in royal entries; the 1533 entry into Lyons, for example, had had seven revolving planets on one pageant,[96] and the "Theatre de la Crosse" provides a further instance of the degree of mechanical proficiency attained in these shows—an ingenuity which makes contemporary indoor scenic designs appear pallid by comparison.

The most difficult elements of the festivities which the councilors had to organize must have been the events concentrated around the river.

95. I make no detailed comments on the song and verse of this entry. Only one song is extant, and the verse, for the most part, has little aesthetic quality.

96. On the third pageant the seven planets "incessamment viroient et tournoient" (Godefroy, I, 804 ff.).

They involved many people, performing tasks which were not only diverse but also impossible to calculate in advance. Three hundred Brazilians, for example, however well-prepared, would no doubt act differently every day. The water festival also, which so readily recalls the famous water tapestry of the series at the Uffizi Gallery, Florence,[97] must have depended on spontaneity, though the songs of the sirens and Arion and the speeches of Neptune and Thetis were probably rehearsed in advance. The sea fight, on account of the expense, could only be performed twice, since the Portuguese ships were destroyed on each occasion. These seem to have been the two parts of the triumph which aroused the most publicity and pleased Henri most, since further sea fights were organized for his pleasure during his stay at Rouen. In spite of their popularity, however, they do seem to form a kind of joyous interlude in a festival which otherwise hangs together satisfactorily.

Long after the most important French royal entries had passed away, the compendious mind of Claude François Menestrier began to formulate rules for them. The principal matter with which organizers have to concern themselves, he says, must be the unity of the entry, both thematic and aesthetic.[98] We have already shown how the King himself provides the links between the various political, moral, and religious comments. But how did the authors of the entry conceive the aesthetic unity? They leave us in no doubt as to what their intentions were. We are told, quite categorically, that the citizens of Rouen had chosen a manner of entry most appropriate to the recent victories of Henri II. He was to be given a triumph which scrupulously reproduced all the elements of an ancient Roman triumph. The triumphal chariots had been designed "a l'immitation expressé des Romains triumphateurs, chose bien deue à ung si magnanime et victorieux prince comme est le nostre."[99] The epigram,

97. The water tapestry perhaps did not record a particular festival but was rather a synthesis of many such shows. Savages had not fought at Fontainebleau as Miss Frances Yates points out (*The Valois Tapestries* [London, 1959], p. 54). They had fought at Rouen. There are many further similarities between the Rouen water festival and the tapestries: cf. the island and American Indians (or Brazilians?) in Fig. I; the sirens, the bridge, Neptune, and the Tritons in Fig. III of *The Tapestries*. G. Mourey, *Le Livre des fêtes françaises* (Paris, 1930), p. 52, thinks that the "Whale" tapestry depicts the Rouen festival.

98. Menestrier, *Réflexions,* p. 127.

99. *La Deduction,* D,iii.

"contenant L'epitome de L'Entrée," which is addressed to the reader and brings the prose account to a close, is even more explicit. It describes the proceedings as "Pareil triumphe à tous ceulx des Caesars." [100] Moreover, there are hints that although they wished to give the impression of an authentic Roman triumph, modeled on those of Caesar and Paulus Emilius as described by Suetonius, Appian, and Plutarch, they wished to outdo these ancient examples in pomp and magnificence; Henri II was more worthy than Scylla, more deserving of his crown of glory than Dentatus, Scevola, Trebius, or Fabius.

> Il vous fault bien d'autres triumphans arcz
> Que ceulx qui ont esté faictz pour Césars:
> Car la paix plus grans font ses mérites
> Que des Césars par cruelz exercites.[101]

The extraordinary length of the procession in front of Henri II is thus explained. The equipment of the soldiers who marched before him was "pareil à celuy dont l'antique chevalerie Romaine souloit user"; their skill rivaled that of Roman gladiators; their number was a measure of Henri's triumph. Just as Caesar's legions had preceded his triumphal chariot into Rome, so those who had fought with Henri carried high the spoils of victory. The elephants, symbols of magnificence, had carried Caesar's riches and models of the places he had won; [102] their slow, majestic walk was accompanied by numbers of soldiers joyously carrying aloft banners on which were painted images of the countries they had conquered. They had vases of precious stones, lighted torches of celebration, and laurel wreaths waving in their hands. Their prisoners, in chains, tramped be-

100. *Ibid.*, R,ii^v.

101. *L'Entrée*, p. II. According to Merval's introduction to *L'Entrée*, p. 8, the following lines formed part of the verses hung over the King's gallery:
> Là pouvoit le triumphe plus grand
> Que les Romains n'ont fait en leur vivant
> Au Scipion L'Affricain, Le vainqueur.

For details on the triumph, the following two articles of R. Schneider should be consulted: "Le thème du triomphe dans les entrées," *Gazette des beaux arts* (1913), pp. 85–107; "Notes sur les livres à gravures et la décoration de la Renaissance en Normandie," *Mélanges Lemonnier* (Paris, 1913), pp. 127–141.

102. According to M. E. Deutsch, *The Apparatus of Caesar's Triumphs* (n.p., n.d.), models of the places Caesar had captured were made in ivory, gold, silver, tortoise shell, and acanthus wood, according to the appropriateness of his five triumphs.

hind them. Musicians, trumpeters especially, sang out the long recital of victories to the crowd. Young and beautiful girls strewed flowers of honor. Priests gratefully sacrificed lambs to the gods, who would also receive a share of the booty. All these elements [103] provided a fitting escort for the victorious commander who followed on his triumphal chariot, crowded with spoils, wearing laurel wreaths in his hair and bearing the palm of peace in his hand. In the same way, not forgetting any one of these details, the citizens of Rouen had carefully prepared for the coming of the "Char d'Heureuse Fortune," which carried the living image of Henri II.

Throughout the prose account of the 1550 entry, the exactness and accuracy of the imitation is emphasized; and yet, much of the information for such an elaborate copy, as well as the inspiration for the idea, derived from sources other than the writings of Plutarch, Suetonius, and Appian. The entry owes something to medieval tradition, a great deal to the Italian and Imperial revivals of ancient customs, and much to evidence found in printed and painted sources. In Florence, the triumph of Paulus Emilius had been recreated in its entirety to honor Lorenzo the Magnificent. In 1500 Caesar Borgia had been given the triumph of Julius Caesar in Rome.[104] Such practices, together with the growing cult of the military hero and the importance that contemporary political thought gave to the Prince, had a significant effect on court festivals, particularly upon the royal entry. French kings—Charles VIII, Louis XII, François I, and their followers—as they were received in triumph into the Italian cities they had conquered, saw a modern vision of the ancient world spread out before them. Triumphal chariots passed through arches of extraordinary proportions and incredible intricacy, faithfully reproducing the Doric, Corinthian, and Ionic orders established by the Greeks. There were few "tableaux vivants" to greet the royal visitors. Instead the arches were adorned with statues of antique design and pictures in which all the diffi-

103. Suetonius mentions elephants, carriers of torches, and shows for the citizens, such as circuses, wrestling matches, naumachia, chariot racing, and beast baiting; see *The History of the Twelve Caesars* (London, 1672), pp. 24–25. Plutarch details scaffolds, statues, pictures, images, chariots, spoils, vases, trumpeters, animals for sacrifice, captives, and triumphal cars, ed. cit. pp. 222–227. Appian refers to "boeufs, chariots dorez, images et representations de ceulx qui n'y estoient pas, peintures des navires gagnez, des cités edifiées, Rois vaincuz," *Des Guerres des Romains,* trans. Claude de Seyssel (Lyons, 1544), pp. 230–231.

104. See P. Kristeller, *Mantegna* (London, 1901), p. 288.

culties of perspective seemed to have been overcome. (Italian buildings, too, were often decorated with friezes of ancient triumphs, and eating vessels were embossed with triumphal cars and the spoils of war.) [105]

Moreover, from the fifteenth century onwards, ancient monuments, elements of the triumph—arches and triumphal cars—and principles of ancient architecture increasingly made their way into printed works. The triumph of Caesar, with every detail intact, was engraved down the side of Simon Vostre's *Heures à l'usage de Lyons*.[106] *The Triumph of Maximilian* recorded in Burgkmair's remarkable woodcuts has been available in print since 1526.[107] Triumphal chariots adorned the texts of Petrarch's *Trionfi*.[108] Tory's *Champfleury*[109] depicts "Hercule Gaulois" as he would appear in the Paris entry in 1549; it shows a triumph of Apollo and the Muses (fol. 29ᵛ) and another of Bacchus, Ceres, and Venus led as captives, with the same trophies as those which accompanied Caesar's triumph (fol. 30). *Le Songe de Poliphile* of Francesco Colonna, first translated into French in 1545,[110] provided an inexhaustible source of information with its chariots—Europa drawn by centaurs blowing the trumpets of Victory (pp. 55ᵛ-56), Leda pulled along by elephants and accompanied by musicians (pp. 57-58), and Diana's car drawn by unicorns (pp. 59-60)—its erudite descriptions of ancient monuments, and its fine engravings of buildings, arches, fountains, grottoes, and so on. Further knowledge concerning the structure of columns for arches and the building of wheels and chariots could be gleaned from the first French translation of Vitruvius which Jean Martin had published in 1547, some of the engravings being the work of Jean Goujon. The entries at Lyons in 1548 and at Paris in 1549 (to which both Martin and Goujon contrib-

105. There are many illustrations of such triumphs in W. Weisbach, *Trionfi* (Berlin, 1919).

106. (Paris, 1502–1503); reprinted (Paris, 1920).

107. There is a new edition of *The Triumph of Maximilian I* with introduction and notes by Stanley Appelbaum, printed by Dover Books (New York, 1964).

108. See A. Venturi, "Les Triomphes de Pétrarque dans l'art représentatif," *Revue de l'art ancien et moderne*, XX (1906), 81–93, 209–221.

109. Geofroy Tory, *Champfleury* (Paris, 1549) is the edition I have used; see fol. 29ᵛ.

110. The translator was Jean Martin; according to Pierre du Colombier, *Jean Goujon* (Paris, 1949), Goujon did not contribute any engravings, though many historians maintain that he did.

uted) had made specific use of many of these sources (notably *Poliphile* and Vitruvius), concentrating their architectural interests on the triumphal arches, statues, and fountains.[111]

The Rouen entry of 1550 shows that these sources were not unknown or ignored—the permanent arch of the Golden Age built on the bridge spanning the Seine is proof of this. Throughout the prose account its author is at pains to point out architectural accuracy and complexity. At the beginning of his work he claims that if he were to narrate the details of all the shows "il seroit plus tost traiter les regles et preceptes d'architecture." [112] He does, however, indicate that the columns holding up the round pavilions are Corinthian and that the chariot of Fame was "enrichy de moulleures, Frizes, cornices, Metopes, Triglisses, consolators, et aultres membres d'architecture dores argentes et enrichis, des compartimens, Masquines, Feuillages, Begerres et Grotesques." [113] He mentions that Hector is supported by "quatre harpyes bronzées et racroupies sur stilobatés, au lieu de colonnes persanes, ou Cartatides" [114] and that the "Theatre de la Crosse" is supported on Doric columns. Similarly, he never forgets to praise the excellence of perspective. His intent is to prove that the inventions at Rouen can easily compete, in exactitude and proficiency, with the revivals from antiquity shown at Paris and Lyons.[115] Nevertheless, it does seem that, while being aware of the great interest expressed everywhere—in books, engravings, and buildings—towards ancient architecture, Rouen was primarily concerned to make its own contribution to the general enthusiastic renewal of ancient art conform less to the example of Paris and Lyons and more to a specific type of triumph. For this reason, it turned for inspiration to further sources still: to Mantegna's triumphs of Caesar and d'Aurigny's *Livre de la police humaine.*[116]

111. The affinities between the printed accounts of Lyons (1548), Paris (1549), and their possible influence on Rouen have been discussed by Du Colombier, *ibid.*, pp. 68–69.

112. *La Deduction*, B,iii.

113. *Ibid.*, D,iii.

114. *Ibid.*, M,ivᵛ.

115. Regarding the Lyons entry, cf. Paradin, p. 612, "en laquelle fut toute l'antiquité non seulement representée, mais aussi veincue, en grans et somptueus spectacles."

116. Gilles d'Aurigny's work, published in 1545, went into several editions; for details, see Jung, *Hercule*, p. 79.

The nine pictures of Mantegna depicting Caesar's triumphs might have been seen by the inventors of the Rouen festival in the Palace of San Sebastiano where they had been housed since 1501. They could also have had firsthand knowledge of them through the engravings of Nicolas Hogenberg or Robert Péril.[117] Whatever the source of their information, the Roman triumph which they produced is too close in detail to Mantegna's conception to have been simply created from the sources of Plutarch, Suetonius, or Appian. In Mantegna's version the "Picture Bearers," surrounded by trophies, not only carry standards and banners showing the places of victory, but one of them also carries a tiny marble statue—a parallel to the Virgin which was carried behind the "Char de Religion." The "Vase Bearers" in Mantegna's work and in the Rouen engravings have the same attitudes, suggesting that the latter was a copy of the former. The "Elephants" carry the same lighted vases and torches. "The Captives" in Mantegna are more varied, but they appeared similarly attired and in chains. In the "Musicians" where Mantegna presents castles and forts on the end of pikes, the Rouen engraver simply copies the Italian painter and throughout introduces the same turbaned individuals as companions to the triumphal cars—figures dressed in the same style with antique headdresses. The final picture, "Caesar on his Chariot," in which Caesar, holding both palm and scepter, is being crowned with laurel by a winged figure, also reminds us of the Rouen engravings; one has only to substitute the features of Henri II, and "Le Char d'Heureuse Fortune" appears before us.

Le Livre de la police humaine, originally amplified and expanded by Gilles d'Aurigny, was translated from the Italian by Le Blond. D'Aurigny's work became very popular and provided a convenient source of thematic inspiration for organizers of court festivals. It is especially interesting to us in this context since it provides some of the main themes of the Rouen entry, stressing the political force of war ("Nulle discipline ou excitation n'est plus utile et necessaire à ung Roy ou Empereur, que l'exercice de la guerre, ou il se doibt bien plus fier qu'a toutes ses richesses, et thresors"); the need for a prince to excel in military skills, and the overriding importance of reputation ("Un prince se doibt plus efforcer de laisser à ses enfans honneste renommée, que beaucoup de biens, pour ce

---

117. *Les Fêtes de la Renaissance,* ed. Jean Jacquot (Paris, 1960), II, 425.

que les biens sont caducz et perissans, mais bon bruyt est immortel"); and
finally, reminding readers of the joys of peace and of the necessity for a
monarch to be liberal, particularly towards men of letters.[118] It might be
argued that almost any political handbook of the century could have produced this kind of inspiration; but not every political treatise consistently
illustrates its themes, as does d'Aurigny, with reference to Julius Caesar
who "surmonta tous les mortelz par l'excellence de l'ame."[119]

Thus, the first half of Henri II's entry and elements from the second are
made up from highly complex source materials, which argue organizers
of rare talent and up-to-date knowledge. Traditional themes which could
easily fit into their scheme were not, however, ignored. The equestrian
portrait of the King, for example, which figures prominently in the verse
account's miniature of the "Char d'Heureuse Fortune," was probably suggested by a reading of the official account of François I's entry into
Rouen in 1517, where a similar statue on horseback "avoit esté ordonnée
pour aucunement en suyvir et emuler le triumphe des romains."[120]
So too the spilling of Hector's blood with such good effect may well
be an adaptation of the medieval "pressoir mystique," symbolizing the
blood spilt by Christ for the final redemption of man.[121] Similarly, the
vision of François I in Paradise, enjoying good opinion and offering good
counsel, repeats an age-old theme in the newer context of a garden whose
representation is organized following the strict rules of perspective. Thus
new inspiration is balanced by tradition. And yet it is the Roman atmosphere of the entry which remains uppermost in the mind. It led the author
of the prose account to say that it was "non moins plaisant et delectable
que le tiers triumphe de Pompée,"[122] and furthermore it inspired the
artists working on the stained glass windows of St. Vincent in Rouen to
introduce triumphal chariots into one of them. Although the original
window has been destroyed, a surviving drawing shows it to have used

118. The references to d'Aurigny have been cited in the following order: II, 68ᵛ,
16ᵛ–17, 92; I, 20, 92ᵛ; II, 9, 69–69ᵛ.

119. *Ibid.*, II, 13.

120. This constituted the fourth pageant for François I's entry into Rouen. The
tradition of using earlier accounts of entries for inspiration was well established by
this time; see Chartrou, *Les Entrées solennelles,* pp. 66 ff.

121. See Emile Mâle's discussion of this, *L'Art religieux à la fin du Moyen Age*
(Paris, 1931), pp. 117 ff.

122. *La Deduction,* O,iv ᵛ.

themes similar to those employed at Rouen in 1550. Other windows which show traces of such influence can be found at St. Patrice (Rouen) and in the Church at Blou.[123] The authors at Rouen in 1550 had anticipated Brantôme's judgment on the court and reign of Henri II: "qu'on pouvoit accomparer à l'empire de César Auguste, qui fleurit si bien à Rome en toutes grandeurs, magnificences, esbattemens et plaisirs, apres avoir mis fin aux guerres civiles."[124]

It is now the moment to ask who was the author of this entry? Many names have been suggested—Maurice Scève, who organized the Lyons entry in 1548, Jean Goujon, who did some work at Paris in 1549, and Brévedent, the prominent Rouen town councilor who designed the entry of Charles IX in 1563.[125] Since there is no great amount of evidence to support the claims of any of these candidates, let us consider what can be learned from the prose account. We know that:

Les Conseillers Eschevins de la ville de Rouen, non contentz de maistres ouvriers habitans en icelle ville, quoy qu'il y en ait grand nombre de suffisantz, avoient mandé venir de loingtain pays, souverains et excellentz maistres en leur art consommez ... pour nouvelles et estranges inventions et dessaigns excogiter.[126]

These remarks seem to refer principally to the artists who were actually to create the shows, not necessarily to those who had invented the general scheme into which the work of sculptors, carpenters, and painters would fit. Rouen seems to be following a fairly general practice of having recourse to specialist artists, experienced in erecting shows for royal entries and willing to move around from town to town in advance of the King.[127] Such a procedure might well explain the resemblances we have already noted in the printed accounts of Lyons (1548), Paris (1549), and Rouen (1550). It might be that the engravers were not copying from each other, but that the artists designing the detail of the shows were the same.

123. Details provided by Mâle, *L'Art religieux*, pp. 240, 282. He also points out (p. 279) a sixteenth-century house at Gisors which was decorated with reliefs representing the triumph of Caesar.

124. Brantôme, III, 280.

125. See Denis' list, *Une Fête brésilienne*, pp. 20–21; Merval's introduction to *L'Entrée*, p. 5.

126. *La Deduction*, Q,i^v.

127. See Jacquot, *Fêtes*, II, 475.

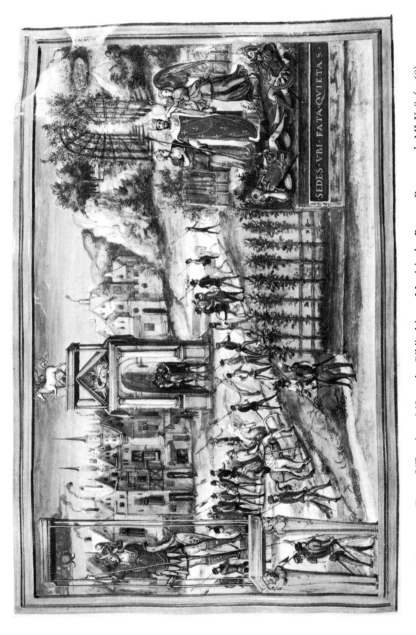

SEDES·VBI·FATA·QVIETAS·

Figure 21. From *L'Entrée* … MS at the Bibliothèque Municipale, Rouen, Press mark Mˢ Y28 (1268).

FIGURE 22. From L'Entrée ... MS at the Bibliothèque Municipale, Rouen, Press mark M⁵ Y28 (1268).

Is there any other evidence in the prose account which might provide us with clues as to its authorship? The author's erudition and his desire to show it off dominate all the descriptions. He shows himself to have a good knowledge of history,[128] both contemporary and past; he quotes from Virgil and Ovid;[129] and has been at pains to learn the technical and architectural terms necessary to give an accurate image of the works he is describing whether they are large, like the show at the Cross, or miniatures, such as the castles carried by the elephants. The "grand et sumptueulx Theatre [de la Crosse],"

à double plancher, porte sur quatre pillastres quarrez, et composez de pierre brutte, renforcée d'or moullu, et de bronze clair, et en la superficie, meubrises, et diversifies, parait mixte, engravez de subtiles voynes traversantes, de couleur de Jaspe, et porphyré, Et neantmoins la proportion et beauté convenables a tel ouvrage, diligemment observez, le fronc de chacun plancher et pillastre, estoient assouvyz de stilobates chapiteaulx, Tuscans, d'oriques, et composez de proportion diagonée, d'architraves, moulures, frizes, coronices, et frontispice, estendu d'or et argent bruny . . .

and he continues for several sentences more describing the detail of the friezes and the ornaments.[130] At times his knowledge seems quite gratuitous, such as his superfluous remarks describing the powerful effects of Orpheus' playing, or the extraordinary display of strange names which he gives to the sea monsters: "Vous eussies veu Sergestus agilement conduire son Centaure, Gyas sa Clymere, Cloanthus Scyllam, Menesteus Pistrin, et autres plusieurs Argonautes, comme Typhis, Zétes, Calays Thelonis, Phoceus, Canopes et Peloras.[131] It is as though his enthusiasm, both at the show and at his own erudition, continually gets the better of him. The exhilaration which marks his writing throughout is never more apparent than when he imagines "Echo" taking part in the water show, helping the harmonious sounds produced by the marine creatures to reverberate along the Seine.[132]

By far the most interesting and revealing feature of the text, however, is the insistence on the theme of arts and letters. This theme is cleverly

128. *La Deduction*, D,iii.
129. *Ibid.*, O,ii,iii.
130. *Ibid.*, N,ii.
131. *Ibid.*, P,iv; see also the ingenious play on the name *Marguerite*, P,ii^v.
132. *Ibid.*, M,i.

woven into the general scheme of the entry with constant reminders for Henri II that he should be liberal towards men of letters (by the harangue delivered before him on the cathedral steps) and with particular stress in the final two pageants on the presence of François I, "Prince clement, pere des ars et sciences." The late King with his "plus que humain sçavoir des bons autheurs," can teach Henri II most about the art of kingship, for as d'Aurigny had often repeated, government can only be effective if it is founded on the advice of good men of letters, and the King's name and deeds will only last for posterity if they are recorded by wise men. The author of the prose account more than makes these points clear; he lingers over them for some time, explaining in minute detail how generous François I was towards his fellow men of letters:

[il] n'a espargné ses thresors, faisant venir de pays estranges livres antiques et doctes lecteurs en toutes langues et sciences qu'il à honnorablement stipendie et promeu en estatz condignes a leurs merites, Au moyen de quoy les langues grecques Hebraiques Latines et autres florissent en France plus qu'elles n'ont iamais par le passé.[133]

The great attention given to these matters suggests that the author had a vested interest in persuading Henri II to emulate the magnanimity of his father. As though to encourage him further, he reminds the King that he has already shown himself worthy of all scholars' admiration by increasing the number of readers at the University of Paris. Such pointed congratulation implies that further gratifications should be made.

Opinions are divided as to the extent of Henri's generosity to men of letters. Contarini claims that he was "bien moins libéral et magnifique que son père." Brantôme, on the other hand, writes "il aymoit les gens de lettres et les entretenoit comme le roy son père." [134] The citizens of Rouen, it would seem, are as yet a little uncertain on this point, but the town is prepared to give solid encouragement, in the form of an image two feet high of the goddess Minerva, "Imperatrice des armes, et inventrice des ars et sciences." Our enthusiastic author devotes three and a half pages of his quarto text to explanations of this image. In lines stiff with classical allusions, erudite comments, and ingenious parallels, he develops his thoughts on power and knowledge, constantly underlining the important

133. *Ibid.,* O,ii. The theme of letters is also particularly stressed at the beginning of *L'Entrée,* p. II[v].

134. Contarini, printed in Baschet, p. 436; Brantôme, III, 285.

fact that both should operate together, and simultaneously, in a well-ordered monarchy.

In spite of the attention given to the significance of the choice of Minerva as a present, perhaps the most important mention of the theme occurs in the harangue made to the King by Claude Chappuys. The orator is himself the author of the speech which neatly sums up the entire series of shows and their significance, putting in pride of place all that the King's generosity can achieve for his people and his Church. Is it not possible that the orator Chappuys is himself the author of the prose text and even the inventor of the general scheme for the entry? He is obviously so conversant with all the detail of the shows, understanding so readily their implications, that he can produce a succinct summary of them for the King. The same enthusiasm, knowledge, and perspicacity which we have noted in the general descriptions marks his harangue. Furthermore, an ardent Frenchman, he was used to composing works which combined literary effectiveness with political comment. He had started by writing a panegyric of François I in 1538; then in 1540 he had written a *Complainte de Mars sur la venue de L'Empereur en France;* four years later he had once more protested against the encroaching power of Charles V in a satirical poem *L'Aigle qui a faict la poulle devant le Coq,* stating categorically, "Le coq tousiours partout prospérera," and ending with the prophecy that its "children" will survive, "En menassant d'Hercules les colomnes." A *Discours de la Court,* 1543, reveals his knowledge of court circles, of their intrigues, and of the political pretensions that were voiced there. His meticulous description of the *Sacre et Couronnement de Henri II,* 1547, prodigiously detailed and erudite, has great affinities of style and method with the prose account of the Rouen entry. Contemporary evidence also implies that he was intellectually capable of conceiving such a festival. Marot had called him "Un des bons poètes de son temps"; and, more significantly, Macrin had asked "Qui est plus cultivé, plus érudit que lui?" [135] In addition, by 1550, although "chantre de la Cathédrale," he had concentrated his attention on town affairs increasingly and had become one of the outstanding personalities in Rouen, his name figuring ever more frequently in the local records.

Conjecture on this subject becomes virtual certainty when we turn to

135. Quoted by Roche, *Claude Chappuys,* p. 24.

the municipal records for 12 June 1550. A special meeting of the councilors had been called to consider the question of the King's entry into
the town. Before arranging anything they decided to:

faire semondre M. Chappuy, chantre en l'eglise cathédrale N.D.de Rouen,
Croismare et Preudhomme chaniones en icelle église, Me Pierre de Couldray,
notoire et secrétaire du Roy, sr de Fréville, Me Robert le Fèvre Médecin, Me
Michel Desarpens, Gallopin, curé de Raoul-Feugère, Me Nicolle Malherbe,
Me Joseph Taseye, pour inventer quelque chose propre pour l'entrée du Roy,
de la Reine et à la décoration de la ville.[136]

From what we know of all these worthy gentlemen, Chappuys seems the
most likely to have thought up the idea of which the "ediffices, structures
et preparatifz, excedassent les autres de nostre aage et equipolassent les
antiques en beaulté." [137]

It is perhaps appropriate to end this analysis of Henri's entry into Rouen,
as he did, on a lighter note; revealing the forms of art which probably
appealed to the court's personal taste as opposed to those expressions of
feeling and opinion which more properly belonged to state occasions.
Rouen was renowned for its long tradition of political and social satire—
Picot's work on *La Sottie en France*,[138] for example, is almost entirely
devoted to an analysis of plays created and performed in Rouen, plays
which contained sharp comment on the war between France, England,
and Spain, for instance, in *Les Trois Gallans et Philipot* (c. 1545).[139] Most
often, these political satires were organized by the Conards of Rouen who,
in 1541, had dared to display the political jugglings of Henry VIII,
Charles V, and Pope Paul III.[140] Louis XII had been particularly fond of
such performances, which he felt helped him to discover exactly what his
people thought about his régime. Henri II seems to have inherited this
feeling, for, against the wishes of the town councilors who had denied
players of farce the privilege of showing the King their talents,[141] he
asked to see

136. *Ibid.*, p. 55.
137. *La Deduction*, Q,i[v].
138. E. Picot, *La Sottie en France* (Paris, 1878).
139. *Ibid.*, p. 71.
140. Petit de Julleville, *Les Comédiens en France* (Paris, 1885), p. 252.
141. See Merval's introduction to *L'Entrée*, p. 18: "M.Mustel advocat du Roy au
Bailliage de Rouen a remonstré que le Roy de la Bazoche, Régent du Palais a

la triumphante et ioyeuse chevauchée des Conardz: Lesquelz eux mettans à tout debvoir et obeissance superforcerent par diverse sumptuosité d'accoustrementz et monture, Par traynée de Chars de triumphe, Par nouvelles inventions, Subtilz et problemes dictons, et Par plaisantes moralitez, donner entiere recreation au Roy.[142]

So, in healthy contrast to the magnificent and pompous events of the previous days, the Abbé, chief of the Conards, rode triumphantly through Rouen, as was the custom, on a chariot drawn by four horses; he ridiculed people and institutions for their amusement and their embarrassment; "Aux conards est permis tout dire / Sans offenser du prince l'ire." [143] Experts agree that *La Farce de Veaulx* was performed on this occasion.[144] The play was apparently concerned with the sad state of the Conards' finances, and, as far as I can discover through the maze of abstruse allusions, contains no specific political comment.

A similar strange juxtaposition had occurred on the day before Henri visited the local Parlement, when the King's fool, Brusquet, had delivered a mock "plaidoirie, offerte comme distraction dans le parquet de la grand' Chambre du Palais de Justice, à Catherine de Médicis et à Marie de Lorraine." [145] Nothing—King, church, courts of justice—was sacred in the hands of the youth of Rouen. Their hilarity and their abundant satire was to survive until the serious-minded, humorless Cardinal de Richelieu took over the reins of government in France. Their satirical yet sane observations and their joyous antics bring the complex happenings of this royal entry to a close, reminding us that in the last analysis Rouen, while resurrecting a form from the past, had nevertheless concentrated attention on recent themes and had created, essentially, an occasion which in no way breaks away from the legacy of local traditions.

---

présenté requeste à la court tendant afin d'estre receu avec sa compaignye à l'entrée du Roy, sur quoy a esté ordonné que le Régent du Palais ou Roy de la Bazoche sera esconduit de la requeste par luy faicte d'aller en ceste qualité avec ladicte ville en ladicte entrée et que au contraire deffense luy seroit faicte d'y aller pendant le temps que le Roy y seroit."

142. *La Deduction,* R,iᵛ.

143. M. Floquet, *Histoire des Conards de Rouen* (Rouen, 1839), p. 115.

144. Published in Leroux de Lincy and Michel, *Recueil de farces* (Rouen, 1837), Vol. II.

145. Ch. Robillard de Beaupaire, *Le Trésor immortel* (Rouen, 1899) p. xlij.

Calderón, Cosme Lotti, Velázquez, and the Madrid Festivities of 1636–1637

J. E. VAREY

I N THE SUMMER AND AUTUMN of 1636, Spain was waging war against France on two fronts. In the Jura Spanish troops were besieged in the fortress of Dole, but Spanish reinforcements were at hand, led by Thomas Francis, Prince of Carignano and son of Charles Emmanuel I of Savoy, who had come over to the Spanish cause in 1635. In Italy, meanwhile, the Spanish troops were gaining the upper hand. In the course of this article I shall be concerned not so much with the exact nature and pattern of these historical events but with the impact made in Madrid by news of them and rumors concerning them.

News reached Madrid in early September that the French had been driven out of the states of Milan and that the Marqués de Leganés had entered Piedmont and taken Fontana, Arona, and Gattinara. Further news soon arrived of a great victory in Picardy, and Spanish troops were said to be nearing Paris. On 15 September the raising of the siege of Dole was announced, and Philip IV proclaimed his jubilation in an official decree. It is clear from the newsletters of the period that in early September a great wave of optimism flooded the capital.

On Sunday, 21 September, the King went in solemn procession to the church of Nuestra Señora de Atocha to give thanks for the victories of his arms. At the same time, the Princess of Carignano was on her way to Madrid. The Princess was French, being the daughter of Charles of Bourbon, Comte de Soissons, but she was also the wife of Prince Thomas of Savoy, whose troops had won such apparently significant victories in Flanders. A further joyful event was the approaching birthday of the heir apparent, Prince Baltasar Carlos, who was to be seven years of age on 17 October.[1]

I

On 14 October 1636, Philip IV decreed that Madrid should organize festivities in honor of the birthday of the Prince and, at the same time,

1. For the impact of the news of these events in Madrid, see the letters of the Jesuit chronicler in "Cartas de Jesuitas," *Memorial histórico español* (Madrid, 1851–1915), XIII, 479–517 (hereafter cited as *MHE*); and also the anonymous chronicler edited by Antonio Rodríguez Villa, *La Corte y Monarquía de España en los años de 1636 y 37,* vol. II of the *Curiosidades de la historia de España* (Madrid, 1886), II, 43–55 (hereafter cited as "Rodríguez Villa"). In *MHE*, XIII, 482–484, and at Biblioteca Nacional de Madrid, MS. 2.367, fol. 25ʳ, there is a copy of the *Respuesta de la ciudad de Dola, de el condado de Borgoña, a la carta del príncipe de Condé, general del rey de Francia;* a printed version exists, *Escrivense los progressos, y entrada de su Alteza del señor Infante Cardenal en Francia por Picardia, en nueue de Iulio deste año; y la retirada del exercito de Francia, y sus coligados del Estado de Milan, y la valerosa y fuerte resistencia que hizo la ciudad de Dola en Borgoña al Principe de Condè General de las armas de Francia en su assedio, con la respuesta de vna carta que aquel Parlamento, y Corte escriuiò al referido Principe* (Madrid, 1636), and a copy may be found at Biblioteca Nacional de Madrid (hereafter referred to as "B.N.M."), MS. 2.367, fols. 151ʳ–154ᵛ. A letter giving details of the siege of Dole appears in *MHE*, XIII, 504–506. The decree of Philip IV dated 15 September 1636 is printed in Rodríguez Villa, II, 55. For details of the journey of the Princess of Carignano, see Andrés Sánchez de Espejo, *Relacion ajustada en lo possible, a la verdad, y repartida en dos discursos. El primero, de la entrada en estos Reynos de Madama Maria de Borbon, Princesa de Cariñan. El segundo, de las fiestas, que se celebraron en el Real Palacio del buen Retiro, à la eleccion de Rey de Romanos* (Madrid, 1637), fols. 1ʳ–8ᵛ (hereafter cited as "Sánchez de Espejo"); and the anonymous *Venida a España de la Princesa de Cariñano muger del Principe Thomas de Saboya,* B.N.M., MS. 2.367, fols. 9ʳ–10ᵛ.

celebrate the expulsion of enemy troops from Milan and the arrival in Madrid of the Princess of Carignano; the festivities would not only show respect for the person of the Princess but would also be a token of gratitude for the services to the Crown of Prince Thomas. The decree was forwarded to the Town Council of Madrid, together with a list of the elements of the festivity which Madrid was expected to provide: a bullfight, seating accommodation for the spectators, costumes, and *carros triunfales,* or pageants. In accordance with the usual practice, each aspect of the festivity was put under the control of two members of the Town Council, the construction of the pageants falling to the lot of Claudio de Cos and don Gonzalo Pacheco de la Vega.[2] On 16 October, the Town Council received a letter from the Council of Castile asking for a statement of the possible cost of the festivities. The Town Council replied that it was impossible to give this information as too many factors were still unknown; there had, for instance, been no decision on the design of the pageants nor on their allegorical purpose.[3]

Perhaps because of the lack of enthusiasm displayed by the Town Council, a Jesuit chronicler recorded on 28 October that the festivities might be put off until the result of the election of the Holy Roman Emperor by the Diet of Ratisbon was known in Madrid, where it was confidently expected that the Imperial crown would go to Ferdinand, King of Hungary and Bohemia and brother-in-law of Philip IV (being married to Philip's sister, Maria).[4] This view does not appear to have been widely held and certainly preparations for the festivity were quickly put in hand. From a list of expenses (Appendix A-1) we know that on 25 October Domingo de Susvilla received the first installment towards the cost of constructing a covered shelter in which two pageants were to be built. He contracted to complete the task within eighteen days and received his final payment on 18 November. On 25 October Cosme Lotti, a Florentine

---

2. The decree of 14 October, together with the accompanying papers, is copied in the *Libros de acuerdos* of the Town Council: Archivo Municipal de Madrid (hereafter cited as "A.M.M."), *Libros de acuerdos,* Vol. LIV, fols. 266ᵛ–268ʳ.

3. "... Algunas cosas no se le a dado forma ni modelo dellas por que no se dice los carros que an de ser ni de que istoria ni fabrica ni el adorno dellos ..." (A.M.M., *Libros de acuerdos,* Vol. LIV, fols. 269ʳ–272ᵛ).

4. *MHE,* XIII, 522, 526.

who had served in the Spanish court since 1626 as a theatrical designer and a designer of gardens and fountains,[5] was paid a first installment of 550 ducats towards the 2,000 for which he had contracted to provide two pageants for the festivities, the design having been approved by the Conde-Duque de Olivares. Lotti received further installments on 6, 17, and 26 November. On 19 and 27 November Andrés de la Vega was paid for providing 108 persons, together with their costumes, who were to accompany the pageants; the final payment was not made until 6 February 1637. Pedro de Padilla received payment on 22 and 27 November for the trappings for the forty horses which were to draw the pageants, and on 24 and 27 of the month Juan de Lezona was paid for the horse collars. The traces were painted and gilded by Juan Bautista Sánchez and Miguel López, payment being made on 27 November, and the bridles and other accessories were gilded by José de Lubiando, who received his payment on 28 November. Further payments in respect of the horses are listed for 2 and 3 December; the payment of 2 December is for fifty sets of trappings, but that of 3 December mentions twenty-four horses only. On 28 November Juan de Baraona and Andrés de la Vega received payment for the costumes of forty *saluajes* (savages, or wild men) who were to precede the pageants in the procession.

It is clear from these accounts and from the dates of the respective final payments that the pageants must have been ready by the end of November, and, indeed, the payment made to Juan de Absete on 6 February 1637 states that the work on the pageants was completed by 14 November 1636. Yet the great entertainment of which the pageants formed a part was not used to welcome the Princess, who made her entry into Madrid on 16 November.[6]

5. For some details of the life of Lotti, see Emilio Cotarelo y Mori, *Actores famosos del siglo XVII. Sebastián de Prado y su mujer Bernarda Ramírez* (Madrid, 1916), pp. 111–112, n. 2; Vincencio Carducho, *Dialogo de la pintura* (Madrid, 1633), fols. 152ᵛ–153ʳ; Dr. Ulrich Thieme and Dr. Felix Becker, *Allgemeines Lexikon der bildenden Künstler von der Antike bis zur Gegenwart* (Leipzig, 1907–1950), XXIII, 409–410; Juan Agustín Ceán Bermúdez, *Diccionario histórico de los más ilustres profesores de las bellas artes en España* (Madrid, 1800), III, 52.

6. Sánchez de Espejo, fol. 7ʳ. Sánchez de Espejo errs in giving the date as 27 November. The next date in his *relación*, Saturday 22 November (fol. 9ʳ) is correct, so the error in the date of entry is a misprint, not corrected in the *Fè de erratas*. For a description of the entry of the Princess, see Rodrigo Méndez Silva, *Dialogo com-*

Various reasons can be adduced for the postponement of the festivity. The main reason appears to have been the decision of the Crown that an arena should be created on the Prado alto de San Jerónimo (to the east, that is to say, of the northern section of the present Paseo del Prado). The area is clearly to be seen in the *Topographia de la Villa de Madrid,* published in 1656 by Pedro Teixera (the relevant section is reproduced in Figure 23). It lies to the west of the façade of the newly-built palace of Buen Retiro and to the east of the line of trees bordering the Paseo de San Jerónimo, as Teixera calls it, known in 1636 as the Prado de San Jerónimo. The square building on the western side of the Prado alto is a *pelota* court. Two further illustrations give a clearer idea of the space available and the surrounding buildings. Figure 24 is of a painting, attributed by Elías Tormo to Juan Bautista del Mazo, and dated 1637–1656. Figure 25 is of a copy of a painting said to date from the time of Charles II and formerly in the possession of the Marqués de Castel-Rodrigo. The former shows, in the bottom right-hand corner, the Torrecilla del Prado, and in the latter can be seen also the bridge over the stream which ran down the side of the Prado de San Jerónimo, dividing it from the Prado alto. Both paintings were clearly made after 1637, for the Prado alto is shown as reasonably level.[7] In 1636 the ground was uneven, and, for the projected festivities, it was necessary to remove a hillock, "there," says the chronicler León Pinelo, "since God created the world." Both León Pinelo and Sánchez de Espejo stress the speed with which the work was carried out and give the impression that it was begun in February 1637, after the return of the King from his residence at El Pardo.[8] But the accounts show quite clearly that the work was begun in October 1636.

On 16 October it was argued in the Town Council that the Council of

pendioso de la antiguedad, y cosas memorables de la Noble, y Coronada Villa de Madrid, y recibimiento que en ella hizo su Magestad Catholica con la grandeza de su Corte a la Princesa de Cariñan, Clarissimo consorte del Serenissimo Principe Thomas, con sus Genealogias (Madrid, 1637), fols. 11r–12r.

7. For a study of the plan of Teixera, see Luis Martínez Kleiser, *Guía de Madrid para el año 1656* (Madrid, 1926), pp. 95–98; and for the two paintings, see *Exposición del antiguo Madrid. Catálogo general ilustrado,* published by the Sociedad Española de Amigos del Arte (Madrid, 1926), pp. 287, 323.

8. Antonio de León Pinelo, *Anales o historia de Madrid desde el Nacimiento de Cristo hasta el año de 1658,* B.N.M., MS. 1.764 (a copy), fol. 308v (hereafter cited as "León Pinelo"); Sánchez de Espejo, fol. 13v.

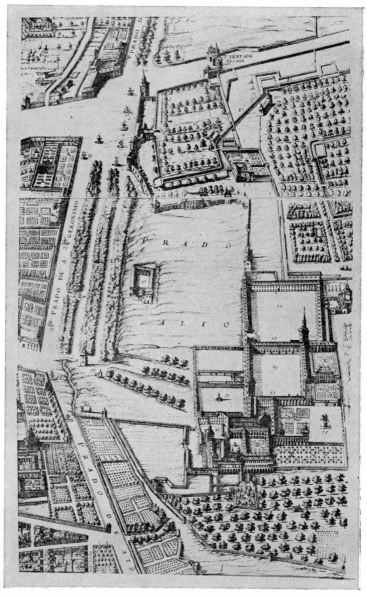

FIGURE 23. Detail from Pedro Teixera, Topographia de la Villa de Madrid, 1656, showing the Prado alto de San Jerónimo.

Castile be asked to request the King to order the festivity to take place in the Plaza de Palacio, or in the Plaza Mayor, or in the Buen Retiro itself; thus, said a *regidor,* would much expense be saved.[9] But on 25 October the *ingeniero* Juan de Ramsdique received a first payment towards the cost of leveling the ground, and further installments followed on 5 and 22 November. On 22 November he received a second payment for subsidiary works which would allow the pageants access to the arena, and further subsidiary works were paid for on 29 November and on 5 and 20 December. Francisco Martín and Diego de Magadán were paid for paving the arena on 22 December.[10] Clearly the task was longer and more complicated than had been anticipated, and it was also proving difficult to collect the immense amount of timber needed for the temporary structure surrounding the arena. On 24 November a chronicler records that the King had that day visited the site and ordered that 2,000 men should be put to work at once and that all carts and mules entering Madrid should be commandeered to carry the necessary materials. On 29 November a second chronicler writes that the festivities are being put off, although the countryside is being scoured for timber, the work on the arena is being carried out by night and by day, and a whipping post has been set up to encourage the laborers. On 30 November it is stated that a commissioner has been sent into the countryside to seek a further 50,000 planks.[11]

Bad weather also played its part. When the entry of the Princess took place on 16 November, there was a temporary pause in the incessant storms.[12] But the rains returned, heavy flooding occurred in Madrid on 14 December, and it was not until the last week in January that the skies cleared.[13] A further occurrence which undoubtedly influenced the post-

9. A.M.M., *Libros de acuerdos,* Vol. LIV, fols. 272^r–272^v.

10. 25 October: "... allanar y bajar la Plaza del Prado alto de San Geronimo ..."; 22 November: "... para ensancharla y quitarla otros pedaços de tierra para que entrasen en ella los carros triunfales ..." (A.M.M., Archivo de la Secretaría [hereafter cited as "AS"], 2-58-1^{26}).

11. For 24 and 30 November, see the anonymous *Noticia* which covers the years 1636–1641, B.N.M., MS. 2.339, fols. 74^r, 76^r; for 29 November, see Rodríguez Villa, pp. 66–67.

12. "Al zelo del Real afecto lisongeo el tiempo, y elementos, suspendiendo lo continuo de las aguas antecedentes, haziendole vn hermoso dia de Mayo" (Sánchez de Espejo, fol. 7^r).

13. B.N.M., MS. 2.339, fol. 80^r; *MHE,* XIII, 543; "A los rigores de este invierno y

ponement of the festivities was the death on 4 December of the infant Princess, Maria Antonia Dominica Jacinta.[14] A short period of court mourning would necessarily follow. On 20 November rumors reached Madrid that the election of the Emperor had taken place, and these were repeated on 9 December, when it was thought that the festivities might take place on 21 December,[15] but the combination of these various factors made the postponement of the festivities inevitable.

The Princess had arrived at an awkward time of the year for a festivity which of necessity had to be held out-of-doors; the weather was unusually inclement; and the decision to hold the festivity on the Prado alto had not only cost a great amount of money—as one percipient member of the Town Council had foreseen—but had meant that the preparations were not completed by the time the Princess arrived in Madrid. The definite news of the election of the King of Hungary as Holy Roman Emperor allowed the Conde-Duque de Olivares to find a face-saving formula.

II

The election had taken place on 22 December 1636 in the Diet of Ratisbon, and the news was brought to Philip IV at El Pardo on 13 January by don Felipe Ladrón de Guevara, son of the Conde de Oñate and Ambassador of Spain at the Court of Vienna. The news was greeted with three nights of festivities, plays, and fireworks, 13, 14, and 15 January.[16] On 14 January, Olivares wrote to the Town Council of Madrid, commanding that all necessary steps be taken to ensure that the *máscara*— as the postponed festivity was now called—could be performed as soon as the King should command.[17] Olivares returned to Madrid from El

---

a una larga porfía de continuas aguas que hemos tenido, ha sucedido un tiempo muy apacible y tan lindos días como se pueden desear" (Rodríguez Villa, p. 79; *noticia* of 31 January 1637). The sailing of the galleon from Dunkirk which was to convey the Princess from Spain was also delayed by the bad weather; cf. Rodríguez Villa, p. 66; B.N.M., MS. 2.339, fol. 81ʳ.

14. *MHE*, XIII, 540.

15. B.N.M., MS. 2.339, fols. 73ʳ, 78ᵛ–79ʳ.

16. Sánchez de Espejo, fols. 12ᵛ–13ᵛ; A.M.M., *Libros de acuerdos*, Vol. LV, fols. 10ᵛ–11ʳ; *MHE*, XIV, 14, 17.

17. The letter is copied in A.M.M., *Libros de acuerdos*, Vol. LV, fol. 10ᵛ.

Pardo on the morning of 7 February, the King and Queen following later in the day. The anonymous chronicler announces on the same day that great festivities will take place during Carnival, and that the most important will be held on Carnival Sunday, 22 February.[18]

The preparations were now speeded up, and a significant number of the documents which have been preserved date from 25 January to 18 February. Juan de Ramsdique, now a sick man, received through an intermediary two further payments, on 24 January and 9 February, towards the cost of preparing the arena. On 26 January, Juan de Villoria received payment for the construction of a wooden bridge over the stream which ran down the center of the Prado in order to permit the passage of the pageants; and two days later payment was made for a door to permit their access.[19] Other documents deal with lances, the construction of platforms, the painting of the decorations, the making, painting, and gilding of a balcony from which the Queen would view the festivities, and the provision of rush mats in a covered way along which the Queen would walk to reach a second balcony constructed on the façade of the Church of San Jerónimo from which she would watch the arrival of the pageants.[20] One of the most interesting of these documents reveals that a last-minute decision had been taken to replace the horses which were to draw the pageants with oxen (Appendix A–2). A supplementary list of moneys spent and owing shows that the forty sets of harness were indeed made for the horses but in fact never used.[21] The document quoted in the Appendix reveals that the oxen were to have a covering of buckram (*anjeo*), painted carmine and silver, which would give them the ap-

18. Rodríguez Villa, pp. 87–88.

19. 26 January 1637: "... Se libraron a Juan de Villoria maestro de obras 1.600 reales por haçer vna puente de madera mas abajo de la de piedra del arroyo questa en el Prado de San Geronimo para el paso de los dichos carros ..." (A.M.M., AS, 2–58–1[26, 32]). The *obligación* to construct the bridge is in A.M.M., AS, 2–58–1[57].

20. A.M.M., AS, 2–58–1[3, 10, 13, 15, 17, 18, 20, 21]; various dates are listed between 26 January and 6 March. On 29 January the Corregidor of Madrid ordered the painters and gilders to finish their appointed tasks within three days, on pain of death (B.N.M., MS. 2.339, fol. 92[v]).

21. "... Las quales dichas colleras y las guarniciones arriba dichas se hicieron para los caballos que habian de tirar los carros, y por no hauer serbido se lleuaron las colleras a la guardarropa de la Villa y las guarniciones estan en poder de el Cochero maior del Rei" (A.M.M., AS, 2–58–1[30]).

pearance of rhinoceroses. The change from horses to oxen was therefore presumably made in order to make it possible for the animals drawing the pageants to form, as it were, a vivid and striking extension of the pageant itself. The conditions for making the trappings were proclaimed on 11 February; they were to be supplied by 10 A.M. on 15 February, the morning of the performance itself.

The arena in which the festivity took place is described in detail by Sánchez de Espejo and León Pinelo. The arena measured 600′ by 530′ and was larger than the Plaza Mayor.[22] It was surrounded by a two-storied wooden structure, divided into 488 separate apartments. There was also a large glass-fronted balcony, hung with tapestries and destined for the use of the Queen, the Princess of Carignano, Prince Baltasar Carlos, and his cousins. Before the lower of the two stories was a scaffold, running round the arena and fronted with timber. All the woodwork was skillfully painted or made to imitate silver, bronze, jasper, and marble; the general effect was of a contrast between carmine and silver. The apartments and scaffolds were decorated with masks, swags of fruit, and other imitation architectural detail, "belying," as Sánchez de Espejo says, "by the richness and nobility of its outward appearance, the base and vulgar nature of the materials" ("desmintiendo a la vista en lo hidalgo y rico del traxe lo villano y grossero de la materia de que se componia"). The arena was lit by over 6,000 torches and glazed lanterns. Each apartment had its torch, and before the scaffold in the four corners of the arena were 200 free-standing candelabra, in the form of trees. Fire precautions were taken, and pumps were ready in case of emergency. The roads leading to the arena were blocked to prevent the access of coaches, and special entrances were constructed for the horsemen, masquers, and pageants.[23]

22. The *pie castellano* measures 0.2786 m.

23. León Pinelo, fols. 308ᵛ–310ʳ; Sánchez de Espejo, fols. 13ᵛ–15ᵛ; *MHE*, XIV, 36–37; Rodríguez Villa, pp. 99–100; *Relacion de las cosas mas particulares sucedidas en España, Italia, Francia, Flandes, Alemania, y otras partes, desde Febrero de 1636. hasta fin de Abril de 1637* (n.p.,n.d.), a printed *gaceta*, at B.N.M., MS. 2.367, fol. 177ʳ; *Sumario y compendio de lo sucedido en España, Italia, Flandes, Borgoña y Alemania, desde Febrero de 636. hasta 14. de Março de 1637* (n.p.,n.d.), another printed *gaceta*, at B.N.M., MS. 2.367, fol. 183ʳ. See also "Estudios históricos. Fiestas en Madrid en 1637," published anonymously in the *Semanario pintoresco español*, ser. 2ᵃ, II (1840), 195–196. The editor of this anonymous, and apparently contempo-

Rehearsals of the tourney took place in the Buen Retiro on 10 and 13 February,[24] and on Sunday 15, the King, accompanied by Olivares, went to the house of the Genoese banker, Carlos Stratta y Baliano.[25] In the previous year a huge and timely loan to the Crown had had a significant effect on the progress of the war; Stratta was made a Grandee of Castile, and the King's visit to his house on the occasion of this festivity was a further mark of particular esteem. Here the King was offered a collation, received costly presents, and dressed for the tourney.[26]

III

The entertainment began at 8 P.M. with eight drummers on horseback, dressed in white; these were followed by four trumpeters, also on horseback and dressed in carmine and silver. Musicians played and, headed by the officials in charge of the festivity, there entered fifteen groups (*cuadrillas*) of horsemen, each group comprising twelve gentlemen. All were dressed in a livery of black and silver, and, as they entered the arena two by two, bearing torches in their hands, each was followed by his lackeys also dressed in the same colors. The King then made his entry from the house of Carlos Stratta and took command of the sixteenth group. The horsemen then divided into two main bodies, headed respectively by the King and by Olivares. The King and Olivares also wore the black and white, although their costumes were more richly embroidered than those of their followers.[27]

---

rary, description was probably Ramón de Mesonero Romanos, since the piece is reprinted, with an additional paragraph at the end, in his *El antiguo Madrid* (Madrid, 1881), II, 243–250.

24. Rodríguez Villa, pp. 91, 97.

25. The house was "frontero de la iglesia vieja de Santa Cathalina, entre el Hospital de los Italianos y los Clerigos menores" (León Pinelo, fol. 310^r), and belonged to the Marqués de Spínola (Rodríguez Villa, p. 99).

26. Sánchez de Espejo, fols. 15^v–17^v; León Pinelo, fols. 310^r–311^v.

27. "Los vestidos heran marlotas y capellares de tela de plata con bordadura negra, los Generales y Maeses de campo con gabardinas, bandas y botas blancas, y espuelas de plata. Cada cauallero lleuaba su acha y dos criados. S.M. vistio su traje español bordado de plata. Los caualleros eran duzientos; las galas y riqueza la maior que se ha visto" (León Pinelo, fols. 311^v–312^r).

At this point the two pageants were drawn into the arena.[28] Each measured thirty-two feet in length, twenty-two feet in width, and forty-six feet in height. The two pageants carried, respectively, allegorical figures of Peace and War. The main decorations of the former were based on olives and flowers and those of the latter, on palms and laurels. Jupiter held the reins of the pageant of Peace, for he represented Life, whilst the pageant of War was in the hands of Saturn, representing Death. Religion rode in the pageant of Peace, and Justice in that of War, and the music of each pageant was suitably chosen, that of the former consisting of sweet harps and violins, and that of the latter being the martial clangor of trumpet and drum.

The main construction on each pageant was a large urn, decorated with the heads of heroes in low relief, with four sirens round its base. Below them were six emperors on horseback. In the front part of the pageant was a large shell, with seats for twenty-two persons, each of whom represented a virtue, the nature of which was indicated by the insignia he or she carried. Behind the urns, at the rear of the pageant, was a tall pyramid made of reflecting glass and variously colored. On its point was an antique urn, over which fluttered a carmine pennant. The base of the cart was surrounded by a gilded balustrade, the wheels hidden by a richly decorated pageant-cloth.

The pageants, each bearing one hundred lighted torches, were drawn into the arena by the oxen disguised as rhinoceroses and clad in their carmine and silver; they were accompanied by men bearing torches and preceded by forty savages and satyrs with maces. Before the pageants, as we have seen from the monetary accounts, walked Cosme Lotti himself, clad in his rich costume of carmine and silver. The theme of the decorations of the arena and of the pageants, then, was based on carmine and silver, whilst the colors of the horsemen were predominantly black and silver, or black and white.

The two pageants approached the Queen's balcony and then retired to two specially prepared entrances. The groups of horsemen, now divided

28. The Queen was able to see the pageants as they passed through the streets from the glazed balcony specially built on the façade of the Church of San Jerónimo. From here a covered way led to the apartment in the arena from which she viewed the dramatic performance and the jousting. The making of the covered way was ordered on 2 December 1636 (A.M.M., *Libros de acuerdos*, Vol. LIV, fol. 298ʳ–298ᵛ).

Figure 24. The Palace of Buen Retiro, attributed to Juan Bautista del Mazo.

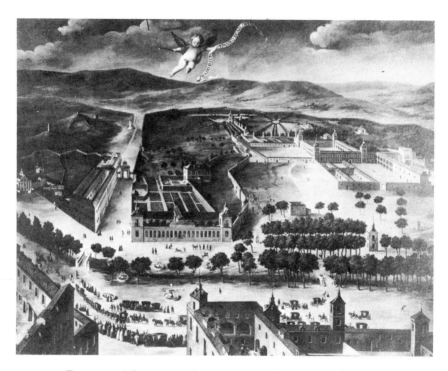

FIGURE 25. The Palace of Buen Retiro, by an unknown artist.

into two bands, galloped round the arena in mock skirmish, group by group, and then two by two. After the excitement and noise of the tourney, the two pageants then approached the Queen's balcony again, musicians played, and the actors performed a short dramatic piece, "a dialogue explaining the nature of the festivity," according to León Pinelo—that is to say, according to Sánchez de Espejo, an explanation of the allegory of the pageants themselves. The anonymous chronicler edited by Mesonero Romanos entitles the piece a "Colloquy of Peace and War." [29] The petition for payment by Alonso de Olmedo (Appendix A–4) speaks of an "auto, loa y colloquio," but it is not likely that the performance would have been as long as an *auto sacramental*. The performance obviously included songs and instrumental music; it may well have been preceded by a *loa,* or introduction; and the main spoken element was probably a "Colloquy" or "Dialogue" between Peace and War, between Jupiter and Saturn, and, perhaps, between Religion and Justice. According to Sánchez de Espejo, the author of this dramatic entertainment was Pedro Calderón de la Barca. The festivity ended at midnight with the King and some of his gentlemen tilting at the quintain (*estafermo*).[30]

IV

The festivities continued throughout the following week and up to Carnival Tuesday. On Monday 16 February the Condesa de Olivares offered an entertainment in the Ermita de San Bruno, with dances, a mock Galician wedding, a *loa* by Quiñones, and a play written and presented by amateur actors ("compuesta y estudiada por hijos de vezino"). On Tuesday 17, the festivities were transferred to the Ermita de la Magdalena and organized by the Conde-Duque, with a masque performed by twelve ladies and interludes and plays presented by three companies

29. "Representaron los comediantes que en ellos yban vn Dialogo explicando la fiesta" (León Pinelo, fol. 313ʳ); "... para representar ... lo significado dellos [i.e., of the pageants]" (Sánchez de Espejo, fol. 18ʳ).

30. The description of the festivity and of the pageants is based on Sánchez de Espejo, fols. 17ᵛ–19ʳ (his description of the pageants is printed in Appendix B below); León Pinelo, fols. 311ᵛ–313ʳ; Mesonero Romanos, *El antiguo Madrid,* II, 243–250; Rodríguez Villa, pp. 99–101; *MHE,* XIV, 36–38; B.N.M., MS. 2.339, fol. 98ʳ.

of actors. The following day, Wednesday 18, the festivities again fell to the lot of the Condesa de Olivares; the royal company embarked on the artificial waters of the Retiro (*estanque*), and there was a musical performance in the Ermita de San Isidro. The Town Council offered a bullfight at its expense on Thursday 19 in the newly-built Plaza of the Palace of Buen Retiro (that is to say, within the palace itself and not in the wooden arena of the Prado alto). The most important event on Friday 19 was a literary contest (*certamen literario*) in the Palace of Buen Retiro, presided over by Luis Vélez de Guevara. On Saturday 21 there were Carnival frolics, and on Carnival Sunday 22 a *mogiganga* in the style of Catalonia with four pageants, and interludes, dances, and plays. Monday 23 saw a performance of a play entitled *El robo de las Sabinas* by Francisco Rojas Zorrilla and Juan and Antonio Coello, performed by the company of Tomás Fernández, as well as a *máscara,* a bullfight, and a reed-spear tournament. Finally, on Thursday 23 February the Town Council presented a burlesque procession, and the company of Pedro de la Rosa performed a play by Pedro Calderón de la Barca on the subject of Don Quixote, a play which is unhappily lost.[31]

V

The monetary accounts relating to the festivities continue for many months. Of special interest is the document reproduced in Appendix A–3: the inspection and valuation on 6 March 1637 of the painting and

---

31. For an account of these festivities, see Sánchez de Espejo, fols. 19^v–25^v; León Pinelo, fols. 313^r–314^v; *MHE,* XIV, 36–38, 45–46 [the editor of the *Cartas* in a long footnote on pp. 38–39 summarizes the festivities but gives the dates incorrectly]; Rodríguez Villa, 102–114; B.N.M., MS. 2.339, fols. 98^v–100^v; B.N.M., MS. 2.367, fols. 177^r–177^v, 183^r–183^v (two printed *gacetas*); J. Domínguez Bordona, "Noticias para la historia del Buen Retiro," *Revista de la Biblioteca, Archivo y Museo,* X (1933), 83–90; "Académie burlesque célébrée par les poètes de Madrid au Buen Retiro en 1637," in Alfred Morel-Fatio, *L'Espagne au XVIe et au XVIIe siècle* (Paris-Madrid, 1878), pp. 603–684; *Academia burlesca en Buen Retiro a la Magestad de Philippo Quarto el Grande,* ed. Antonio Pérez Gómez (Valencia, 1952); *Academia que se celebro en el buen Retiro a la Magestad del Rey D. Phelipe Quarto el Grāde N.S. En la Villa de Madrid—Año de 1637,* B.N.M., MS. 10.293, fols. 93^r–118^v. I hope elsewhere to study in greater detail the dramatic performances of this period.

gilding done under such pressure—and under pain of death—earlier in the year. The work was inspected and the document is signed by three artists: Cosme Lotti, Pedro Martín de Ledesma (who is described as "sculptor and gilder"), and Diego de Silva Velázquez. Velázquez was at this time "pintor de cámara." [32] The signatures from this document are reproduced in Figure 26. Later in March there are payments to some of

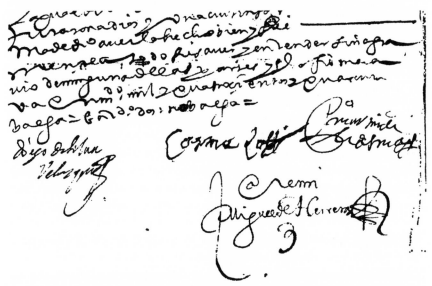

Figure 26. From Archivo Municipal de Madrid, Archivo de la Secretaria, 2–58–1[15].

the actors who took part in the theatrical performance on the pageants (Appendixes A–4, 5), and on 21 July the first list of expenses was drawn up.[33] In August Doña Ana Caro de Mallén, the author of a verse description of the festivities,[34] having lost an order for the payment to her of one hundred ducats, applied for a new copy of the order; on 18 September

32. For details of his work in the palace, see the very important article by José María de Azcárate, "Noticias sobre Velázquez en la Corte," *Archivo español de arte*, XXXIII (1960), 365.

33. A.M.M., AS, 2–58–1[1].

34. Ana Caro de Mallén, *Contexto de las reales fiestas que se hizieron en el Palacio del Buen Retiro. A la coronacion de Rey de Romanos, y entrada en Madrid de la Señora Princesa de Cariñan. En tres discursos* (Madrid, 1637), ed. Antonio Pérez y Gómez (Valencia, 1951).

the Town Council agreed to pay one hundred ducats to Doña Ana and
a further one hundred ducats to Andrés Sánchez de Espejo, as payment
for his *relación*.[35] The accounts extracted in Appendix A–1 were drawn up
on 19 September, but the colossal expenditure on timber is responsible for
a series of documents in the years 1637–1638,[36] and although another
attempt to produce a financial statement was made on 15 April 1638,[37]
there are nevertheless documents in the file which reach as far as the year
1640.[38] The financial burden of the festivities was truly heavy.

VI

The companies of players who appeared on the pageants were headed
by Alonso de Olmedo and Pedro de la Rosa (Appendix A–1). Many bio-
graphical details concerning these two well-known actor-managers are
available to us; it is sufficient for the present purpose to point out that
Alonso de Olmedo's plea that he was being kept unnecessarily in Madrid
while his troupe and family were awaiting him in Valladolid (Appendix
A–4) is substantiated by reference to documents published by Alonso
Cortés. In February 1637 Olmedo was invited to perform in Valladolid
and was given 4,000 *reales* in order that he might make the journey from
the capital. He finally arrived in Valladolid from Rioseco in June 1637.[39]
    Although Sánchez de Espejo refers to three companies of players, the
number of troupes engaged in the performance on the pageants was two,

35. Doña Ana writes: "Yo hice vn libro de las fiestas que V.S. hizo por los años
de S.A. el Principe nuestro señor, buenos sucesos de Dola y benida de la Serenissima
Princesa de Cariñan ..." (A.M.M., AS, 2–58–1[63]). The order for payment is at
A.M.M., AS, 2–58–1[24].

36. A.M.M., AS, 2–58–1[6, 7, 8, 9].

37. *Ibid.*, 2–58–1[27, 28].

38. *Ibid.*, 2–58–1[80]. Notarial copies of *cartas de pago* in respect of work done for
the festivity in 1636–1637 are to be found in the Archivo de Protocolos, Madrid:
Manuel de Robles, *protocolos* 5.812 (1636) and 5.813 (1637); Miguel de Herrera,
protocolos 6.583 (1636) and 6.584 (1637). The documents repeat some of the information copied at Appendix A–1.

39. Narciso Alonso Cortés, *El teatro en Valladolid* (Madrid, 1923), pp. 92–94.
Compare also the statement of Olmedo printed by N. D. Shergold and J. E. Varey,
Los autos sacramentales en Madrid en la época de Calderón: 1637–1681 (Madrid,
1961), p. 1.

as is clearly shown by the documents published in the Appendix. A third company—that of Tomás Fernández—was certainly engaged in performing plays during the festivities,[40] but we also know from a chronicler that Tomás Fernández was wounded in the face between 8 and 15 February 1637 on the orders of don Juan Pacheco, for having refused to perform a play to celebrate the recovery from a fever of the latter's ladylove.[41] Nevertheless, apart from the companies of Rosa and Olmedo, other players took part in the performance as *sobresalientes,* and it may be these players to whom Sánchez de Espejo refers as a third company. Among them was Vicenta López, who performed the role of Peace. She was the wife of Francisco de Sotomayor, whose petition is reproduced at Appendix A–5.

Vicenta López and Francisco de Sotomayor first make their appearance as members of the company of Cristóbal de Avendaño in 1626. In a *loa* written by Quiñones de Benavente for Roque de Figueroa in 1628, Sotomayor appears as a member of the latter's troupe, and the *loa* further states that Sotomayor had been nominated an *autor de comedias* but had failed to collect a company. In 1631 both husband and wife were again in the company of Figueroa and continued with the same troupe in 1632, when they were received into the Cofradía de la Novena, the actors' guild. Vicenta is stated to perform the second female roles in Quiñones de Benavente's *Loa segunda con que volvió Roque de Figueroa a empezar en Madrid.* According to Cotarelo y Mori, husband and wife left for Italy in November 1636 in the troupe of Figueroa; this is, however, by no means certain, as the anonymous author of the *Genealogia, origen, noticias de los comediantes de España* states that Sotomayor attended meetings of the actors' guild in Madrid on 14 March 1632, 25 February 1635, 12 December 1636, and 15 March 1637. Cotarelo also gives the date on which the death of Sotomayor was recorded by the chaplain of the guild, 30 September 1637, and supposes that Sotomayor died in Naples. From his petition, reproduced at Appendix A–5, it is clear that Sotomayor and Vicenta López were in Madrid at the end of 1636—thus substantiating the

---

40. N. D. Shergold and J. E. Varey, "Some Palace Performances of Seventeenth-Century Plays," *Bulletin of Hispanic Studies,* XL (1963), 212–244, print various payments for plays performed during the festivities; Fernández, as we have seen, performed *El robo de las Sabinas.*

41. Rodríguez Villa, p. 90.

dates put forward by the author of the *Genealogia*—and not in the company of any *autor de comedias*. This information also permits us to affirm the tentative date of autumn 1636–Carnival 1637 assigned by Hannah E. Bergman to Quiñones de Benavente's *Jácara que se cantó en la compañía de Olmedo,* in which Vicenta appears as one of the actresses.[42] In March 1638 Vicenta López was in the company of Antonio de Rueda in Madrid, having contracted to perform the leading female roles; however, she fell ill, and her life is stated in the document to be in danger. She was replaced by another actress. The document does not refer to her as the wife of Sotomayor, and this may be taken as substantiation of Cotarelo's assertion that the latter had died previous to this date. Vicenta López was indeed seriously ill, and her death is recorded in 1639. One child, Isabel de Sotomayor, was born of the marriage.[43]

In his petition Alonso de Olmedo insists on the physical danger which Vicenta López and her companions ran as they sat aloft on the pageants. No doubt the ground was somewhat uneven, despite the efforts of Ramsdique and his men, and no doubt the top-heavy structures swayed and lurched as they passed in procession into the arena. Vicenta López' ten days of rehearsals and the physical risks she ran, together with her professional services, were assessed by the Town Council at 200 *reales*.

VII

The entertainments of 15–24 February 1637 were clearly intended to demonstrate the wealth of Spain and the power of the Spanish Crown.

42. Hannah E. Bergman, *Luis Quiñones de Benavente y sus entremeses* (Madrid, 1965), pp. 326–328, 548–549.

43. For details of the lives of Francisco de Sotomayor and Vicenta López, see *Genealogia, origen, noticias de los comediantes de España,* B.N.M., MSS. 12.917–12.918, I, 76, and II, 93; Cristóbal Pérez Pastor, *Nuevos datos acerca del histrionismo español en los siglos XVI y XVII. Segunda serie* (Bordeaux, 1914), pp. 58–59; Emilio Cotarelo y Mori, *Actores famosos del siglo XVII. Sebastián de Prado y su mujer Bernarda Ramírez* (Madrid, 1916), pp. 35–36; Shergold and Varey, *Los autos sacramentales en Madrid,* p. 9; Hugo Albert Rennert, *The Spanish Stage in the Time of Lope de Vega* (New York, 1909), pp. 510–511, 603; Emilio Cotarelo y Mori, *Tirso de Molina. Investigaciones bio-bibliográficas* (Madrid, 1893), p. 206; Bergman, *Luis Quiñones,* pp. 548–549; Luis Quiñones de Benavente, *Colección de piezas dramáticas, entremeses, loas y jácaras,* ed. Cayetano Rosell (Madrid, 1872–1874), I, 224, 232.

The description of a theatrical performance in the Alcázar in November 1636, for instance, enables Sánchez de Espejo to publish to the world the noble way in which Spain venerates its kings.[44] For this reason the pageants of 15 February were necessarily lavish and on the grand scale, outdoing, says a chronicler, the splendors of ancient Rome.[45] The festivity was intended to dazzle the eye by its lavish detail, the brilliance of the illumination, the sharp color contrasts of black/white-silver and carmine/silver.[46] The pageants were expressly designed for their purpose, with the shell-like structures at the front facing the Queen, the urn with the principal figures at the center, and the tall pyramids at the rear. The decorative motifs are clichés of the period; the flowers and olives of peace and the palms and laurels of war could find their parallels in the works of any contemporary poet or dramatist. The balanced allegory bears a strong resemblance to that employed in the *autos sacramentales* (the religious plays performed on carts during the feast of Corpus Christi), the similarity arising from the fact that the *autos* of this period, like this theatrical performance, were based on two separate carts. The dramatist, influenced by this basic factor, tends to play one cart against another, thus producing the balanced structure with which we are familiar in the *autos* of Valdivielso, Lope de Vega, and Calderón. Calderón, a past master of staging techniques, would undoubtedly have felt at home when he came to turn his hand to the *Dialogue* or *Colloquy* performed on the pageants.

The purpose of the festivity is clearly not susceptible of simple definition. The treatment of the Princess of Carignano was by no means as happy as might be assumed, considering the importance of Prince Thomas to the Spanish cause. In mid-December the Princess was informed that she was to leave her four children behind in Spain, presumably to ensure

44. "... La Magestad y grandeza de respetos con que venera España sus Reyes ..." (Sánchez de Espejo, fol. 9ᵛ).

45. "Dos carros triunfales muy grandes, de tan admirable inuencion y arquitectura, Agujas, Basas, y Pedestales, que la antiguedad Romana no vio tan hermosas maquinas" (a printed *gaceta* at B.N.M., MS. 2.367, fol. 177ʳ).

46. The contemporary accounts refer to the same color as both *carmín* and *leonado* (literally, "tawny"). It is interesting to note that when the royal family rode to Atocha to give thanks on 21 September, they and Olivares were dressed in the same combination of colors: "Los Reyes, y Principes de leonado y plata: y el Exceletissimo señor Conde Duque de los mismos colores" (the printed *gaceta* at B.N.M., MS. 2.367, fol. 176ʳ).

them a Spanish upbringing, but perhaps as unofficial hostages. She was given this news early enough so that she would not depart "disconsolate and troubled." On 6 January 1637 she was said to be much happier than she had felt for some days past, but that week she had had a passionate quarrel with the Condesa de Olivares.[47] The temperature inside the glazed balcony from which the ladies viewed the festivities may well have been a little chilly. The Princess was undoubtedly used by Olivares. The account of Sánchez de Espejo, himself a dependent of Olivares, stresses the "liberality" of her treatment. Spain had just gained significant victories in the province of Milan, and here was a princess of French origin, even if married to an ally, come to the capital of Spain. Her treatment was deliberately intended to recall the treatment received by the captive King of France, Francis I, after the battle of Pavia. Let the French know, writes Sánchez de Espejo, that if Philip IV with his might can overcome them, with his magnanimity and with his clemency he can welcome a Bourbon to Spain.[48] Olivares is endeavoring to make these temporary victories in Italy, and in Flanders, into another sixteenth-century epic. The malicious, however, murmur that he is also trying to impress his rival, Richelieu, with Spain's wealth.[49]

We have seen that Olivares insisted that the festivity should take place on the Prado alto, under the windows of the palace of Buen Retiro which he had himself created. It may be that one reason for this insistence is that he intended the Town Council to bear the expense of leveling the Prado alto, a suggestion which perhaps accounts for some of the opposition he met from Madrid.[50] But the work took much longer than had been anticipated. The Princess arrived and was received with only minor fes-

47. *MHE,* XIII, 547; XIV, 2-3.

48. One of the reasons for which Sánchez de Espejo writes is, he says (fol. 1ʳ), "para que los estrangeros entiendan, que si es Rey poderoso, si, para subjugarlos; es pues Magestuoso para honrar cumpliendo con tanta magnificencia con los Titulos, que su piedad quiere calificarlos por empeños de su grandeza."

49. "Dicen los discursistas que tan grande acción ha tenido otro fin que el de recreación y pasatiempo, que fue también ostentación, para que el Cardenal Richelieu nuestro amigo sepa que aun hay dinero en el mundo que gastar y con que castigar a su Rey" (Rodríguez Villa, p. 101).

50. Sánchez de Espejo, fol. 13ᵛ, reveals that there were criticisms of the decision to level the Prado alto: "Començòse a igualar con admiracion de todos, si bien con coartada censura de los que no penetrauan el fin ..."

tivities; the Prince's birthday came and went; the rains poured down, but, to judge from the chroniclers, did not dampen the enthusiasm aroused in Spanish breasts by the recent victories. The election to the Imperial Crown gave Olivares an opportunity to use the lavish spectacle which he had created. The use of the festivity for this purpose had been thought of as early as October, but it only became a serious possibility after the arrival of the Princess in mid-November.[51] Hence the title of Sánchez de Espejo's account, describing the festivity as a two-pronged affair, stretching from November to February, and hence his insistence on the liberality of the Spanish Crown, its continent-wide connections, and the sweep and grandeur of the ideas of its chief minister, Olivares.

The festivity was certainly intended also to consolidate the position of the Conde-Duque. In the tourney he takes a place second only to the King, and, indeed, in heading the rival troop, he places himself almost on a par with his sovereign. Both Sánchez de Espejo and the authors of both the *gacetas* spare no opportunity to praise his farsighted genius. The success of the entire festivity is attributed to him, and all shortcomings are glossed over.

VIII

Here, then, is a theatrical festivity intended to amuse, but one which also has a political aim. It brings together Velázquez, putting an expert valuation on painting work done in a great hurry; Cosme Lotti as a designer of pageants; and Calderón as the author of a short dramatic piece, now unhappily lost.[52] The *Dialogue* or *Colloquy* is not a typical genre for Calderón to use, but it would not be dissimilar to the *loas* which preceded the Corpus performances. It would be interesting to have seen if Calderón made political capital out of the possible contrasts between

51. A printed *gaceta* suggests that as early as September the intention had been to await the arrival of the expected news from Ratisbon (B.N.M., MS. 2.367, fol. 177ʳ), but this is written with the advantage of hindsight and only serves to confirm what has been said.

52. The assertion of Emilio Cotarelo y Mori, *Ensayo sobre la vida y obras de D. Pedro Calderón de la Barca* (Madrid, 1924), pp. 182–184, that Calderón took little part in these festivities can thus be seen to be invalid. Cotarelo was only aware of the reference to the performance of the lost play on the subject of Don Quixote.

Peace and War, between Religion and Justice, and if he referred to the sinfulness of war between Christian peoples, a point which was much in the minds of many of his audience. His antithetical concepts would use to their full value the symbolism inherent in the design of the pageants, and no doubt he too would have endeavored to stress the liberality and magnificence of the Crown of Spain. It is unfortunate that the *Colloquy* or *Dialogue of Peace and War* should be unknown to us; perhaps it still remains to be discovered in a Spanish archive or library.[53]

Appendixes

A–*Manuscript sources*

In the transcription of these documents, abbreviations have been resolved, and modern practice has been followed with respect to double consonants and capitalization; some necessary punctuation has been added.

A–1. *Extracts from a series of accounts, dated 19 September 1637*

[The expenses directly related to the pageants are here extracted. Where payment was made in installments, the first payment only is copied in full. The entries have been arranged in chronological order.]

"... A Domingo de Susvilla, maestro de obras, 6.000 reales por los mismos que vbo de hauer por la primera paga y por quenta de 14.000 reales en que se obliga a haçer el colgadizo y zerramiento que se hiço en el alto del dicho Prado para la fabrica de los carros triunfales: lo qual se obligo a hacer dentro de 18 dias por libramiento de Madrid de 25 de octubre de 1636." (Additional payments on 31 October and 18 November.)

"... En 25 del dicho mes de octubre de 1636 se libraron a Cosme Lot, yngeniero de S.M., 550 ducados por la primera paga y por quenta de 2.000 ducados en que se obligo a hacer los dos carros triunfales para las dichas fiestas a satisfaçion del Sr. Conde Duque." (Additional payments on 6, 17, 26 November.)

"... En 19 del dicho mes [November] y año se libraron a Andres de la Vega 11.000 reales por la primera paga y por quenta de los 21.000 reales en que estuvo obligado a dar 108 bestidos y otras tantas personas para los

---

53. I am, as always, greatly indebted to don Agustín Gómez Iglesias, Archivist of Madrid, for the unfailing generosity with which he has placed at my disposal the documentary riches of his archive.

carros triunfales que se hizieron para las dichas fiestas, conforme a vna memoria." (Additional payments on 27 November 1636 and 6 February 1637.)

"... En el dicho dia, mes y año dichos [22 November 1636] se libraron a Pedro de Padilla, guarniçionero, 2.000 reales por la primera paga y por quenta de 4.000 por el preçio de 40 guarniciones como las de arriua y rendajes y sus mangas para 40 cauallos para tirar los carros triunfales para las dichas fiestas por precio de 200 reales cada par de guarniçiones." (Additional payment on 27 November.)

"... En 24 del dicho mes y año [November 1636] se libraron a Juan de Leçona, maestro de hacer sillas, 2.700 reales por quenta de las 40 colleras para otros tantos cauallos que tiraron los carros triunfales en las dichas fiestas, a raçon de a 135 reales cada collera." (Additional payment on 27 November.)

"... En 27 del dicho mes y año [November 1636] se libraron a Juan Bautista Sánchez y Miguel López, pintores, 550 reales por tantos en que se obligaron a pintar y platear los tirantes de los 40 cauallos para tirar los carros para la mascara de las dichas fiestas."

"... En el dicho dia, mes y año [28 November 1636] se libraron a Juan de Baraona y a Andres de la Vega 240 ducados de a onçe reales por los vestidos que se obligaron a haçer de los saluajes que fueron 40 y otras 40 personas para salir delante de los dichos carros triunfales en la dicha noche para las dichas fiestas."

"... En 28 del dicho mes y año [November 1636] se libraron a Jusepe de Lubiando, dorador, 450 reales por adereçar 40 frenos de los cauallos que an de tirar los dos carros triunfales y ponerlos baruadas y alacranes y estanarlos para las dichas fiestas."

"... En 2 del dicho mes de diziembre del dicho año de 1636 se libraron a Francisco Beltran de Echauarri, Secretario de S.M. y su Contador de relaciones y Guardajoyas de la Reina Madre, 5.000 ducados de a 11 reales para los 50 bestidos que lleuaron los cauallos que tiraron los dichos carros triunfales y 100 bestidos de los lacayos que vistio esta Villa, los 4.000 por los mismos que pago el Secretario Diego Suarez por quenta de los 17.500 que deuia a esta Villa, y los otros en la forma que las demas partidas de arriua."

"... En 3 del dicho mes de diziembre del dicho año [1636] se libraron a Francisco de Mesa, frenero, 336 reales por 24 frenos que se obligo a haçer

para las dichas fiestas, a raçon de a 14 reales cada freno, para los 24 cauallos que tiraron los dichos carros triunfales."

"... En 6 de febrero del dicho año de 1637 se libraron a Juan de Absete 425
reales que gasto en dar de almorçar y comer a Cosme Lot, yngeniero, a
cuyo cargo estubo el hacer los dichos carros triunfales, por que no se
apartase de la dicha fabrica y asistiese a que se trauaje en ellos, desde 27
de octubre de 1636 hasta 14 del noviembre del dicho año, por mandado
del Sr. Conde de Montaluo."

"... En 17 del dicho mes y año [February 1637] se libraron al dicho Domingo Sanz de Viteri 3.525 reales que conforme vna quenta se le deuian
por otra tanta cantidad que monto el bestido que por mandado de S.M.
se dio a Cosme Lot, yngeniero, para yr delante de los carros triunfales, y
6 baras de tafetan encarnado para las banderillas de los dichos carros ..."

"... En 11 del dicho mes y año [March 1637] se libraron a Pedro de Luna y
Pedro del Rio, trauajadores, 1.030 reales para ellos y los demas que sacaron
los carros triunfales a la Plaça y los que asistieron el dia y noche antes de
la de la mascara."

"... En 31 de marco del dicho año [1637] se libraron a Francisco de Sotomayor 500 reales por su muger por la ocupaçion y trauajo que tubo en la
representaçion y estudio de la loa que hiço en los carros triunfales para
las dichas fiestas."

"En el dicho dia 31 de marco del dicho año [1637] se libraron a Alonso de
Olmedo y Pedro de la Rosa, autores de comedias, 1.000 reales a cada vno
por la ocupacion y trauajo que tubieron con sus compañias en la repre-
sentacion de los dichos carros en las dichas fiestas."

                                        (A.M.M., AS, 2–58–1[26])

A–2. *11 February 1637. Trappings of the oxen.*

"Condiciones con que se an de hacer quarenta bestidos que an de lleuar
los bueyes que an de tirar los carros triunfales. Son las siguientes:

"Cada bestido a de ser vna manta de bara y quarta de ancho y tres baras
de largo de anxeo, lo qual a de yr pintado de plata y carmin conforme la
muestra que en la traça del bestido esta dispuesta.

"Ansimismo a de lleuar todo el rastro del buey de cartones ajustados con
los cuernos de lo mismo en figura de reynoçeronte y en el rostro vna como
tronpa finxida de carton. Sobre el pescueço an de ser como tocador que

caiga a los lados con sus espinas de carton. Y debajo de la barua lo mismo conforme el dicho dibujo que esta para este efeto hecho. Todo ello de plata y carmin a satisfacion de los Sres. Corregidor y Comisarios. Lo qual se a de entregar para el domingo 15 deste mes a las diez de la mañana sin hacer falta, lo qual se pregone y remate luego en quien por menos lo hiçiere. En Madrid a 11 de Febrero de 1637 años. —CLAUDIO DE COS. —DON GONÇALO PACHECO DE LA VEGA":

[In the left-hand margin:] "Lo que dice la condicion que sea la caueça de carton, a de ser del mismo anjeo pintado, con los adornos de carton. [Rúbrica]."

The conditions were proclaimed and bids received and accepted on 11 February from Domingo Sobrino, Simón de Ballenilla, and Antonio Gutiérrez.

(A.M.M., AS, 2–58–1[16])

A–3. *4–6 March 1637. Valuation of painting and gilding.*

(*a*) Undated list of additional painting works carried out by Francisco de Barrera, Antonio Ponce, Lorenzo Sánchez, and Domingo de Yangues.

(*b*) 4 March 1637. Order of the Town Council of Madrid that this work should be inspected and valued.

(*c*) 6 March 1637. "En la villa de Madrid a 6 dias del mes de março de 1637 años ante mi el escriuano Cosme Lot, yngeniero de S.M., y Diego Belazquez, pintor de su Real camara, y Pedro Martin de Ledesma, escultor y dorador, dixeron que en cumplimiento del auto proueido por los señores Corregidor y Comisarios ellos an bisto toda la obra de demasias que hiçieron los contenidos en el dicho auto, lo qual tasan y baluan en la forma siguiente:

"Primeramente tasaron el lienço grande del çielo del balcon de la Reina nuestra Señora, dorada la moldura, pintado y el corte del lienço en 3.300 reales.

"Mas tasaron las dos tablas que pintaron y doraron entre el bastidor de las bidrieras y el lienço del çielo del dicho balcon y las dos tarvas de los dos lados que siruieron de pilastras y los demas adornos que vbo en esta parte de pintura y dorado en 1.400 reales.

"Mas de dorar todos los marcos de las bidrieras por dentro y fuera esceto los plomos que no los doraron los dichos, lo tasan en 1.000 reales.

"Mas tasaron el dorar el balcon de hierro con su pasamano alto y bajo y el pedrestral de hierro que tenia en 1.100 reales.

"Mas tasaron 4 tablas que doraron en el dicho balcon por la parte de afuera con sus faxas de oro y festones y demas adorno del dicho balcon en 500 reales con el dorado y pintado de las dichas tablas.

"Mas de pintar y dorar 6 pilastras que se pusieron por la parte de adelante de la bidriera tasaron en 500 reales.

"De vna tabla que pintaron y doraron que hace friso debajo del balcon de hierro con sus fajos y brutescos de oro en 200 reales.

"Mas de vna cornisa que esta ençima de las pilastras de dorarla, y pintarla, en 150 reales.

"Mas tasaron el pedrestral que reçiuia los frontispicios y esfera con los demas adornos que de alli arriua ay de trofeos de guerra y otras cosas pintadas en 1.200 reales.

"Mas tasaron el pintar y dorar 8 candeleros de oro y berde en 88 reales.

"Mas tasaron el pintar 2 lienços finxidos de ladrillo que estubieron por la parte de afuera del balcon con el lienço y bastidores que pusieron y pintaron en 150 reales.

"Mas tasaron el pintar 40 escudos de las armas de los reinos a 36 reales cada uno que montan 1.440 reales.

"Mas tasaron de toda costa las 42 mantas pintadas y plateadas para los bueyes a 100 reales cada vna: 4.200 reales.

"Mas tasaron 6 mantas que fueron pintadas de cola y en lugar de plata, labores blancos, a toda costa a 55 reales cada una: 330 reales.

"Mas tasaron la pintura y dorado de los 18 escudos de armas que se pusieron en la Plaça para las quadrillas de armas y geroglificos, pies y candeleros a 160 reales cada uno que montan 2.880 reales.

"Mas de 425 pares de cartelas que pintaron y platearon a real cada par montan 425 reales.

"Mas de 151 luminarias pintadas de blanco y colorado de a 12 acheros cada una a 4 reales, que montan 600 reales.

"La qual dicha tasacion y declarazion juraron a Dios y vna cruz en forma de derecho auerlo hecho bien y fielmente a todo su sauer y entender sin agrauio de ninguno de las partes, y lo firmaron ... DIEGO DE SILUA VELAZQUEZ. —COSME LOTTI. —PEDRO MARTIN DE LEDESMA. Ante mi: MIGUEL DE HERRERA."

(A.M.M., AS, 2-58-1[15])

A-4. *March 1637. Petition of Alonso de Olmedo.*

(*a*) Undated. "Alonso de Olmedo, author de comedias, digo que el Corregidor y don Gonçalo Pacheco y otros Comisarios de la fiesta grande del Retiro me mandaron y apremiaron a que acudiese con toda mi compañia juntandola con la de Pedro de la Rosa, asimismo author de comedias, y me hizieron estudiar para los carros triunfales un auto, loa y colloquio de don Pedro Calderon, para cuio efecto me mandaron y no me consintieron hazer particular ninguno ni 4 dias representar en el publico, de que se me han seguido de daño mas de 500 ducados, ansi por las perdidas de los particulares como por las representaciones de los corrales y por 160 ducados que he dado de raciones a mi compania por que acudiesen a la dicha fiesta, y hauiendo acudido a la Villa de Madrid y Comisarios a que me den la satisfacion y paga del dicho trauajo y dinero que tengo gastado, no tan solamente no lo hacen pero ha 20 dias que me tienen en esta Corte gastando mi hacienda y teniendo mi compañia en la ciudad de Valladolid para hazer las fiestas del Santisimo Sacramento, y por paga se me manda acuda a cobrar 400 reales de una persona que dicen deuerlos a la Villa de Madrid, sin otro recado alguno, y no me dan satisfazion ni mandan se me paguen las demas cantidades de maravedis que se me deuen entreteniendome en que se verá en la Junta, despues de hauer salido con toda mi compañia en los carros triunfales, a pique de perder la vida todos los que iuan en el, y hauiendo estudiado el auto y loa y musica que se me fue mandado por la Villa de Madrid y sus Comisarios, mandandome ensayar, poniendome alguaciles para el efeto. Por tanto pido y suplico a V. S. Illma. me mande se me de la satisfacion y paga conueniente a mi trauajo y perdidas, con la breuedad que V. S. Illma. puede considerar, estando en esta Corte gastando mas de lo que tengo de hauer y mi compañia y muger y hijos en Valladolid sin tener quien los socorra si yo no voy, que en ello reciuira particular merced con justicia. —ALONSO DE OLMEDO."

(*b*) 24 March. Declaration of the two Commissioners: "Andres de la Vega tuuo a su cargo por concierto que con el se hico todo lo principal de la fiesta de los carros de la mascara que refiere este memorial por scriptura que otorgo en esta raçon, y en ella se obligo pagar lo que costasen dos compañias de representantes al respecto de lo que se hico en otra ocasion con Prado, y porque quando se quiso poner en execucion y pidio a Olmedo y Rosa que fuesen a lo referido y tuuieron noticia de la cantidad, que eran 400 reales, respondieron ser poca y respecto de la breuedad de el tiempo y la falta tan grande que esto podria hacer, el Corregidor y Comisarios acudieron a hacer instancia con estas dos compañias para que saliesen en dichos carros, como lo hicieron, ofreciendoles que se les daria justa satisfacion, y porque el dicho Andres de la Vega se obligo a bestir y satisfacer en la manera que se dice asta 46 personas, las 10 de ellas puso el y las 36 las dichas dos compañias, y a todos se les dieron sus vestidos en conformidad de su contrato y me consta que dexaron de representar 3 dias al comun y vn particular, conforme a lo qual y con bista de la scriptura Vm. mandara lo que fuere seruido. Madrid, 24 de março de 1637 años. —CLAUDIO DE COS. —DON GONCALO PACHECO DE LA VEGA."

(*c*) 30 March 1637. In the light of this information, the Town Council agreed to give 500 *reales* to Alonso de Olmedo, and a similar sum to Pedro de la Rosa.

(A.M.M., AS, 2–58–1[48])

A–5. *22 March 1637. Petition of Francisco de Sotomayor.*

(*a*) Undated. "Francisco de Sotomayor y Biçenta Lopez, su muger, deçimos que estando en nuestra casa sin representar ni en conpania de ningun autor, el Corregidor de esta uilla y don Cristobal de Medina y don Gonçalo Pacheco me mandaron contra mi boluntad reciuiese un pliego de papel y l[e] estudiase y ansimismo la musica de los carros triunfales de la fiesta que se içio a S.M., y acudiese a ensayar en casa de los autores que içieron la dicha fiesta y saliese en la parte mas alta del carro representando La Paz, y abiendo salido en la dicha fiesta y en la parte que me fue señalado y ocupadome todos los dias neçesarios en los ensayos y ydo a dar la muestra en casa del Corregidor a los dichos Comisarios, y de todo este trauajo y ocupaçion aunque [e] acudido a que pag[u]en a la dicha Biçenta Lopez mi muger y a mi, no lo an echo, teniendome [e]ntretenido mas de 20 dias y abiendo pagado a todos los demas que sirbieron la dicha fiesta y no estauan con autor, pido y suplico a V.S. Illma. mande se pag[u]e el dicho trabajo y ocupaçion con toda breuedad por estar de camino para yr fuera desta Corte a buscar mi bida, que en ello reçiuire merced y benefiçio. —FRANCISCO DE SOTOMAYOR."

(*b*) On 22 March the Town Council agreed to award Francisco de Sotomayor 200 reales.

(*c*) 24 March. Declaration of the two Commissioners: "Andres de la Bega tuuo a su cargo por concierto que con el se hiço todo lo principal de la fiesta en los carros, y porque parecio ser necesario que Bicenta Lopez tomase a su cargo el estudio de vn pliego de papel que toco a ella, de horden de el Corregidor y comisarios se le encargo que lo hiciese, como lo hiço, ocupandose a lo que es los ensaios 10 dias y asistio la noche de la mascara en la parte y como se refiere, y se le ofrecio pagar lo que fuere justo. Y parece que se le podria dar 300 reales o lo que Vm. fuere seruido. Madrid y março 24 de 1637. —CLAUDIO DE COS. —DON GONCALO PACHECO DE LA VEGA." [The date of either document (*b*) or (*c*) is probably in error.]

(A.M.M., AS, 2–58–1[49])

B–*Printed source*

Description of the pageants, extracted from Andrés Sánchez de Espejo, *Relacion ajustada en lo possible, a la verdad, y repartida en dos discursos. El primero, de la entrada en estos Reynos de Madama Maria de Borbon, Princesa de Cariñan. El segundo, de las fiestas, que se celebraron en el Real Palacio del buen Retiro, à la eleccion de Rey de Romanos* (Madrid, María de Quiñones, 1637), fols. 17ᵛ–18ʳ.

"Figurò aquel protento Italiano, quimerico ingeniero (Cosme Loti) q̃ por su rara inuentiua, y biẽ fingidas tramoyas haze a la vista arbitro del objeto, q̃ desmentidamente le representa dos carros triunfales de quarenta y seis pies de alto, sin los remates, veinte y dos de ancho, y de circunferẽcia 32. dedicado, vno a la paz, y otro à la guerra, y ambos Historiados con los despojos de su triunfo, Palmas y Laureles este, oliuas y flores aquel. La vriga del de la paz era Iupiter, figurado por la vida. Saturno del de la guerra, significado por la muerte. La vrna de arriba, que era remate al carro, era assiento en vno de la Religion; y en otro de la Iusticia, abaxo tenia vna vasa, en cuyos lados rematauan quatro Sirenas, ò bichas en orden, a la mas baxa donde estauan seis Emperadores a cauallo por la parte delantera, de la qual auia vna concha que hazia gradas à 22. personas, representadas en otras tantas virtudes del sequito de cada vna, conocidas por la insignia que lleuauan en su mano, a la espalda, dos piramides de espejos cristalinos, y diferentes colores. En la cima auia vn jarron de forma antigua, al qual hazia remate vna vanderola, rodeados ambos de ricos balaustres, q̃ con vn semicirculo cogian en medio vn globo esferico, coronado, y figurado por la Monarquia de España, en este, y aquel lado. La vrna de ambos estaua orlada, de cabeças de medio cuerpo, de Heroes diferentes, que atandose con ella le venian a hazer adorno, iban en cada vno tres tronos, y en ellos assentados tres figuras, adornadas de festones y f[r]uteros las vasas. Los rodapies ricos de trofeos armas y mas coronas, y cõ vistosa cenefa debaxo. Tirauã estos carros 48. bueyes, transformados de aparentes pieles de diferentes animales cõ yugos y cordeles plateados, y mas de ciẽ luzes entre achetas y achas, cada vno en seguro pedestal, y plateado achero con igual correspõdẽcia, de manera, q̃ no pareciesse cõfundido incẽdio lo q̃ era distinta claridad, ayudada de 200. achones de boraz materia, q̃ no pudiesse apagar casual accidẽte de viẽto, ò agua, q̃ a pie lleuauã otros tantos ministros del triunfo en forma de satiros enanos, y salbajes. Y si, Marciales, y belicos instrumẽtos de musica, en el vno, acordadas y apacibles citaras, y biolones en el otro: y ambos cõ tres cõpañias de Comediantes ricamente vestidas para representar à la Reina nuestra señora, Principe nuestro Señor, Señora Princesa de Cariñan, Damas, Cõsejos, y Embaxadores (como se hizo despues de la mascara) lo significado dellos en vn dialogo de aquel luzidissimo ingenio, q̃ por su Cortesano juizio, y Palaciega atenciõ entre los llamados, es de los escogidos D. Pedro Calderõ."

The Plague, the Theater, and the Poet

ANN HAAKER

S EVENTEENTH-CENTURY ENGLAND offers us a unique opportunity to examine the history of a great human disaster—the plague of 1636–
1637. The reaction of poets and actors to such a scourge is a fascinating
subject. The story is unfolded in two 1640 documents which also reveal
the most detailed evidence to date of the relationship between an early
theater and its playwright: a Requests Proceedings Bill of Complaint filed
on 12 February by the Salisbury Court Theater against Richard Brome,
once the servant of Ben Jonson, as well as Brome's answer of 6 March.[1]
The documents tell the complete story, from Brome's first encounter with
Salisbury Court up to his final break with the theater five years later in
order to join William Beeston at the Cockpit Theater. In 1910 Professor
C. W. Wallace and his wife discovered the partially damaged parch-
ments[2] at the London Record Office and, with the aid of the Record

---

1. Listed in the Wallace Collection in the Henry E. Huntington Library as *Requests Proceedings, Charles I*, Bundle 58, Part III, No. 622 [near the bottom in
another set of documents]; and *Requests Proceedings, uncalendared, Charles I*,
Bundle 76, Part IV. They are now catalogued in the Public Record Office as Reg.
2/622 and 723.

2. A note appended to the transcript of Brome's answer reads: "The writing on
the upper right quarter and entire right edge is badly damaged by damp. On part

Office officials, were able to make a complete transcript of them.[3] The stipulations of Brome's 1635 and 1638 contracts are briefly outlined in Professor Wallace's article "Shakespeare and the Blackfriars." [4] Further information, pieced together from correspondence with Professor Wallace, has been brought to light by C. E. Andrews in 1913 and later by Professor G. E. Bentley in 1956.[5] Comments concerning hardships experienced by both playwright and theatrical company during the severe plague of 1636, temporary emergency settlements, an implied rivalry among theaters, and the real reason why Brome left Salisbury Court have heretofore been left to conjecture or have remained unknown.

The complaint was filed by the actors and owners making up Queen Henrietta's Company, which occupied the Salisbury Court Theater [6] when it reopened 2 October 1637. That establishment had been closed for over a year and a half because of the plague. The complainants accused "one Richard Brome of London gent' well knoweinge That it would bee very beneficiall for him . . . to write and Compose playes for the Actors, and

---

of the upper right portion the ink is entirely gone, and only the transparent white impression left in the skin can be read by holding the parchment against a window pane toward a sharp light. Right margin stained by damp and possibly by ink. Officials removed stains from back, and placed an infusion of galls on the obscure writing down the right margin. There are also ten holes eaten by decay through the document in a virtual line to the left of the middle. But words & parts of words there are easily supplied by context. By patient labor for nearly four days by us both, we have been able to read every word of the document, even the transparencies and all but obliterated portions on the right margin. We believe the transcript is therefore absolutely correct in every letter. Lond. 22 July, 1910. C. W. W."

3. Now at the Henry E. Huntington Library among the C. W. Wallace manuscript papers, purchased by the library in 1962 from Professor Wallace's sister, Victoria E. Berggen.

4. *The Century Magazine*, LXXX (1910), 751.

5. Clarence E. Andrews, *Richard Brome: A Study of His Life and Works* (Yale Studies in English; New Haven, 1913), pp. 14–15; G. E. Bentley, *The Jacobean and Caroline Stage* (Oxford, 1956), III, 52–53, hereafter cited as "Bentley"; summary of correspondence in R. J. Kaufmann, *Richard Brome, Caroline Playwright* (New York, 1961), pp. 29–30.

6. Listed in the complaint as: "Richard Heton, John Robinson, Nathaniell Speed gent Tenants and Owners of the playhowse in Salsbury Courte London, And Richard Perkins Anthony Turnor Wm Sherlocke John Yonge John Sumpner Edward May Curtis Grevell Wm Wilbraham Tymothy Reade and Wm Cartwrighte the yonger gent her ma:^ts Comedians att the Playehouse."

Owners of the said howse" who made means "to enterteyne him in that buissines." After many parleys between the dramatist and the former owners and actors at Salisbury Court Theater,[7] a contract had been drafted 20 July 1635, stipulating that Brome, for the next three years, should write three plays each year exclusively for the Salisbury Court Theater. For his services he would receive fifteen shillings weekly plus one day's profit for each new play "In pursuance of which Artickles hee the said Richard Brome did putt hymselfe into the said Buissines."

In his answer to the complaint Brome requested "the advantage of excepcon to the insufficiencies and defects in lawe of the said Bill of Comp^lt." Contrary to the complaint, Brome claimed that as early as January 1634, when he was writing for Prince Charles's men at the Red Bull, where he was "very well intertayned and truly paied without mur*muring or wranglinge,*" his services were sought by representatives of the Salisbury Court Theater. Richard Gunnell, initiating the King's Revels at Salisbury Court, saw how well Brome's plays were being received at the Red Bull Theater and asked Brome to compose plays for their company. To this Brome agreed, even though in 1634 the Red Bull Company was at the pinnacle of its reputation and was even chosen to accompany His Majesty on his summer progress.[8] Richard Gunnell, however, died that year.[9] Some of Brome's plays were, nevertheless, performed at Salisbury Court; one of them, *The Sparagus Garden,* brought the new company an estimated profit of over a thousand pounds, according to Brome. Pleased with the success of Brome's plays, the rest of the company sought to enhance its reputation and employed Brome exclusively as their poet. According to Brome's answer, it was, however, only "theire specious pretences and promises of reward and bountifull retribucon and love [that] did intice and *Inveagle this d*efend^t *to depart* and leave the company of the Red Bull players being the Princes highnes servants." Brome further states that only the hope and confidence engendered by the company's "large pretence of Love and courtesie" induced him to agree to write three plays yearly. He was at first "vnwilling to vndertake . . . more then hee *could*

7. "Anthony Berrye [Bray] Wm Cartwrighte thelder Xpofer Goade and George Stutevill, and yor subiects Curtis Greuell John Yonge Edward Maye Tymothy Reade Wm Wilbraham and William Cartwrighte the yonger."

8. Bentley, I, 311.

9. *Ibid.,* II, 454, 457.

well performe." He was assured, however, that the stipulation for three plays yearly was only an insurance that Brome would dedicate "all his labour and playes totally vnto theire sole proffitts" but that no more plays would be exacted or expected than he "could or should bee able well and conveyniently to doe or perform*e.*" With this understanding Brome signed the first contract. Clearly, Brome placed too much "trust and confidence" upon the "true and faire intent and plaine meaning of all parties" during the parleys preceding the signing of the contract.

Brome admitted agreeing to each of the articles of the contract, but his answer included such interesting tidbits as:

theire Company did agree to pay ffifteene shillings weekly vpon every Saturday vnto this def^t and to *permytt this defend^t and* [sic] *to have the* cleere benefitt of any one dayes playing vnto himselfe [with]in the space of Tenn dayes after the first playing of any such play at this defend^{ts} elecc*on.*

He added, however, "that his purposes and intenes were alwayes *faire to performe the said* Articles on his parte Albeit the same were left in effect vnto himselfe vpon trust." Moreover, he emphasized, the company "did often tymes *confidently affirme vnto* this defend.^{t} as aforesaid That this defend.^{ts} best indeavo^{rs} in wrighting playes for them should bee always accepted" and "also that they would bee more gratefull and beneficiall vnto this def.^{t} for his endeavo^{rs} then by theire said written Articles and Agreement they had engaged *themselves to bee."*

The complainants, on the other hand, contended that Brome signed the first contract and received full payment until the following year when, because of the plague, "publique Acteinge of playes on the stage in or about London were prohibited." The company consequently stopped payments "as in such Cases is vsuall" during closure of theaters but offered a temporary agreement 26 October 1636 "to accepte of Tenne pounds for satisfaction of all demaunds for salary from the tyme of the said prohibicon vntill Allowance should bee obteyned for Acteinge of playes againe." To this Brome agreed, and the amount was "well and truly payed." At the end of the three-year term Brome had been paid "all the said salarye after the rate of ffifteene shillinges p weeke for all the said tyme of Cessation which Continued a full yeare and a halfe saue onely ffiue pounds which payment they made in hope and vppon the promises" that Brome would fulfill his part of the contract. But, Brome, after "haveinge gotten soe much Money of yor subiects," failed to deliver the nine plays agreed upon, "beinge then in Arreare with them ffower playes." Moreover, the complaint reads, Brome within the three-year period did "sell and deliu*er* one of the playes which hee made for yo' Subiects in the said tyme vnto Christopher Beeston gent and Willia*m* Beeston or one of them which was to yo' subiects greate preiudice"[10] even though Brome promised to deliver the plays in arrears and to "applye himselfe wholly vnto yo' subiects."

It would seem that at first both Brome and the Salisbury Court Company adhered to the contract in good faith. Accordingly, *"within the first three* quarters of the yeare after the date of the said Articles," i.e., around 20 March 1636, Brome "did Compose and Deliver vnto the said Comp.¹ᵗˢ"" two plays. For the first play, the answer continues, Brome received one day's clear profit. According to Brome, his labors brought the company "into theire first and cheefest extimacon accompanyed *with very great* proffitts and gaynes." The second play, however, did not fare so well. Around April 1636 the plague increased "in and aboute London." For this second play, performed "neere *or aboute the tyme of* theire restraint from playing by reason of the said sicknes," Brome never received the clear day's profit "to the Damage *of ffive pounds and* vpwards." The theaters were closed 12 May 1636. And so began successive "wranglings."

That theater owners, actors, and playwrights alike suffered during the plague has been well known. A set of 1632 documents[11] discloses the early difficulties of Richard Gunnell, who, in copartnership with William Blagrave, built and managed the Salisbury Court Theater for the purpose of training boys to supply actors for His Majesty's servants of the Blackfriars. Christopher Babham, who later shared partnership with Richard Gunnell, accused Gunnell, in a Court of Requests Proceedings Bill dated 2 October, of throwing over the business and treating the boys badly during the pestilence of the same year. Unable to meet his debts, his credit no longer good, Gunnell, according to the bill, was compelled "in stead of

10. *The Antipodes* (1640). In a note to the reader appended to the play Brome writes that the play was *"intended for the* Cockpit Stage, *in the right of my most deserving Friend Mr.* William Beeston, *vnto whom it properly appertained."* See *The Antipodes*, ed. Ann Haaker (Lincoln, Nebr., 1966), p. xi. All quotations are from this edition.

11. The following quotations are from a transcript of a *Court of Requests Proceedings, Charles I,* Bundle 524 (13 Part I) uncalendared, found among the Wallace manuscript papers. This document will be published in a forthcoming article.

beare to *p*vide whey for theire the boys' ordinarie drink." Suffering further from quartan ague, Gunnell finally was forced to leave London in order to avoid persecution by his creditors and to regain his health. Babham was left with the expense and responsibility of dieting fourteen boys and furnishing them with new clothes. In August, the complaint continues, Babham accepted the boys, raggedly appareled, with no more than seven shirts and "five sheets and a half to lodge them in." Some of the boys were sick; one had died from ill diet, "some of them beeing forced to steale others to begg for want of sustenance." For over three months Babham provided for the boys, "all wch time the sicknes continuing there could bee no profitt made of theire said quality of playing towards their maintenance." Richard Gunnell answered the bill on 3 November. Far from shirking his responsibilities, he had hired a house at Hackney, near London, where he took the boys for the season, along with the rest of his family. He denied all charges in the bill, but the many difficulties arising from the plague are apparent. The numerous petitions, during the 1636–1637 plague, of theatrical companies requesting permission to resume acting further attests the plight of the theaters.[12] In a 1639 document, endorsed "Heton's draught of his Pattent," Heton claimed he "disbursed good somes of money for the maintayning and supporting the said Actors in the sicknes tyme, and other wayes to keepe the said Company together, wthout wch a great part of them had not bene able to subsist, but the Company had bene utterly ruyned and dispersed." [13]

Brome, however, denied in his answer of 1640 that it was usual, unless so specified in the contract, to cancel all payments during a plague and consequently intended "in the tyme of vacancy *of* the said playing" to write in compliance with the contract "more newe playes . . . for theire future vse and Comoditie when they should play againe." But *"in* recompence and requitall thereof" he "expected the due and true performance and payment of the said ffifteene shillings weekly." The company's refusal to adhere to the agreement during the plague forced Brome to seek compensation elsewhere. Both owners and actors of Salisbury Court, Brome complained, "intending . . . to deceive and defraude this defend.^{t} of the said weekly payment did first begyn to quarrell *and take* occasions of

12. Bentley, II, 663–664.

13. Heton's draft for his patent has been published by P. Cunningham in *Shakespeare Society Papers*, IV (1894), 97–98; also published in Bentley, II, 684–687.

distast against this def.'" About May 1636, furthermore, representatives of the company told Brome "to take what course hee could or would for himselfe for they neither could nor would contynue the weekly payment." In fact, the company offered Brome the first articles "to bee Cancelled so as this def.ᵗ was tourned of by and amongst them and to *put to* his shifts in that hard sadd and dangerous tyme of the sicknes boeth for himselfe and his famyly." The following August, Brome, "by necessitie constrained and being left in such distres and want," repaired to William Beeston and "acquainted him with his then *present* case and Condicon whoe then lent this defendᵗ Six pounds at his need vpon this defendᵗˢ Agreement to Compose and write a play for the Cockpitt Company." The Salisbury Court Company, however, "being in hope that the sicknes would in a shorte tyme afterwards seace," offered Brome "money and did ear*nestly* solicite this defᵗ to desert the said William Beeston and [his] Company and to retourne to the comp.ᵗˢ againe." Brome, remembering their former treatment, at first refused, but "vpon theire earnest perswasion and promises of better vsage afterwards, and partly vpon threates of suites and troubles . . . did resolve to make further tryall of them." The complainant, Richard Heton, further promised to release Brome from his agreement with William Beeston and to "give him the said Mʳ Beeston *satiffaccon.*" In due course the company agreed to pay Brome the ten pounds for payments in arrears. The payment, however, was not made until Brome *"brought* them a new Play and then it was made vpp with severall small sumes and pettie dribling payments which did small pleasure vnto this def.ᵗ"

In any case, Brome disclosed, the plague still continued, and the weekly payments were still stopped. Once again Brome, in desperate straits, sought the aid of Beeston. This time, however, the Salisbury Court Company retaliated by bringing the case before Sir Henry Herbert, Master of the Revels, "to here and examine the cause betweene them." As a result Sir Henry Herbert awarded Brome a payment of "six shillings weekly and ffive pounds for every new play which hee should bring vntill such tyme as the sicknes should cease and the p.ᵗˢ should have leave to play againe." This award, Brome continued, the company "did but in parte performe." By the time the company played again, 2 October 1637, "they were then Indebted . . . the sume of Eleaven pounds Eleaven shillings six pence or thereaboutes."

When Brome's first contract came to an end around 20 July 1638, the Salisbury Court Company maintained they had made full payment to Brome "after the rate of ffifteene shillinges *p* weeke for all the said tyme of Cessation which Continued a full yeare and a halfe saue onely ffiue pounds." They further charged that Brome not only was in arrears for four plays but also had violated the contract by selling and delivering to Beeston one of the plays due them. Brome, on the other hand, claimed that he "brought the said Company in six new playes wth in the space of three yeares . . . and more hee was not able possibly to performe aswell through sicknes as by other hinderance which hee then had."

The company must have thought it advantageous to keep Brome, for they offered him another contract in August 1638. This second contract was drawn up by Richard Heton, the manager of Queen Henrietta's Company, which, as we have already indicated, occupied Salisbury Court when the theaters opened in 1637. Though this company promised Brome better treatment and more salary, the demands upon him were in fact even more exacting.[14] Brome remained accountable for plays in arrears from the last contract. The provisions demanded Brome's exclusive services to the company acting at Salisbury Court Theater for the next seven years, for which he would receive twenty shillings weekly and one day's profit for each of the new plays completed. The payment, however, was subsequent to "yo[r] subiects and theire successors theere Continued playeinge att the said playhowse without restraint." Brome would be required to write three

---

14. It would seem that Brome's discontent was not unique. A similar dogmatic tone pervades Heton's patent and instructions (1639) for Salisbury Court: "My selfe to be sole governo[r] of the Company. The Company to enter into Articles wth me to continew there for 7 yeares, upon the same condicons they haue had for a yeare and halfe last past, and such as refuse to be removed, and others placed in their roomes; for if they should continew at libertie as they now are, And haue power to take her M[ts] service alonge wth them, they wold make use of o[r] house but untill they could p'vyde another upon better termes, and then leave us as in one yeare and halfe of their being here they haue many tymes threatned, when they might not exact any new imposicons upon the housekeepers at their pleasure . . . This setling of the service and Company upon condicons certane, and of a knowne governo[r], would be the occasion to avoyd many differences and disturbances that hapen both betwene the Company and housekeepers, amongst the Company themselves, and many generall discontents—to the great credit of the house, and p'fitt of the Company." *Shakespeare Society Papers,* IV (1894), 95–97; also in Bentley, II, 684–685.

plays each year, and no play would be published without the consent of the company. If, moreover, Brome should fail to produce the allotted three plays, he would forfeit half his salary until the plays in arrears were brought in. Of the four plays in arrears under the first contract, two were to be prepared "as that they mighte bee studdied to bee presented vnto publique veiwe vppoñ the stage att the said howse in the tearme of St Mickaell tharchangell next ensueinge," for each of which Brome would receive fifty shillings. This offer was to be considered full satisfaction for the five pounds which the company owed Brome under the first contract. The third play was to be completed at Brome's convenience any time within the next three years of the seven-year term. Should Brome effect the conditions prescribed for the three plays, he was then to be released of his obligations for the fourth play in arrears.

To this new contract, the owners alleged that Brome not only "Condiscended vowed and promised the *p*formance theereof" but "willed that the same might bee reduced into writeinge." Accordingly the company:

putt [the second contract] into writeinge by waye of Artickles indented Wheerevnto the said Richard Brome seemed very desirous to seale and Execute the same in due fforme of Lawe but from tyme to tyme delayed the same with Asservacoñ of his willingnes to *p*forme the said Agreement and to seale the said Artickles.

Acting upon Brome's promises, the complaint continues, the Salisbury Court Company paid Brome twenty shillings weekly from August 1638, "vntill a fortnight after Easter last past," i.e., April 1639. It was on 5 April 1639 that William Beeston was sworn "Gouuernor & Instructer of the Kings & Queens young Company of Actors" at the Cockpit Theater.[15] Accordingly the complaint reads: "But nowe soe it is May . . . Brome by and throughe the *p*swasions and inticement of the said Wm Beeston or soñe other by him" deprived the company of "such Benefitte and proffitte as shall or may accrue and Coñe vnto them by the said Broñes studdye and *p*formance in the said Buissines; And vppon the said Beestons promise to bee his good freinde and to give him more salarye then yor subiects." Brome failed to present the plays in arrears. By Michaelmas, or 29 September 1638, only one play instead of two was presented to the company, though Brome had been paid his fifty shillings and one day's profit. "But

15. Bentley, II, 372.

the said Brome beinge tampered withall by the said Beeston" refused to
compose any more plays for the company, "But wholly applies himself
vnto the said Beeston and the Companie of players Acteinge att the playhowse of the Phoenixe in Drury Lane."

In conclusion, the complaint accused Brome of having received twenty
shillings per week from 20 July 1638 "vntill the thirty sixte daye of Aprill
followeinge or thereabouts beinge Nine monthes and vpwards," amount-
ing to over forty pounds. In all, Brome's dereliction was reckoned a
"daṁage of ffiue hundred pounds att the leaste." Of interest is the statement that the complainants

haue noe releiffe in the ℘misses att the Coṁan Lawe for that the said Artickles
and writeinges are casually lost & mislayed or are Coṁe to the hands of the
said Brome And ℘tely by reason the wittnesses which should proue the truthe
of the preṁisses are some of them late dead and the rest of them gone beyonde
seas or into places remote and to yoʳ subiects vnknowne Theerefore in this
Case yoʳ subiects are properly to bee releaued in the premisses in Course of
Equitie.

Regarding the second contract Brome answered that he had composed
a new play in Hillary term 1638 (i.e., 29 September), and another new
play before Easter 1639. Salisbury Court Company, however, slighted both
plays, again threatened to stop weekly payments, and "used such scornefull
and reproachfull speeches concerning this def.'" that Brome, realizing
"that they tooke occasions daily to wearie the defend.ᵗ from and out of
theire ymployment," once again left them "to theire owne dispose through
theire owne only default." Concerning Beeston, Brome added: "And true
it is that this def.ᵗ si*thence* that tyme hath contracted and made other
agreements with the said William Beeston with whome hee hopeth to
enioy the fruites of his laboʳˢ more beneficially and peaceably." He repeated that he had requested their aid when he was in their employment,
"being very sicke," but was uncharitably refused and that "for theire
further tryall" he did "twoe or three tymes weeke after weeke importune
and solicite them *with* Letters Imagininge that might . . . worke remorse
and pittie from them." He was, however, sent word that his services were
terminated and that he must "shift for himselfe." He was refused "any
payment or releefe . . . in *his* said great sicknes want and misery." When
Brome, nevertheless, made arrangements "through there meere default
. . . to provide for himselfe," the complainants "do now out of mallice

and evill will only molest and vex this def.ᵗ with suites of Lawe intending thereby to Crush and Ruyne him."

Brome then summed up the entire proceedings:

1) He stated that in the beginning it was the Salisbury Court Company who sought his services, not he theirs;

2) He denied receiving all of the payments of fifteen shillings weekly that had been due him under the first agreement before the plays were prohibited because of the plague;

3) He denied that it was customary to stop all payments during calamities unless so specified in the contract itself;

4) He denied having received at the end of the three-year term all fifteen shillings weekly full payment for all the time of the sickness;

5) He admitted, however, to an earlier written agreement for ten pounds but added: "The same was paied by such driblets and petty payments . . . *and* not before a new Play received . . . so as it did him little pleasure as aforesaid";

6) He maintained that he was behind with them only with regard to

twoe Playes In lieu of which hee hath made divers scenes in ould re*viv*ed playes *for them* and many prologues and epilogues to such playes of theires, songs, and one Introduccon at theire first playing after the ceasing of the plague all wᶜʰ hee verily beleeveth amounted to asmuch tyme and studdy as twoe ordynarie playes might take vpp *in* writing which hapened by the accidents and through theire owne defaults as aforesaid;

7) Referring to the new play "wᶜʰ the Comp.ˡᵗˢ suppose this def.ᵗ to haue sould vnto the said Christopher or William Beeston," however:

this def.ᵗ confeseth it *to bee* true that the stopage of his weekly meanes and vnkind carriages aforesaid forced this defend.ᵗ to Contract and bargaine for the said new play with the said William Beeston but yet the said Compˡᵗˢ and theire Company had it and acted it and by comon estimacon gott a Thousand pounds and vpwards by it;

8) He further admitted agreeing to the new contract for twenty shillings weekly, but after considering their uncharitable treatment and stoppage of weekly salary in time of sickness,

his labors and playes Cavelled at and reiected and himselfe discharged and *left* at libertie . . . whereby theire was no further proceedings therein so as each partie was left to himselfe wherevpon this defᵗ did apply himselfe vnto the said William Beeston as hee hopeth was and is law*full for* him so to doe.

9) He denied receiving twenty shillings weekly from July 1638 until April 1639 and denied being behind in any plays, all things considered, and requested "to bee hence dismissed with good Costs for his vniust vexacon and charge in that behalfe most iniuriously sustayned."

Just how the court determined the final settlement is not known, but it is certain that Brome never returned to Salisbury Court. Moreover, the hopes he may have had for good entertainment at the Cockpit were short-lived. On 11 September 1640 the theaters once again closed, after a steady increase in the number of deaths from 1 July, and presumably did not open until 6 November. Then came the Civil War, and in 1642 all theaters were closed for the duration of the Commonwealth until 1660. In the preface to the 1653 edition of Brome's plays, Alexander Brome wrote of Brome as dead and again in an introductory verse to his 1659 edition of Brome's *Five New Playes* fittingly described him: *"Poor* he came into th' world, and *poor* went out." [16]

The effect of these 1636–1640 "murmurings" and "wranglings" is perhaps most evident in Brome's plays. His pique with the Salisbury Court Company is clearly perceptible in the note appended to *The Antipodes* (1640), the play which he was accused of writing for Beeston while still under contract with Salisbury Court:

Courteous Reader: You shall find in this book more than was presented upon the stage, and left out of the presentation, for superfluous length (as some of the players pretended). I thought good all should be inserted according to the allowed original; and as it was, at first, intended for the Cockpit stage, in the right of my most deserving friend, Mr. William Beeston, unto whom it properly appertained; and so I leave it to thy perusal, as it was generally applauded, and well acted at Salisbury Court.

Farewell,

RICHARD BROME.

His continued admiration and friendship for Beeston are also expressed in *The Court Beggar,* written for the rival Cockpit Theater in late 1639 or 1640.

These sentiments are obvious. One wonders, however, how many in the

16. Alexander Brome, *Five New Playes* (London, 1659).

audience knew the full implications of some of the lines from Brome's plays. Blaze's opening lines in *The Antipodes* recall long months of confinement; the only visitors were the callous researchers taking their count, and finally the physician:

> To me, and to the city, sir, you are welcome,
> And so are all about you: we have long
> Suffer'd in want of such fair company.
> But now that time's calamity has given way
> (Thanks to high Providence) to your kinder visits,
> We are (like half pin'd wretches that have lain
> Long on the planks of sorrow, strictly tied
> To a forc'd abstinence from the sight of friends)
> The sweetlier fill'd with joy.

The lines are redolent with memories of bonfires in the streets and junipers, vinegar, rue, and rosemary perfumes combating repellent putrification. They recall the tolling bells and the surprised cry of pets and stray animals which were ordered to be dispatched, as well as the advice published by the College of Physicians, their various cures and preventatives concocted to meet the demands of both the wealthy and the penniless, such as Brome. Everyone in that audience at the Salisbury Court Theater must have responded to the promise of a desperately needed cure for sorrows and memories. A lord who loves the quality of playing and a psychologist devise such a cure in a play that will both instruct and, above all, provide mirth. To these suggestions the audience could readily respond.

How many in the audience recognized the implications behind the lines which closely resembled situations mentioned in the lawsuit? Letoy remarks: "As for the poets, / No men love them, I think" (I.v.74–75). Later he explains that in the antipodes, depicted in a play within the play, all is antipodal to real life as experienced by the audience: "Yes, poetry is good ware / In the Antipodes, though there be some ill payers, / As well as here; but law there rights the poets" (III.ii.14–16). In the same scene a lawyer taking the case for an unpaid poet cavils in much the same way as the company must have caviled at Brome just before he left them: "Umh, I cannot read your hand; your character / Is bad, and your orthography much worse. / Read it yourself, pray" (ll. 19–21); and later the lawyer, speaking the poet's lines, says:

Here's a large sum in all, for which I'll try
His strength in law till he *peccavi* cry,
When I shall sing, for all his present bigness
Jamque opus exegi, quod nec Jouis ira, nec ignis.

(ll. 70–73)

In *The Court Beggar,* which alludes to *The Antipodes* in its epilogue, Courtwit announces his project that "no Playes may be admitted to the Stage, but of their making who Professe or indeavour to live by the quality" and that the author be bound to serve truly and faithfully for a whole term. To this Mendicant answers: "Here's trim businesse towards, and as idle as the Players going to Law with their Poets" (Act II, sig. P⁴). This certainly alludes to the now rival Salisbury Court Company. When one knows the full story of the court proceedings between the Salisbury Court Theater and its poet Richard Brome, one can detect darts engendered in all the frustrations of misery and want but converted into laughter provoking lines and situations by the gentle satirist who "Never spilt Ink, except in Comedie."¹⁷

Heaton vs. Brome

Bill

[The following transcript has been checked against the original documents at the London Public Record Office and against Professor Wallace's transcription made in 1910 (see footnote 2 on Wallace's appended comment on his transcription). In the right margin of Brome's Answer the "transparent white impressions" which are illegible except by holding the parchment against a sharp light are italicized. The "per" symbol is denoted by an italicized "p"; flourishes are expanded and italicized; the superior "a" over the "nn" in words like "covenñtees" is standardized and italicized, e.g., "covenantees." The one deletion in the documents is recorded within broken brackets, and letters or words supplied by the editor are recorded within brackets. Otherwise the transcript retains the essential characteristics of the original.]

Lane Duodecimo die februarij
 xv.ᵗᵒ Anno R Rs Caroli xv.º /
  To the kings most Excellent Ma:ᵗⁱᵉ
In all humble manner Complayninge shewe vnto yoʳ most Excellent Ma:ᵗⁱᵉ

17. *Ibid.*

yo[r] Loyall and obedient Subiects Richard Heton, John Robinson, Nathaniell
Speed gent tenants and Owners of the playehowse in Salsbury Courte London, And Richard Perkins Anthony Turnor W[m] Sherlocke John Yonge John
Sumpner Edward May Curtis Grevell W[m] Wilbraham Tymothy Reade and
W[m] Cartwrighte the yonger gent her Ma:[ts] Comedians att the Playehouse;
That wheereas one Richard Brome of London gent' well knoweinge That it
would bee very beneficiall for him the said Brome to write and Compose playes
for the Actors, and Owners of the said howse did by himselfe and others whom
hee imployed, theerein make meanes vnto yo[r] said subiects or some of them the
then Owners and Actors in the said howse to enterteyne him in that buissines;
And after many Parleyes and treaties theerein It was att the last by Artickles
of Agreem[t] indented bearinge date on or about the twentieth day of July in the
yeare of ou[r] Lord one thousand sixe hundred thirty and ffive agreed by and betweene Anthony Berrye W[m] Cartwrighte thelder Xpofer Goade and George
Stutevill, and yo[r] subiects Curtis Greuell John Yonge Edward Maye Tymothy
Reade W[m] Wilbraham and William Cartwrighte the yonger the then Owners
and Acto[rs] of and in the said howse on thone pte, And the said Richard Brome
on thother pte that hee the said Brome should for the terme of three yeares then
next ensueinge with his best Arte and Industrye write euerye yeare three
playes and deliu[er] them to the Companye of players theere Acteinge for the
tyme beinge And that the said Richard Brome should not nor would write
any playe or any pte of a playe to anye other players or playe howse, but ap-
plie all his studdye and Endeauo[rs] theerein for the Benefitte of the said Companie of the said playehouse; And that the said Covenantees should paye vnto
the said Richard Brome the some of ffifteene shillinges p weeke dureinge the
said Terme of three yeares And pmitte the said Brome to haue the Benefitte
of one dayes proffitte of playeinge such newe playe as hee should make accordinge to the true intent and Meaninge of the said Artickles (the ordinary
Chardges of the howse only deducted); In pursuance of which Artickles hee
the said Richard Brome did putt hymselfe into the said Buissines, and receiued all his said paye of ffifteene shillinges p weeke thencefoorth vntill it
pleased god that by reason of the visitacõn of the plague in the yeare followeinge publique Acteinge of playes on the stage in or about London were
prohibited By reason wheereof the said Covenantees did forbeare (as in such
Cases is vsuall) to paye the said ffifteene shillinges p weeke Salarye vnto the
said Brome for a while wheerevppon the said Brome did Cõme to an Agreem[t]
with the said Covenantees to accepte of Tenne pounds for satisfaction of all
demaunds for salary from the tyme of the said prohibicon vntill Allowance
should bee obteyned for Acteinge of playes againe the which agreem[t] was
Comprized and sett downe in a note or Memorand vnder the hands aswell of
the said Companie or somme of them as of the said Brome beareinge date on or
aboute the Sixe and Twentieth day of October in the yeare of our Lord God
one thousand Sixe Hundred Thirtye and Sixe (as in and and [sic] by the said
writeinge or note (relacõn theerevnto beinge had) and readye to bee produced

Appeareth; the which Tenne Pounds was by the said Companie or some of them well and truly payed vnto or for the said Richard Brome; And neuerthelesse Att the end of the said Terme of Three yeares yo' subiects or some of them made full payment vnto the said Brome of all the said salarye after the rate of ffifteene shillinges *p* weeke for all the said tyme of Cessation which Continued a full yeare and a halfe saue onely ffiue pounds which payment they made in hope and vppon the promises of the said Brome That hee would *p*forme all his said Covenants on his *p*te to be *p*formed in All things But soe it was most gratious Souereigne; That the said Brome haveinge gotten soe much Money of yo' subiects as aforesaid did fayle to deliuer vnto yo' subiects the nomber of playes which in tyme hee was by his Artickles to haue deliuered them (beinge then in Arreare with them ffower playes; And moreover yo' subiects discouered That the said Richard Brome did in the three yeares before mencoñed sell and deliuer one of the playes which hee made for yo' Subiects in the said tyme vnto Christopher Beeston gent and William Beeston or one of them which was to yo' subiects greate preiudice Howbeeit vppon the said Bromes promise to deliuer the other playes behinde as aforesaid and applye himselfe wholly vnto yo' subiects; It was in the Monthe of August in the yeare of ou' Lord one Thousand Six Hundred Thirtye Eighte Concluded and Agreed by and Betweene yo' subiects and the said Richard Brome in manner and fforme ffoloweinge; That is to saye That hee the said Richard Brome should for the space of Seaven yeares thence next ensueinge write and present vnto yo' subiects and the Companie of players Acteinge att the said howse for the tyme beinge three playes yearely and euerye yeare; And that hee shoulde not write invent or Compose any playe Tragedye or Comedye or any *p*te theereof for any other playhowse, And that hee should not suffer any playe made or to bee made or Composed by him for yo' subiects or theire successors in the said Companye in Salsbury Courte to bee printed by his Consent or knowledge priuitye or dirreccoñ without the Licence from the said Companie or the Maio' *p*te of them; And that if hee the said Brome should not bringe in three newe playes of his owne Composeinge and makinge within euerye yeare of the said Seauen yeares; That then halfe his paye or Salarye heereafter mencoñed should bee deteyned and kepte from him vntill hee had broughte in such playes as hee should bee behinde and in Arrere with them; And that the said Richard Brome should bringe in two of the said Newe playes where with hee was soe in Arreare soe Conveniently as that they mighte bee studdied to bee presented vnto publique veiwe vppoñ the stage att the said howse in the tearme of St Mickaell tharchangell next ensueinge the tyme of the said Artickles for eache of which the said Brome was to haue of yo' subiects or theire successors in the said Companie ffiftye shillinges appeece in full satisfaction and dischardge of the ffiue pounds soe Arreare and due vnto him as aforesaid for the said playes in Arreare Dureinge the said first mencoñed three yeares, And that hee should bringe the third playe of the said ffower playes behinde in manner as aforesaid, Att any tyme within three yeares next ensueinge the said Agreem^t; And that in case the said Brome $p$formed the said last menconed Agreem^t in every-respecte; That then the ffowerth playe of the said playes behinde with yor subiects as aforesaid should be remitted to him freelye; And that yor subiects vppoñ $p$formance of the said Agreem^t on his the said Bromes $p$te to bee $p$formed; And in case yor subiects and theire successors theere Continued playeinge att the said playehowse without restraint that then they should paye vnto or for the said Richard Brome the some of twenty shillinges p weeke and $p$mitte and suffer him to haue one dayes proffitte of the said seuerall newe playes (excepte as before is Excepted) in manner as in the said first recited Artickles of Agreement is menconed and expressed vnto which Agreem^t hee the said Richard Broome Condiscended vowed and promised the $p$formance theereof; And willed that the same might bee reduced into writeinge to that ende and purpose Wheerevppoñ yor subiects did Cause the said last menconed Agreem^t to bee putt into writeinge by waye of Artickles indented Wheerevnto the said Richard Brome seemed very desirous to seale and Execute the same in due fforme of Lawe but from tyme to tyme delayed the same with Asservacon of his willingnes to $p$forme the said Agreement and to seale the said Artickles Wherevppoñ and in exspectacoñ of the $p$formance theereof yor subiects did Continue payment of the said Twenty shillinges p weeke accordinge to the said later Agreem^t from the tyme of the said later Agreem^t makeinge vntill a fortnight after Easter last past; And yor subiects Exspected that the said Brome would haue sealed the said Artickles of Agreem^t or att the Leastwise haue stood vnto and $p$formed the same in euerye respecte accordingly; But nowe soe it is May it please yor most Excellent Matie That the said Richard Brome by and throughe the $p$swasions and inticement of the said Wm Beeston or some other by him in that behalfe imployed to defeate yor subiects of such Benefitte and proffitte as shall or may accrue and Come vnto them by the said Bromes studdye and $p$formance in the said Buissines; And vppon the said Beestons promise to bee his good freinde and to give him more salarye then yor subiects by the Agreem^t aforesaid Hee the saide Richard Brome did voluntaraly faile to present vnto yor subiects any more of the said playes for which hee was in Arreare with yor subiects. as aforesaid then onely one playe insteede of two which hee was to bringe in in the Terme of St Michaell tharchangell one Thousand Six Hundred thirty Eight And vppoñ the hopes aforesaid; Howebeit yor subiects payed or Caused to bee payed vnto the said Richard Brome accordinge to the said last menconed Artickles the some of ffifty shillinges and $p$mitted him to haue one dayes proffitte of the said playe soe by him newlye made as aforesaid And the said Brome promised to Compose make and present vnto yor subiects the residue of the said Playes in Arreare and behinde hand with yor subiects as aforesaid; But the said Brome beinge tampered withall by the said Beeston as aforesaid hath and doth refuse and denie to Compose make or present vnto yor subiects the said three playes which by the first Artickles hee is in Arreare in and behinde hand with yor subiects as aforesaid But wholly applies himself vnto

the said Beeston and the Companie of players Acteinge att the playhowse of
the Phoenixe in Drury Lane; And notwithstandinge hee hath receiued of yor
subiects some or one of them his Salarye and wages of Twenty shillinges *p*
Weeke from or about the twentith day of July 1638 vntill the thirty sixte daye
of Aprill followeinge or thereabouts beinge Nine monthes and vpwards which
amounts to ffortye pounds and vppwards better due for the said premisses
yett hee refuseth and denieth to present vnto yor subiects the residue of the said
playes in Arreare and behinde hand with yor subiects as aforesaid or any satisfaction for the aforesaid Salarye of Twenty shillinges *p* weeke received as
aforesaid, which tendeth vnto yor subiects Losse *p*reiudice and damage of ffiue
hundred pounds att the leaste as is well knowne vnto the said Brome And is
Contrary to all righte Equity and good Conscience In tender Consideracon of
all which premisses and foreasmuch as yor Subiects haue noe releiffe in the
*p*misses att the Comon Lawe for that the said Artickles and writeinges are
casually lost & mislayed or are Come to the hands of the said Brome And
*p*tely by reason the wittnesses which should proue the truthe of the premisses
are some of them late dead and the rest of them gone beyonde seas or into
places remote and to yor subiects vnknowne Theerefore in this Case yor
subiects are properly to bee releaued in the premisses in Course of Equitie To
the end theerefore That the said Richard Brome may vppon his oathe trulye
and fully sett foorth and declare the truthe of the said first and later Agreem^t
And whther hee hath not fayled in the p^rmmisses *p*formance of eache of them
and wheerein; And whether the same tended not to yor subiects damage and
howe much; And that hee might shewe cause if hee can whye hee should not
make yor subiects satisfaction for the same; And ffinally That yor subiect may
bee releiued in all and eu*er*ye the p^rmisses in such sorte as to Equitye and
Conscience shall obteyne It may theerefore please yor most Excellent Matie
(the p^rmisses duly Considered) to graunte vnto yor Ma^{ts} most gratious Writte
of Priuie seale or other Comaunde to bee directed vnto the said Richard Brome
Comaundinge him and att a Certeyne daye and vnder a certeyne paine theerein
to bee Limited *p*sonally to bee and appeare before yor Highnes Honble Counsall
att White Hall att Westm*inster* then and there to answer the p^rmisses And to
stande to and abide such farther order theerein As to yor said Honble Counsaile
shall seeme fitte, And hee as in duty bounde shall eu*er* praye Etc.

                          P Harlowe

Heaton vs. Brome

Answer

Sexto die Marcij
Anno R Rs cur nõ *p*dct Caroli
xv^{to}

The answeare of Richard Brome gent Defend:^t
to the Bill of Complainte of Richard Heaton
and others Comp:^{lts}./

The said defend.^t saving to himselfe the advantage of excepcon to the insufficiencies and defects in lawe of the said Bill of Comp^{lt.} saieth, that Eighteene monethes or thereaboutes before the < Sat > Date of the said Articles in July 1635 in the bill m[en]c̄oned one Richard Gunnell and others for themselues and on the parte and behalfe of the said Comp:^{lts} being of the Company knowne by *the name* of Salisbury *Courte* Actors in or neare White ffryers did make meanes vnto this defend.^t And vpon theire specious pretences and promises of reward and bountifull retribucon and love did intice and *Inveagle this* defend^t *to depart* and leave the company of the Red Bull players being the Princes highnes servants, And where this defend.^t was then very well intertayned and truly paied without murm*uring or wranglinge and to come and* write and compose and make playes for the said Comp.^{lts} and theire said Company vpon which Inticements and Inveaglements this defend^t vpon hope and *confidence of the Comp^{lts} performance of theire* said vndertakings and promises aforesaid did Com[pos]e and make for the said Comp.^{lts} divers Playes which the said Comp.^{lts} and theire company did *Act which playes proved very fortunate and succesfull to the* said Comp:^{lts} and theire said Company and bein[ge] in the Infancie of theire setting vpp and first playing at Salisbury Courte afore*said did bring them into esteeme and fame And one of the said playes* stiled and called the Sparagas Garden was wor[th] *to* them by generall Coniecture and estimacon and as by theire owne bookes and writings *beinge produced this defend^t verely* bele*eveth* may *appeare the sume of* One thousand pounds and vpwards, And this d[efen]d^t further saieth hee beleiveth it to bee true that the Comp.^{ts} finding how vsefull and p[rofitable] this *defend^{ts} labours in that* kind *might and was apparently* like to prove vnto them the Complaiñts out of a large pretence of Love and courtesie as aforesaid did first intreate and perswade this defend.^t to agree to write three playes for the Comp.^{lts} and *theire* said *Company* yearely for the space of three yeares together w[hich] this defend.^t at the ffirst proposicon thereof was vnwilling to vndertake as being more then hee *could well performe,* But some of the Comp.^{lts} *on the* behalfe of the residue of them did vndertake and asu[red]ly affirme vnto this defend.^t that howsoever they had desired to have three playes yearely for three *yeares countynuance together to bee* vndertaken *and* promised by this defend.^t yett vpon trust and confidence and by the true and faire intent and plaine meaning of all parties the plaintiffes *neither should nor* would exact *nor* expect from this de*fendant the* performance or composicon of any more playes th[en so] many only as this def.^t could or should bee able well and conveyniently to doe or perform*e* and that *theire* mayne *purpose in expressing* such a *nomber of* Playes was but only to oblige this def.^t to dedi[cate] all his labour and playes totally vnto theire sole proffitts vpon which trust true it is that this defend^t by Articles in writing *Indented made betweene* the said Comp^{lts} or some of theire company on the[ire] parte, And this defend.^t on the other parte, and bearing date in or aboute the said moneth of July 1635 as this def.^t beleiveth did *agree to compose and write* three playes yearly by the space of three yeares together then next following for the said Comp.^{lts} or the said Company And that hee would write for noe other Company but apply *his labors totally vnto them as* aforesaid In Consideracon whereof the said Comp.^{lts} or som[e of] them or some of theire Company did agree to pay ffifteene shillings weekly vpon every Saturday vnto this def^t and to *permytt this defend^t to have the* cleere benefitt of any one dayes playing vnto himselfe [with]in the space of Tenn dayes after the first playing of any such play at this defend^{ts} eleccon (the Comon charge d*educted as by the said Articles* wherevnto this defend^t for certaintie thereof only refer[re]th himselfe may more at large appeare. And this defend^t further saieth that his purposes and intente were alwayes *faire to performe the said* Articles on his parte Albeit the same were left in effect vnto himselfe vpon trust as aforesaid And the said Comp.^{lts} or some of the cheife of the said Company did often tymes *confidently affirme vnto* this defend.^t as aforesaid That this defend.^{ts} best indeavo^{rs} in wrighting playes for them should bee alwayes accepted, and that they would expect no more from him then hee *could well and conveyniently* doe therin as aforesaid, and also that they would bee more gratefull and beneficiall vnto this def.^t for his endeavo^{rs} then by theire said written Articles and Agreement they had engaged *themselves to bee Wherevpon* this defend.^t alsoe sheweth that Hee in pursuance and parte of performance of the said Articles on his parte did Compose and deliver vnto the said Comp.^{lts} or theire Company Twoe playes *within the first three* quarters of the yeare after the date of the said Articles, and true it is that this defend^t. for the ffirst of the said Twoe playes had one dayes cleare proffitt as they affirmed by *theire Accompt deducting* as aforesaid according to the said Articles, But this defend.^t also saieth that albeit this defend^{ts} said labo^{rs} brought the said Company into theire first and cheefest estimacon accompanyed *with very great* proffitts and gaynes as aforesaid Yett the plague shortly afterwards increasing here in and aboute London this def.^{ts} second play was first played by the said Company neere *or aboute the tyme of* theire restraint from playing by reson of the said sicknes And this def.^{ts} said Cleere dayes proffitt of the said second new play was never allowed vnto him to the Damage *of ffive pounds and* vpwards. And this defend.[t] also saieth that the Comp.[lts] and theire said Company being shortly afterwards wholly restrained from playing And this defend.[t] intending in the tyme of va*cancy of* the said playing to Compose and prepare more newe playes for them according to the said Articles and agreement for theire future vse and Comoditie when they should play againe. *And in* recompence and requitall thereof this def.[t] expected the due and true performance and payment of the said ffifteene shillings weekly from the said Comp.[lts] Company according to theire *Agreement* aforesaid in the Vacancy in which tyme hee was to write for them aswell aswhen they had permission to play theire being noe excepcon at all either in the said treatie Agreement or Articles *of* any tyme or such casualty whatsoever nor intencon to this defend[ts] knowledge Neither is there any such mencon made in the said Bill of Complaint that this Deft should not bee paied in *case of* such restraint But the Comp.[lts] or theire said Company intending Covenously or fraudulently to deceive and defraude this defend.[t] of the said weekly payment did first begyn to quarrell *and take* occasions of distast against this def.[t] and did deny to pay the same ffifteene shillings weekly to this defend.[t] against all equitie and good conscience and expresly against theire Agreement *and Articles* aforesaid And the said Company or some parte of the cheifest of them on the behalfe of the residue in the said tyme of Vacancy willed this defend.[t] to take what course hee could or would for himselfe for they neither could nor would contynue the weekly payment of ffifteene shillings vnto him as aforesaid And aboute the moneth of May 1636 as this defend[t] remembereth the tyme this defend.[t] was offered by the said *comp.*[lts] or Company or some of them That the said Articles bearing date in July as aforesaid should bee delivered vpp vnto this defend.[t] to bee Cancelled so as this def.[t] was tourned of by and amongst them and to *put to* his shifts in that hard sadd and dangerous tyme of the sicknes boeth for himselfe and his famyly wherevpon true it is that aboute the Moneth of August then next following this defend.[t] by necessitie constrained and being left in such distres and want as [afo]resaid by theire sole defaults did repaire vnto the said William Beeston in the bill named and acquainted him with his then *present* case and Condicon whoe then lent this defend[t] Six pounds at his need vpon this defend[ts] Agreement to Compose and write a play for the Cockpitt Company whereof when some of the Comp[lts] and theire Company vnderstood being in hope that the sicknes would in a shorte tyme afterwards seace Then true it is that some of them offered this def.[t] money and did ear*nestly* solicite this def.[t] to desert the said William Beeston and [his] Company and to retourne to the Comp.[lts] againe which this def.[t] at the present refused in regard of his said former badd and vn*charitable* vsage yett vpon theire earnest perswasion and promises of better vsage afterwards, and partly vpon threates of suites and troubles this def.[t] did resolve to make further tryall of them And *therevpon* the Comp[lt] Richard Heaton on the Companyes behalfe did vndertake agree and promise to take this defend.[t] of from the said William Beeston And to give him the said M[r] Beeston *satiffaccon* whereby this defend[t] might bee freely released from him And likewise they then agreed and promised to pay this def.ᵗ Tenn pounds in hand in Recompence and towards the satisfaccon of the then Arrera*ges of* the said weekly payment of ffifteen shillings due and behinde vnpaied vnto this def.ᵗ vpon the said former agreem.ᵗ and Articles but the same was not all paied vnto this def.ᵗ vntill he *brought* them a new Play and then it was made vpp with severall small sumes and pettie dribling payments which did small pleasure vnto this def.ᵗ And this def.ᵗ also saieth that afterwards the *sicknes* still contynueing the said ffifteene shillings per weeke was still stopped from this def.ᵗ whereby this def.ᵗ was in a kind enforced to treate againe and to make some agreement wᵗʰ the said William Beeston *touching* the premises wherevpon the comp.ˡᵗˢ or some of their Company became suitors to Sʳ Henry Herbert knight Master of the Revells to here and examine the cause betweene them and the said Master of the Revells taking the *trouble* vpon him did afterwards Award that the def.ᵗ should bee paied six shillings weekly and ffive pounds for every new play which hee should bring vntill such tyme as the sicknes should cease and the p.ˡᵗˢ should have leave to play againe which Award the p.ˡᵗˢ and Company did but in parte performe for when they began to play againe which was in the month of October 1637. they were then Indebted vpon that Award and Accompt to this def.ᵗ the sume of Eleaven pounds Eleaven shillings six pence or thereaboutes And this def.ᵗ also saieth that hee brought the said Company in six new playes wᵗʰin the Space of three yeares next after the said first agreement and Articles and more hee was not able possibly to performe aswell through sicknes as by other hinderance which hee then had. And this def.ᵗ vpon the last agreement in the bill menconed for Twenty shillings a weeke videlt in Hillary Terme 1638 Composed another new play for the said Comp.ˡᵗs and before Este*r tearme* 1639 this def.ᵗ brought them another new Play written all but parte of the last sceane But this def.ᵗ found that divers of the Company did so slight the last menconed playes and used such scornefull and reproachfull speeches concerning this def.ᵗ and divers of them did advise the rest of them to stopp all weekly payments towards this def.ᵗ so as this def.ᵗ vnderstood that they tooke occasions daily to wearie the defend.ᵗ from and out of theire ymployment which this def.ᵗ well perceiving did againe leave them to theire owne dispose through theire owne only default as aforesaid And true it is that this def.ᵗ *sithence* that tyme hath contracted and made other agreements with the said William Beeston with whome hee hopeth to enioy the fruites of his laboʳˢ more beneficially and peaceably. And this *def.*ᵗ also saith that this def.ᵗ of late tyme when hee was in the compˡᵗˢ ymployment being very sicke did send vnto the said Comp.ˡᵗˢ or some of them and theire Company for some weekly meanes *at* that tyme to supply his necesitie, but they vncharitably refused to lend him any And for theire further tryall this def.ᵗ did twoe or three tymes weeke after weeke importune and solicite them *with* Letters Imagininge that might and would worke remorse and pittie from them wherevpon some of the company by the assent of the residue as hee conceiveth sent him word that they had *given him* this def.ᵗ wholly over and meant to ymploy him noe further and wished him to shift for himselfe againe as aforesaid and refused vtterly to yeild any payment or releefe vnto this def.ᵗ in *his* said great sicknes want and misery saying they would have no more to doe with him whereby this def.ᵗ was againe enforced through there meere default as aforesaid to provide for himselfe as *aforesaid* which when the Comp.¹ᵗˢ observed this def.ᵗ to haue done, they do now out of mallice and evill will only molest and vex this def.ᵗ with suites of Lawe intending thereby to Crush and Ruyne him And *This def.ᵗ doth* deny that hee either by himselfe or others made meanes to the Comp.¹ᵗˢ in the begining for his said ymployment or that this def.ᵗ received all his pay of ffifteene shillings per weeke vpon the *said first* agreement and Articles vntill the Playes were prohibited or that it is usuall to stopp the Poetts weekly meanes or paym:ᵗˢ when such accidents happeneth vnless it bee so agreed made or expresed in or by *theire* Contracts or agreements, Or that full payment of the said ffifteene shillings *p* weeke at the end of the said Tearme of three yeares was made and paied for all the tyme of the sicknes as in and by the sa*id bill* of Comp.¹ᵗ is thereof vntruly pretended And this def.ᵗ saieth that theire was an anagreement [*sic*] made betweene this def.ᵗ and the Company as is aboue mențoned for the payment of Tenn pounds as aforesa*id wᶜʰ* hee beleeveth was reduced vnto writing as the bill thereof specifieth and wherevnto this def.ᵗ for certaintie thereof only also referreth himselfe but the same was paied by such driblets and petty payments as afor*esaid and* not before a new Play received as aforesaid so as it did him litle pleasure as aforesaid And this def.ᵗ saieth that hee is only behind with them twoe Playes In lieu of which hee hath made divers scenes in ould re*vive*d playes *for them* and many prologues and Epilogues to such playes of theires, songs, and one Introduccon at theire first playing after the ceasing of the plague all wᶜʰ hee verily beleeveth amounted to asmuch tyme and studdy as twoe ordynarie playes might take vpp *in* writing which hapened by the accidents and through theire owne defaults as aforesaid And as to the new play wᶜʰ the Comp.¹ᵗˢ suppose this def.ᵗ to haue sould vnto the said Christopher or William Beeston this def.ᵗ confeseth it *to bee* true that the stopage of his weekly meanes and vnkind carriages aforesaid forced this defend.ᵗ to Contract and bargaine for the said new play with the said William Beeston but yet the said Comp¹ᵗˢ and theire Company had it and acted it and by comon estimacon gott a Thousand pounds and vpwards by it And this def.ᵗ also saith true it is that there was an other agreement made between the Company or some of them and the def.ᵗ for the Composing of Playes for the rate of twenty shillings weekly wᶜʰ agreemᵗ was intended to bee reduced into writing as by the bill of Comp.¹ᵗ is menconed, but this defᵗ saieth as herein before he hath said that in the tyme of *the* sicknes hee was so unkindly and vncharitably vsed by the Comp.¹ᵗˢ and theire Company or some of them, and his weekly meanes stopped and his laboʳˢ and playes Cavelled at and reiected and himselfe discharged and *left* at libertie as aforesaid, whereby theire was no further proceedings therein so as each partie

was left to himselfe wherevpon this def[t] did apply himselfe vnto the said
William Beeston as hee hopeth was and is law*full for* him so to doe And this
def[t] denyeth that hee received twenty shillings weekly from July 1638 vntill
Aprill 1639 or that this def[t] is in effect any playes behinde vpon agreementt
with the Comp.[its] as by the said bill of *Comp.[it]* is thereof also vntruly pretended without that, that any other [ma]tter or thing suggested by the said
bill and materiall to bee answeared vnto, and herein before not answeared
Confessed Avoyded Traversed or denyed i*s true* in such manner and forme
as the same is therein alleadged All which matters this defend.[t] is ready to
Averr and prove as this hono.[ble] Courte shall award And humbly prayeth to
bee hence dismissed with good Costs for his vniust vexacon and charge in that
behalfe most iniuriously sustayned/

Andr. Browne

"The Eloquence of Masques": A Retrospective View of Masque Criticism

Review Article

INGA-STINA EWBANK

T HERE WAS NO DOUBT about the view he took of "the eloquence of masques" when, in the evening of Twelfth-night 1617/8, James I interrupted the performance of Ben Jonson's *Pleasure Reconciled to Virtue* by shouting out: "Why don't they dance? What did you make me come here for? Devil take you all, dance." [1] Little did this most vociferous and least inhibited of all masque critics think, as Buckingham sprang to the rescue by cutting an impromptu "score of lofty and very minute capers," that some 350 years later an American scholar would write of the same entertainment: "this is the masque above all others in which Jonson has made the revels integral to his text." [2] Some witnesses of that Twelfth-night performance simply thought the masque so bad as to indicate that Jonson "should returne to his ould trade of bricke laying againe"; others, with rather more attempt at discrimination, praised the visual effects,

1. *Calendar of State Papers, Venetian*, XV, 113–114. See G. E. Bentley, *The Jacobean and Caroline Stage* (Oxford, 1941–1956), IV, 671, and Ben Jonson, *Works*, ed. C. H. Herford and P. and E. Simpson, 11 vols. (Oxford, 1925–1952), X, 580–584 (hereafter cited as "*Works*").

2. Stephen Orgel, *The Jonsonian Masque* (Cambridge, Mass., 1965), p. 164.

particularly the antimasque, but did not like the poetry. And some were more impressed by the diplomatic complications around the occasion—the wrangling for precedence among the foreign ambassadors—than by anything about the masque as a work of art.[3] None of these commentators would have cared much for the terms in which, in the last ten years, *Pleasure Reconciled* has been rated high for its union of ritual structure with visual and verbal symbolism.[4]

I have quoted these extremes of diverging opinion about a single work not so much to illustrate the change in approach to the masque from Jonson's generation to ours as to introduce the problem of how, as critics, we approach the masque at all. What equipment do we bring to an examination of something which is at once an offspring of pagan rite, a sophisticated Renaissance celebration of social and divine order, and a harbinger of modern experiments in drama [5]—and which on the way manages to form the foundation of English opera? What criteria of goodness or badness do we apply to something which is both a social activity, "tied to rules of flattery," [6] and a work in which all the arts are interdependently combined into a banquet of sense—often, too, a work where so many of the records of its visual and aural effects are irrevocably lost that what we have left is no more than "broken meats of a banquet that is over"? [7] Truly *The Cambridge History of English Literature* may lament that even Jonson's masque texts are "not much more than the stick of the rocket after the firework has flamed and faded." [8]

To review masque criticism is first of all to be reminded of the obvious point: that most masque critics have cut the Gordian knot from the angle

3. See Bentley, *The Jacobean and Caroline Stage*, IV, 670–671.

4. See, e.g., W. Todd Furniss, *Ben Jonson's Masques,* in *Three Studies in the Renaissance* (New Haven, 1958), pp. 89–179, esp. 169–176.

5. Both "total theater" and "happenings" are in many ways anticipated in the way the masque involves its audience *and* all their senses—even the sense of smell, as we see in Bacon's reference to "some sweet odours suddenly coming forth."

6. Beaumont and Fletcher, *The Maid's Tragedy*, I.i.11–12.

7. *The Cambridge History of English Literature* (Cambridge, Eng., 1910), VI, 329 (hereafter cited as "*C.H.E.L.*"). The quotation is from the Rev. Ronald Bayne's chapter (XIII) on "Masque and Pastoral." Cf. Orgel's statement that "*Pleasure Reconcild to Vertue* is very nearly self-sufficient as a work of literature" (*The Jonsonian Masque*, p. 151).

8. *C.H.E.L.*, VI, 329.

they know best. Sir Francis Bacon had been professionally involved in organizing masque occasions, sometimes as "chief contriver"; [9] hence his essay "Of Masques and Triumphs" is a pragmatic discussion of how to make such occasions most pleasurable and least expensive, a kind of guide or commission to intending "contrivers":

. . . since princes will have such things, it is better they should be graced with elegancy than daubed with cost. Dancing to song is a thing of great state and pleasure . . . the alterations of scenes, so it be quietly and without noise, are things of great beauty and pleasure . . . Let the songs be loud and cheerful . . . Let the suits of the masquers be graceful and such as become the person when the vizars are off . . . But chiefly, let the music of them be recreative . . . Some sweet odours suddenly coming forth without any drops falling, are, in such a company, as there is steam and heat, things of great pleasure and refreshment . . . But all is nothing, except the room be kept clear and neat.[10]

Stephen Orgel, writing in the 1960's on *The Jonsonian Masque,* is a literary scholar and critic; hence his learned and illuminating study is concerned to show how "Jonson transmuted the occasional elements of his commission into integral parts of what was, for him, a poem." [11] Most modern critics strive, at least theoretically, for as comprehensive a view of the masque as possible:

The text becomes a scenario, to be fulfilled by the arts of choreography and stage design, or a libretto, in which at key moments the supremacy passes to the melodic line or the harmony of the instrumental ensemble. . . . Considered as verbal structures, the best masques occur during the Jacobean period, when Italian stagecraft was still a not quite familiar toy, and spoken language still held its pre-eminence over the singing voice. . . . The Caroline masques, on the other hand, more and more triumphant as feats of stage engineering, deteriorate as literature into twaddle. Whether this progress is properly to be regarded as a fulfillment or a degeneration depends, perhaps, on one's point of view, but if one thinks of the masque as ideally a composite of music, poetry and the arts of the dance and stage architecture, with poetry occupying the

9. See Mary Susan Steele, *Plays and Masques at Court during the Reigns of Elizabeth, James and Charles* (New Haven and London, 1926), p. 179.

10. Quoted from the Morley ed. of *The Essays or Counsels Civil and Moral of Francis Bacon* (London, 1887), pp. 212–215. The essay "Of Masques and Triumphs" first appeared in the 1625 ed. of Bacon's *Essays.*

11. Orgel, *The Jonsonian Masque*, p. 187.

central position, then certainly the peak achievements occur during the early years, and most of them are Jonson's.[12]

Mr. Barish's discussion of the masque forms only a small part of a full-length study of *Ben Jonson and the Language of Prose Comedy,* but it is one of the most discriminating discussions available. Naturally, however, his view has a literary bias. It is a bias which is shared by all those who think of poetry as "occupying the central position" in the masque and which is decried, sometimes bitterly, by representatives of other disciplines. Otto Gombosi starts his essay on "Some Musical Aspects of the English Court Masque" with an uncompromising statement: "The masque . . . was not what most literary historians make it appear"; and he continues: "By virtue of its origin the masque was, in the first place, dance, and naturally, dance music—and by virtue of its history, in the second place, spectacular entertainment. Only in the third place was the masque literature." [13] So he rebukes Enid Welsford for making the dance central in her definition of the masque and yet "curiously neglecting" dance and dance music in her book, *The Court Masque.*[14] Similarly John P. Cutts criticizes standard works on the masque because they have too little to say about the music.[15] Perhaps, at least for my purpose of looking at how, and how well, masques have been evaluated, the most important aspect of this partisanship—each critic wanting to claim the masque for his or her own particular sphere—is that it suggests that the masque is *worth* claiming.

This has not always been so. With few exceptions, it was only in this century that the masque as a form began to be at all taken seriously or to be seriously studied. The opening flourish of Bacon's essay—"These things are but toys"—was, it would seem, taken only too literally. There had been some serious discussion of the masque from a musical point of view in Dr. Charles Burney's *General History of Music* (1789),[16] and the

12. Jonas A. Barish, *Ben Jonson and the Language of Prose Comedy* (Cambridge, Mass., 1960), pp. 241–242.

13. Otto Gombosi, "Some Musical Aspects of the English Court Masque," *Journal of the American Musicological Society,* I (1948), 3.

14. *Ibid.,* p. 4, and Enid Welsford, *The Court Masque* (Cambridge, Eng., 1927).

15. John P. Cutts, "Le Rôle de la musique dans les masques de Ben Jonson," in *Les Fêtes de la Renaissance,* ed. Jean Jacquot (Paris, 1956), I, 285–302, esp. 301.

16. Charles Burney, *A General History of Music,* ed. Frank Mercer (London, 1935), II, Chap. VII. Among other things, Burney reproduces Whitelocke's account of the performance of Shirley's *Triumph of Peace* (pp. 293–300).

staging of the masque was to receive attention in a volume, *Inigo Jones and Ben Jonson*, brought out by the Shakespeare Society in 1848;[17] but in 1834 Isaac Disraeli could still claim that most commentators on the masque had spoken "with a perfect ignorance of the nature of these compositions."[18] Disraeli gets a great deal of malicious fun out of the "illegitimate opinion" held by Warburton, who "said on Masques, that 'Shakespeare was an enemy to these *fooleries,* as appears by his writing none'"; but his own opinions are not much more legitimate for—though he claims to have pursued "extensive researches" on the masque—he speaks of *Comus* as "composed by Milton to celebrate the creation of Charles the First as Prince of Wales." Such information and insights as he does have, he seems to have acquired from Gifford's piece on the masque in his *Memoirs of Ben Jonson*.[19] Gifford's essay—in which, with some acerbity, he defends both Jonson as a masque writer and the masque in general against Malone's condemnation of "bungling shews" in which "the wretched taste of those times found amusement"[20]—seems to have been the major attempt at critical appreciation of the masque in the nineteenth century. Seventy-four years after its first appearance it was reprinted as "A Comment on Ben Jonson's Masques" in Henry Morley's edition of *Masques and Entertainments by Ben Jonson*.[21] In the same year Gosse could still see the masque as "the lighter labours of a very goodly company"; and he did not think much of the form, despite what Jonson made of it: "The confinement of the form, its inherent stiffness and insipidity, did not alarm the fighting elephant of Elizabethan song."[22]

17. This is a composite volume, containing *Inigo Jones. A Life of the Architect,* by Peter Cunningham; facsimiles of drawings by Inigo Jones, accompanying *Remarks on Some of his Sketches for Masques and Dramas,* by J. R. Planché; and an edition of *Five Court Masques,* by John Payne Collier.

18. Isaac Disraeli, *Curiosities of Literature* (London, 1866), III, 4. (From the essay entitled "Masques.")

19. In *The Works of Ben Jonson,* ed. W. Gifford (London, 1816).

20. Jonson, *Works,* ed. W. Gifford and F. Cunningham (London, 1875), I, clxxix-clxxxi.

21. *Masques and Entertainments by Ben Jonson,* ed. Henry Morley (London, 1890).

22. *The Academy,* 22 February 1890, pp. 138–139: an account of a paper by Edmund Gosse, on "The Masques of Ben Jonson," read at a meeting of the Elizabethan Society on 5 February 1890. Gifford, too, is fond of the image of Jonson the masque writer as an agile elephant in a china shop: "it must be granted that here, at least, he *writhed his lithe proboscis* with playfulness and ease" (Jonson, *Works,* ed. Gifford and Cunningham, I, clxxix).

Neither Dowden, in a rather slight essay entitled "The English Masque," nor Schelling, writing the history of *Elizabethan Drama* early in this century, could get away from the notion of masques as toys.[23]

But the generation of Schelling and Dowden also saw the beginnings of serious scholarship on the masque. When, in 1897, H. A. Evans published an edition of sixteen masques by various authors from Daniel to Davenant[24] (which until the appearance of *A Book of Masques in Honour of Allardyce Nicoll* was the only readily available collection of masques), he could build his introductory essay on Alfred Soergel's dissertation, *Die englischen Maskenspiele*.[25] This pioneer work was fairly soon followed by two other monographs which still remain standard works on the masque and its development: Rudolf Brotanek's *Die englischen Maskenspiele* (Vienna and Leipzig, 1902) and Paul Reyher's *Les Masques anglais* (Paris, 1909). Meanwhile, W. W. Greg's *List of Masques . . .* had provided a bibliographical foundation for work on the masque;[26] and E. K. Chambers, in *The Mediaeval Stage,* had made a study of the origins of the masque in folk drama and festival—to be followed up by a clear and authoritative account of the Elizabethan and Jacobean masque in *The Elizabethan Stage*.[27] Two shorter studies from the early part of the century, R. Bayne's chapter on "Masque and Pastoral" in *The Cambridge History of English Literature* (1910) and Percy Simpson's work on "The Masque" in *Shakespeare's England* (1916), summarize what was so far known rather than adding anything new—though Bayne makes an interesting point, which has never yet been fully developed, about the rela-

23. Edward Dowden, *Essays Modern and Elizabethan* (London, 1910), pp. 334–350; F. E. Schelling, *Elizabethan Drama* (Boston and New York, 1908), II, 93–138, esp. 117. About the same time W. W. Greg, in Chap. VII of *Pastoral Drama and Pastoral Poetry* (London, 1906), argued that the masque was too elusive a form to be rigidly defined, ranging from "mere pageants on the one hand" to "what may be called miniature plays on the other" (p. 369).

24. *English Masques,* ed. H. A. Evans (London, 1897).

25. (Halle, 1882). I have not seen this work.

26. W. W. Greg, *A List of Masques, Pageants, etc. Supplementary to a List of English Plays* (London, 1902). Studies of specific aspects of the masque had also started to appear—see A. H. Thorndike, "Influence of the Court-Masques on the Drama, 1608–15," *PMLA,* XV (1900), 114–120; J. W. Cunliffe, "Italian Prototypes of the Masque and Dumb Show," *PMLA,* XXII (1907), 140–156.

27. E. K. Chambers, *The Mediaeval Stage* (Oxford, 1903), Vols. I–II, esp. Chap. XVII; *The Elizabethan Stage* (Oxford, 1923), Vol. I, Chaps. V–VI.

tion between Jonson's masques and the comedies of Aristophanes.[28] Information about the staging of masques was also accumulating. In a chapter of *The Elizabethan Playhouse* (1912) W. J. Lawrence had discussed "The Mounting of the Carolan Masque"; but the major breakthrough came with Lily B. Campbell's study of *Scenes and Machines on the English Stage* (1923), followed the next year by Percy Simpson's and C. F. Bell's magnificent edition of the Chatsworth collection of Inigo Jones's designs.[29] In *The Development of the Theatre* (1927) Allardyce Nicoll analyzed the importance of the masque for the development of staging methods and theater architecture in England, regretting that the format of his book allowed only a "rapid and all too brief account of the masques."[30] This account was superbly expanded in the richly illustrated *Stuart Masques and the Renaissance Stage* (1937), which will be an essential tool as long as masques are studied.

In 1927 came the first full-length study in English of the masque as a form: *The Court Masque* by Enid Welsford. The author stressed that her aim, following on Brotanek, Reyher, and others, was "to interpret and to coordinate rather than to accumulate facts." Brotanek's and Reyher's studies in many ways complement each other. Brotanek's is a straightforward account of the history and the development of the masque form, with much emphasis on the structure of individual masques and with a final chapter on foreign influences. Reyher covers the same ground but arranges his survey around a series of central topics, concentrating all the time on seeing the masque in its total social and artistic context—"car une étude sur le 'Masque' en soi, isolé du milieu social, de la littérature, du drame, de l'art de l'époque, me fait l'effet d'un contre-sens et presque d'un non-sens" (p. viii). Making full use of the records and accounts in Domestic State Papers, he is the first to evoke the sense of occasion around each masque.

Where, however, Brotanek and Reyher are mainly descriptive, Miss Welsford is more analytic. As indicated by the subtitle of her book, "A Study in the Relationship between Poetry and the Revels," she is writing

28. *C.H.E.L.*, VI, 362–363.

29. Percy Simpson and C. F. Bell, *Designs by Inigo Jones for Masques and Plays at Court* (Oxford, 1924).

30. Allardyce Nicoll, *The Development of the Theatre* (London, 1927), pp. 127–130.

more than a study of the history of the masque (she does this, too, and is especially informative on the continental analogues of the masque); she is preoccupied with "the significance of the masque," and her ultimate aim is to examine, through the masque, a theory of art—that of the artist as "a strayed reveller" (p. 405). This gives her book a unity and interest greater than the admittedly rather heavy studies of Brotanek and Reyher. But it also involves dangers such as distortions of emphasis, most clearly seen, perhaps, in her chapter on "The Influence of the Masque on the Drama," where the masque has come to seem more or less directly responsible for any symbolical element in Elizabethan-Jacobean drama.[31]

The significance which Miss Welsford finds in the masque is that it gives us "a clue to the connection between the social utility and the aesthetic value of a work of art" (p. 404). Always emphasizing the central position of the dance in the masque, she sees it as at once a symbolic and a social art form. Her book here forms the bridge into recent masque criticism, which in many ways can be seen as an elaboration and extension of Miss Welsford's argument. Her insight is an anticipation of Northrop Frye's placing of the masque in relation to drama:

The further comedy moves from irony, and the more it rejoices in the free movement of its happy society, the more readily it takes to music and dancing. As music and scenery increase in importance, the ideal comedy crosses the boundary line of spectacular drama and becomes the masque. . . .

It thus differs from comedy in its more intimate attitude to the audience: there is more insistence on the connection between the audience and the community on the stage.[32]

It is also a forerunner of the emphasis given to the masque by Miss M. C. Bradbrook in *English Dramatic Form,* where she sees the masque as the culmination of a pageant-stage tradition, converting social reality into poetic image and image into social reality: "Oberon the Fairy Prince,

31. Compare this to the very businesslike accounts of masques-in-plays given by Reyher and Chambers. Reyher, *Les Masques anglais* (Paris, 1909), pp. 497–498, has a list of plays which contain masques, and so has R. S. Forsythe, *The Relations of Shirley's Plays to the Elizabethan Drama* (New York, 1914), pp. 79–80. Various studies of masques in plays have been referred to in my essay on this subject in *A Book of Masques in Honour of Allardyce Nicoll* (Cambridge, Eng., 1967), pp. 407–449.

32. Northrop Frye, *Anatomy of Criticism* (Princeton, 1957), pp. 287–288.

played by Henry Prince of Wales, represented *himself;* it was an imaginative way of sweeping the small courtly audience into his kingdom-to-be." [33]

It is obvious from these two quotations alone that the climate created by the preoccupation of criticism with literature as symbolic structure has been favorable to the masque. The distance which masque criticism had traveled in a quarter of a century can be measured by comparing the essay on "Masques and Entertainments" in Volume II of the Herford and Simpson *Ben Jonson* (1925) with the masque commentary in Volume X (1950). In the earlier volume the bibliography of works on the masque is very short; and, though there is much valuable analysis of Jonson's work in the genre, the attitude to the masque itself is summed up by the concluding comment that "the spectacle remains impressive of the Titan playing with bubbles and butterflies and rainbows" (p. 334). The later volume not only has a much longer bibliography, but it also has sections on aspects of Jonson's masque newly revealed as important. Significantly, the last reference in the last section—on "Classical Allegory and Symbolism"—is to an article by E. W. Talbert on "The Interpretation of Jonson's Courtly Spectacles." This article is, perhaps, the clearest expression of the new seriousness in dealing with masques—particularly, of course, Jonson's: ". . . the voice of Jonson's courtly spectacle, I submit, is that of the panegyric *laudando praecipere;* the sense, that of precepts *de regimine principum* enlarged by the ethical-political *credo* of a staunch Renaissance humanist." [34]

If the masque is capable of becoming a symbolic work of art which is also a kind of humanist Mirror for Magistrates, then we can no longer hold it to be "a contemptible form of the dramatist's art." [35] It is above all through studies of the allegorical and emblematic tradition in which it belongs that the masque has returned to respectability. Naturally this has mainly been true for Jonson's masques, which have tended to be used as sticks to beat other masque writers with: thus, for example, W. Todd Furniss compares Daniel's *Vision of the Twelve Goddesses* to Jonson's masques and finds it lacking in "the interrelationship of theme and

33. M. C. Bradbrook, *English Dramatic Form* (London, 1965), p. 58.

34. E. W. Talbert, "The Interpretation of Jonson's Courtly Spectacles," *PMLA* (1946), 473.

35. C. V. Wedgwood, *Seventeenth-Century English Literature* (London, 1950), p. 63.

imagery and action." [36] But there are exceptions, such as D. J. Gordon's study of Chapman's *Masque of the Middle Temple and Lincoln's Inn*.[37]

Examinations of the masque as an important form of symbolical art have followed two frequently intersecting paths: one pursuing the symbolical aspects of the staging and execution of the masque and the other its symbolical meanings—with the implications in terms of philosophy and *Geistesgeschichte* which this entails. Both these paths are, of course, very close to those trodden by the many scholars and critics who, in the last few decades, have explored the relation of Elizabethan literature, and particularly drama, to traditions and modes of thought inherited from the medieval past.

"Pageantry is itself the quintessence of emblematic art," Glynne Wickham points out; [38] and it is through its kinship with pageantry—royal entries and civic occasions, especially the Lord Mayor's Show—that the masque has often been seen as part of the general dependence of the Elizabethan theater on the emblematic tradition. As early as 1918–1920, R. Withington, in *English Pageantry: An Historical Outline,* had provided material for explorations in this direction; and Erwin Panofsky's *Studies in Iconology* (1931) had become a bible for anyone interested in emblematic art. But it was left for the forties and fifties to make the connection with the stage: in works like G. R. Kernodle's *From Art to Theater* (1944), S. C. Chew's *The Virtues Reconciled* (1947), and Alice C. Venezky's *Pageantry on the Shakespearean Stage* (1951); in a series of articles in the *Journal of the Warburg and Courtauld Institutes,* and in several publications issued from the Centre National de la Recherche Scientifique in Paris, under the editorship of Jean Jacquot.[39] The relevance

36. Furniss, *Ben Jonson's Masques,* p. 105.

37. D. J. Gordon, "Le 'Masque Mémorable' de Chapman," in *Les Fêtes de la Renaissance,* I, 305–317.

38. Glynne Wickham, *Early English Stages 1300 to 1660* (London, 1963), II, i, 209.

39. See esp. the articles by D. J. Gordon cited in notes 42 and 45, below; and *Les Fêtes de la Renaissance,* cited in note 15, above. Allardyce Nicoll had already discussed the connection between the masque and the tradition of the emblem and the *impresa* (Chap. VI, "Court Hieroglyphics," in *Stuart Masques and the Renaissance Stage*); and Reyher (*Les Masques anglais,* pp. 391 ff.) had pointed to the indebtedness of masque writers to the *Iconologia* of Ripa. This line of study has brought forth many works on Jonson's use of classical allegory and symbolism and

of such work to the staging of the masque is best seen in Glynne Wickham's analysis of the masque as a testing ground on which takes place

a head-on collision of two fundamentally opposed attitudes to art: the typically mediaeval contentment with emblematic comment on the significance of the visual world versus a new, scientific questing for the photographic image.[40]

Wickham has a most illuminating analysis of Inigo Jones's gradual move away from the pageant type of staging to the point where—seen objectively—he might well have felt entitled to appear on the title page of *The Masque of Augurs,* sharing the credit for the "invention" of the masque.[41] The famous quarrel between Ben Jonson and Inigo Jones—in which masque critics have usually been on Jonson's side and seen Jones's victory as being at the root of the decadence of the masque into merely scenic splendor—is, then, not simply a black and white issue between poet and architect; it becomes a clash between the Old Drama and the New, the Old Philosophy and the New. The deeper implications of this clash have also been finely analyzed by D. J. Gordon, who—with a different emphasis from Wickham's—shows that what was at stake between the combatants was a difference between two conceptions of *design:* verbal and visual.[42]

Gordon's essay shows, too, that in pursuing the problem of the scenic representation of the masques, we are back with their *meaning:* the study of what Jonson called their *"bodies,"* or "outward celebration," leads sooner or later to their *"souls,"* or "inward parts" or "more remov'd

---

particularly on his dependence on Renaissance mythographers. See, e.g., D. C. Allen, "Ben Jonson and the Hieroglyphics," *PQ,* XVIII (1939), 290–300; E. W. Talbert, "The Classical Mythology and the Structure of *Cynthia's Revels,*" *PQ,* XXII (1943), 193–210; E. W. Talbert, "Current Scholarly Works and the 'Erudition' of Jonson's *Masque of Augurs,*" *SP,* XLIV (1947), 605–624. Much of this is summed up in Starnes and Talbert, *Classical Myth and Legend in Renaissance Dictionaries* (Chapel Hill, 1955). See also C. F. Wheeler, *Classical Mythology in the Plays, Masques and Poems of Ben Jonson* (Princeton, 1938).

40. Wickham, *Early English Stages,* p. 209.

41. *Ibid.,* p. 272.

42. D. J. Gordon, "Poet and Architect: The Intellectual Setting of the Quarrel between Ben Jonson and Inigo Jones," *Journal of the Warburg and Courtauld Institutes,* XII (1949), 152–178. This essay also has a very useful appendix on the terminology used by other writers of masques.

mysteries."[43] What it is that thus links the outward and the inward parts of the masque is perhaps most clearly articulated in the "discussion générale" which concludes the symposium of essays edited by Jean Jacquot under the title *Les Fêtes de la Renaissance*—in a dialogue which might itself well have come out of such a Jonsonian masque as *Pleasure Reconciled to Virtue.* M. Chastel points out that in the sixteenth century the arts did not always, in practice, collaborate. But if there is a sort of unity between them, then it exists in a cosmic vision common to all the arts— "une orientation commune qui se traduisait . . . par un certain symbolisme." To which Miss Frances Yates replies:

L'harmonie des sphères s'exprime en musique, en peinture, en morale, en politique, en architecture.
CHASTEL:
Et dans la fête.[44]

At this stage, then, the study of masque symbolism is also a study of the underlying philosophical assumptions. Much fascinating work has been done in this field, notably by D. J. Gordon who, in essays on *The Masque of Blackness,* on the "Haddington Masque," and on *Hymenaei,* has analyzed the imagery of these masques and its ideological background.[45] Thanks to these insights it has by now become almost a commonplace to see the Jonsonian masque as a flower of humanist thinking and art, with poetry, music, and dance joining to form a celebration of the order of the universe and the divinity of kingship[46]—*and* to judge other masques according to how they approach or depart from this norm.

It has also become a commonplace of criticism to see the ideal masque as having a basically didactic function: the antics of the antimasque merely affirming by contrast the beauty and harmony and order which the main masque establishes. This has had the effect of lessening the distance

43. See *Hymenaei, Works,* VII, 209.

44. *Les Fêtes de la Renaissance,* I, 462.

45. "The Imagery of Ben Jonson's *The Masque of Blacknesse* and *The Masque of Beautie,*" *Journal of the Warburg and Courtauld Institutes,* VI (1943), 122–141; "Ben Jonson's 'Haddington Masque': the Story and the Fable," *MLR,* XLII (1947), 180–187; "*Hymenaei:* Ben Jonson's Masque of Union," *Journal of the Warburg and Courtauld Institutes,* VIII (1945), 107–145.

46. See, e.g., John C. Meagher, "The Dance and the Masques of Ben Jonson," *Journal of the Warburg and Courtauld Institutes,* XXV (1962), 258–277.

between Jonson and Milton, between *Pleasure Reconciled to Virtue* and *Comus*.[47] For "when men thought in emblems, the purpose of a masque did not need to be mere amusement." Thus writes A. H. Gilbert, in *The Symbolic Persons in the Masques of Ben Jonson* (1948), which is not only a useful handbook to Jonson's mythological figures but also, in its introductory essay, a program declaration for those who evaluate the masque as a poetic-didactic form. (This view was to be intelligently developed in Dolora Cunningham's essay, "The Jonsonian Masque as a Literary Form." [48]) The main points of Gilbert's argument also form a standard against which he can measure the decadence of the masque:

Jonson in his masques brings to its consummation in practice the Renascence theory of poetry . . . "feigning notable images of virtues." . . .

It was Ben's good fortune that he lived just as the age of emblems—to which his genius was so well matched—reached its culmination. When symbolism began to lose its vitality, such masques as he believed in could no longer be written.[49]

It is on this standard that W. Todd Furniss bases his judgments in his monograph on *Ben Jonson's Masques* (1958). It is difficult to escape a sense of *déjà vu* as one is confronted with Furniss' starting point—"a world centering in the office of monarchy, which is itself patterned on a universal philosophy . . . the picture . . . of an ideal monarchy" (p. 99)— and with his argument, that the best masques are ritual celebrations of kingship, their core consisting of kingly images which "fall into categories which correspond to the links in the Great Chain of Being." Furniss' division of the masques which he examines into four groups—Golden Age, Pastoral, Triumph, and Combats of Concepts—makes new and valuable connections among the varied forms of Jonsonian masque. But the disadvantage of this sort of approach is that the connections are made too tight, that variety is underplayed. For, we are told, "the enormous variety shown on the surface of Jonson's masques has frequently deluded

47. I have not been able to deal within the scope of this essay with criticisms of *Comus*—which would need a whole article to themselves.

48. In *ELH*, XXII (1955), 108–124. Reprinted in *Ben Jonson: A Collection of Critical Essays*, ed. Jonas A. Barish (Englewood Cliffs, 1963).

49. A. H. Gilbert, *The Symbolic Persons in the Masques of Ben Jonson* (Durham, N. C., 1948), pp. 27–28. Cf. also Gilbert's article "The Function of the Masques in *Cynthia's Revels*," *PQ*, XXII (1943), 211–230.

his readers. We must try to see the pattern common to them all" (p. 107). As one who has been deluded, one wonders if, in criticism of this type, we are not in danger of altogether losing the sense of the masque occasion: if, to the audience and the participators (made up of largely the same people from one occasion to the next), some of Jonson's power did not rest precisely in his variety. *Lovers Made Men,* which both structurally and musically (*"the whole Maske was sung* . . . Stylo recitativo" [50]) must have seemed one of the most interesting masques, is used as a whipping boy because, not having been performed before the king, it lacks "a symbol of some greater universal order. *Lovers Made Men* is an amusing fable illustrating pleasantly a commonplace about love; it lacks the emotional power that the presence of royalty gives to other masques" (p. 168).

It is greatly to the credit of Stephen Orgel (*The Jonsonian Masque,* 1965) that in his book he has rethought the whole nature and—and this is to him the key word—function of the masque. Despite its title, the book is much concerned with developments of the masque before Jonson (and it includes an original appreciation of Sidney's *Lady of May*). Mr. Orgel challenges the notion, held by Miss Welsford and others, of the dance as the essence of the masque; he sees it instead as " a unique kind of relationship between its action and its audience." Jonson's work is the perfection of the attempt of the masque "to breach the barrier between spectators and actors, so that in effect the viewer became part of the spectacle" (p. 6). After Orgel it will hardly be possible to see the masque as drama *manqué* and Jonson's contribution to the genre as measurable in terms of his "transforming the formal Court Masque from a mere spectacle into something at least resembling drama." [51] While Orgel's own notion of

50. Jonson's description (*Works,* VII, 454). This masque is sometimes referred to as the first English opera. Cf. Edward J. Dent, *Foundations of English Opera* (Da Capo Reprint ed.; New York, 1965), p. 26, and *Grove's Dictionary of Music and Musicians,* ed. Blom (London, 1954), where it is described as "an epochal work from the musical standpoint." None of the music for this masque, which was composed by Lanier, is extant; but cf. Andrew J. Sabol, *A Score for "Lovers Made Men"* (Providence, R. I., 1963).

51. T. M. Parrott, "Comedy in the Court Masque: A Study of Ben Jonson's Contribution," *PQ,* XX (1941), 440.

the relationship between masque and drama is questionable,[52] his stress on the masque as an occasion is salutary.

Yet, Orgel's criterion for the masque remains literary—that is, the masque is good if the occasion has been transformed into a unified poetic whole: "It is a remarkable testimony to the integrity of Jonson's imagination that any failure to achieve the necessary unity of form tends to be evident from the quality of the verse in the main masque" (p. 81). We have come a long way since H. A. Evans could say that "the majority of modern readers" know the masque "simply . . . as a promising hunting-ground for some of the most graceful lyrics of the seventeenth century"; [53] and Orgel has some very fine analyses of Jonson's masque verse. It is also true that Jonson published his texts as literature and spoke of the poetry as the "soul" of the masque; but one cannot help feeling that Orgel is too insistent that, for the masque to be good, the *words* must do all the work. Hence he has it in for the antimasque of *Love's Triumph,* because it has no text at all, only a prose description of the dances; and, conversely, he praises *Pleasure Reconciled to Virtue* because in this masque Jonson "no longer relies on descriptions of setting."

Thus the most recent study of the masque has landed us back in the dilemma of criteria. The "literary" view of the masque is now a much wider one than Gosse's, when he envisaged the company of masque writers ("Ben Jonson stands up, burly and mountainous, in the midst of them, with Shakespeare holding his right hand and Milton his left")[54] and wider than what Dowden had in mind when he said: "The distinction . . . of the English masque . . . is the lofty invention of its poets." [55] It is not limited to detachable poetic beauties but includes an awareness of Renaissance symbolism in all its aspects. But, it would seem, it is still too

52. He overestimates, I think, the uniqueness of the masque in "breaching the barrier" between spectators and actors: a great deal of such "breaching" must have gone on in the Elizabethan playhouse. He also tends to make too rigid a separation of "drama" and "theater," implying that dramatic moments must be verbal (see, e.g., p. 126, on *Blackness*); and, finally, the concluding pages, on how "the masque movement has borne fruit in the modern theatre," are misleading in their generalizations.

53. Introduction to *English Masques,* p. li.

54. *The Academy,* 22 February 1890, p. 138.

55. Dowden, *Essays Modern and Elizabethan,* p. 334.

narrow a framework to allow full credit to what the visual and musical effects must have meant in the masque as a whole. Are these important only when they directly support a verbal symbol?

To read the descriptions of performances which masque writers have attached to their texts is to be reminded how utterly the masque must have been bound up with nonverbal elements. Daniel, in his Preface to the Reader in *Tethys' Festival* (1610), grovels before the architect (who, of course, was Inigo Jones): "But in these things wherein the onely life consists in shew; the arte and invention of the Architect gives the greatest grace, and is of most importance: ours, the least part and of the least note in the time of the performance thereof." [56] This, like the whole form of this masque, may be a defiance of Jonson—who was later to say "That next himself only Fletcher and Chapman could make a Mask." [57] Yet, Jonson himself, in the descriptive parts of his earlier masques, communicates a very strong sense of the importance of the visual elements. The feeling of delight at the performance itself, and the nostalgia that "our revels now are ended" (so often a part of these descriptions), turn Jonson's description at the end of *Hymenaei*, for example, into the sort of passage which makes us realize how difficult it is for us to try to recover the impact of the masque. And it is worth noticing, too, that this is the masque the printed text of which opens with Jonson's famous distinction between the outward show which perishes and the "inward parts" which "lay hold on more remov'd mysteries." Clearly to Jonson himself, as both a creator and a critic of masques, there was nothing so irreconcilable in these attitudes. [58] For him the conflict came when Inigo Jones wanted to let the "body" feed on the "soul."

In the *Hymenaei* passage referred to above, Jonson also speaks of the "divine rapture of the musique." Recent musicological research has made

56. *The Complete Works in Verse and Prose of Samuel Daniel,* ed. Alexander B. Grosart (London, 1885), III, 307.

57. See *Works,* I, 133.

58. Barish, *Ben Jonson and the Language of Prose Comedy,* p. 242, has an interesting comment on the Jonson-Jones rivalry as mirroring a conflict within Jonson himself "between the platonizing effort to read sensible things as symbols of a higher reality, on the one hand, and the more pragmatic, more theatrical attachment to things of sense for their own sake, on the other."

it clear that we have not fully understood the nature of that "rapture"—not exhausted the contribution of song, instrumental music, and dance to the total effect of the masque—even when, in a "literary" fashion, we have referred to the harmony of the songs, seen the dances as emblematic,[59] and pointed to the symbolic contrast between the cacophonies of the antimasque and the harmonies of the main masque. It is, I think, in the field of musicology that some of the most important work on the masque is being done at the moment. A. J. Sabol's essay prefaced to his *Songs and Dances for the Stuart Masque* (1959) forms a balanced and, to a nonmusicologist, convincing analysis of the importance of the choreographic pattern in the structure of the masque, in which the order of the dances forms the basis of the design.[60] To criticize Jonson for having no words in the antimasque of *Love's Triumph* (as Orgel does), and to leave it at that, is to forget about the effect,

When sodainely they leape forth below, a Mistresse leading them, and with anticke gesticulation, and action, after the manner of the old *Pantomimi,* they dance over a distracted *comoedy* of *Love,* expressing their confus'd affections, in the Scenicall persons, and habits, of the foure prime *European* Nations.[61]

59. Most "literary" discussions of the masque will nowadays speak of the dances and the music as projections of the idea of cosmic order and refer to Sir John Davies' *Orchestra.*

60. Andrew J. Sabol, *Songs and Dances for the Stuart Masque* (Providence, R. I., 1959). On the music and / or dance of the masque, see also, e.g., Dent, *Foundations of English Opera;* Gombosi, "Some Musical Aspects"; W. J. Lawrence, "Notes on a Collection of Masque Music," *Music and Letters,* III (1922), 49–58; Ernest Ulrich, "Die Musik in Ben Jonsons Maskenspielen und Entertainments," *Shakespeare Jahrbuch,* LXXIII (1937), 53–84; Ian Spink, "English Seventeenth-Century Dialogues," *Music and Letters,* XXXVIII (1957), 155–163; and several articles by John P. Cutts, especially, "Jacobean Masque and Stage Music," *Music and Letters,* XXXV (1954), 185–200; "Ben Jonson's Masque *The Vision of Delight,*" *N & Q,* N.S., III (1956), 64–67; "Robert Johnson and the Stuart Masque," *Music and Letters,* XLI (1960), 11–26, and "Le Rôle de la musique." I should like to thank Mr. H. N. Davies for much help on the musical aspects of the masque and for drawing my attention to many works in this field which I would not otherwise have known of.

61. *Works,* VII, 736. Inigo Jones's sketches for all but two of these lovers have been preserved. See Simpson and Bell, *Designs,* Nos. 68–78; and cf. *Works,* X, 677–679.

The qualities of the lovers, Jonson says, "in varied, intricate turnes, and involv'd mazes, exprest, make the Antimasque"; and we hardly need words here any more than we do in a modern dramatic ballet.[62]

Sabol also has a most illuminating analysis of the function of songs, many of which were functional in the structure, and of the importance of the instruments used. Campion, who wrote some of the music for his masques and who, because of his own musical background, is more articulate than other masque writers in his descriptions of the use of music, so describes the devices he used in *Lord Hay's Masque* as to enable Sabol to make the following analysis:

Even though there is no antimasque, he achieves variety in three principal ways: by placing several ensembles of instrumentalists in various portions of the hall and requiring them to play sometimes in alternation and sometimes together; by relying considerably upon the movement of musicians—singers and instrumentalists—as well as masquers (there are several processions); and by adapting different kinds of songs to various plot situations.[63]

How are we to tell, with so little in the way of scores preserved, that similar functions were not performed by the musical arrangement in other masques where maybe the words alone carry little effect of conflict or variety? The recent important discovery (or rediscovery) by Murray Lefkowitz of documents on the musical aspects of Shirley's *Triumph of Peace*—such as the make-up of the choir and the names and voice parts of all the singers, the instrumentation of the "symphony" of musicians, several diagrams of the soloists, chorus, and symphony during the musical numbers, etc.—is not only of historical interest to musicologists but fully substantiates Mr. Lefkowitz's claim of having "added immeasurably to our knowledge concerning this masque and to performance practice in general." [64] In the case of *The Triumph of Peace,* putting the Longleat papers together with Shirley's text and description, with Inigo Jones's designs, and with William Lawes's score, we have indeed "the most com-

---

62. Cf. Dent, *Foundations of English Opera,* p. 25, on the dances of the antimasque as "the foundation of the modern dramatic ballet."

63. Sabol, *Songs and Dances for the Stuart Masque,* pp. 10–11.

64. Murray Lefkowitz, "The Longleat Papers of Bulstrode Whitelocke; New Light on Shirley's *Triumph of Peace*," *Journal of the American Musicological Society,* XVIII (1965), 42–60. Lefkowitz has also discussed the music of *The Triumph of Peace* in his book *William Lawes* (London, 1960), Chap. IX.

plete extant records of the production of any English Court Masque."
Placing too much emphasis on the musical aspects of the masque, we may
run the risk of seeing it merely as a steppingstone on the road to opera
(but this is probably no more dangerous than seeing it as drama *manqué*).
The best of the musicological discussions of the masque recognize this:
thus Sabol points out that, while historically the masque is a preparatory
form for opera (so that in the Restoration the terms coexist), it yet is "an
independent art form in its own right which served a distinct social purpose quite different from that of opera" (p. 17).

It is to the critics' view of that social purpose we must finally turn, for
ultimately each masque, in a way different from any other art form, is a
product of its occasion. Or, as Chapman put it in the preface to his only
surviving masque:

> . . . *all these courtly and honouring inventions (having poesy and oration in
> them, and a fountain to be expressed, from whence their rivers flow) should
> expressively arise out of the places and persons for and by whom they are
> presented; without which limits they are luxurious and vain.*[65]

Scholars and critics have provided us with many aids towards recovering,
imaginatively, the social occasions of masques—at best with such splendid
pieces of evocation as Miss C. V. Wedgwood's essay, "The Last Masque." [66]
Nichols' *Progresses,* the systematic use of state papers and other contemporary evidence by Herford and Simpson, E. K. Chambers, and G. E.
Bentley, and M. S. Steele's useful handbook of court dramatic performances (*Plays and Masques at Court,* 1926) are the most obvious aids.
Reyher, as I have already mentioned, makes much of the social context
of the masque, especially in his Chapter III, "Le Monde du ballet," and
also in section 3 of Chapter IV, where he deals with "le ballet et les
événements du jour." As early as 1913 Mary Sullivan, in *Court Masques
of James I,* an intelligent if one-sided book, studied the political and diplomatic bearings of some of James's court masques. More recently D. J.
Gordon's essays have dealt with (among many other things) the political
implications of some masques: of *Hymenaei,* where—under the bridal

---

65. *The Plays and Poems of George Chapman,* ed. T. M. Parrott (London, 1910–
1914), II, 444.
66. On the performance of Davenant's *Salmacida Spolia* on the eve of the Civil
War. See *Truth and Opinion* (London, 1960), pp. 139–156.

theme—the theme of English-Scottish union is more apparent; in Chapman's Middle Temple masque, where the reference both to the Raleigh situation and to the political ramifications of the marriage celebrated are more removed mysteries.[67] Few modern critics have forgotten that, in all the masques performed at court, the monarch *is* the occasion, for good or for ill. As G. K. Hunter says (discussing the inevitable compliment to the sovereign which prevented the masque from acquiring an independent plot): "This fragility was no doubt one of the charms of the masque, but it was a charm which separated it from drama, and which makes it remote from us today, except as an historical document." [68] And a historical document, from this point of view, the masque must presumably remain—in the hands of poets as well as critics. Presumably that "memorable scene" of tragedy on the scaffold outside Whitehall in January 1649 put an end to a world of masque occasions. It was less incongruous for "the 'obdurate virgin' of threescore and ten, the hoary headed Cynthia of Whitehall" to be addressed as "Queen and huntress, chaste and fair" than for her twentieth-century namesake, at the performance of William Empson's masque of *The Birth of Steel,* to accept Minerva's address, "Royalty I am yourself." [69] Actual masque occasions may have been as messy and full of unintentional irony as the one emerging from Harington's satirical description of the performance of a masque before James and the visiting king of Denmark in 1606; but the king as a drunk and stupid watcher counted nothing against the king as a symbol.[70] Carlyle did not think much of the masque as art, but in his comment on Jonson's masques there is a (modern) nostalgia for that irretrievable symbol:

Certainly it is a circumstance worth noticing that surly Ben, a real Poet, could employ himself in such business, with the applause of all the world; it indicates an Age very different from ours. An Age full of Pageantry, of grotesque Symbolising,—yet not without something in it to symbolise.[71]

67. D. J. Gordon, "Le 'Masque Mémorable' de Chapman."

68. G. K. Hunter, *John Lyly: The Humanist as Courtier* (London, 1962), p. 115.

69. See Gifford's description of Elizabeth I, quoted in Hunter, *ibid.,* p. 142; for the masque performed before Elizabeth II when she visited Sheffield University in 1954, see William Empson, *Collected Poems* (London, 1955), pp. 85–89.

70. Mary Susan Steele, *Plays and Masques at Court,* p. 151.

71. From *Historical Sketches of Notable Persons and Events in the Reigns of James I and Charles I* (London, 1898), p. 74. Quoted in *Works,* XI, 566.

Where, then, in the end do we stand with the masque? And with its critics? Sabol's is only one of many voices, but perhaps the most articulate one, asking for an integrated view: "Masques perhaps should not be evaluated solely for their literary merit, or for their music, or even their scenic designs or dancing, but rather on the integration of all these elements." [72] This is a tall order, and few of us have the equipment necessary for such an integration. And when we add to the combination of art forms the essential masque element of *occasion,* then I doubt if even the most painstaking research could put us in the position of judging rightly the absolute worth of one masque over another. The final prospect seems gloomy. But it is, I think, lightened by Miss Welsford, speaking of how to evaluate the masque:

In attacking this problem critics are apt, first to assume that the arts in their most highly developed forms are to be adjusted to one another, and then to show that this adjustment is undesirable if not impossible. But they disregard the possibility that the arts may be combined *at low pressure,* and that there may be a peculiar beauty in the combination, which compensates for the fact that each art has had to sacrifice something of its own proper excellence. The masque shows how this may happen, and under what conditions it is desirable. The arts draw nearer to each other as they draw nearer to life, nearer to their rudimentary function as an enhancement of ordinary social activities. The libretto, the stage design, and the musical composition might be mediocre; but the masque itself was electric with the mirth and vitality of the ballroom.[73]

Perhaps, then, masque critics should be esteemed according to the success with which they have been able to interpret and express that "mirth and vitality." Perhaps, on the other hand, those qualities remain ultimately inexpressible. Perhaps Jonson, who in many ways was the greatest masque critic of them all, arrived at the truth, rather than at his intended irony, when he cried out:

> O Showes! Showes! Mighty Showes!
> The Eloquence of Masques! What need of prose
> Or Verse, or Sense, t'express Immortal you?

72. Sabol, *Songs and Dances for the Stuart Masque,* p. 18.
73. Enid Welsford, *The Court Masque,* pp. 404–405.

Reviews

MACK, MAYNARD. *King Lear in Our Time*. Berkeley and Los Angeles: University of California Press, 1965. Pp. x, 126. $3.75.

ELTON, WILLIAM R. *King Lear and the Gods*. San Marino: The Huntington Library, 1966. Pp. xii, 369. $8.50.

IT IS GOOD TO HAVE Professor Maynard Mack's splendid essay on *King Lear*, "We Came Crying Hither," in a more permanent form. It constitutes in a slightly revised version the third chapter of his Beckman Lectures. It is preceded by an account of what actors and producers have done to the play. Professor Mack's principles are impeccable, and his strictures are courteously worded; but the chapter suffers to some extent from the fact that his acquaintance with most modern productions is at second hand. He might, even so, have made more use of available dramatic criticism—e.g., Una Ellis-Fermor's detailed account of Olivier's performance. The reader would find it difficult from these pages to obtain a clear idea of two of the best Lears of our time (Gielgud's and Redgrave's) and why Wolfit's production destroyed the effect of his own fine performance.

Professor Mack concludes this chapter with a question which expects an affirmative answer:

Does it mean that something like the whole play might be actable and know-able, if we were to come to it with other ends in view than rationalizing the irrational, regularizing the irregular, and unifying on a particular plan what cannot be unified on such a plan?

He gives the answer to this question in his second chapter, in which, after discussing sources (including Shakespeare's own plays) and the survival of Morality and homiletic techniques in *King Lear,* he suggests that

the play calls for a performing style that has absorbed both epic disengagement and psychic intimacy, renders the implausible event more plausible, moves easily from personification to personality, effectively marries the tragic to the absurd, and, above all, represses the urge to regularize and unify by twentieth-century psychological principles a play whose actual mode of unity is partly medieval and homiletic.

The book as a whole is not merely a timely lesson to theater directors: it goes far to explain the special appeal of the play in the postwar world. *King Lear* "begs us to seek the meaning of our human fate not in what becomes of us, but in what we become," Professor Mack writes with his usual perception, eloquence, and grace.

Professor Elton's impressive inquiry into the meaning of *King Lear* starts from the question of how far modern critics are justified in calling it a "Christian" play—"a drama of meaningful suffering and redemption, within a just universe ruled by providential higher powers." At the end of the book, after a detailed discussion of the evidence, he comes to the conclusion that the optimistic Christian interpretation is probably invalid since Lear is not saved, regenerated, or redeemed, since providence "can-not be shown to be operative," and since "the devastating fifth act shat-ters, more violently than an earlier apostasy might have done, the founda-tions of faith itself."

On the way to this conclusion—with which, as I shall show, I do not wholly agree—Mr. Elton brings up a massive array of learning, a knowl-edge of the relevant literature, an understanding of the theological ideas current in Shakespeare's day, an appreciation of the poetry and dramatic structure of the play, and plenty of common sense. His seven hundred footnotes will be a valuable quarry for future editors of the play.

He takes from Sidney's *Arcadia* four attitudes to providence: the *Prisca Theologica,* good pagans, such as Pamela, who exhibit virtues which "foreshadow Christian ones"; the atheistic view, represented by Cecropia;

the superstitious view of Basilius; and the *Deus absconditus* view—that providence is mysterious and unintelligible to mortal eyes. Mr. Elton then considers Edgar and Cordelia as virtuous pagans, Goneril, Regan, and Edmund as atheists, Gloucester as an example of the third category, and Lear himself as an example of the fourth.

Other chapters are concerned with the dechristianization of *King Leir,* the use of the double plot, and "irony as structure," in which Mr. Elton finds "annihilation of faith in poetic justice and, within the confines of a grim, pagan universe, annihilation of faith in divine justice." We may readily agree that Shakespeare did not believe that every tragedy should inculcate "a particular Providence, and shewing it plainly protecting the Good, and chastizing the Bad." *King Lear* and *Othello* might have been written to show the absurdity of Dennis' conception of tragedy. Cordelia's death is particularly gratuitous since it depends on Edmund's long silence and the forgetfulness of the surviving characters. Albany's prayer for her safety is given a deliberately dusty answer.

All this is true, but it does not inevitably lead to Mr. Elton's conclusion. A Christian, after all, need not believe that God intervenes to protect the good, nor suppose that the virtuous triumph in this life. Some critics have doubted whether a Christian tragedy is possible since heavenly rewards and punishments are apt to convert the dramatist's sounds of woe to hey nonny nonny. *Murder in the Cathedral* and *Samson Agonistes* both end in triumph. A Christian, therefore, who wishes to write a satisfactory tragedy will either write about a pre-Christian world, or, if he is concerned with a Christian world, he will, as it were, retract his belief and keep it on the fringe of his theme. Hamlet expresses a belief in a special providence, and flights of angels are called upon to sing him to his rest; but the Christian ethic is contrasted only implicitly with the "duty" of revenge. The Moor is a Christian and he—if not Shakespeare—assumes that he will spend an eternity in hell. In the world of *King Lear* any question of a future life is ruled out. The flagrant injustice of this life cannot be reversed by the operations of divine justice. Shakespeare, it may be suggested, started from the dramatic hypothesis that would be available to a pagan. He shows that the will to power is self-destructive, and that the violation of the natural law leads to anarchy. Lear and Gloucester, whose initial sins open the door to the worse sins of the evil characters, are brought to their ruin; and the innocent Cordelia is hanged. But no mem-

ber of the audience doubts that it is better to be Cordelia than her sisters
and better to be Edgar than his brother. The Christian ethic is vindicated,
without any support from the Christian hope. May it not be that a virtue
which is its own reward is ethically superior to—and more Christian than
—one which looks forward to a reward in heaven?

It should be added that Mr. Elton is particularly good in his analysis of
topoi and that he throws light on two of Edgar's famous remarks. "The
gods are just" he takes to be Edgar's attempt to ease his brother's "last
moments by offering extentuating comfort in the only terms Edmund is
able to comprehend."

KENNETH MUIR

A Book of Masques in Honour of Allardyce Nicoll. Cambridge, Eng.:
Cambridge University Press, 1967. Pp. xv + 448. $12.50.

THIS HANDSOME VOLUME has appeared too late for review, but it should
not go unnoticed in a number of *Renaissance Drama* devoted primarily to masques and entertainments. The book includes, in addition to a general introduction by Gerald Eades Bentley and a study of
masques in plays by Inga-Stina Ewbank, editions of the following works:
Samuel Daniel, *The Vision of the Twelve Goddesses* (1604), ed. Joan
Rees; Ben Jonson, *Oberon, the Fairy Prince* (1611), ed. Richard Hosley,
Love Freed from Ignorance and Folly (1611), ed. Norman Sanders, *Lovers Made Men* (1617), ed. Stanley Wells, and *Pleasure Reconciled to Virtue* (1618), ed. R. A. Foakes; Thomas Campion, *The Lords' Masque*
(1613), ed. I. A. Shapiro; Francis Beaumont, *The Masque of the Inner
Temple and Gray's Inn* (1613), ed. Philip Edwards; *The Masque of
Flowers* (1614), ed. E. A. J. Honigmann; William Browne, *The Masque
of the Inner Temple (Ulysses and Circe)* (1615), ed. R. F. Hill; Thomas
Middleton, *The Inner Temple Masque, or Masque of Heroes* (1619), ed.

R. C. Bald; James Shirley, *The Triumph of Peace* (1634), ed. Clifford Leech, and *Cupid and Death* (1653), ed. B. A. Harris; Thomas Nabbes, *The Spring's Glory* (1638), ed. John Russell Brown; and Inigo Jones and William Davenant, *Salmacida Spolia* (1640), ed. T. J. B. Spencer. Spelling and punctuation have been modernized. There are forty-eight pages of plates.

S. S.

MEAGHER, JOHN C. *Method and Meaning in Jonson's Masques.* Notre Dame: Notre Dame University Press, 1966. Pp. ix + 214. $6.50.

SOME NOTICE too should be taken of this book, which also appeared too late to be included in Mrs. Ewbank's review article. Jonson's masques, Professor Meagher writes, "were from the beginning more extravagant spectacles than the masque had ever been before, and this must undoubtedly account in part for their immediate and long-lived success. . . . But Jonson would have us be more careful about being distracted by mere show. If his masques are, as it has generally been conceded, the finest flower of the (pre-Miltonic, if you will) English masque tradition, their proper understanding must begin in discovering from what roots and in what air they grew. This book is an attempt at placing the Jonsonian masques in their rather complicated context in order to elucidate their meaning and explicate their design, but it is far from being a comprehensive study. . . . I am attempting only to isolate a few important patterns in a vast and fascinating design."

S. S.

Notes on Contributors

Sydney Anglo, who teaches at the University of Swansea, has published several articles on English court festivals of the fifteenth and sixteenth centuries. The Clarendon Press will shortly bring out his book, *The Great Tournament Roll of Westminster*.

David M. Bergeron, Assistant Professor of English at the University of Louisville, is engaged in several projects concerned with English civic pageantry.

Michael R. Best, who is teaching at the University of Victoria in British Columbia, has a special interest in Lyly and has also published "A Theory of the Literary Genesis of Lyly's *Midas*" in *R.E.S.* (1966).

Inga-Stina Ewbank is Lecturer in English Literature at the University of Liverpool. In addition to numerous articles on Elizabethan drama, she is the author of *Their Proper Sphere: A Study of the Brontë Sisters as Early-Victorian Female Novelists*.

Ann Haaker, Associate Professor of English at California State College

335

in Fullerton, has edited Brome's *The Antipodes* for the Regents Renaissance Drama series.

ROBERT KIMBROUGH, Associate Professor of English at the University of Wisconsin, is author of *Shakespeare's* Troilus and Cressida *and Its Setting.*

MARGARET M. McGOWAN, who teaches in the School of European Studies of the University of Sussex, is author of *L'Art du ballet de cour en France, 1581–1643,* published in 1963.

SCOTT McMILLIN, who teaches English at Cornell University, is preparing a transcript of the Hatfield House papers discussed in his article for a Malone Society *Collections* volume.

JOHN C. MEAGHER, who teaches English in St. Michael's College of the University of Toronto, has just published *Method and Meaning in Jonson's Masques.*

KENNETH MUIR, who is King Alfred Professor of English Literature at the University of Liverpool, is editor of *Shakespeare Survey*. He has edited *King Lear* for the New Arden Shakespeare.

PHILIP MURPHY is editing *The Lady of May* as a doctoral dissertation at the University of Wisconsin.

STEPHEN ORGEL, who is in the English Department of the University of California at Berkeley, published *The Jonsonian Masque* in 1965.

J. E. VAREY, Professor of Spanish at Westfield College of the University of London, specializes in seventeenth-century Spanish drama and is general editor of the Coleccion Tamesis series.

ANDREW VON HENDY, who is Assistant Professor of English at Boston College, has published articles on *The Kingis Quair* and on Northrop Frye's criticism.

Books Received

The listing of a book does not preclude its subsequent review in *Renaissance Drama.*

Bibliography of English Printed Tragedy 1565–1900, compiled and edited by
CARL J. STRATMAN, C.S.V. Carbondale: Southern Illinois University Press,
1966. Pp. xx + 843. $15.00.

BONAZZA, BLAZE ODELL. *Shakespeare's Early Comedies: A Structural Analysis.*
New York: Humanities Press, 1966. Pp. 125. $5.75.

BOWERS, FREDSON. *On Editing Shakespeare.* Charlottesville: University Press
of Virginia, 1966. Pp. xi + 210. $2.45 (paper).

BROME, RICHARD. *The Antipodes,* ed. ANN HAAKER. Regents Renaissance
Drama. Lincoln: University of Nebraska Press, 1966. Pp. xxi + 138. $3.00
(paper, $1.00).

CHAPMAN, GEORGE. *The Widow's Tears,* ed. ETHEL M. SMEAK. Regents Renaissance Drama. Lincoln: University of Nebraska Press, 1966. Pp. xxvi +
119. $3.00 (paper, $1.00).

COLIE, ROSALIE L. *Paradoxia Epidemica: The Renaissance Tradition of Paradox.* Princeton: Princeton University Press, 1966. Pp. xx + 553. $12.50.

338   BOOKS RECEIVED

Davis, Joe Lee. *The Sons of Ben: Jonsonian Comedy in Caroline England.* Detroit: Wayne State University Press, 1967. Pp. 253. $8.95.

Editing Sixteenth Century Texts, ed. R. J. Schoeck. Papers given at the Editorial Conference at the University of Toronto, October 1965. Toronto: University of Toronto Press, 1966. Pp. xi + 137. $5.00.

The Elizabethan Age, ed. David L. Stevenson. New York: Fawcett Premier Books, 1966. Pp. 319. $.95 (paper).

Elizabethan Poetry: Modern Essays in Criticism, ed. Paul J. Alpers. New York: Oxford University Press, 1967. Pp. ix + 524. $2.50 (paper).

Frye, Prosser Hall. *Romance and Tragedy: A Study of Classic and Romantic Elements in the Great Tragedies of European Literature.* Lincoln: University of Nebraska Press, 1961. Pp. x + 372. $1.25 (paper).

Hawkes, Terence. *Shakespeare and the Reason.* New York: Humanities Press, 1965. Pp. xiv + 207. $6.00.

Hogrefe, Pearl. *The Life and Times of Sir Thomas Elyot, Englishman.* Ames: Iowa State University Press, 1967. Pp. xiii + 410. $6.50.

Holloway, John. *The Story of the Night: Studies in Shakespeare's Major Tragedies.* Lincoln: University of Nebraska Press, 1963. Pp. ix + 187. $1.25 (paper).

Jonson, Ben. *Three Comedies: Volpone, The Alchemist, Bartholomew Fair,* ed. Michael Jamieson. Baltimore: Penguin Books, 1966. Pp. 487. $1.45 (paper).

Jorgensen, Paul A. *Lear's Self-discovery.* Berkeley: University of California Press, 1967. Pp. x + 154. $4.50.

Kyd, Thomas. *The First Part of Hieronimo* and *The Spanish Tragedy,* ed. Andrew S. Cairncross. Regents Renaissance Drama. Lincoln: University of Nebraska Press, 1967. Pp. xxxiii + 186. $3.00 (paper, $1.00).

Laguardia, Eric. *Nature Redeemed: The Imitation of Order in Three Rennaissance Poems.* New York: Humanities Press, 1966. Pp. 180. $5.75.

Laver, James. *Costume in the Theatre.* New York: Hill and Wang, 1967. Pp. xii + 212. $1.95 (paper).

McCrary, William C. *The Goldfinch and the Hawk: A Study of Lope de Vega's Tragedy,* El Caballero de Olmedo. Chapel Hill: University of North Carolina Press, 1966. Studies in the Romance Languages and Literatures, Number 62. Pp. 181. $4.00 (paper).

McCready, Warren T. *Bibliografía Temática de Estudios sobre el Teatro Español Antiguo.* Toronto: University of Toronto Press, 1966. Pp. xix + 445. $12.50.

MacLure, Millar. *George Chapman: A Critical Study.* Toronto: University of Toronto Press, 1966. Pp. ix + 241. $6.50.

Marlowe, Christopher. *The Jew of Malta,* ed. T. W. Craik. New Mermaid
Series. New York: Hill and Wang, 1967. Pp. xxi + 106. $1.25 (paper).

Medieval and Renaissance Studies, ed. O. B. Hardison, Jr. Proceedings of the
Southeastern Institute of Medieval and Renaissance Studies, Summer 1965.
Chapel Hill: University of North Carolina Press, 1966. Pp. ix + 187.
$6.00.

Middleton, Thomas. *Michaelmas Term,* ed. Richard Levin. Regents Renaissance Drama. Lincoln: University of Nebraska Press, 1967. Pp. xxv + 139.
$3.00 (paper, $1.00).

Moore, Don D. *John Webster and His Critics, 1617–1964.* Baton Rouge:
Louisiana State University Press, 1966. Pp. x + 199. $4.00.

Narrative and Dramatic Sources of Shakespeare, Volume VI, ed. Geoffrey
Bullough. New York: Columbia University Press, 1966. Pp. xiv + 578.
$10.00.

Phialas, Peter G. *Shakespeare's Romantic Comedies: The Development of
Their Form and Meaning.* Chapel Hill: University of North Carolina Press,
1966. Pp. xvi + 314. $7.50.

Prosser, Eleanor. *Hamlet and Revenge.* Stanford: Stanford University Press;
London: Oxford University Press, 1967. Pp. xiv + 287. $7.50.

The Reader's Encyclopedia of Shakespeare, ed. Oscar James Campbell and
Edward G. Quinn. New York: Thomas Y. Crowell, 1966. Pp. xv + 1014.
$15.00.

Roberts, John R. *A Critical Anthology of English Recusant Devotional Prose,
1558–1603.* Pittsburgh: Duquesne University Press, 1966. Pp. x + 322. $6.95.

Rojas, Fernando de. *La Celestina or The Spanish Bawd,* trans. J. M. Cohen.
New York: New York University Press, 1966. Pp. 248. $5.00. (Orig. publ.
1964.)

Sannazaro, Jacopo. *Arcadia & Piscatorial Eclogues,* ed. Ralph Nash. Detroit:
Wayne State University Press, 1966. Pp. 220. $7.95.

Satin, Joseph. *Shakespeare and His Sources.* Boston: Houghton Mifflin, 1966.
Pp. xiii + 623. $3.95 (paper).

Seng, Peter J. *The Vocal Songs in the Plays of Shakespeare: A Critical History.* Cambridge, Mass.: Harvard University Press, 1967. Pp. xix + 314.
$8.95.

Shakespeare, William. *The First Part of the History of King Henry the
Fourth,* ed. H. M. Richmond. Indianapolis: Bobbs-Merrill, 1967. Pp.
xxxii + 176. $1.45 (paper).

———. *Henry the Fourth, Part I,* ed. Charlton Hinman. Shakespeare Quarto
Facsimiles, No. 14. London: Oxford University Press, 1966. Pp. xi + 88.
$5.20.

————. *Henry VI, Part One,* ed. Lawrence V. Ryan. Signet Classic Shakespeare. New York: New American Library, 1967. Pp. 222. $.50 (paper).

————. *Henry VI, Part Two,* ed. Arthur Freeman. Signet Classic Shakespeare. New York: New American Library, 1967. Pp. 224. $.50 (paper).

————. *Richard the Second,* ed. Charlton Hinman. Shakespeare Quarto Facsimiles, No. 13. London: Oxford University Press, 1966. Pp. xvi + 84. $5.20.

———— and John Fletcher. *The Two Noble Kinsmen,* ed. Clifford Leech. Signet Classic Shakespeare. New York: New American Library, 1966. Pp. 268. $.50 (paper).

Shakespeare: Modern Essays in Criticism, Revised Edition, ed. Leonard F. Dean. New York: Oxford University Press, 1967. Pp. x + 476. $2.25 (paper). (Orig. publ. 1957.)

Shakespeare Studies II, ed. J. Leeds Barroll. Cincinnati: Shakespeare Studies, 1966. Pp. 388. $8.00.

Spalding, K. J. *The Philosophy of Shakespeare.* New York: Hillary House, 1966. Pp. viii + 191. $2.50.

Stevenson, David Lloyd. *The Achievement of Shakespeare's* Measure for Measure. Ithaca: Cornell University Press, 1967. Pp. xi + 169. $5.75.

Three Jacobean Tragedies, edited by Gāmini Salgādo. [Comprises Tourneur, *The Revenger's Tragedy;* Webster, *The White Devil;* Middleton and Rowley, *The Changeling.*] Baltimore: Penguin Books, 1965. Pp. 364. $.95 (paper).

Tourneur, Cyril. *The Revenger's Tragedy,* ed. Lawrence J. Ross. Regents Renaissance Drama. Lincoln: University of Nebraska Press, 1966. Pp. xxxii + 130. $3.00 (paper, $1.00).

Tudor and Stuart Drama, compiled Irving Ribner. Goldentree Bibliographies. New York: Appleton-Century-Crofts, 1966. Pp. viii + 72. $1.35 (paper).

Williams, John Anthony. *The Natural Work of Art: The Experience of Romance in Shakespeare's* Winter's Tale. Cambridge, Mass.: Harvard University Press, 1967. Pp. 47. (Paper.)

Corrigenda

Owing to a printer's error, a number of the legends to the illustrations in the article "Pictures for the Reader: A Series of Illustrations to Comedy 1591–1592," by Louise George Clubb, in the 1966 number appeared incorrectly. The errors are in Figure 4, pp. 268–273; the corrected legends are in parentheses: *Inganni* 9 (37ᵛ), 15ᵛ (41), 22 (45), 23 (47ᵛ),

27 (59), 27ᵛ (56), 32ᵛ (77ᵛ), 37 (10ᵛ), 37ᵛ (17ᵛ), 41 (21), 45 (34ᵛ), 47ᵛ (50), 56 (9), 59 (15ᵛ), 77ᵛ (22), 10ᵛ (23), 17ᵛ (27), 21 (27ᵛ), 34ᵛ (32ᵛ), 50 (37); *Torti* 5 (*Prigione* 38), 17 (*Prigione* 6), 141 ([5]), 203 (141), 76 (17), 118 (203); *Prigione* 6 (*Torti* 118), 38 (*Torti* 76).